P9-DVC-992

32471
3

0327

THE JOHN HARVARD LIBRARY

Bernard Bailyn
Editor-in-Chief

Frank Norris, 1901 or 1902

A NOVELIST
IN THE MAKING

A COLLECTION OF STUDENT THEMES
AND THE NOVELS
Blix AND *Vandover and the Brute*

FRANK NORRIS

EDITED BY JAMES D. HART

THE JOHN HARVARD LIBRARY

THE BELKNAP PRESS OF
HARVARD UNIVERSITY PRESS
CAMBRIDGE, MASSACHUSETTS
1970

For my brother-in-law,
Joseph M. Bransten,
with affection and admiration

CONTENTS

ILLUSTRATIONS

ORIGINALS IN THE BANCROFT LIBRARY,
UNIVERSITY OF CALIFORNIA, BERKELEY

EDITOR'S NOTE

This book treats Frank Norris' beginnings as a novelist. It opens with a biographical and critical introduction covering his early life and literary attempts through his year at Harvard (1894–1895), with a brief consideration of the mature writings in the succeeding seven years before his death. Next comes the publication for the first time of forty-four themes that Norris wrote at Harvard, most of which were early versions or studio sketches for his novels *Blix, McTeague,* and *Vandover and the Brute.* The themes reveal hitherto unrecognized relations among these novels, and show that they possess a basic philosophy about the nature of man and an almost symbolic use of California as a setting. Lastly, the volume reprints the two least known and most unavailable of these early novels, *Blix* and *Vandover and the Brute.*

All but one of the themes reproduced here were obtained from Frank C. Preston, Frank Norris' literary executor, to whom I am indebted for permission to publish them. Mr. Preston found the papers in the attic of the Oregon home once occupied by his mother, Jeannette Black Preston, who had previously been married to Frank Norris until his death in 1902. The other theme formerly belonged to Franklin Walker, who generously turned it over to The Bancroft Library of the University of California to add to the collection donated by Mr. Preston. At the time that he was working on his biography of Frank Norris, Professor Walker received this theme from Charles G. Norris, the author's brother, who may have given other themes to admirers and may for a similar purpose have cut the autograph from themes here numbered 8 and 30.

The printed text of the themes eliminates material that is readable but crossed out on the manuscript. It does not include Norris' conventional heading of the course title, his signature, his manner of dating, and his college status. It also regularizes his trivial mispellings and corrects some rudimentary flaws, such as the failure to place a period at the end of a sentence or a capital at the beginning. But more substantial irregularities, such as Norris' peculiar hyphenation or absence of commas in a series, have been preserved to give the feel of his obviously rapid composition. Fourteen of the themes were untitled by Norris, and the titles given them here are indicated by brackets in the list of themes. The main comments made by the faculty reader are grouped together at the end of each theme, but his minor markings, such as additional punctuation, spelling corrections, or the placement of a question mark or X in the margin next to a particular section of a composition, are generally omitted.

The text of *Blix* is that of the Argonaut Edition of Norris' collected works issued by Doubleday, Doran & Company, Inc., in 1928, which is an exact copy of the first book publication of the novel by Doubleday & McClure Co. in 1899. Typographical errors are silently corrected. The slightly different and earlier text serialized in the *Puritan* from March through August 1899 was of aid in making some of these corrections and has itself been the subject of comments incorporated in notes. The text of *Vandover and the Brute* is also that of the Argonaut Edition, which corrected minor errors of the first edition printed in 1914. New typographical errors made in the later edition are silently corrected here. The British spellings with "our" endings and "s" where Americans would use "z" are presumably the publisher's addition, since Norris' manuscripts do not employ these spellings.

Like most writers on Frank Norris, I am indebted to three major students of his life and works. First of these is Professor Franklin Walker, whose biography published in 1932 has never been superseded and whose other important scholarship on Norris includes an edition of the author's *Letters,* issued in 1956. The present work has also profited from Professor Walker's sensitive and keen-eyed reading of the Introduction in manuscript. Next is Robert D. Lundy, who in 1956 wrote an influential doctoral dissertation on "The Making of *McTeague* and *The Octopus,*" which unfortunately remains unpublished. Most recent is Professor Donald Pizer, whose thorough scholarship is set forth both in his edition of *The Literary Criticism of Frank Norris,* published in 1964, and in his 1966 study *The Novels of Frank Norris.*

I am also indebted to Kimball C. Elkins of the Harvard University Archives for his aid on a variety of matters concerning Norris' period at Harvard.

J. D. H.

Berkeley, California
April 1970

A NOVELIST IN THE MAKING

INTRODUCTION

Like many California authors, Frank Norris was not born in the state. He liked to pretend that he was, however, as when on the appearance of his first novel he told a journalist, "I was 'bawn 'n raise' in California." [1] He doubtless said so because he believed that a novelist could write successfully only about that which he knew intimately, and his own intimacy might imply lifelong association with the subject. But the California he chose to depict was not the conventional setting portrayed in the sensational or sentimental tales of the gold rush and of "Indians, road agents, and desperadoes" turned out by hack writers, who, he said, "strut in fringed leggings upon the street corners, one hand held out for pennies." [2] As he explained to the encouraging reviewer of his first novel: "I have great faith in the possibilities of San Francisco and the Pacific Coast as offering a field for fiction. Not the fiction of Bret Harte, however, for the country has long since outgrown the 'red shirt.' The novel of California must be now a novel of city life, and it is that novel I hope some day to write successfully." [3]

Norris was born in Chicago in 1870. His father was a wholesale jeweler, who was so prosperous that one year he could take his family on a grand tour of Europe and winter in the English seaside resort of Brighton.

1. Franklin Walker, ed., *The Letters of Frank Norris* (San Francisco: The Book Club of California, 1956), p. 22.
2. Frank Norris, *The Responsibilities of a Novelist* (New York: Doubleday, Doran & Co., 1928), pp. 48–49.
3. *Letters*, p. 23.

I

At home the Norrises lived in a Michigan Avenue mansion, behind which lay their stable containing elegant carriages and sleighs. But because the damp and snowy climate made life difficult for the elder Norris, who had a lame hip, he decided to move his family and business to California. In 1884 they settled in San Francisco.

Young Frank was just fourteen then, an impressionable age. Later, when he decided to be a novelist, he came to regard San Francisco as an ideal setting for fiction. "Imagine a novel of Chicago," he remarked scornfully. "But consider San Francisco. It is not necessary to hesitate a moment. 'Things can happen' in San Francisco." Then he ticked off the fascinating features of this site: the great bay itself; the mansions of Nob Hill overlooking the water; the artists' quarter of Telegraph Hill; the teeming Tenderloin of Kearny Street; exotic Chinatown; the lurid Barbary Coast; the old Spanish military reservation, now the Americans' Presidio; Fisherman's Wharf; and the famous restaurants, ranging from the elegant French menu of the Poodle Dog through the simple Mexican of Luna's, to the raffish bars with their back rooms closed off for private parties. He declared, "there is an indefinable air about all these places that is suggestive of stories at once. You fancy the names would look well on a book's page. The people who frequent them could walk right into a novel or short story and be at home." This, then, was to be his setting. True, it was simultaneously discovered and featured by a local fin-de-siècle group of writers and artists called Les Jeunes, but though Norris, who was sometimes associated with this group, found its members delightful people, he seemed also to consider them trivial, implying that their view of San Francisco, as presented by the ingenious Gelett Burgess, was as flabby as were that artist's boneless Goops. The kind of treatment Norris wanted was something quite as romantic but more incisive and significant. He cried out: "Who shall be our Kipling? Where is the man that shall get at the heart of us, the blood and bones and fiber of us, that shall go a-gunning for stories up and down our streets and into our . . . parlors and lodging houses and saloons and dives along our wharves and into our theaters; yes, and into the secretest chambers of our homes as well as our hearts?" [4]

The environs of San Francisco and the sea that spreads beyond it represented something very special, something virtually symbolic to Frank Norris. His first novels even have subtitles to point up this setting or to suggest the atmosphere of the area with which they are suffused. *Moran of the Lady Letty* is subtitled *A Story of Adventure off the California Coast*, and *McTeague* is also called *A Story of San Francisco*. *Blix* has no subtitle, although the very first page emphasizes the city, which later becomes almost as much of a character as are the two lovers who roam through it. Similarly *Vandover and the Brute* does not mention San Francisco in the subtitle that Norris gave it on his manuscript— "A Study of Life and Manners in an American City at the End of the Nineteenth Century"—but the city is identified on the opening page, and several of the novel's characters derive their very names from the city's streets: Haight, Geary, Ellis, and Laguna.

Condy, the hero in *Blix* modeled after Norris himself, was forced to admit to his fellow San Franciscans that Chicago was where he was born and reared, but he always added, "I couldn't help that, you know." For Norris, like Condy, life really began in California. Years later toward the end of Norris' days, he placed his final novel in his native city, at the same time that he was

4. Donald Pizer, ed., *The Literary Criticism of Frank Norris* (Austin: University of Texas Press, 1964), pp. 28–30.

championing Dreiser's *Sister Carrie*, another novel with a Chicago setting, but for a long while he had eyes only for California, and especially for what Californians in those days called "The City."

When the Norris family first moved to California in 1884, they lived briefly in Oakland, across the bay, then stopped at the Palace Hotel in San Franrcisco, and finally settled into a house on Sacramento Street that was bought from Henry T. Scott, the vice-president and treasurer of the Union Iron Works. It was a fitting residence for the elder Norris, who described himself in the city directory as a capitalist. When the younger Norris used the house as the model for the one in which Vandover lived, he moved it a block south and probably aggrandized the real garden, but otherwise he hardly changed the appearance of this comfortable dwelling with its Corinthian-columned entrance flanked by bay windows. He was to call it home until the last five years of his life, even though he was away from it a good deal. His first absence, a temporary one, occurred when his parents sent him to a stylish preparatory school, the Belmont Academy, about twenty-five miles down the Peninsula—a school with which another future California novelist, Jack London, was later associated in the menial capacity of washing and ironing the clothes of the students and their teachers. From that boarding school Norris soon moved back to the city to nurse an arm broken in a football game.

At home he enjoyed influences that proved more significant than those of the boarding school. Every night his mother, a statuesque former actress of strong will and personality, dramatically read aloud from the fiction of Scott and Dickens and Robert Louis Stevenson, or the poetry of Shakespeare, Scott, and Browning. These readings stimulated the literary interests of a boy who long before had kept a diary, so that by the time

4

he was fifteen he had begun to write tales himself and even tried his hand at a poem. These works were more the product of Sir Walter Scott than of the surroundings of the former Henry T. Scott house, but that setting also affected him. As Norris later wrote, looking back on himself as a childish storyteller: "Every instant at the day he is dramatizing. The cable-car has for him a distinct personality. Every window in the residence quarters is an eye to the soul of the house behind . . . A ship is Adventure. An engine a living brute; and the easy-chair of his library is still the same comfortable and kindly old gentleman holding out his arms." [5] Each of these five objects entered his fiction in, respectively, *McTeague, Blix, Moran of the Lady Letty, The Octopus,* and *Vandover and the Brute,* although they also appeared in his other novels. As the apprentice writer contemplated his neighborhood setting, if perhaps without yet a clear design for fiction, his eye met a variety of appealing sights. Less than a block below his home lay Van Ness Avenue, the city's most elegant residential street. One block farther east was Polk Street, the marketplace for ladies from the Avenue and adjacent stylish streets, itself the home of small tradespeople who lived above their places of business: butcher shops and groceries, drugstors with jars of colored liquids in the windows, saloons and cigar stands, plumbers' rundown offices, cheap restaurants, sweet-smelling candy stores, and a harness maker's shop. The street itself was noisy with the clatter of passing cable cars, and on its busy sidewalks ladies like Mrs. Norris examined the produce and gave orders to the local merchants for the daily needs of their great houses.

At home young Norris often whiled away a dull or rainy afternoon playing at warfare between lead soldiers with his younger brothers, Charles and Lester. The

5. *Literary Criticism,* p. 67.

campaigns they waged were turned by the older brother into reenactments of the battles in Scott's novels or of incidents from other fiction and from history. Like the elaborate games enjoyed by the admired Robert Louis Stevenson and his stepson, these contests moved beyond the surface of the table to the written word. Before long Norris was creating a romance-cycle of "Gaston le Fox," and so as to carry it out more fully he sketched battle plans and drew pictures of the armored knights involved in its adventures. His skill as an artist was considerable and his enthusiasm great.

His mother, perhaps because she had been thwarted in acting, encouraged her elder son toward an artistic career, first as painter, later as poet, and still later as novelist. After a brief period at Boys' High School, a public institution that prepared for both a college course and a commercial career, Norris in 1886 was allowed to enroll in classes at the San Francisco Art Association, where he later placed Vandover. There Virgil Williams, Stevenson's old-time friend, taught Norris to draw by depicting casts of ancient statues and conventional still-life arrangements, but the young artist was happier when he and another student sneaked off to the Presidio to sketch from life the cavalry horses found there. His work was good enough for the parents to decide that their oldest son deserved more serious training, and for this reason they determined to go to Europe in 1887. His father was largely retired from business and, like his mother, needed a change of scene following the sudden death of Lester, their youngest son. They visited London briefly and then went on to their objective of Paris, where Norris enrolled in the Atelier Julien. After a time his father tired of living abroad without the settled routine of business and returned to the United States; before a year was out his mother and her young son Charles had followed, leaving Norris, on the verge of his eighteenth birthday, alone to study and experience life in Paris.

At the Atelier young Norris studied under Bouguereau, the painter of fleshy nudes. He was thus introduced to quite different models from those provided by Virgil Williams. Each Monday forty nude girls were brought before the hundred or so students and auctioned off to those who wanted their services. When the studio could not hold him, even with such attractions—and often it could not, for he was a rather self-indulgent dilettante—he browsed among the bookstalls on the left Bank, got a job as a member of the claque at the Opéra, learned to fence, sketched animals in the Jardin des Plantes, and ranged widely through the modern French fiction of Zola, Flaubert, Daudet, De-Maupassant, and the Goncourt brothers. At his pension he labored on a huge canvas depicting the Battle of Crécy. To ensure its complete accuracy, he not only read and reread Froissart but made careful sketches and notes on the armor exhibited in the Musée de Cluny and the Hotel des Invalides. But if his knowledge was thus enhanced, his artistic fervor diminished, and the canvas remained as blank as Vandover's projected chef d'oeuvre, "The Last Enemy." Unlike Vandover, however, while the canvas remained white, the preparation for working on it led Norris to another art: writing. As background for his painting, he wrote and illustrated an article about armor, "Clothes of Steel," which he sent home to his mother. She proudly arranged for its printing at the end of March, 1889, in a San Francisco newspaper, the *Chronicle*. This was Norris' first published writing.

Norris' study of medievalism also led him to write a long story, "Robert D'Artois," which he mailed to his young brother as a souvenir of the toy soldier wars they had fought in San Francisco and Paris. These two compositions convinced his father that Norris was idling away his time at writing, whereas painting, and painting at a particular studio, was the object for which he had been left in Paris. So the artist *manqué* was summoned home. He returned in 1890 a sophisticated boulevardier, his youthfulness and nationality disguised by a moustache, long sideburns, and exotic clothes. At home he began to write a narrative poem in the vein of Scott, replete with feudal adventures. Although his mother encouraged his writing, his father decided that Norris needed a steadier activity and should study for a business career, probably in the wholesale jewelry business or perhaps in rental of the houses that the elder Norris, like Vandover's father, was building for speculation. He insisted that his son prepare for admission to the University of California.

Although unable to pass the entrance examination in mathematics, Norris moved to Berkeley in the fall of 1890 as a limited status student. Curiously enough, the dapper bohemian who wore black silk underwear turned into an enthusiastic college man. He was pledged to Phi Gamma Delta, became an ardent member, and wrote the ritual for the pig dinner that his beloved Fijis still celebrate as "The Norris." He played a banjo decorated with his own lively drawings, participated in college pranks and escapades, reveled in the freshman-sophomore battles, and openly admired the football heroes, whose games suggested to him the qualities of medieval knightly contests. He spent a good deal of time at Haggerty's saloon near the campus, and sometimes on Saturday nights he traveled the "cocktail route" along Kearny Street in San Francisco.

His class experiences were not always so happy. Twice at Berkeley he wrote petitions to the president and the faculty to request special academic dispensations, one of which was granted, even though part of the time he was on probation for poor grades. Although he spent four years at the university, he never managed to fulfill the mathematics requirement and thus never received an A.B. But he did well in his French courses and enjoyed history. Most of all he liked the geology and zoology courses taught by the dynamic Professor Joseph LeConte, whose purpose was to reconcile post-Darwinian science and traditional religious belief. One of Norris' college contemporaries described LeConte's approach: "As interpreted by him, science appears to have a loftier mission than is commonly attributed to it. It is seen in its relations to philosophy, to ethics and to poetry." [6] In developing his views, LeConte contended that God is immanent throughout existence in the form of an indestructable Energy, part of which appears as Nature. He taught that there were stages in animal evolution, of which the most recent and highest was that exhibited by man, who not only carries within him earlier evidences of evolutionary change but also possesses the unique power to exercise free will in striving toward a loftier spiritual objective. These conceptions may have been unsatisfactory as science and insufficient as logic, but they entranced Norris, as they did other students who, after listening to LeConte's dramatic presentations, often burst into spontaneous applause. Eventually LeConte's ideas, further simplified and dramatized by Norris, reappeared in the writer's masculine characters, who undergo a struggle between their lower, animal-like, sensual nature and their higher ideals. Often they fall victim to a latter-day beastliness unless they can redirect their brute power toward moral ends under the encouragement and guidance of a good woman.

6. Donald Pizer, *The Novels of Frank Norris* (Bloomington: Indiana University Press, 1966), p. 13. Pizer treats LeConte's theory thoroughly.

Although the science courses provided Norris with theses suitable to his developing desire to become a novelist, he found useless the very classes on composition and literature that should most have aided him toward his goal. The manner of teaching English at the University of California so outraged him that he later wrote an excoriating article for a San Francisco journal in which he pitied the student, "with his new, fresh mind, his active brain and vivid imagination, with ideas of his own, crude, perhaps, but first hand," who "is set to work counting the 'metaphors' in a given passage . . . He classifies certain types of sentences in De Quincey and compares them with certain other types of sentences in Carlyle. He makes the wonderful discovery—on suggestion from the instructor—that De Quincey excelled in those metaphors by similes relating to rapidity of movement. Sensation!" [7]

The values of the Department of English so irritated him that even after becoming a professional author, he continued to detest rhetoric and once exclaimed, "We don't want literature, we want life"; but they did not dissuade him from the intention he had announced to the university administration of "preparing myself for the profession of a writer of fiction." [8] This career he began by publishing pieces in campus and San Francisco papers over the affected name of "Norrys." On the masthead of a humorous student journal, however, he listed himself as either "B. Norris, '94" or "B. F. Norris," for his name, like that of his father, was legally Benjamin Franklin Norris, though he never used the "Jr." that would have been proper. Not until No-

---

7. *The Wave*, XV, no. 48 (Nov. 28, 1896), p. 2.
8. *Letters*, pp. 30–31; "An Early Frank Norris Item," *Quarterly News-Letter* of the Book Club of California, XXV, no. 4 (Fall 1960), p. 84.

vember of his sophomore year did he sign any of his work as Frank Norris.

His first publications at college were poems set in the Middle Ages, in keeping with the octosyllabic verse narrative *Yvernelle* that he had begun before going to Berkeley, and whose printing in an elegantly illustrated edition was subsidized by his fond mother at Christmastime in 1891. Thus Norris' first book, like his first article, was published only because his mother was determined to see it in print. But soon Norris was getting established on his own with contributions accepted by student papers and San Francisco journals. During his two years as an upperclassman he contributed only three pieces to student publications, two of them to the yearbook, of which he was an assistant editor, while nine others appeared in established magazines: *The Overland Monthly*, *The Argonaut*, and *The Wave*.

These works were immature, yet they foreshadowed what Norris was soon to write as a professional author, even though they still showed debts to the disparate authors whom he had recently read with enthusiasm—Kipling, Zola, Richard Harding Davis—mixed with the ideas of the admired LeConte. "The Son of a Sheik" tells of a sophisticated young Arabian who is sent from Paris by a newspaper to serve as its war correspondent in North Africa, where he is suddenly swept up by ancestral passions and throws himself into a native uprising. The subject and technique are influenced by Kipling, but the basic idea illustrates LeConte's thesis about the possibilities of man's reversion to savagery. "The Finding of Lieutenant Outhwaite," another story indebted to Kipling, concerns mistaken identities among the "chasseurs d'Afrique." It is narrated by a character named Vandover, a smart, sophisticated young society man like Richard Harding Davis' Van Bibber, from whom he probaby got his name, although the setting has been transferred from the Four Hundred of New York to Coronado, a fashionable southern California resort. The most interesting story of all, and by far the longest, is "Lauth." Set in medieval Paris, it concerns an intellectual scholar named Lauth who is led to kill a man, and at sight of the blood he has shed, "all the animal savagery latent in every human being awoke within him." Lauth himself is later killed, yet before he dies, he reverts entirely to his animal nature. His "nails became claws, the teeth fangs," and his friends find him "stripped, grovelling on all fours in one corner of the room, making a low, monotonous growling sound, his teeth rattling and snapping together." [9] This deterioration of man into a brute foreshadows the degraded, drunken Vandover and, like him, illustrates LeConte's views.

These stories went far beyond what was required in Norris' composition course at Berkeley, and he evidently felt that if he was to write fiction of greater length and substance, he would need better tutelage than could be found in California. For that purpose he turned to Harvard. The idea that he might enter business had faded while Norris was at Berkeley, and he had drifted away from his father. The withdrawal was mutual, for family friction had led Mr. Norris to take a solitary trip around the world in the summer of 1892, which he had terminated in his old home of Chicago rather than back in San Francisco. In time his separation from his wife led to a divorce, and he became totally cut off from his San Francisco family when he remarried and established a new family in Chicago, to whom upon his death in 1900 he reportedly left nearly a million dollars. Frank Norris' enrollment at Harvard for

9. *Collected Writings Hitherto Unpublished in Book Form* (New York: Doubleday, Doran & Co., 1928), pp. 119, 144.

the academic year 1894–1895 was thus his own action, although his mother probably encouraged the decision, not only because she thought of her native New England as the center of culture but because she was intent that her son should have the best preparation for a cultural career. The idea of being "a Harvard man" evidently appealed to him, too, for a few years later he told a book reviewer that he was a member of Harvard's class of '95, although in fact he had once again been admitted to a university as a "Special Student," a category encompassing ten percent of Harvard's 1,667 undergraduates. To be near him, his doting mother moved with young Charles to a Cambridge boarding house, while Norris installed himself in a dormitory in the Yard. He registered under the name of Benjamin Franklin Norris, but the handwriting of his final initial was so elaborate that at first he was catalogued as B. F. Morris. In three courses in the French Department— a survey of French literature, advanced speaking and writing, and "Difficult Modern French"—his grades were mostly B's, and in George Lyman Kittredge's famous course on Shakespeare he earned the grade of C+. The most important course he enrolled in was composition, in which he rose from a B+ at midyear to a final A.

This class, called English 22, was taught by Lewis E. Gates, then an instructor. Aged thirty-four, Gates was a popular but demanding teacher with very firm opinions, which he communicated forcefully to his many students. His critical views, set forth six years later in *Studies and Appreciations,* emphasized the need to bring romanticism into association with common life so as to create a "renovating imaginative realism." He was only incidentally an impressionist, although he was often called one, for he demanded that impressionism be synthesized with historical criticism.

13

The 248 other students who completed English 22 with Norris that year were mostly sophomores who wished to devote more time to writing than was required in the regular sophomore composition course. The university catalogue described the chief aim of the course as to give training in four kinds of writing: description, narration, exposition, and argument. It further stated: "The lectures discuss the purposes and methods of each kind of writing; selections from standard authors are read in the class-room and examined in detail; and the student is taught to determine by observation and analysis the principles on which success in each kind of work depends, while at the same time he is gaining practical skill in writing and a feeling for style. The lectures also deal with the elements and qualities of style and the elements of Logic."

The class met on Tuesday, Thursday, and Saturday afternoons (the Saturdays were not excused), and for each meeting a theme, no longer than one page, was required. The thrice-weekly compositions were intended to cultivate regular habits of work and ease of composition, and students were advised to treat subjects they met from day to day in order to promote the "habitual observation of life." In addition, a fortnightly theme was required so as to give more ample evidence that the students could "cultivate correctness and vigor of expression." The catalogue indicated that during the first half-year the students would presumably deal with subjects assigned by Gates, whereas during the second half-year each student would be asked to treat a single topic, or a series of closely related topics, selected with the instructor's approval. Gates seemingly interpreted these requirements loosely. Some of the themes were read aloud in the classroom, at which time the students were expected to discuss them.[10]

10. *Harvard University Catalogue, 1894–1895*, pp. 12–13.

Norris later gave his own description of the class, contrasting it to composition instruction at Berkeley. As he pointed out, "they order this matter better at Harvard. The literary student at Cambridge has but little to do with lectures, almost nothing at all with text books. He is sent away from the lecture room and told to look about him and think a little. Each day he writes a theme, a page if necessary, a single line of a dozen words if he likes; anything, so it is original, something he has seen or thought, not read of, not picked up at second hand. He may choose any subject under the blue heavens from a pun to a philosophical reflection, only let it be his own." [11] The program worked admirably in leading Norris on to the writing of novels, and it is even said to have allowed a classmate, Joseph Sharts, to write the novel *Ezra Caine* directly for the course, though Norris seems to have exaggerated a good deal when he declared that "the character of the themes produced under this system is of such high order that it is not rare to come across one of them in the pages of the first-class magazines of the day." [12] One more famous author got her basic training in Gates's course that year. In addition to Norris, English 22 enrolled another Californian—Gertrude Stein, who was a student at Radcliffe. She entered the class for women which, though identical, was taught by Gates at a different hour and location. Her surviving themes [13] show that her work as a twenty-year-old sophomore was immature in ideas and techniques when compared with the capable compositions of Frank Norris. She was often asked to "rewrite"; he never was. It is no wonder that she received a grade of C while he and Sharts were

11. *The Wave,* XV, no. 48 (Nov. 28, 1896), p. 3.
12. *The Wave,* XV, no. 48 (Nov. 28, 1896), p. 3.
13. Collected by Rosalind S. Miller in her *Gertrude Stein: Form and Intelligibility* (New York: The Exposition Press, 1949).

among the five men accorded A's. Nevertheless, from her forty-five surviving themes she salvaged a sentence for *The Making of Americans,* an incident for *Three Lives,* and a setting and a situation for *Ida.*

The main reader of Gertrude Stein's compositions was William Vaughn Moody, later a noted poet and teacher, while the major reader of Frank Norris' themes was Herbert Vaughan Abbot, just nine years past his Amherst A.B. and soon to receive a professorship at Smith College. But it was Gates who set the tone and the standards for his assistants as well as for their students, and he seems to have read at least some of the writings of the better students, for as he reported to President Eliot that November, "I spend nine ⅓ hours a week correcting college themes." [14]

Gates praised literature that could "bring us closer to life," [15] although he also wanted it to "vanquish the repellent imperfections and defects of actual experience." He asked literature to show, "in the unwrought dross and tortured material of commonplace existence, God in the making." He believed that a writer should express "the necessary frank hospitality toward all kinds of experience, the quick insight into motive and character, and the wide and close familiarity with the drama of life." [16] Presumably Gates found these virtues in the embryonic novels that Norris was writing in his class. He seems to have read several of Norris' fortnightly themes toward the end of the year, and considering the high grade that they earned, he very likely read and discussed some of them before the class. It was for this reason that four years later Norris dedicated *McTeague* to Gates, explaining to his one-time professor that,

14. Letter of November 2, 1890, to President Eliot, in Harvard University Archives.

15. *The Nation,* LXXII, no. 1869 (April 25, 1901), p. 344.

16. Lewis E. Gates, *Studies and Appreciations* (New York: The Macmillan Co., 1900), p. 65.

"though [you] may have forgotten the theme, I have not forgotten Eng 22, and your very good encouragement & criticism during the short time I was with you. I doubt very much if *McTeague* would ever have been expanded to its present—rather formidable dimensions —if it had not been for your approval of the story in its first form. In a way you must share with me in the responsibility of its production now, as you certainly was its Godfather and sponsor." [17]

Abbott, too, in his lesser way was a beneficial reader for Norris. Time and again Abbott praised him for being "Vivid" or for setting forth "specific details." These were just the qualities that Norris himself admired when in *Blix* he praised the work of his alter ego Condy for its use of exact, revealing details. Nevertheless, curiously enough Norris in his finished novels sometimes employed the same detail to characterize two quite different persons, so that Condy and the dissimilar figure of "the other dentist" in *McTeague* wear, respectively "waistcoats too extreme" and "astonishing waistcoats," just as Condy and McTeague stammer respectively, "Hah! who–what–wh–what are you talking about?" and "What? What? Huh? What is it?" [18] But if not seen in conjunction, these details are just the concrete sort that Abbott admired. Indeed, he liked Norris' themes so much that he usually forgave minor errors in the papers, to the extent that there are no checkmarks against misspellings from haste ("scrorched in Theme 13) or ignorance ("develloped" in Theme 29), nor did he comment when "Photograph's" appeared on a signboard cited in Theme 43, where one cannot be certain whether the unnecessary apostrophe is the painter's or Norris'. Without needed correction Norris

17. Letter of February 22, 1899, *Letters*, p. 27.
18. *McTeague* (New York: Doubleday, Doran & Co., 1928), pp. 43, 199; *Blix*, Ch. II.

did not improve his bad spelling, so that sometimes it carried over into the printed works, where "jewellry" turns up in *Vandover and the Brute,* although the author should have known better because of the family business. Abbott also passed over errors in diction that later even escaped Norris' editor at the publishing firm, so that the first chapter of *Blix* ends with young Snooky having "clamoured down to the outside door"—a surprising situation, for though the young girl is noisy enough, surely she was meant to have "clambered."

In all, forty-four of Norris' themes have survived. The course description and calendar indicate there should have been fifty-five daily themes and six longer, connected fortnightly themes. All Norris' extant themes are daily ones, as they generally vary from 40 to 325 words, in keeping with the course requirement to the effect that no daily theme could be longer than would fit on the side of a conventional sheet of ruled paper. To make the longer themes fit, Norris adjusted his handwriting, and when he composed one theme that even small handwriting could not cramp onto a page (Theme 36), he resorted to the typewriter. The six longer fortnightly themes have disappeared, perhaps because they were cannibalized to fit into the more ambitious fiction he was simultaneously writing outside of class.

As a student who knew he was moving toward the career of a professional author, Norris planned to make use of all his writings, and in fact most of his themes did turn up, in one form or another, in his published writings, the same text sometimes being reworked for more than one novel. Although not all the themes appear verbatim in his later published novels, or are even closely paraphrased, they almost all relate rather intimately to Norris' three novels set in San Francisco: *Blix, McTeague,* and *Vandover and the Brute,* the first two published in 1899, the last in 1914. Twenty-seven of the themes have some relation to *Vandover and the Brute*, eleven are related to *McTeague*, and seven bear upon *Blix*. Of the forty-four themes, only seven seem to have no relation to these novels. Four of those came in a sequence from December 4 through December 10, another on December 18, the sixth on January 5, and the last, much later on March 22, interrupting a sequence related to *Vandover and The Brute*.

The subject matter and even some text that later appeared in *Blix* and *Vandover and the Brute* may be found in all the other themes written in the first semester. After the Christmas recess, the themes suddenly turn to the story that finally became *McTeague*. There is a difference in tone between the materials of the first semester that relate to *Vandover and the Brute* and those of the second semester that pertain to *McTeague*. The Harvard themes pertaining to *Vandover and the Brute* are light and flip, set within the secure boundaries of the San Francisco residential district in which the Norrises lived or in the Harvard Yard. They herald the early and "good" Vandover up to the time of his seduction of Ida. In contrast, the themes related to *McTeague*, which range from a character sketch of the protagonist on the opening page of the novel to Trina's death, near its end, do not touch on the happier days of Mac's marriage to Trina but generally treat the violent, animalistic aspects of their lives. The handling of drunkenness in the plot summary of Theme 32 suggests that it will be the major motivation of McTeague's downfall. That alcoholism is to be a dominant concern of Norris' fiction appears plain, because it is not only the subject of the first composition of the New Year (Theme 20), but it also turns up in other spring semester themes. After Norris wrote out the plot summary of *McTeague* on March 8, he returned to its Polk

19

Street environment in a theme toward the end of April, but the remainder of his themes during the last two months were concerned with the atmosphere and situations of *Vandover and the Brute*, and the very last one clearly derived from Zola and laid in France used the setting and language that were to appear on the opening page of that novel.

As a student who knew he was moving toward the career of a professional author, Norris planned to make use of all his writings, and in fact most of his themes did turn up, in one form or another, in his published work, the same text sometimes being reworked for more than one novel. Twenty-seven of them have some relation to *Vandover and the Brute*, eleven are related to *McTeague*, and seven of them bear upon *Blix*.

These three theme-related novels are themselves variously related. First, they are all set in San Francisco. When Vandover leaves that city for four years, his absence is disposed of in eight pages. But the three novels are interrelated in ways that go far beyond their common setting. Not only descriptions and scenes, but also situations and characters that Norris first sketched in the themes are shared by the novels. *Vandover and the Brute*, for example, was seemingly in Norris' mind at the beginning of his Harvard course, for the earliest surviving themes present situations related to it, even though few of them were finally worked into the text. But the incipient novel appears to have had larger dimensions than it ultimately achieved, as indicated by even so early and trivial a fragment as Theme 4, where Norris writes about a little boy who later appears under the name of Howard in both *Vandover and the Brute* and *Blix*, in each case as the heroine's naughty little brother. The relevance of several compositions to both of these novels and, even more significantly, the relations between the novels themselves, suggest that initially they may not have been separate works. If this were so, the finished *Blix* might actually be the expansion of a subplot removed from *Vandover and the Brute*, the expansion consisting mainly of set local-color descriptions, as well as material from the stories Norris had been told by Captain Joseph Hodgson (the prototype of the novel's Captain Jack) and from his own journalistic activities and courtship. Of course, if these elements were not in the original subplot, it would have been a very thin affair, like that of the romance between Landry and Page in *The Pit*, perhaps not even so developed as the curious love stories of Miss Baker and Grannis or of Maria and Zerkow in *McTeague;* that is, it would have been only a lightly sketched romance of two simple characters used to contrast with the actions of the more fully delineated figures in the main plot. But the Harvard compositions merely provided setting or slight situations for *Blix*, not any plot line. Of course, much that appears in the finished *Blix* could not have been conceived at the time that Norris was first thinking of *Vandover and the Brute*, for many of its events are fictionalized treatments of the courtship of his future wife, which occurred two years after he left Harvard, yet the general relationships between the novels are both curious and striking.

Use of the college themes alone does not explain the duplication of material in these novels. When he tried to launch his literary career in earnest, Norris discovered that publishers considered *Vandover and the Brute* and *McTeague* too unpleasant in subject and treatment to introduce an unknown Californian to the general reading public, and he found that he would have to prepare his way with more conventional fiction. So Norris wrote a melodramatic adventure tale, *Moran of the Lady Letty*, to precede *McTeague*, and he issued a gay romance, *Blix*, which was to come before *Vandover and the Brute*. Indeed, *Vandover and the Brute* had to wait for posthumous publication. By the time that Charles G. Norris put it into print, he seems not to have noticed that his brother had already used some of its text in *Blix*. Obviously Frank Norris did not intend to employ the same material twice in two published novels, but perhaps in a period when he despaired of ever publishing *Vandover and the Brute* he simply pillaged passages for the newer *Blix*.

The relations among the characters of the two finished novels are intriguing. Condy, the hero of *Blix*, is of the same age and class as Vandover and his friends Charlie and Dolly, coming from San Francisco's eligible young society men. Although Condy's group appears to be a little less rich than Vandover's (Condy's mother lives in hotel rooms rather than in a mansion like the elder Vandover), and it appears to be a little more elegant (his friends meet at the Bohemian Club rather than at a fast cafe, The Imperial), both sets seemingly are at home in the same society, and both young men go to the same sort of debutante parties. All this, of course, was closely related to Norris' own experiences, and he may only have been drawing on them twice over. For example, Condy and he were not only both born in Chicago and reared in San Francisco, but each lost his father (Condy by death, Norris by desertion), and each was educated at the state university, after which each spent a year at an Ivy League university in New England before returning to San Francisco to join the staff of a local journal, for which each wrote hack work as well as stories affected by Kipling, Richard Harding Davis, and DeMaupassant.

Furthermore, Condy's real love is for a young woman identical with the one to whom Vandover is initially betrothed, and both are like Jeannette Black, whom

22

Norris married. The resemblance indicates not merely that Norris was unable to create distinctively different kinds of heroines (although he was never good at subtle characterization of women), but also that possibly these characters were conceived as one. If this were so, it would help to explain Charles Norris' wonder that after a careful introduction and characterization of the heroine in *Vandover and the Brute*, the author let her drop from the novel's action, for he may have removed her part of the plot into the separate novel, *Blix*. In *Vandover and the Brute* the heroine is called Turner Ravis; in *Blix* she is known as Travis Bessemer. In the later novel she bears the nickname that gives the book its title, a nickname that seems intended primarly to make the character distinctive, as it runs counter to Norris' usual practice of naming. Although most of Norris' major male characters (McTeague and Vandover among them) have no first names, his women always do, and the "good" women are endowed with both first and last names. Turner and Travis are the same age, and both are almost ten years younger than their beaux, Vandover and Condy, just as Jeannette Black was a decade younger than Frank Norris. Turner is "a frank, sweet-tempered girl and very pretty," while Travis is "so pretty, so unaffected, and so good-natured." Both fit Condy's description of Blix as "a *man's* woman, a regular pal to him"—a concept Norris liked so much that he used the first phrase as the title of a lesser novel, published in 1899 along with *McTeague* and *Blix*. Drawing upon LeConte's theories, Norris portrayed these women as pure powers who lead the men they love to achieve the best that is within them, causing them to conquer their normal inclinations to brutality, sensuality, or vice, and assisting them to rise above their crude masculinity to a higher, more spiritual state.

23

INTRODUCTION

Norris may well have written these novels at different times to serve as basic contrasts to one another, depicting divergent ways of life, but the striking associations revealed by the Harvard compositions suggest
that these contrasts would have been even more effective if encompassed within one novel. The reader would
then discover significant relationships in situations that
are now quite separate. For example, one would find
more in the changing situation of the heroine Turner.
After Vandover's corrupt behavior makes him persona
non grata in society and Turner breaks with him, she
is pursued by other young men in their social group.
Were *Blix* and *Vandover and the Brute* a single novel,
one of these young men might well have been Condy.
The novel would then have shown that while one artist,
the painter Vandover, sinks in the scale, the other, the
novelist Condy, rises. Both start off with weak wills,
but Vandover becomes more and more addicted to
gambling and drinking as he pursues cheap women,
while Condy cures himself of gambling by turning to
a pure love. Condy's widowed mother also tacitly provides him a good background, whereas Vandover both
lacks the beneficent influence of a mother and absents
himself too much from the favorable influence of his fiancée Turner. While Condy has a constant and happy
association with Travis, as they roam the city like
"pals" with a chumminess untinctured by sexual attraction, Vandover chases after different women just for sexual excitement. The very settings of San Francisco are
contrasted, in that Vandover and the fast girl Ida meet
in the fetid atmosphere of a tawdry cafe, whereas Condy
and the fresh young Travis meet in the quaint, simple
atmosphere of Luna's restaurant.

Though it is easy to see that in a simplified form
Blix might well have served as the subplot of *Vandover
and the Brute*, it is far less apparent, yet not improb-

24

able, that in an early stage *McTeague* may also have
been conceived in relation to *Vandover and the Brute*.
Before Ida Wade is seduced and deserted by Vandover,
she talks to him "endlessly about a kindergarten in
which she had substituted the last week." Ida's closest
friend is Bessie Laguna, a shadowy figure who is gaily
dressed, loose, eager for fun, and probably also a substitute teacher since she is described as Ida's counterpart." [19] The first of Norris' themes that were later
worked into *McTeague* are those of January 7 and 8,
which concentrate principally on Bessie, a kindergarten
teacher married to a drunken, brutal sexual sadist, who
bears the name of McTeague but who is not the same
person as the dentist who marries Trina in the finished
novel. The McTeague in these two themes is unidenti-
fied by occupation, social class, or anything other than
his depraved behavior under the influence of drink. He
lives on Polk Street, presumably at the same time that
Vandover and Condy inhabit the city's nearby better
residential area, so that their paths could cross when
Vandover and his friends go out on the town. These
themes center on what happens to Bessie when she contracts a miserable marriage with McTeague, presumably after enjoying sexual relations with him, just as
did her friend Ida with the callous Vandover.

McTeague himself begins to assume clearer shape in
subsequent compositions. In Theme 25 of January 11 it
again appears that he, like Vandover, is given to drunkenness, though there is still no indication that he is an
ignorant, unlicensed dentist, very different in social level
from some of the other sporty men with whom the fast
women associate. It is possible that the McTeague in
Themes 23, 24, and 25 of January 7, 8, and 11 could
once have belonged to a fashionable set. Not until after
the long examination period holiday at Harvard does

19. *McTeague*, p. 59, 64.

25

the McTeague who gives his name to the finished novel begin to make an appearance. By then his story has moved farther away from an environment into which Vandover might venture. The first theme of the new semester, Theme 26 for February 15, coming more than a month after the last one dealing with McTeague, is a rough initial draft of the first page of the new novel. Over that vacation Norris' mind seems to have moved away from the McTeague who was in a position to marry the kindergarten teacher Bessie to a McTeague conceived as a loutish, unlicensed dentist. On February 18 came a theme that was not worked into the finished novel but whose depiction of a starving squalid hag, like the drunken woman of the theme of January 3, suggests what could happen in old age to a debased Bessie. The next day Norris turned in a theme about the death of McTeague's wife, for the first time named Trina. In the finished novel Trina becomes a scrubwoman in the kindergarten in which she once was imagined as the teacher, a downfall as great as Vandover's, in which he becomes a scrubman on the properties he once owned. However, there is no evidence in this theme whether Trina is a scrubwoman or a teacher, although we know that Norris' treatment of her murder was based on newspaper stories of a drunken husband stabbing to death his wife, a charwoman in a San Francisco kindergarten in October 1893.

In Theme 20, written only a day after the one presenting Trina's death, Norris backed up to sketch in a little more of McTeague's character, as well as to present his brother-in-law, Marcus Schouler. This composition was reworked into a passage in the first chapter of the finished novel but differs from the published text in apparently treating the McTeagues as already married, perhaps indicative of a faster-moving plot, not dwelling so long as does the finished novel on their

26

happy married days. A week later, in Theme 30, Mc-
Teague and Trina are depicted at an art exhibition, the
very same one that in *Vandover and the Brute* is attended by Ida and other women of her sort who make
pretensions to culture. For his next theme Norris
turned away from his dominant figures to create a character sketch of a typical lower-class worker on Polk
Street, which is to become the milieu of McTeague and
Trina, and the setting for the novel that surely by now
is wholly their own. Finally, on March 8, Norris wrote
a theme to outline the entire plot of the novel *Mc-
Teague* as he then conceived it. Trina is still a kindergarten teacher, and the outline differs from the finished
work in several other significant ways. But even if it
is not precisely the novel in miniature, the composition
is the outline of an independent tale whose characters
pursue paths separate from those they seemingly traveled in earlier themes. Even though the characters in
all three novels are now thought of as living but a
block or two apart in the city of San Francisco, the
McTeagues spend their squalid lives within the confines of Polk Street, while Vandover and Turner Ravis
and Condy and Travis Bessemer go their ways on Van
Ness Avenue and its stylish cross streets. The characters are wholly separated in the finished novels to which
they belong, no matter whether they started out with
some associations. Closely related as the three novels
may once have been, they certainly took on their own
lives as individual works and each was composed independently in final form. To some extent all three novels
came out of the year at Harvard. *Vandover and the
Brute* was probably pretty well finished in Cambridge,
and even *McTeague* may have been brought far toward
completion by the end of that college year. *Blix*, however, belongs mostly to a later day.

Norris returned to San Francisco for the summer of

1895. There he continued to work over the fiction written at Harvard while looking around for a journalistic job. During the whole of that year he published only two minor pieces. The first was a little sketch in the April issue of the *Harvard Advocate*, which was fitted into *Vandover and the Brute;* the other occupied a page in the autumn number of *The Argonaut*, published in San Francisco. It was his thinnest year of publication. Presumably Norris did not find the kind of job he wanted in San Francisco, so with a romantic dash, perhaps purposefully following the style of Richard Harding Davis, he arranged with a leading local newspaper, the *San Francisco Chronicle*, to print what he sent home from a trip abroad as a special foreign correspondent— the trip doubtless paid for by his mother. He went to England, from there to Madeira, and then in November he sailed to South Africa aboard a ship carrying adventurous young Englishmen to help Sir Leander Jameson and Cecil Rhodes achieve their dream of a united South Africa. From Cape Town and beyond he sent back a few dispatches accompanied by pen-and-ink sketches to illustrate such subjects as the famous diamond mines and a Zulu war dance. He was on the scene at the time of Jameson's Raid and close to the action. Although Norris suffered no wounds, he was stricken by a South African fever that was to weaken him for the remainder of his short life. By February he was back in California to recuperate and resume the writing of fiction. Norris spent six weeks of the early spring of 1896 slowly regaining his health. At first he stayed at home, but when he was well enough to leave his mother's care and the bay area itself, he decided to relax in the bracing air of the Sierra Nevada on a visit to a gold mind operated by a college friend. There he acquired the knowledge needed for the mining scenes toward the end of *McTeague*, though even with this added information, Norris' manuscript was still not ready for publication. His health regained, in April Norris assumed the assistant editorship of *The Wave*, a San Francisco journal to which he had intermittently contributed while he was a Berkeley student.

The Wave, which initially bore the facetious subtitle *A Weekly for Those in the Swim*, had been founded six years earlier with money from the Southern Pacific Railroad, to promote the Del Monte Hotel, its fashionable new spa south of San Francisco. The paper had grown beyond its original purpose to become a spritely tabloid journal of liberal editorials, bright theatrical and sports reporting, social gossip, interesting interviews, local color features, parodies, and short fiction and poems. For twenty-two months Norris was associated with *The Wave*, during most of which period he hardly missed contributing to an issue, even though he sometimes wrote only minor bits under the pseudonym of Justin Sturgis, or simply took care of the magazine's hackwork in much the way that his counterpart Condy did in *Blix*. Some of Norris' sketches depicting local character types or local scenes and situations were only about as long as his major Harvard themes. Indeed, some of *The Wave* pieces are quite similar to the Cambridge compositions. For example, Tug Wilson of Theme 31 emerges in *The Wave* of May 2, 1896, as a plumber's apprentice named Jonesie, whose habits and behavior also much resemble those of the protagonist of *McTeague*. To that novel Norris seriously returned in 1897, and its development beyond the form sketched out in the Harvard summary may be seen in *The Wave* short story of October 1897, "Judy's Service of Gold Plate," an early version of the story of Maria and Zerkow that introduced the theme of gold and greed in *McTeague*. "Fantaisie Printanière," a story printed in November, further develops McTeague's cruelty to Trina as portrayed in the Harvard themes, anticipating the finished novel. Other contributions to *The Wave*, such as "His Dead Mother's Portrait," "At Home from Eight to Twelve," "The 'Fast Girl,'" and "The End of the Act," are lifted entire from *Vandover and the Brute*.

Norris not only used his Harvard themes as contributions to *The Wave*, but some reporting for *The Wave* in turn served to embellish or extend his Harvard writings. So it was that an assignment handed to him in 1896 suggested a situation that he could use for *Blix*. The first adventure enjoyed by Condy and Travis in *Blix*, and the one from which so many others depend, is the visit he pays as a San Francisco reporter to a "great whaleback steamer taking on grain for famine-stricken India," just the sort of ship about which Norris had been sent to write an article on June 12, 1897. The exciting anecdote that the first mate tells to Condy is actually the one that Captain Hodgson told Norris, which he originally published in *The Wave* of September 24, 1898, as "The Drowned Who Do Not Die."

Norris doubtless considered himself lucky when he chanced on such a good assignment as that about the grain-laden ship, for years later it still inspired him as a subject for *The Octopus* and a projected novel, "The Wolf," which was to conclude his trilogy about wheat. But too many of the weekly chores for *The Wave* were of the kind that Condy said allowed him to "fake his copy from a clipping on the subject." By the end of 1897 Norris could not stand to work up any more of these short pieces. For that kind of stint, he maintained, he was "written out." He was only too willing to give up the position when he found a suitable new job and the journal located a satisfactory substitute.

The substitute was his friend Gelett Burgess. Fresh from his ingenious editing of the little magazine *The Lark*, Burgess had an observant eye and a nice turn of phrase. He applied them both not only to the local subject matter covered by *The Wave* but to his predecessor. He was correct when he referred to Norris' writings for *The Wave* as "the studio sketches of a novelist in the making." [20] Just a bit beyond the Harvard themes in scope and maturity of achievement, they too were early drafts and models for Norris' novels. More finished work began to emerge from Norris' studio at the beginning of 1898, when *The Wave* published serially Norris' first completed novel to appear in print. From January 8 to April 9 each issue carried one installment of *Moran of the Lady Letty*. It was a short adventure yarn, far more suited to *The Wave* than was *McTeague* or *Vandover and the Brute*, either of which might otherwise have been finished off quickly and submitted to the editor. *Moran of the Lady Letty* was turned out so rapidly that Norris often wrote a section only a week before publication, but the serial was effective enough not only for *The Wave* but also for a major New York publisher, S. S. McClure, who purchased it for book publication and hired its author to work for the firm. Norris thus found himself in the same situation as did Condy, whose novelette in an adventurous vein interested the fictitious Centennial Company of New York.

Moran of the Lady Letty is a fast-paced, high-spirited adventure tale of the sort told by the character Captain Jack Hoskins in *Blix*, having been based on yarns spun by his prototype, Captain Hodgson, to whom the work was dedicated. Just 150 pages long (the length that the Centennial Company told Condy was then much wanted by the New York market), it narrates the remarkable experiences encountered by a young San Francisco socialite of the same age and social set as

20. Oscar Lewis, ed., *Frank Norris of "The Wave"* (San Francisco: The Westgate Press, 1931), p. 8.

Condy, Vandover, and Norris himself. Shanghaied from the San Francisco waterfront and not altogether unwillingly forced to ship to Lower California, the hero, a recent Yale graduate, enjoys an escape from "his conventional life" as "a taxpayer, a police-protected citizen," into a series of melodramatic adventures with members of his city's Chinatown. He learns to make his way on a shark-fishing schooner, and eventually is left alone aboard ship with Moran, a huge, blonde, sea-roving, savage viking of a girl, possessed of the "purity of primeval glaciers." Their schooner is buffeted by whales, and in a wild fight with vicious beachcombers they capture a treasure in ambergris. Gradually the hero, like Vandover, loses his civilized character as "clubman and college-man," and "the half-brute of the stone age" leaps to life with "savage exultation." But unlike Vandover, as he becomes more primitive, he paradoxically grows to manhood. In this farrago of fantastic melodrama the nautical incidents come from Captain Hodgson, the tone of high society and derring-do are out of Richard Harding Davis, the philosophy of the cleft man is based on recollections of LeConte's classes, while the amalgam and the belief that nowhere "else but in California could such abrupt contrasts occur" are pure Norris. [21]

Even before *Moran of the Lady Letty* appeared from the presses of the New York publisher, for whom the author himself had gone to work in March 1898, Norris was attracted to adventures of his own. McClure's "half promise in the matter of war correspondence for the syndicate in case of 'unpleasantness' " in Cuba turned to reality by late spring. Norris was delighted to be dispatched in company with the admired Richard Harding Davis and his contemporary Stephen Crane, whose

21. *Moran of the Lady Letty* (New York: Doubleday, Doran & Co., 1928), pp. 244, 261, 285–286, 251.

books Norris had enthusiastically reviewed for *The Wave*. He soon discovered, however, that there was no truth in the popular idea of a war correspondent as a "tanned and toughened fellow who sits on his horse upon a hill top, watches a battle through his field glasses and then gallops off to the nearest telegraph station to get his stuff on the wire." [22] Instead, he did a lot of waiting at a Key West hotel, the headquarters for newspapermen on their way to Cuba. But once there, he saw plenty of action. Near San Juan Hill he witnessed one battle at the end of which "the dead were everywhere; they were in the trenches, in the fields of pineapple, in corners of the blockhouse, and in grisly postures halfway down the slope of the hill." [23] Norris returned to New York untouched by bullets but stricken with malaria, which seemed to revive his South African fever. He was not capable of work, so in the early fall he returned home to San Francisco, hoping to wallow "in the longest grass I can find in the Presidio Reservation and on the cliffs overlooking the Ocean and absorb ozone and smell smells that *don't* come from rotting and scorched vegetation, dead horses, and bad water." [24]

After nearly two months in a hospital and abed under his mother's care, Norris felt well enough to visit the Bohemian Club, where he enjoyed sitting idly behind the big window and observing passersby, particularly if they were pretty women. As his strength grew, he made ferryboat trips to Berkeley to loll away more time at his old fraternity house. Best of all, he was able to resume the exploring expeditions that he and Jeannette Black had enjoyed a year earlier. In this spirit he began to write an autobiographical novel about their

22. *Letters*, pp. 6, 11.
23. *Collected Writings*, p. 259.
24. *Letters*, p. 19.

romance. He had first met Jeannette two years before, in the fall of 1896, at a subdebutante dance when she was only seventeen. Tall, lively, charming, easygoing, fresh, and full of fun, she seemed to him a chum rather than a woman to love. They shared enthusiasms as they tramped about her native city, discovering its quaint byways and spacious vistas, amusing themselves with a variety of high-spirited jokes and jinks. That was the way they had spent much of the two years that Norris worked on *The Wave*. To the surprise of them both, their relationship gradually changed into love, and when in the fall of 1897 her family sent her to a finishing school in St. Louis, he contrived to have *The Wave* assign him to a story that would permit a trip there. As he confessed in *Blix*, in keeping with his masculine preference for experience over literary concerns, "Life was better than literature, and love was the best thing in life."

Back together again in San Francisco in the fall of 1898, Frank Norris and Jeannette Black resumed their relationship, reliving their frolicsome courtship while he wrote *Blix*. Presumably its heroine is a fair sketch of Jeannette, although she is given a medical career to make her appear like the dedicated kind of woman that Norris admired, at least in his fictive ethic. Condy represents the flip side of Norris, although his interest in gambling is perhaps exaggerated so as better to allow the novel to show the effect of a good woman on a morally lax man. But Condy is so much the puppy that one can hardly imagine him being—as Norris was— nine years older than the woman who reforms him.

Blix cannot be taken very seriously. It it is a trivial tale in keeping with the popular taste of the times, but its light-heartedness makes it much more appealing than that other example of popular tastes, the melo-dramatic *Moran of the Lady Letty*, whose situations and scenes are sometimes so overwrought as to be almost parodies of themselves. *Blix* is a charmingly pleasant story of light romance, amusing escapades, and colorfully appealing scenery. At the same time it is a self-centered boyish book, earnest about morality and gentlemanly standards, and tinctured by a patronizing juvenile snobbishness. Underlying the work, and set forth with an equally youthful gravity, is a basic thesis that every so often becomes jarringly obtrusive. Norris' animating novelistic philosophy emphasizes the transcendent, invigorating influence of nature on man, which leads him in this novel to praise the purity discovered "in that fine, clear, Western morning, on the edge of the Continent," where innocent lovers can stride forward, "young and heady and tumultuous with the boisterous, red blood of a new race." Such passages culminate on the last pages in a portentous paean to life which contrasts the wholesome West of America with the businesslike East to which the young couple must turn their faces as they plan to achieve their fulfillment in a sterner world beyond the simple, happy region of romance they have known.

Once again the thesis is Norris' own, but some of the situations and settings derive from his favorite writers. Travers herself is not only Jeannette Black but also a Gibson Girl out of Richard Harding Davis' books, just as Condy owes something to Davis' attractive young men. Some of the rhetoric describing their adventures, like their mutual admiration for literature distinguished by telling technical details, derives from Kipling's fiction, particularly *Plain Tales from the Hills* and *Many Inventions*, which Blix reads in preference to going to the theater with Jack Carter, and *The Seven Seas*, which she reads aloud with Condy. Even Norris' own city is seen partly through the eyes of Kipling, who described a visit there with great verve in *American Notes*, published only a few years earlier, while Norris was still a sophomore at Berkeley. Kipling therefore set the style for admiration of the bright lights of Kearny Street, of the cable cars that "take no count of rise or fall but slide equably on their appointed courses . . . and, for aught I know, may run up the side of houses," and best of all, of the fresh, lovely young women of San Francisco who "look you between the brows as a sister might look at her brother." All in all, Kipling decided that "San Francisco is a mad city, inhabited by perfectly insane people whose women are of a remarkable beauty." [25] That was Norris' San Francisco as well, and Travis was his local heroine à la Kipling, for "even in San Francisco, where all women are more or less beautiful," she "passed for a beautiful girl."

Just as important in shaping Norris' view of San Francisco was Robert Louis Stevenson, who had also enjoyed a love affair there only a decade before Kipling's visit. About the city he wrote an attractive if mannered piece, "San Francisco, A Modern Cosmopolis," whose key words are "romance," "quaint," and "foreign." It apparently affected Norris so much that in *Blix* he repeated its error that the trade winds purify San Francisco's climate. Stevenson also evoked San Francisco for Norris in two chapters of his novel *The Wrecker*, in one of which, entitled "Faces on the City Front," he described the same sort of prowling through picturesque parts of the city that captivated Norris. It is therefore no wonder that Condy praises this tale of Loudon Dodds' opium ship without identifying it, as though he expects any reader to know the novel intimately. Certainly Vandover does, for he also has remembered it for a long while and refers to it more than once. Indeed, the novel so influenced Norris that

25. Rudyard Kipling, *Letters from San Francisco* (San Francisco: The Colt Press, 1949), pp. 12–13, 56, iii.

its portrait of the mate on the brig *Flying Scud* helped to shape one of his major characters, for like the later McTeague, this sailor "was a huge viking of a man, six feet three and of proportionate mass, strong . . . musical and sentimental . . . on board he had three treasures; a canary bird, a concertina, and a blinding copy of the works of Shakespeare." [26]

Ultimately, of course, *Blix* told Norris' own story, in keeping with his belief that one best treats the setting and situation that one knows best. Having worked on the novel during the summer, he took its manuscript East in the fall when he felt well enough to return to his job at McClure's, but within a few months he wrote to a friend: "New York is not California, nor New York City San Francisco, and I am afraid that because of the difference I shall never become reconciled to the East, or ever come to really like New York . . . There is not much color here and very little of the picturesque. I have almost forgotten how a mountain looks and I can never quite persuade myself that the Atlantic is an Ocean—in the same sense as the Pacific." [27] But Norris continued at his editorial post and moved ahead with his fiction. The year 1899 was an important one, for he published three new novels. While *Blix* was being serialized from March to August in *Puritan*, a woman's magazine edited by a former associate on *The Wave*, the installments of his next romance, *A Man's Woman*, began to appear in the *San Francisco Chronicle* and the *New York Evening Sun*. This is an adventure story of Arctic exploration, again derived from that copious source of tales, Captain Hodgson, and from printed memoirs of polar explorers. First in an icy locale unfamiliar to him, then in a generalized city that lacks the specificity essential to Norris' settings, he places a

26. Stevenson, *The Wrecker*, ch. 24.
27. *Letters*, p. 31.

37

determined, high-spirited nurse—a kind of cultivated Moran, not unlike what her medical studies might have made of Blix—and an even more forceful man, the heroic explorer, who engage in a clash of wills before she is able to admit her love of him. It is the most contrived of his novels, "kind of theatrical," as he admitted. When writing *Moran of the Lady Letty*, he had been "flying kites, trying to see how high I could go without breaking the string," but this newest story, he had to confess, was an even more artificial affair, "very slovenly put together . . . with a lot of niggling analysis to try to justify the violent action of the first few chapters." [28]

A few months before this potboiler was serialized, his New York publishers finally issued Norris' first major novel, *McTeague*. Mulled over for a long time and partially written down four years earlier at Harvard, the novel was relatively free of the influences of the popular writers that were discernible in his other fiction. However, the impact of one novelist—Zola—was evident, and the other significant influences were his two professors, LeConte and Gates. It has been common to view *McTeague* as embodying Zola's naturalism, providing an amoral, detached, objective treatment of natural man as controlled by his instincts and passions, and shaped by an alien social and economic environment with which he cannot cope. Although Norris admired Zola and exuberantly signed some personal letters as "the boy Zola," he actually thought of Zola as a romantic writer and seems not to have intended to subscribe to his concept of naturalism. Rather, Norris thought of naturalism as a mode of fiction that is marked by reportorial accuracy in its serious quest for the "truth" of human experience, which might often be

28. *Letters*, pp. 22, 48.

38

seen as horrid but should not necessarily be viewed as deterministically shaped.

Zola's theory meant less to Norris than Zola's practice. He liked the novels, not the tracts, and of the fiction he particularly admired *L'Assommoir* because it presented a detailed, precise view of a lower middle class environment. Norris' interest in this kind of technique was evident even so early as the spring of 1895 when for an English 22 assignment he submitted the theme "Instantaneous Photographs," depicting life along the small shopping street of a large city. This exercise suited Professor Gates' injunction that a writer's work should be firmly rooted in particulars of observed scenes, that it ought to express a genuine, firsthand experience. This is just what Norris aimed at in his particularization of the life led by McTeague on Polk Street. Indeed, he once thought of calling his novel "The People of Polk Street," to show that the characters were influenced by their environment.[29] It is the street's unchanging appearance and unvaried routine, affected by the cable cars starting up each day at the same hour and leaving the street silent when they shut down at the same hour late each night, which provide the security needed by the ignorant McTeague to make a pattern of his life. Robert D. Lundy has carefully worked out the way in which, after introducing a single "fictional element, the dentist's offices, into the street, Norris meticulously drew the rest of its profile from life, observing the most trivial details, from the actual locations of shops to the real names of their owners."[30] By showing the myriad interrelationships of the lives passed in this microcosm, Norris creates the sense

29. *Letters,* p. 23.
30. Robert D. Lundy, "The Making of *McTeague* and *The Octopus*," unpub. diss. University of California, Berkeley, 1956, p. 146.

of an organic world. His treatment of life on Polk Street provides the novel not only with a convincingly realistic pattern but also with a symbolic one. No longer is he aping Stevenson's or Kipling's San Francisco, nor making an American translation of Zola's bourgeois milieu; this is now clearly Norris' own world. So firmly is it fixed and so precisely is it patterned that, as in real life, even the most extraordinary situations can be believably encompassed. Into this world he introduces LeConte's thesis about the contrasting animal and spiritual natures of man, simplifies and exaggerates it in the figure of McTeague, and in the climax to the novel shows how the brute whose "evil instincts . . . were so close to the surface" could leap to life and violently disrupt the quiet street by a bestial, sadistic murder.[31]

The novel that should have been published directly after *McTeague* was *Vandover and the Brute*, for both works were begun at the same time and intermittently added to and revised over the same period of years. Closely related in inception, they are similar as well in thought and treatment. Both portray the animal urges that lie just below the surface of civilized man and that easily rise up in displays of violence or vice, and both show the degeneration of men who give way to their animality. The brute that is within man appears in the title of one work and at the opening of the other, where one learns that McTeague's father often "became an irresponsible animal, a beast, a brute, crazy with alcohol," as McTeague himself finally does too.[32] Although the conception of both titular characters derives from LeConte's ideas, *Vandover and the Brute* illustrates them in a purer way, since Vandover is less affected by outer forces and more constantly animated by instinctive desires. His strong sensuality prevents

31. *McTeague*, p. 26.
32. *McTeague*, p. 2.

him from cultivating his spiritual potentialities, and his weak-willed, "yielding disposition" causes him to drift irresponsibly through life.

Despite the difference in temperament and background between McTeague, the unlicensed dentist who was a former car-boy in the mines, and Vandover, the San Francisco society man who was a former Harvard student, they are equally incapable of coping with life. Both lose their goods and their homes, become isolated from society, and sink finally to an animal level— the one a frightened brute who "felt an enemy, scented the trackers"; [33] the other down on all fours, ploddingly performing the basest chores at the orders of a young child. When Vandover drops into brutishness, he succumbs to a state of mind not unlike that of the simple McTeague: he enjoys only the habitual gratification of animal instincts by food, drink, and sex, and he so completely loses his intellectual powers that, when turned out of his lavish apartment, he shakes his head incredulously, grows confused, and falls into a furious rage.

When the ponderously slow-witted McTeague is aroused by liquor or can no longer stand "being made small of," he resorts to violence. Vandover too, though initially just as easygoing in his own way, lapses into angry confusion when overcome by drink or irritation. His response is attributable less to temperament than to a disease, which has been regarded by some as a curious unscientific bit of folklore that Norris ingenuously picked up for his novel. The only diagnosis of Vandover's sickness comes from a hotel doctor, whom Ellis calls in when he finds Vandover on his hands and feet, "perfectly naked, going back and forth along the wall, swinging his head very low, grumbling to himself." Ellis reports the doctor's diagnosis of Van-

33. *McTeague*, p. 362.

dover's affliction as "Lycanthropy-Mathesis," in which either Ellis or Norris seems to have garbled the doctor's statement by linking the two words. Ellis admits that he "never heard the name before" but assumes it to be "some kind of nervous disease." Since the first word indicates a kind of insanity in which the victim imagines himself to be a wolf, this ailment at first appears as fantastic as Ellis' own diagnosis, to the effect that Vandover's trouble stems from indulging in too much sexual activity. Such a cause is obviously as specious as the scary stories that once were told to prevent young boys from masturbating. But what Ellis thinks must not be confused with what Norris knew. Norris did not pick up information from old wives' tales but, like Condy, prided himself on getting technical matters correct. He obviously intended to show that Vandover was syphilitic. It would have been easy for him to get the needed information about this disease from Dr. Albert J. Houston, his college classmate and fraternity brother, who had recently provided the medical knowledge for *A Man's Woman*—a debt Norris recognized by the dedication of that novel.

From Dr. Houston, Norris could also have learned the "mathesis," or scientific knowledge, about paresis, a paralysis that may result from a syphilitic attack on the brain. The early manifestations include headaches, sleeplessness, and tension. These are followed by an inability to coordinate hand movements precisely, by a failure to concentrate or recall, and by general abandonment of the niceties of cultivated manners, which can culminate in a delusion that leads to beastlike behavior. Although the symptoms of Vandover's disease may not be commonly known, the cause is clearly indicated by Norris. The innocent Dolly Haight picked up syphilis from Flossie when "she kissd him full on the mouth" with such force that she caused his cut lip to bleed heavily. Such a means of becoming syphilitic is more a product of schoolboy lore than a common likelihood, but Norris uses it not only for melodramatic horror but to establish Flossie's infectuousness and the basis of Vandover's deterioration. Soon after kissing Dolly, Flossie has sexual relations with Vandover, and surely Norris intends the reader to understand that Vandover becomes not merely psychically but physically diseased. More dreadful yet is the effect on still another innocent friend of Vandover. Presumably the horror that leads the basically decent but "fast" girl Ida to commit suicide is her discovery that she is pregnant, four months after Vandover has lured her into intercourse with him. But there is also the suggestion that the syphilis, revealed much later in Vandover, has been transmitted to Ida and already discovered by her.

Like other novels by Norris, *Vandover and the Brute* not only treats the contrast of brutal and higher natures within an individual but commonly employs contrasts between characters. From the first the "easy, irresponsible" Vandover submits to the dictatorship of Geary, his Harvard classmate from San Francisco, who was "very shrewd and clever, devoured with an inordinate ambition," and "particularly pleased when he could get the better of anybody, even of Vandover." Similarly, the animalism of Vandover is contrasted with the simple purity of his friend Dolly Haight, another boy without a mother's influence but who is basically good, like Condy. The contrasts appear not only among the major characters. The fine, spirited, friendly Turner with whom Vandover goes to church on a Sunday morning is the exact opposite of Flossie, the woman with whom he spends a night although her "slightest actions suggested her·profession." We are told that Turner "influenced him upon his best side," while "Flossie appealed only to the animal and the beast in him." Even lesser figures, only momentarily associated with Vandover, are brought into tacit contrast, like the fast girl Grace and the Salvation Army "lassie," both of whom he encounters aboard ship. They all represent Norris' simplification and dramatization of LeConte's thesis.

The elementary conception of that thesis is put forth in all his works in a manner so single-minded and heavy-handed that Norris needed the specificity enjoined upon him by Professor Gates to save them from bathos. The precise details of settings, situations, and behavior, which he had often practiced in his Harvard themes, gave his novels an essential density and particularity that lent a realistic cast to the badly overstated thesis. He obviously knew intimately the people and places of which he wrote, for even when he was away from them at Harvard, he could describe with nicety the uptown San Francisco avenue that Vandover travels of a Sunday morning on his way to meet Turner; the gay, warm, noisy life of the Imperial bar; and the Sunday breakfast of a middle class family. To a substantial degree *Vandover and the Brute*, like some of Norris' other novels, is a mosaic of small scenes and descriptions such as he had learned to write for English 22. These snippets of situations and settings seem so real that they give a needed sense of actuality to the novel, which serves it far better than the author's orotund commentary about the dual nature of man. They also furnish a firm base for the symbolic significance attached to Vandover's various surroundings, indicating his diverse states of being: the Old Gentleman's home just off Van Ness Avenue; Vandover's apartment suite with its oak mantel, tiled stove, and window seat heaped with cushions; the blank white monotony of the Lick House bedroom, whose furniture was a "set" and whose floor was covered with a dull red carpet; and the room

dual nature of man.

in the Reno House, where "newspapers were pasted upon the ceiling and a great square of very dirty matting covered the floor."

When he has the exact realistic particulars, Norris can make any scene effective, and even the melodramatic shipwreck is convincing because of its substantial details, which Norris doubtless learned from Captain Hodgson. But when the novel becomes abstract, as it does for a while after Vandover's return from Coronado, the thesis obtrudes and the text becomes unduly sensational. At such places the image of a railroad engine frequently appears, which was later to dominate *The Octopus*. Not only is an engine used to open *Vandover and the Brute* realistically, but it recurs as a symbol throughout the novel, speeding "straight forward, driving before it the infinite herd of humanity, driving it on at breathless speed through all eternity, driving it no one knew whither, crushing out inexorably all those who lagged behind the herd and who fell from exhaustion." When Norris' oversimplified ideas are aggrandized with this spacious symbolism of titanic forces, they emerge in a rush of inflated rhetoric. The portentous diction is cast in what Norris at the end of *Blix* first developed as his epic style, depending on stock words and phrases that generally come in pairs and triplets: gigantic, vast, primordial; irresistible, changeless, unhampered; vague, unknown, mysterious; remorselessly, irresistibly; and squat, deformed, hideous. Such language plunges Norris into a mysterious but obsessive state of being, in which he strives to summon up "the deep murmur, that great minor diapason that always disengages itself from vast bodies, from mountains, from oceans, from forests, from sleeping armies."

Sometimes there is a more careless sort of repetition in *Vandover and the Brute*. It derives not from supposedly epic purposes but merely from the incompleteness of the novel. Because the work remained unrevised, Norris described two drunken sprees of Ellis in identical words, once near the beginning, once toward the end of the novel, presenting two pictures in which "the skin around his eyes was purple and swollen, the pupils themselves were contracted," as "suddenly he swept glasses, plates, castor, knives, forks, and all from off the table with a single movement of his arm." Sometimes text from the Harvard themes, slightly reworked, turned up in *Vandover and the Brute* and another novel as well, although Norris at one time presumably intended a single use for what was possibly thought of as a single novel. Thus, in *McTeague* it appears that "Trina's cousin Selina, who gave lessons in hand painting at two bits an hour, generally had an exhibit on the walls . . . it usually was a bunch of yellow poppies painted on black velvet and framed in gilt. They stood before it some little time, hazarding their opinions and then moved on slowly from one picture to another. Trina had McTeague buy a catalogue and made a duty of finding the title of every picture." [34] In *Vandover and the Brute* another couple, Ellis and Bessie Laguna, visit the same Mechanics Fair art gallery because "Mrs. Wade, Ida's mother, who gave lessons in hand painting, had an exhibit there which they were interested to find: a bunch of yellow poppies painted on velvet and framed in gilt. They stood before it some little time hazarding their opinions and then moved on from one picture to another; Ellis bought a catalogue and made it a duty to find the title of every picture." Similarly, Ida's house and the house for which McTeague and Trina long are essentially identical. Fragments of *Vandover and the Brute* were doubtless mined for use in *McTeague* and *Blix* and for sketches published in *The Wave*. Not only was some of the text transferred

34. *McTeague*, pp. 169–170.

INTRODUCTION

to other works, but at least a little of the manuscript
may have disappeared before publication, as evidenced
by the lack of a transition between Chapters XV and
XVI. No substantive matter seems to be missing, but
Chapter XVI opens too abruptly, with a reference that
implies a missing antecedent. That gap, however, is
trivial by comparison with the fate of the entire manuscript of *Vandover and the Brute*, which not only was
said to have been lost for a time before publication, but
which has since disappeared completely.

Of the several hundred pages that must have comprised the book, only Norris' handwritten title page sur-
vives. As though it were a printed page, he appended
the date 1895, indicating that the work was completed
in that year. Though he may have tinkered with it beyond that time, the text of the novel does not provide
clear evidence. Probably Norris put *Vandover and the
Brute* aside in 1895 while working on *McTeague*, then
had to hold it in reserve even longer when publishers
indicated that they needed a short, light novel before
attempting to introduce a new author with a long,
frankly realistic, unpleasant book. So the manuscript
was again put away until Norris had been safely established as the author of *Moran of the Lady Letty*
and *Blix*, and until *McTeague* itself had been issued.
In November 1899, the year in which the last two
books appeared, his New York publishers still seemed
unwilling to print *Vandover and the Brute*. However,
they went so far as to send it to Grant Richards, the
London firm that had already issued two of his novels
and was to follow with all the others. Norris rather
anxiously inquired, "What do you think of it?" and
then admitted, "I am afraid it is hardly available for
any publisher just yet," [35] implying that the text was
still in need of reworking. The reception was obviously

35. *Letters*, p. 49.

47

unfavorable, for the manuscript came back to its author and was stored away once more. From time to time it must have been looked at, but probably without hope of publication, for there is no evidence that he polished it further, and in 1901 he even picked out parts of a passage for *The Pit*, the last novel he ever wrote.

In a way, *Vandover and the Brute* thus formed part of Norris' literary career almost from its beginnings to its end. Sadly enough, the distance between the two was not great. The unpublished novel continued to have a life after the death of its author from peritonitis in 1902. In 1903 Charles G. Norris privately admitted to Norris' biographer, Franklin Walker, that the manuscript had remained in the hands of Frank's widow until his publishers should find it acceptable, but in a Foreword to the first edition, printed in 1914, he contended that publication was deferred because the manuscript had been packed in one of many uninventoried crates stored in a large San Francisco warehouse and therefore the chore of searching for it was put off for a time. According to this story," while the question of opening these crates one by one was being discussed," [36] the warehouse was burned to the ground in the San Francisco earthquake and fire of 1906. Then, Charles Norris declared, another six or seven years elapsed before "a letter was received from the storage company stating that certain furniture and boxes had been moved away from the warehouse just before the building caught fire. These had been transferred to a safer place, and when a readjustment took place, it was discovered that a few of the crates had not been properly labelled and the contents of one or two of them failed to identify

36. The private admission is documented in notes by Franklin Walker on his interviews with Charles G. Norris, The Bancroft Library; the public statement occurs in the Foreword by Charles G. Norris to *Vandover* and the Brute (New York: Doubleday, Doran & Co., 1928), p. v.

the owner." Among those contents was the missing manuscript, which bore neither the author's signature nor the owner's name, so that it was kept by the warehouse management "for seven years until a junior member of the firm one day began to read the manuscript, recognized its author's style at once, and a complete identification resulted."

Not only could the style be recognized by more formal literary critics than junior managers of storage companies, but the professionals were readier then to accept another so-called naturalistic novel by Norris than they had been during his lifetime or directly after his death. In 1899 *McTeague* had been attacked as a coarse, brutal story, and one reviewer of the time even insisted "we must stamp out this breed of Norrises!" [37] Moreover, some years later Professor Gates had told Charles G. Norris that he would not write a Preface to *Vandover and the Brute* and that he even thought the novel should not be published, perhaps because of what Charles Norris called its "revolting" parts, such as the scenes of drunkenness and the frank descriptions of young men chasing after "chippies" who represent what they call "cheap meat." [38] But by 1914 even the general public had come to accept fiction franker than that which professional critics had once been willing to approve. Dreiser's *Sister Carrie*, which Norris had recommended for publication, helped to break the way. Even Norris' own novel *The Pit*, treating an illicit romance, had been serialized by *The Saturday Evening Post*, from where it moved to the bestseller list. Norris' reputation was so well established at the time of his premature death that within a short period his lit-

37. Franklin Walker, *Frank Norris* (New York: Doubleday, Doran & Co., 1932), p. 222.
38. Ms. of Walker interview with C. G. Norris, May 16, 1930, The Bancroft Library; *Vandover and the Brute*, ch. VII.

INTRODUCTION

erary essays and short stories had been assembled from
various magazines and turned into three new books,
and even a slight parable was salvaged from *The Wave*,
bulked out by elegant typography, and issued as a
separate Christmas book. Under these circumstances a
hitherto unpublished novel was very welcome.

According to the Foreword written by Charles G.
Norris, the pages of the original manuscript of *Vandover and the Brute* "are eloquent of the struggle its
author underwent to bring it to its logical and artistic
conclusion," and the much corrected page that he reproduced in a pamphlet about his brother fits that description well.[39] Nevertheless, the text gives an impression of completeness, and years later, even Charles G.
Norris admitted to his brother's biographer, Franklin
Walker, that the manuscript was in good order, although he also claimed that he had done a great deal
of work to put the manuscript into suitable shape.[40]
First of all he contended that he had deleted a whole
chapter (perhaps the one that once preceded Chapter XV or another that may have followed it) and
expunged words here and there that were thought to
be too frank for the publisher or the public to accept.
He also maintained that he had added about five thousand words of text, but he did not indicate whether
they comprised a single section or several. This would
be a very substantial addition, representing approxi-
mately five percent of the novel. Several critics who
know Norris' writing well have read the work in order
to find the additions. Although one thought he had
discovered them in the first two chapters, this seems

39. Charles G. Norris, *Frank Norris* (New York: Doubleday, Page &
Co.), p. 18.
40. Letter of Jan. 19, 1931, from C. G. Norris to Franklin Walker,
The Bancroft Library.

unlikely because their eight thousand words begin with a passage from a Harvard theme, and other parts are clearly representative of Frank Norris' style. Nowhere does the novel seem to display characteristics of Charles G. Norris' style. The changes and additions he made must have been cleverly done, and they probably were not nearly so extensive as he thought when discussing them seventeen years after the event.

Although Norris' last book to be published, *Vandover and the Brute* was substantially a young man's work, probably untouched after he was twenty-six, that is, two years before his first novel, *Moran of the Lady Letty*, appeared in print. Charles G. Norris considered *Vandover and the Brute* to be a not-quite-finished work that "would have been altered and rewritten were its author here to bring to its revision his riper judgment." [41] This is just what Frank Norris did for *McTeague* in the two years that remained to work over it after he had put away *Vandover and the Brute*. Yet the posthumously published book is almost as good as the one to which the author gave a final revision. The differences in achievement between *Vandover and the Brute* and *McTeague* are in large part comparable to the differences between the sketches for *McTeague* printed in *The Wave* during 1897 and the final novel published in 1899.

Even the finished *McTeague* suffers from a crudity of style and melodrama of situation such as smack of an enthusiastic but still youthful man. The novel has so long been accepted along with Dreiser's *Sister Carrie* as a landmark of American fiction at the opening of the twentieth century that one forgets how young and inexperienced its author was. When the editor of *The Bookman* met Norris in 1899, he was surprised to find

41. Foreword by Charles G. Norris to *Vandover and the Brute*, p. vii.

him "a very pleasant boy." [42] Despite his prematurely white hair, Norris remained boyish until he died in his early thirties. He retained always a kind of youthful playfulness, which led him to refer to his epical *The Octopus* as "The Squid," and which allowed him to introduce a passing portrait of himself into *McTeague* [43] and to arrange that Trina's dental appointments with Dr. McTeague should come on the days and at the hours that English 22 met in the fall of 1894.

Although he was boyish, Norris knew that there was more to life than the happy-go-lucky experiences represented in his counterpart Condy. He enjoyed the easy, romantic days spent wandering about San Francisco's hillsides, breathing in the clean, fog-swept air of its bay, but he knew also the life of Vandover "that began after midnight in the private rooms of fast cafes and that was continued in the heavy musk-laden air of certain parlours among the rustle of heavy silks." He had detected something of Vandover's nighttime feelings in his own nature, and they frightened him. The fiction of his admired Stevenson had dramatically depicted the duality of man's nature and the presence of a Dr. Jekyll and Mr. Hyde in contemporary society. Norris faced such disparate selves both in modern man and himself, and described them in his fiction. Relieved to find that his own so-called lower nature could be held in check by putting himself under the influence of good women, he turned first to his mother, later to his fiancée. But he remained acutely aware that not only adventurous fiction but his own experience bore out what he had learned of mankind in his college course on zoology. From LeConte's class at Berkeley Norris had acquired a thesis about man's ambivalent nature,

42. Franklin Walker, *Letters of Western Authors* (San Francisco: The Book Club of California, 1935).
43. *McTeague*, p. 325.

and from Gates' class at Harvard he had learned the techniques to portray it in writing seriously about his immediate environment. These influences are evident in novels so diverse as *Blix, McTeague,* and *Vandover and the Brute.* Segments of these novels, written during his Cambridge year, all employ the common setting of a city that continually fascinated Norris, and each in its different way illustrates something of his own life extrapolated to general human experience.

The Imperial.

The main Entrance was by the cigar stand in the vestibule. It opened directly into the bar-room paved with marble flags. To the left was the bar, the counter of which was a single slab of polished ~~red-wood~~. Behind it was a large plate mirror.

Cherry

On one side of this was the cash register, on the other a parian marble statue of the diving girl. The glasses and and bottles were arranged in pyramids here and there. The three silent bar-tenders in clean linen coats and white aprons moved about deftly opening bottles and mixing drinks with extraordinary dexterity and occasionally turning ~~to~~ punch the indicator of the cash register. On the other side of the room hung a large copy of a French picture representing a Sabbath, witches, goats and naked girls whirling through the air. Underneath it was the lunch counter where clam-fritters, the specialty of the house could be had three afternoons in the week. Near by was a racing chart, where the day's entries, pools, ~~and~~ weights, and mounts were set forth. By the side of the lunch-counter stood two-nickel-in-the-slot machines.

Manuscript of Theme 39, dated March 27, 1895

THE STUDENT THEMES

1. YOUNG SOCIETY MAN

November 16, 1894

In the winter he was in the Insurance offices of his father or his uncle.

In the summer he could be found at the sea-side, where he played chopsticks on the hotel piano with the forefinger of each hand, while a girl played the accompaniment.

His excitements were of the tennis-court and the drawing room and he believed that education meant knowing things and talking about them. He had never been outside of his state.

Reader's comment: "Not clearly a unit."

• Although this is the earliest theme to survive, it was submitted on the twenty-second class day and was surely preceded by a substantial number of other compositions. Young insurance clerks appear frequently in Norris' work, as in *McTeague* (Ch. I) and *Vandover and the Brute* (Chs. II and IV). Generally they are neither bright nor industrious, but simply pleasant young men. Vandover's friend Ellis, to whom the last line of this text is also applied, appears less sociable than most insurance clerks. The character and text of this theme come straight out of Norris' "Unequally Yoked," first issued in *Berkeleyan Magazine* on September 22, 1893, and republished as "Toppan" in *The Third Circle* (1909). So early in his Harvard course Norris is resorting to writings published while he was a student at Berkeley.

STUDENT THEMES

2. AN UPTOWN AVENUE, SUNDAY 7 A.M.
November 19, 1894

Van Ness Avenue was very still. It was about 7 o'clock. Curtains were down in all the houses. Here and there a servant could be seen washing down the front steps. In the doorways of some of the smaller houses, were loaves of French bread and glass jars of milk, while near them lay the damp twisted roll of the morning paper. There was everywhere a great chittering of sparrows and the cable-cars as yet empty trundled down the cross streets, the conductors cleaning the windows and metal-work.

From far down at the end of the avenue came the bells of the Catholic cathedral ringing for early mass. A defiantly respectable second girl passed him carrying her missal. At the other end of the avenue was a blue vista of San Francisco Bay. On the opposite shore, Mount Tamalpais heaved itself out of the water, like a waking lion.

Reader's comment: "Inventory—Too much passive construction."

• Although marred by a little awkwardness and a lack of punctuation in the sixth sentence, marked by the corrector with a "U," here is the first example Norris' sharp observation of the urban details of his home neighborhood, which distinguishes *McTeague*, *Blix*, and *Vandover and the Brute*. The San Francisco cable cars featured in all three novels also make their first appearance here in Norris' writing. Curiously, Abbott in his comment did not seem disturbed by the fact that this entire theme relates to what is seen by a man identified simply as "him" three sentences from the end. Perhaps the device was acceptable

58

because the man without antecedent is obviously the early Vandover already known to Abbott from prior, related compositions.
By the time this theme was submitted, seven weeks after the
opening of class, Norris would have been at least fifty pages into
the story of Vandover if he wrote it in sequence. The text published in Ch. IV twenty years later is almost identical with this
theme, and a slight repetition occurs in Ch. XIV.

3. AN UPTOWN AVENUE, 11 A.M.

November 20, 1894

It was rather warm and on the sunny side of Van
Ness avenue one saw groups of nurse-maids, with their
charges, some of these in perambulators. But few teams
passed in the street. These were mostly market-deliv-
ery wagons. There were butchers' carts as well, two
wheeled affairs, with high-stepping hacks in the shafts.
The boys who drove them wore big bloody aprons and
smirked at the nurse-maids as they passed. Gardeners
appeared in the front yards, and a China boy here and
there wet down the side-walk. Occasionally a sprinkler
passed laying the dust or more rarely a private carriage
on its way to the park. One saw very well dressed ladies
coming down the front steps of the houses, holding their
grocer's book under their elbows, while they buttoned
their gloves. They were going to market on the little
up-town business street, one block below.

Reader's comment: "Lacks unity. Last sentence good."

• Although this text does not appear as a unit in the finished novels, its atmosphere is redolent of *Vandover and the Brute, Blix,*
and *McTeague.* The China boys and the ladies with their grocer's books also appear in the former novel. The first appearance

here of Polk Street—as yet unnamed—in Norris' fiction seems ordinary enough but it won the approval of Abbott.

4. A LITTLE BOY
November 22, 1894

He played base-ball too well to be a very good boy. He had originally been christened Paul a name which he abhorred because it was so "darn goody-goody." He hated girls and he loathed with a loathing beyond words the pictures of the little boys in the fashion plates.

Reader's comment: "Concise but fragmentary."

• The first sentence and the whole sense of this theme describe young Howard in *Blix* (Ch. I), the heroine's naughty little brother, who is also nearly identical with the young brother of the heroine of *Vandover and the Brute*, as portrayed in Ch. VI.

5. THE END OF THE ACT
November 23, 1894

All the actors of the company began to assemble on the stage for the closing tableau, the leading man began to maneuver for his pose at L. C. where he was to voice the epigrammatic sentiment that gave the name to the play and the escorts in the audience heroically foregoing the finale commenced to get together their ladies' wraps fans and opera glasses.

The curtain, the original red curtain that had been down before the beginning of the first act fell, amid hurried applause and whistles from the gallery. The house-lights were suddenly turned up and the orchestra struck up a lively quickstep.

Reader's comment: "Too loose."

• In April of 1895 Norris published in the *Harvard Advocate* a piece bearing the title of this composition but otherwise unlike it. However, the *Advocate* text was almost verbatim the opera scene in *Vandover and the Brute* (Ch. XIV), which Norris found so satisfactory that he printed it in *The Wave* of November 27, 1897. Later yet he borrowed a little of it for *The Pit*. But the economical Norris never used this composition. It could well have served as part of *Vandover and the Brute*, fitting in, say, in Ch. IV, or it could have turned up in *Blix*, where there are many references to theater parties but no such scenes. In *McTeague* there is a notable theater party, but not nearly so sophisticated as the one in Theme 5 and wholly different from it.

6. AT HARVARD, 1894

November 24, 1894

I came into breakfast the morning after the foot-ball game and saw the Jap. plunged in the Herald. Port Arthur had been taken by his countrymen the day previous after forty hours fighting. Yale had won again and I had no heart for life as yet; but *he* was on a winning side, *he* know how it felt to be victorious, *he* triumphed and as he read eagerly and thirstily, his cheeks flaming with excitement, I (almost) envied him. Port Arthur was taken, his enemies beaten, the back of the war broken, and what a battle it must have been. Think of forty hours of fighting.

"Well," said I as I pulled up my chair opposite him. "It was a great struggle."

He marked his place with his fork before looking up. "Oh yes," he answered, "a great struggle. But if Fairchild had only kicked two inches further and two seconds sooner. — fourteen to twelve, hey? "

Reader's comment: "Well planned."

• On November 21, 1894, Japanese forces had captured the Chinese naval arsenal at Port Arthur, a great victory of the Chino-Japanese War. On November 24 the Harvard-Yale varsity football game ended with the score Yale 12, Harvard 4. Harvard's fullback, Fairchild, missed one field goal because the ball hit the crossbar, and he missed another in the closing seconds of the game, because his perfect kick was completed after the end of the game had been called. This composition was indeed well executed, in the vein of Richard Harding Davis, with the kind of snappy ending that O. Henry was to popularize. Typical of Norris, however, is the sportiveness of treating as an historical incident an event that had occurred on the very day he wrote the composition; it is in keeping with his private joke of scheduling McTeague's appointments for Trina's dental work on precisely the days and hours when English 22 was meeting. Although this clever little piece was not intended for a novel, it was probably composed close to the time that Norris wrote the Harvard scenes for *Vandover and the Brute,* including the one referring to the Harvard-Yale freshman football game (Ch. II), which actually was played on December 1, 1894.

7. THE "LAST LEAF" UP TO DATE

November 27, 1894

The network of dead vines on University looked like the tracings of the nervous system on an anatomical chart. There was just one leaf left, crisp and blood red.

They had been walking through the yard. He was a "Harvard Man." She wore no gloves and carried his cane. I regret to add that they did not know each other's last names.

She plucked the last leaf away and shut it in her card case saying, "I'll press this leaf to remember you by."

"Hum," he said reflectively, digging his heel into the ground. "What's the matter with pressing *me* and remembering the leaf."

Reader's comment: "A good figure."

• Under a title that toys with the image of a venerable Bostonian as presented by Oliver Wendell Holmes, himself the laureate of Boston, Norris offers a sophisticated view of the kind of fast girl who hung around Harvard. Like the preceding theme, this one conveys the mood of some of the scenes of Cambridge life toward the opening of *Vandover and the Brute* (see Ch. II), but it presents a debonair Harvard man with a quip on his tongue rather than one, like Vandover, whose "gorge rose with disgust" at the chippy he had picked up.

8. A FIRE

November 1894

. . . their party had come within two or three blocks of the blaze they were out of breath. Here the excitement was lively. The side-walks were full of people going in the same direction and on all sides one heard guesses as to where the fire should be. On the front steps of many houses stood elderly gentlemen in smoking jackets still holding the evening's paper; forbidding their little sons to go. In the open windows above were other members of the family, looking and pointing their

63

faces tinged with the glow. Then they came to the first engines, violently pumping and coughing, the horses standing near by, already unhitched and blanketed, and feeding indifferently in their nose-bags. Some of the crowd preferred watching the engine than the fire. The party even met some people coming in the opposite direction and with a pang of dissappointment heard them exclaim, "all out now" or else "false alarm."

It was the barn of a big house that was burning. The hoses were laying about the streets like pythons, and upon the neighboring roofs were silhouette groups of firemen with helmets and axes. "Ah," exclaimed a man that stood near by, "I was here when it first broke out. Ought to have seen the flames then.—It's almost out *now*," he added contemptuously.

• The heading, reader's comment, and opening lines of this theme are all missing because that portion of the paper has been neatly cut out, probably by Charles G. Norris to obtain his dead brother's autograph for an admirer of his writing. Although the date of the composition is also missing, it would seem to have fallen between November 19 and 30, 1894, for on the former date Norris submitted some text from Ch. IV of *Vandover and the Brute* and on the latter he submitted some text from Ch. VI, while this theme represents text from Ch. V. The printed text is very close to that of the composition, except that it is more complete and vivid, and Norris has smoothed out an allusion to the engine that the corrector labeled "incoherent." One other emendation indicates a changed point of view: as a young Harvard student, Norris refers to the householders with little sons as "elderly gentlemen," whereas a few years later, more mature himself, these figures are revised to "middle-aged gentlemen."

9. SUNDAY MORNING EN BOURGEOIS
November 30, 1894

It was Sunday morning and the family were at breakfast. Snooky and Howard were eating their mush and melons. "I see father," said Stanley (Harvard '89). "I see there is a scheme to open up the Canadian canal system to U. S. shipping if our government will stand the expense."

"Ma, make Howard stop."

"—the expense for the maintenance repairs etc."

"St–o–p."

"Yes," answered his father. "There is an editorial here about it. It seems the tolls desired from the Canadian traffic are not enough to pay running expenses."

"St–o–p."

"Our vessels will not have absolute liberty. There will probably be resolutions imposed by reason of international comity and the Washington treaty which—"

"Ma won't you please make Howard st–o–p."

"That's it. Go on," exclaimed the old gentleman. "Talk all the time. Interrupt everybody."

"Well I don't c–a–re. Howard's squirting watermelon seeds at me 'n ma won't make him stop."

"O I was not," shouted Howard. "I only just held one between my fingers 'an it kind of shot out."

"Well you walk upstairs lively now young man and get dressed for Sunday school."

Reader's comment: "Prolix."

• This sketch does not appear in Ch. VI of *Vandover and the Brute,* for which it was once obviously intended as part of the

Sunday activities of the Ravis family, whose Howard keeps his name, although Snooky has hers changed to Virginia, while Stanley is switched from Harvard '89 to Yale '88, and from a precise discussion of a particular international economic situation to the vaguer seriousness of "continually professing an interest in economics and finance." But the sketch does become part of the opening of *Blix*, where both Howard and Snooky retain their names and there is a Sunday morning breakfast scene that includes Howard's identical misbehavior.

10. THE NOISES IN THE YARD

December 4, 1894

As I sit here in front of the fire trying to evolve still another daily the noises from the yard come up through the windows and the entry in a steady undertone.

From time to time there is the sound of musical whistled calls from men in the yard to their friends up in Matthew's and Weld and Gray's, and a window raises with a protesting shriek while someone shouts down, "Yes in about half an hour," or some other words. There is the sound of thick soled boots on the walks and an occasional jangle of sleigh-bells. A certain express-man who is delivering a bed-stead over at Weld, raises a strange call half-whistle, half shout which is peculiar to him. From the lower stairway comes a fearful racket. I know it is made by the man who always slides his cane down the stairs after his fox terrier. The next moment I can hear the dog barking outside.

And *this* noise now, I ought to know it, a noise like the sew-saw grating of a gigantic rusty hinge, that sets the nerves in a tangle and the teeth on edge, that makes one feel unhappy and morose and irritable. I think

66

I should know that noise and isn't old John standing on the steps of Matthews waving his hand at its author.

And—but stop. The last noise of all is the ten o'clock bell from Harvard and if this theme is to count it must go in at once.

Reader's comment: "Don't talk 'shop.' Too much an inventory."

• For the first time here Norris does not submit part of the novel he was writing. All of the first nine themes that survive either were incorporated in *Vandover and the Brute* or were so well suited to it that they probably were once considered as its parts. For some reason Norris' work on the novel seems to have bogged down at the end of November. Obviously lacking a subject for his first December theme, he begins it with the time-worn device of describing in the immediate present the situation of being unable to think of what to write about, drifts into a description of whatever is happening around him at the moment, and concludes with a platitudinous reference to the bell calling him away. It is no wonder that Abbott, who must have read this sort of thing many times before, warned Norris not to talk shop and was sufficiently irritated to indicate in the margins his displeasure with the slang use of "daily" for "themes" and to call "raises" an "impropriety" and "sew-saw" a "barbarism."

11. RAIN IN A FOREST

December 6, 1894

Rain in a forest, at the close of a windless autumn day the nadir of depression, the quintessence of dreariness, when the drops drum, drum, drum, upon every shaking leaf, when the green mosses and tree-lichens grow big and spongy with wet and the thick bark of the larger trees turns black with the water and swells to the consistency of muck, when every tiny rattling cataract of rain finds its way into the nether-most corners of the undergrowth and wakes up the drowsy wood-land odors asleep between the layers of dead and fallen leaves, when everything is quiet and hushed, when the robins sit voiceless on each secluded bough, fluffing out their feathers, making themselves larger, dozing with their beaks upon their breasts, when all animal life is drowsing in its farthest coverts and everything is very quiet while the rain drums on unceasingly in endless minor cadence.

Comes a little gust of wind from the East and in an instant all is changed, a great whispering voice seems to pass along the higher foliage the trees shudder and groan and on the ground the leaves go whirling and scurrying about like excited rabbits.

Reader's comments: "A unit of impression. A good figure at the close."

• This mood piece is probably an isolated bit of text written for the occasion only, perhaps even as a specific assignment, because it is far more "poetic" and impressionistic in attitude, style, and subject than the sketches Norris had been submitting as parts of the nascent *Vandover and the Brute*—now for the moment put aside. This theme suggests something of the speciously heightened treatment of nature that Norris was to employ much later in *The Octopus*. It is also the first theme to exhibit a stylistic device that later became typical, use of two or preferably three words, generally adjectives, similar in meaning, to magnify the significance of the subject, such as "quiet and hushed," "dozing" and "drowsing," and "unceasingly" and "endless."

12. A BLIND MAN
December 8, 1894

He did not swing his arms when he walked but let them dangle at his sides and he had long ago lost the habit of turning his head when spoken to. He made clever useless little things out of bits of twine, and people when addressing him, some how made it a point to speak to him in a very loud distinct voice although his hearing was extraordinarily acute.

Reader's comment: "Observant."

• As *Vandover and the Brute* presumably remained in abeyance, Norris continued his stint of daily themes with a little descriptive vignette, this time of a man rather than a landscape. In the first sentence he suggests that the man has been blind for a long time but not forever, a nice detail of the sort that he applies also in his characterization of the stone-deaf character whom Vandover and his friends call "the Dummy."

13. A DESERT RIVER
December 10, 1894

There was a curious smell from the warm slime on the Jeliffe river and a sweet, heavy and sickening odor exhaled into the desert air from the bunches of dead and scorched water-reeds. The river had shrunk during the hot months disclosing its broad black stretch of mud-bank, which rapidly drying under the sun of the Sahara had cracked and warped into thousands of tiny concave cakes.

Reader's comment: "An admirably vivid vocabulary. Unmassed and so not a clear unit of impression."

• This theme is only a slight reworking of the opening paragraph of "The Son of a Sheik," written while Norris was a student at Berkeley and printed in the June 1, 1891, issue of *The Argonaut*. Even though it had been accepted by a publisher, Abbott was right in finding it "unmassed," a criticism that may have had a significant effect on Norris because his his later technique emphasized the heaping up of descriptive impressions. Norris employs another typical device here in the redundant use of "smell" and "odor," which called forth Abbott's stricture: "Avoid using two words for one thing." He also stigmatized the final image as "not clear."

14. MAXIM: MAN'S VICES

December 13, 1894

There is more hope for the man who indulges a little in all the vices in general, women, gambling, drunkenness and the like than for him who gives all his attention to any one of these vices in particular.

Reader's comment: "Assertive. Rejected as a duplicate of December the twelfth's."

• Norris seems to have fancied himself as a writer of maxims. While at Berkeley, for instance, he had published a story, "The Most Noble Conquest of Man," which began: "There are three things that every man, by virtue of his sex, must know all about, and must never under any circumstances be afraid of; these are firearms, women, and horses." However, Norris presumably wrote this Harvard maxim to satisfy an assignment, for Gertrude Stein and other students also submitted epigrams. The moral of this epigram is related to *Vandover and the Brute*, for

although Vandover indulges in all of the vices mentioned—
especially women—it is gambling that undoes him. The subject of a man with a single vice—gambling—is also treated,
though fliply, in *Blix*. The theme of December 12 to which
Abbott referred is missing, a break in the preserved sequence
that may be the result of Frank Norris' brother Charles having
given it away as a gift. He gave the theme of December 10 to
Franklin Walker in 1931, and this one of December 13 he kept
for himself after returning the remainder of the themes to Frank
Norris' widow, having looked through them with a possible
thought to publication.

15. DIALOGUE ON FISHING

December 17, 1894

—"There goes your reel. What is it? Another weed?"
—"Not much. That's a *bite this* time."
—"Steady now, that looks like a big one, don't get
rattled. Let him have all the line he wants . . . now
. . . *strike.*"
—"Whoop! I've got him, get out that landing net."
—"Don't take him in so fast, he's too big for that,
you'll have to play him."
—"By George, he hangs back like an ice-wagon."
"—Only sulking, look out when he starts off.—hi!
There he goes. I told you to look out. You almost lost
him then. Give me your pole. You're going to lose him.
Look out. He's coming up, going to jump. Give him
slack, don't let him fall across a taut line. He's going
to jump, careful, care——*there* he goes, whoop ain't he
a whacker. Gi' me that pole. O gi' me that pole."
—"Go to Hell."
—"That's it, you're getting rattled. He'll get away
from you if you don't keep cool. O I *knew* there was

71

fish here. Now bring him up quiet, where's that landing net"? He's pretty tired, keep him off the boat, bring
him up closer now. O-o Jimminy Christmas ain't he a
bird. Now easy, while I get the net under him, e-e-easy.
O *damn-it-he's-gone*!!"

—"He's got off!"

—"And that was the biggest one yet. I *told* you not
to get rattled."

Reader's comment: "Not individual."

• A more detailed fishing scene appears in *Blix* (Ch. VI). This
theme might therefore be a first draft of it, except that in the
novel the girl Blix catches the fish, and she would hardly say
"Go to Hell." Norris' delight in slang and the private talk of
men is evident in this theme, which is made up solely of conversation. He observes such detail as the natural use of "gi"
when the excitement mounts, as distinct from the proper "give"
employed in a slightly calmer moment, and altogether he shows
a nice feeling for the vernacular conversation of sportsmen while
at the same time revealing their characters through speech.

16. A CHEAP PARLOR

December 17, 1894

The parlor was a little room with bay windows, shut
off from the back parlor by sliding doors. The walls
were white-washed and set off by a gilt picture-mould-
ing. A play carpet with a reddish figures repeated in-
numerably upon a drab ground covered the floor. A
bright green sofa with yellow cushions stood across one
corner of the room. Across the opposite corner was a
cheap piano. To the left of the piano a brass easel held
a crayon portrait of the baby. Across one corner of the

portrait was a yellow drape and drapes of various colors were hung upon the other pieces of furniture. Near the piano was an Alaskan grass-basket filled the photographs. On the bay window was a marble topped table on which were a couple of albums some gift books and a bunch of wax flowers under a glass case. The mantlepiece was of marble and had a sham grate. On one side of it was an inverted section of a sewer-pipe painted with' daisies and poppies and filled with gilded cat-tails tied with a blue ribbon. Over the mantle-piece was a reproduction of Shakespeare reading to the court of Queen Elizabeth.

Reader's comment: "Topographical. Congruous details with conclusion."

• The five preceding compositions submitted over a period of more than two weeks did not treat material related to *Vandover and the Brute* but were merely isolated pieces written to meet course requirements. With this paper Norris returns to his larger subject. However, since this theme fits into Ch. IV at a point shortly after the text used in Theme 2 (submitted on November 19) and before the texts of Themes 8 and 9, respectively related to Chs. V and VI, it appears that at the beginning of December Norris temporarily quit writing the novel that became *Vandover and the Brute* and for the moment was merely drawing on parts of it written earlier. Indeed, he later pillaged part of this very composition to describe the home of the heroine in *Blix* (Ch. II). Although Norris is particularly good at descriptions of rooms and at using them to suggest the status and nature of their inhabitants, this decor fits Blix rather poorly, while serving as a perfect setting for the fast woman Ida of *Vandover and the Brute* (Ch. V). Incidentally, the picture of Queen Elizabeth's court does not appear in *Vandover and the Brute*, but a similar engraving of the court of Lorenzo turns up on McTeague's walls (Ch. I). Naturally, these curious switches could not be known to Abbott, but the adjective he applied to the theme was itself odd, as was his objection to the repetition

73

of "drape" and "drapes" as being "not in good use," while he ignored such an error of haste as "an Alaskan grass-basket filled the photographs" for "filled with photographs."

17. MRS. TEN EYCK ENTERS CHURCH
December 18, 1894

Mrs. Ten Eyck had never been in that particular church before. She came up the aisle slowly, pausing at each step with little hesitating movements of the head and neck like a hen going into a strange barn.

Reader's comment: "Avoid the trailing participial clause. Observant."

• Once again Norris submits a brief descriptive character sketch like that which he turned in on December 8 while presumably marking time on the writing of his novel.

18. GOOD AND BAD WOMAN
December 20, 1894

A woman is always the same with the men she meets. If she is a good woman she will still be good in the company of bad men. If she is bad she will be bad with good men. But with a man it is quite the other way, a good woman will bring out in him all that is best, a bad woman all that is worst.

Reader's comment: "Awkwardly put."

• This rather clumsy, commonplace attempt at epigrammatic composition seems to show Norris still thinking about the subject

74

of Vandover, for it is related to Ch. V and VI, which contrast the influence upon Vandover of Ida, who if not "bad" is gay and easy, and of Travis, the very model of a good woman. It is also related to the talk in Ch. VII of Vandover, Geary, and Haight about a double moral standard for men and women, as well as to Condy's thoughts in Ch. XIII of *Blix* about the good effect pure love has had upon him. Abbott edited the theme to show Norris how maxims might be sharpened, which perhaps helped him with the form that he continued to practice—as, for example, in *Blix* (Ch. XI): "I've always noticed that so soon as a girl is déclassée, she develops a purpose in life."

19. ARTIST'S WORK

December 21, 1894

I think you may set it down as a rule that a true artist always does better than he thinks he will but never so well as he thinks he can.

Reader's comment: "Suggestive."

• This cliché delivered as a profound epigram begins with a conventional opening popular in Norris' day: "I think . . . that . . ." Its subject is related to a theme in *Vandover and the Brute* (Ch. XIII and XIV) and perhaps to Norris' own experience as a student of painting.

20. A MERRY CHRISTMAS

January 3, 1895

The great throng of Christmas buyers, loaded with paper bound packages, gorged the sidewalks to the curbstones, rolling slowly like an immense river and sending up a vast, indistinct roar.

At the corner of one of the smaller streets its progress was for a moment hindered. A little crowd had gathered. The center of its attraction was an elderly woman already gray and comfortably dressed. Her arms were full of bundles, mostly toys. One could see a little red cart, a doll, and a wooden horse, painted gray with great goggled eyes. She was very drunk and swayed as she stood. A strand of gray hair hung across her face and her eyelids were heavy. She took a step forward and fell at full length in the mud of the sidewalk. The packages of toys turned underneath her and she fell upon them breaking the little red cart and the goggled eyed wooden horse.

Readers' comment: "Not a unit of impression. Diction not apt. Sentence structure loose and ineffective."

• In keeping with his sense of the topical, Norris here writes a Christmas theme, but one that presents a horrid holiday situation. Over his own vacation Norris seems to have undergone a significant change. During most of the first semester his themes were relatively light and often related to the pleasant beginnings of *Vandover and the Brute*. Then Norris had a fumbling period beginning with his December 4 theme, out of which he emerges in this first composition of the new year, presenting human degradation suited to the latter part of *Vandover and the Brute* or to the spirit of *McTeague,* now seemingly much on his mind. The subject of drunkenness was to become an important element in both novels. The close observation of people evident in Themes 12 and 17, as well as the sharp detail typified in Theme 16, are here combined, but with the addition of a melodrama that comes of obvious and simplified contrasts, to which Norris was inclined all his life.

21. SHIPWRECKED SCHOONER

January 4, 1895

That evening about half-past ten, the lookout in the crow's-nest sounded upon his fish-horn and the skipper, running forward, lit a huge calcium flare at the schooner's quarter. It was the Cape Horner and presently Vandover made out her lights, two glowing spots moving upon the darkness like the eyes of some nocturnal sea monster. The schooner approached and was laid to and the towering mass of the great deep-sea tramp began to be dimly outlined against the sea and sky rolling slowly and leizurely in the seas that made the schooner dance. In her direction came the sound of voices, the rattle of blocks and the swash of the water as she crushed the waves under her fore-foot.

Reader's comment: "Not clear."

• The name of Vandover is mentioned here for the first time, and here too a theme first treats a situation in which the main character, rather than lesser characters, of *Vandover and the Brute* is involved. If Norris was writing in the sequence of the finished novel, he has progressed from Ch. V in Theme 8 to Ch. IX in this theme. In the finished text of Ch. IX Norris dropped in a new sentence in an unsuccessful attempt to clarify the ambiguous reference to "it" in the second sentence of this theme, whose antecedent was queried by Abbott, but he made a better repair of the third sentence, which Abbott found "incoherent." The passage is understandable in the context of the novel, but in this theme, without preparation or any distinction between the schooner and the Cape Horner, it is no wonder that the reader found the composition unclear.

77

22. MAXIM: ANYTHING CAN BE IMPROVED

January 5, 1895

I think you may set it down as true, that nothing was ever so well done but what it could be done better. If it were not so then it was not worth the doing.

Reader's comment: "Ambiguously phrased."

• Although Norris was to write more themes dealing with Vandover, his interest in the new character McTeague seems to have occurred at about this time. Having temporarily turned away from Vandover, Norris tries his hand at another of his sanctimonious apothegms. As Abbott made clear, Norris was not very good at this sort of writing. For instance, the reader marked the first "it" of the second sentence with "what?" Moreover, Norris tended to be somewhat repetitive, for this piece is not entirely different from Theme 19, and Abbott had earlier criticized Theme 14 for being similar to still another maxim.

23. McTEAGUE

January 7, 1895

The other teachers at the kindergarten often noticed that Bessie's fingertips were swollen and the nails purple as though they had been shut in a door. This was in fact the explanation she offered. But she lied to them. McTeague her husband used to bite her fingertips when he came home after drinking whiskey, crunching them between his strong large teeth, always ingenious enough to remember which were the sorest. If she resisted he

78

brought her down with a blow of his immense bony fist between the eyes.

Often these brutalities inflamed his sensual passions and he threw her, bleeding and stupid from his fists across the bed and then it was abominable, bestial, unspeakable.

Reader's comment: "Morbid and repulsive in subject matter. Your manner is strong and effective but ask yourself why you present us with this subject. To force upon our unwilling attention a repulsive, painful and debasing image has in itself something akin to the brutal."

• For the first time Norris introduces McTeague into his themes. Like Vandover, who appeared only three days earlier in Theme 21, he is a figure from the larger fiction that Norris was writing outside of class assignments. In the novel that was starting to take on final form there now began to loom the story of the tragic marriage of McTeague and the kindergarten teacher Bessie, who was the friend of the loose Ida whom Vandover had seduced. Throughout January and February McTeague figures as the central subject of Norris' themes, with different aspects of his sordid story displayed in Themes 23 through 28, until finally on March 8 his story has become an integral work that can be told in resumé form as Theme 32. The story of Vandover is picked up again only after that of McTeague has been clearly shaped as a separate work.

Theme 23 is reworked in Ch. XVI of *McTeague* so that Bessie changes her name to Trina and her occupation from kindergarten teacher to a beaten housewife who soon becomes a scrubwoman in a kindergarten. In this fallen state it is she who is conceived as pathologically sexual, for whereas the theme states that "these brutalities inflamed his sensual passions," the book attributes the perverse sexuality to her, in that brutality arouses "in her a morbid, unwholesome love of submission, a strange, unnatural pleasure in yielding, in surrendering herself to the will of an irresistible, virile power." In the concluding sentence Norris, for the first time, employs his tripling of ad-

79

jectives for a trip-hammer effect on the reader. Curiously, it is so effective that it leads Abbott to employ the same device in his comment.

24. McTEAGUE

January 8, 1895

Bessie told all sorts of different stories to the other kindergarten teachers to account for the state of her finger-tips after McTeague had been chewing them. The last was that it was a form of gout. Yes *was*n't it funny to have gout in your fingers, but that's what the doctor had said it was. She didn't dare eat any more spiced food. No she didn't suffer much with them.

At last they began to look so bad that she pretended her hands were cold and wore her gloves all the time.

Reader's comment: "An ineffective postscript."

• In Theme 23 Norris had excerpted from his novel a passage not only long enough to satisfy the daily requirement but also complete in itself, concluding with a shocking denouement. In Theme 24, presented a day later, he continues the subject in a less horrifyingly direct style and in a form that makes little sense by itself. Abbott's criticism is wholly justified. Although the text could have served as a continuation of the theme that preceded it, Norris never used it in *McTeague*.

25. McTEAGUE

January 11, 1895

That week McTeague had his first attack of tremens. It came on him quite suddenly on a Thursday evening just after supper as he was shaking up the fire in the kitchen stove. All day he had been burning up with fever; while a certain nervous trembling beginning just between his shoulders had spread to his arms and legs and even at last to his fingers and toes. All at once toward seven o'clock he began to feel cold; cold even inside his body as though his bones had turned to ice. He went out into the kitchen and crouched over the stove. Instead of trembling now, he was shivering. The fire was low and he picked up the poker to arouse it. The poker moved in his hand and grew cold. He looked at it and saw that it was a snake, a thick, black, wet snake, writhing slowly in his fist, its head and neck bent up sharply towards him, its tongue flickering in and out of its mouth. He flung it from him and saw it shrink into a coil as it struck the floor. Then he sprang back stretching out his hands and screaming until the effort brought the blood specks to his eyes. It was not because he knew the coiled horror upon the floor was a snake that he was afraid, a real snake would not have frightened him. It was because he knew that it was *not* a snake that he was afraid, horribly, frantically, unspeakably afraid.

Reader's comment: "A melodramatic subject not relieved by any felicity of treatment."

• The subject of drunkenness, not so important as other vices in the completed *McTeague*, obviously looms large as Norris begins to shape the novel, just as it is a major subject of *Vandover and the Brute* and is also the subject of isolated compositions, like that of January 3. Neither this whole theme nor the typical concluding sentence affected Abbott the way the comparable Theme 23 had done; his displeasure may have kept Norris from using this material in the finished novel.

26. McTEAGUE

February 15, 1895

On Sundays about two o'clock he took dinner at the car-conductor's coffee joint, next to the harness shop on Polk St. He had a gray soup, thick and oily, heavy meat, underdone and very hot on a cold plate, two kinds of greasy vegetables and a sort of suet pudding full of strong butter and sugar.

On his way back to his room he would stop at the corner grocery to get a pitcher of steam beer. Once in his room, he took off his coat and shoes, unbuttoned his vest and having crammed the little stove full of coke, sat at the window in his shirt sleeves and stocking feet, reading his paper, drinking his beer and smoking his huge porcelain pipe, while his food digested, crop-full, stupid and warm. Sometimes even, overcome by the heat of the room, the tobacco smoke and the effects of his heavy meal he dropped off to sleep.

Later on in the afternoon when he awoke he finished his beer very flat and stale by this time and played very mournful airs on his concertina. He always looked forward to these Sunday afternoons as a period of relaxation and enjoyment.

Reader's comment: "Good wording."

• Although Norris rewrote this theme before using it as the opening page of *McTeague*, his protagonist's character and tone are already set four years before the novel's publication. In the final text an office setting, appointment board, operating chair, and seven volumes of *Allen's Practical Dentist* are added to fit McTeague into the profession that is basic to the plot. Norris may actually have conceived McTeague as a dentist at this time and simply not made that clear in the theme; certainly by the March 8 theme his profession is fixed. McTeague already has his concertina but lacks his canary, even though both of these properties belonged to the comparable mate in Stevenson's *The Wrecker*, which Norris greatly admired. This theme was written for the newly conceived novel, yet its atmosphere and a few of its words are still to be found on the third page of Ch. X of *Vandover and the Brute*, and there is an echo of them in the final sentence of Ch. XVII.

27. MISERY

February 18, 1895

The room was large and high and at some forgotten period had been covered with a yellowish paper, at 8 cts. a roll, stamped with a huge pattern of flowers that looked like the flora of a carboniferous strata; the pattern that was repeated to infinity wherever the eye turned. However there were relieving blotches upon it where the water had soaked through the lath and plaster and even in some places it hung down in discolored and unhealthy strips like bilious, coated tongues. The floor was absolutely bare. There were two pieces of furniture; a small cast iron stove, cold and dead, full of the ashes of newspapers that, with every draught of air shook and crackled like a death-rattle.

The other piece of furniture was a mattress or rather huge bag of ticking filled with straw. An old woman of sixty or seventy, dressed in a ragged muddy gown, a man's jacket and a filthy plush bonnet was sleeping on it. She lay sprawled on her back, her legs wide apart, her hands, green with cold, wrinkled like shrivelled apples turned palm downward at her side; her eyes half closed and her mouth stretched open, like a symbol of the famine that dug into her entrails.

By her side was a bit of gnawed candle-end, rounded almost to a ball, by the mumbling of her five yellow teeth.

Reader's comment: "Vivid."

• This theme seems to be only an exercise, depicting a squalid setting and character under the influence of Zola's *L'Assommoir*. The opening sentence was copied almost exactly as the setting of Vandover's room in the Reno House (Ch. XVII), even to the inclusion of the error "a carboniferous strata," which Abbott underlined and marked with an X, but seemingly not to the enlightenment of Norris.

28. McTEAGUE

February 19, 1895

Towards morning Trina died with a rapid series of hiccoughs, that stirred the great pool of blood in which she lay and which sounded like a piece of clock-work running down.

McTeague had killed her in the little room just off the kindergarten school-room where the children hung their hats and coats. McTeague going out had shut the door of this room but had left the street door open so the children, coming in the morning entered as usual.

About nine o'clock a half a dozen babies one a little nigger-girl, came into the school-room with a great chatter going across to the door of the little room to hang up their hats and coats as they had been taught. As they came near the door one of them put her little nose in the air crying "O what a funnee smell" another a butcher's little girl exclaimed "It smells like my pa's shop." The tallest of them swung the door of the little room wide open and they all ran in.

Reader's comment: "Not a toothsome subject."

• Six weeks after writing Themes 23 and 24 Norris has changed McTeague's wife from Bessie to Trina, and by now he probably has much of the finished novel *McTeague* well in mind. The themes between January 11 and February 15 are missing, perhaps because they developed the plot and several scenes in ways so close to the final version that Norris extracted them from his stack of work for use in a last revision. Indeed, Theme 28 is remarkably close to the final text in Ch. XIX of *McTeague*, except for its addition of a cat that sniffs at the closed cloakroom door. However, this theme, like most of the others, is both a first and final draft for the class, and it opens with another version of the first paragraph that has been crossed out. The reader's comment is so oddly inappropriate that one wonders if he could have been playing on the subject of Mc-Teague's dentistry and his great gold tooth, perhaps introduced in an earlier, now lost theme.

29. McTEAGUE

February 20, 1895

McTeague's brother-in-law, Marcus, held advanced and radical ideas, having imperfectly grasped a few half-truths of Political Economy and of theories of population, picked up at some of the ward clubs. He was a clerk at the ribbon counter in one of the Polk street stores. He developed these ideas on all occasions to McTeague, vociferating at the top of his voice, shaking his fists, exciting himself with his own noise.

"The evil is *there*," he would shout. "Self-control,

that's the great secret, the masses must learn self-control. It stands to reason, look at the figures. Decrease the number of wage-earners and you increase wages, aint that true? ain't it? ain't it?"

McTeague understood never a word but would answer stupidly, "Yes, thats it, self-control, yes, yes."

Or it would be a question of strikes.

"It's the scabs that's ruining the cause of labor," Marcus would yell, banging the table with his fist until the beer glasses danced, "white-livered cowards, traitors with their livers, white as snow, eating the bread of widows and orphans. There's where the evil is. It's them the real oppressors of the working man."

Stupefied by his clamor McTeague would answer wagging his head: "Yes that's it. I think it is their livers."

Reader's comment: "Connotative."

• At this time Norris thinks of Marcus as Trina's brother rather than as her cousin and a suitor for her hand, so the theme of rivalry with McTeague has not been conceived. Moreover, Norris has not yet cast Marcus as a veterinarian's assistant but rather as a clerk at a ribbon counter, a job far too dainty for this lusty, brawling man. The final revision of this theme appears in Ch. I of *McTeague*.

30. McTEAGUE AT AN ART GALLERY
February 28, 1895

. . . air opened McTeague and Trina went very often in the evening. They even spent some time in the Art Gallery. A friend of Trina's had an exhibit there, a bunch of yellow poppies painted on black velvet which they were interested to find. They stood before it some little time hazarding their opinions and then moved on from one picture to another. Trina professed to be fond of painting and said she would have taken it up herself only the oil or turpentine or something was unhealthy for her. "Of course," she said, "I'm no critic. I only know what I like." She was much taken with the ideal "heads" pictures of young girls with an abundance of hair and large eyes with the titles of "Reverie" or "Pastoral" or "Faith." They bought a catalogue and Trina made it a duty to find the title of every picture. Mc-Teague wondered helplessly at some of the huge landscapes, asking her if she was sure that "they were all hand-painted."

Reader's comment: "Suggests."

• As with Theme 8, the opening has been cut off, probably to remove Norris' autograph on the rear of the page. The first few words, including the partially preserved "Fair," can be reconstructed from Ch. X of *McTeague*, which is a revision of this text. The final version does not include Trina's comment that painting is unhealthy for her, although it is an aptly ironic foreshadowing of her blood poisoning by the so-called non-poisonous paints with which she decorates toys. Some of this text is also applied to Trina's alter ego, Bessie Laguna, when she visits the same Art Gallery with Ellis in *Vandover and the Brute* (Ch. VII).

31. TUG WILSON

March 5, 1895

Tug worked or was supposed to work in the back room of the plumber's shop, on Polk Street a dark and grimy place, smelling of lead and of greasy dust. The walls were ornamented by a figure cut out from a bill-poster of the Danites and a huge map of the city. On this latter a particularly grimy spot, made by the contact of innumerable index fingers, proclaimed at once the locality of the plumber's shop.

Reader's comment: "Fragmentary."

• This little vignette of Polk Street surely is fragmentary, as the reader remarked, but it is of just such fragments that the realistic mosaic of Polk Street is wrought for the final text of *McTeague*. This particular segment is not found in the novel, any more than is its inhabitant, Tug Wilson, although a nameless plumber's apprentice appears in Ch. I and several times thereafter. However, as "Jonesee," the plumber's apprentice and his grimy shop with its poster and map appear in a sketch in *The Wave* of May 2, 1896. The bill-poster undoubtedly advertised Joaquin Miller's popular play about the Mormons, *The Danites of the Sierras*, first produced in 1877 but several times revived. Norris seems to have written at such speed that when he intended to put down "dark and grimy," he anticipated the second adjective and hastily wrote "dary."

32. McTEAGUE

March 8, 1895

McTeague who is a third class dentist on an uptown business street marries Trina a kindergarten teacher. Their misfortunes begin after a few years. McTeague, having no diploma, is forbidden to practice and begins to drink heavily. For a long time Trina supports the two, until she finally loses her place and in a short while the household falls into great poverty and misery. McTeague goes from bad to worse and finally ends by killing his wife. He manages to escape and goes back to the mines where the first part of his life has been spent. The facts concerning him come to light here and he is obliged to run for it. His way is across an arm of an Arizona desert, here he is ridden down by a deputy sheriff. The two are sixty miles from the nearest human being and McTeague determines to fight, he kills the sheriff and is about to go on when he discovers that even in the fight the sheriff has managed to hand-cuff their wrists together. He is chained to the body sixty miles from help.

Reader's comment: "Gruesome."

• The plot summary for *McTeague* presented here seems complete, if sketchy, but it differs in a number of ways from the final work. First, the initial sentence plunges the protagonist into marriage, suggesting that Norris had not planned to treat McTeague's life as a single man or his courtship, which cover about a third of the finished text. That sentence also identifies Trina as a kindergarten teacher and thus of a higher class than she appears in the final work. The second sentence suggests that there is to be little emphasis on the happy days of their marriage, such as are briefly shown in Theme 30, and a good deal of stress on the concluding sequence of McTeague's escape to the Sierra Nevada and the desert, to which more than half of this outline is devoted, whereas only the last three of the novel's twenty-three chapters treat this denouement. The composition also differs from the novel in larger ways, for it does not introduce the subjects of greed or of animosity and rivalry with Marcus, who is McTeague's captor in the final work. Nevertheless, the theme is important in showing how clearly Norris did have a full novel in mind and in general how close it already was to the work neither completed nor published for four more years.

33. IT WAS ABOUT 2 IN A.M.
March 9, 1895

It was about two in the morning and a strong head wind was blowing, flinging down the steamer's smoke over the ocean like a great veil of crape, and droning a prolonged minor note through the cordage.

On either side the un-numbered multitude of waves were rushing past like a vast herd of horses galloping on with tossing white manes.

The sky was grey and lay close over the ocean while a long pale blur of a light hung low on the Eastern horizon against which the prow of the steamer, inky black, heaved and sank incessantly.

Reader's comment: "Vivid."

• Even after Norris had outlined the basic plot of *McTeague* in Theme 32, he continued to present material that pertains to *Vandover and the Brute* and is unrelated to his newly conceived novel. For the next two weeks he turned in themes associated with *Vandover and the Brute*, though not in the sequence of that work, ranging from this one, which was revised for Ch. IX of the finished text, to Theme 39 of March 27, which relates to Ch. IV. As far back as January 4 Norris had written a theme associated with Ch. IX of *Vandover*. In the present theme Norris refers to a "great veil of crape" that symbolically anticipates the tragic events soon to follow, particularly the actual mourning crepe tied to the front door of Vandover's home after his father's death (Ch. X).

34. VANDOVER VISITS A LAWYER
March 11, 1895

It was at his residence and not at his office, that Vandover saw the lawyer, as the latter was unwell at the time and kept his bed. However he was not so sick but that his doctor allowed him to transact at least some of his business. Vandover found him in his room, a huge apartment, one side entirely taken up by book-cases, filled with works of fiction. The walls were covered with rough stone-blue paper, forming an admirable background to small plaster-casts of Assyrian bas-reliefs and photogravures of Renaissance portraits. Underneath a huge baize covered table in the center of the room were padlocked tin chests and green paste-board deed-boxes.

The lawyer was in bed wearing his dressing gown and occasionally drinking a glass of hot water. He was a thin small man middle-aged with a very round head and a small pointed beard.

Reader's comment: "The details are distinct."

• This material works its way into Ch. XI of *Vandover and the Brute* almost verbatim, after corrections of misspellings and a change to the English spelling "centre" favored by Gates. Curiously, the decor of the lawyer's room also serves as Vandover's ideal in Ch. IX and elsewhere.

35. DEPARTURE AND STEAMER
March 14, 1895

The Santa Rosa cast off the company's docks the next day about noon, in a thick cold mist that was half rain. The old gentleman came to see Vandover off. The steamer which seemed gigantic was roped and cabled to the piers, feeling the water occasionally with her paddle to keep the hawsers taut. About the forward gangplank a band of over-worked stevedores were stowing the last of the baggage and cargo, aided by a donkey-engine, which at every instant broke out into a series of sputtering coughs. At the passenger gang-way a great crowd was gathered, laughing and exchanging remarks with the other crowd that leaned over the railings of the upper decks. There was an odor of cooking mingled with the smell of pitch and bilge and oil from the engines. Just before twelve o'clock the steward went about the decks drumming upon a snoring gong for dinner. At half an hour after the scheduled time the great whistle roared interminably, drowning out the chorus of "Good-bye, good-bye," that arose on every hand. Long before it ceased the huge bulk had stirred almost imperceptibly at first, then gathering head swung out into the stream, and headed toward the ocean.

Readers comment: "Has color."

• This theme was transferred with little alteration to Ch. VIII of *Vandover and the Brute*, although there the steamer is driven by a screw rather than a paddle. However, the steward's gong is still "snoring," despite Abbott's underlining of the word. Obviously Abbott knew that this theme, like others, was an excerpt from a long work rather than a separate piece, because he made no comment on its unexplained allusion to Vandover and his father.

36. THE IMPERIAL
March 19, 1895

Meanwhile The Imperial had been filling up; at about eleven the theaters were over, and now the place was in full swing. The bar-room was crowded with men; they came in by twos and threes, ordered their drinks and leaning over the bar continued the conversation they had begun outside. Afterward they passed over to the lunch counter, and helped themselves to a plate of stewed tripe, or potato salad and ate it in a secluded corner leaning over, so as not to spot their coats; those unaccustomed to the place, remained for a long time before the "bar-room" pictures with half-open mouths, pointing out to each other bits of nakedness, laughing and making jokes. There was a continual clinking of glasses and popping of corks and at every instant the cash-register clucked and rang its bell. Between the bar and the other part of the house, was a door hung with blue plush curtains looped back. Here the waiters passed continually with loaded trays. All the private rooms in this part of the house were full. Men came in walking slowly, looking for their friends, but more often the women and girls passed up and down with a chatter of conversation a rattle of stiff skirts and petticoats and a heavy whiff of musk. There was a constant coming and going and shuffle of feet and hum of talk: A heavy odorous warmth in which were mingled smells of sweetened whiskey and mixed drinks, tobacco, the fumes of cooking and the feminine odor of perfume exhaled into

93

the air. A gay and noisy party developed itself in one of the larger private rooms. There could be heard at every moment, gales of laughter, the rattle of chairs, and glass-ware mingled with the sounds of men's voices and the little screams and cries of women. Every time the waiter opened the door to deliver an order he let out a momentary torrent of noises.

Reader's comment: "Specific details."

• This passage, which with slight revision appears in Ch. IV of *Vandover and the Brute*, is marked by a nicely detailed realism that Abbott approved and which is based on Norris' observation of actual sites. In appearance and atmosphere The Imperial is like one of the great downtown bar-restaurants of dubious reputation that were popular in Norris' time, though the only real resort of that name was owned by one Josie Cronin and located from 1892 to 1896 at 728 Sutter Street, far uptown from the place depicted by Norris. Probably he borrowed its name for one of the downtown establishments that served as his model, whose proper name he would have feared to give because of the improper actions he set there.

37. HOWARD'S SUNDAY MORNING
March 21, 1895

Upstairs, there ensued the usual scene inevitable upon getting Howard off to Sunday school. He just wouldn't wash his hands again, and O! his new shoes were too tight and hurt his sore toe, and he didn't see why he had to wear that darn little old blue necktie and no he wouldn't, he wouldn't, he wouldn't change his shirt; not if he was killed for it. Very well then his nurse told him, if he didn't want to behave the very next time she

94

saw Gracie Walters she would tell her that he had said she was his girl: Ah *now* would he be good and stand still while she brushed his clothes?

Reader's comment: "A suggestive bit of domestic life."

• On the manuscript page of this theme Norris originally made Howard's caretaker an "elder sister" rather than a nurse, and it is to Travis that this part is given when the passage is reworked for Ch. I of *Blix*, although the scene might have been equally well suited to the nine-year-old Howard Ravis and his sister Turner in Ch. VI of *Vandover and the Brute*.

38. A BATTLE SCENE
March 22, 1895

Close in upon their left flank an event or rather a series of events that writhed themselves together into a maze of dizzying complexity suddenly unfolded and widened like the quick rending open of some great scroll. And there came to their sight tremulous billows of smoke and clouds and eddying dust rolling together in one great blur whose outermost fringes were torn by quivering lines of flashing steel and wavering ranks of red. And through it came the roar of many noises, noises of men and noises of arms, noises of feet and noises of horses, noises that boomed, noises that rattled, noises that clanked or shilled or rumbled, and the reek of the sweat of men and of horses, was bitter in their nostrils and the smell of gunpowder was as the smell of salt upon a stormy beach.

Reader's comment: "Virile. 'Noises' is not a good word to repeat, however."

95

• This battle scene (untitled on manuscript, and in which there is no explicit statement that it describes a battle) is a slight revision of a passage in "The Son of a Sheik," a published story on which Norris had drawn for Theme 13. Though written in 1891, the text curiously anticipates the mood and language of Stephen Crane's *The Red Badge of Courage,* published in October 1895.

39. THE IMPERIAL
March 27, 1895

The main entrance was by the cigar stand in the vestibule. It opened directly into the bar-room paved with marble flags. To the left was the bar, the counter of which was a single slab of polished cherry. Behind it was a large plate mirror, on one side of this was the cash register, on the other a parian marble statue of the diving girl. The glasses and bottles were arranged in pyramids here and there. The three silent bar-tenders in clean linen coats and white aprons moved about deftly opening bottles and mixing drinks with extraordinary dexterity and occasionally turning to punch the indicator of the cash register. On the other side of the room hung a large copy of a French picture representing a Sabbath, witches, goats and naked girls whirling through the air. Underneath it was the lunch counter, where clam-fritters, the specialty of the house could be had three afternoons in the week. Nearby was a racing chart, where the day's entries, pools, weights, and mounts were set forth. By the side of the lunch-counter stood two nickel-in-the-slot machines.

Reader's comment: "Specific."

• This description of Vandover's favorite resort appeared with little change as the opening of Ch. IV in *Vandover and the Brute,* just preceding the passages derived from Theme 36. The painting over the lunch counter was a reproduction of Luis Ricardo Falero's *Depart pour le Sabbat,* painted in 1878.

40. "SMOKE?" SAID I

April 6, 1895

"Smoke?" said I pushing my cigar-case toward him. He made a vague movement as if he would have re-arranged an imaginary cloak and sombrero looking down the while into the dregs of his glass, then he shook his head with a tragic frown: "I don't smoke," he answered. "I have no petty vices."

Reader's comment: "Neat."

• Perhaps because of the nature of the assignments, neither this theme nor the four that follow it form parts of *Vandover and the Brute* or *McTeague,* though this trivial dialogue, ending in something like a maxim, remotely relates to the problem of a man who has a single major vice, dealt with in Theme 14.

41. A DRUNK AND HIS FLASK

April 22, 1895

It was in an alley behind a big hotel, and the man, an old man, with a battered derby hat that had turned green, was drunk; blind drunk, reeling about as if in the fore-castle of a wreck, running his head stupidly against the side of the houses, trying to hold on by the wheels of old carts and by the sides of manure bins. He was looking for the flask he had dropped and a group of hack men and cab-drivers at the mouth of the alley were watching him, laughing and very amused because he couldn't find it. Bye and bye the man came down, full length, helpless as a falling tree and lay prone and inert, face downwards, blowing his fetid breath into the mud and filth of the alley.

Then one of the cab-men picked up the flask from where it had fallen and came back sniffing at it. It was half-full of a raw rasping gin, a veritable liquid fire. He went up to his rig and pouring some of the stuff on a chamois cloth, began to rub the nickel trimmings of his harness with it. "Good to clean metal work," he observed grimly.

Next day I had occasion to use his cab. The nickel plate on the trimming was all corroded and eaten off.

Reader's comment: "Specific."

• The melodramatic portrayal of a drunk on a busy city street is reminiscent of Theme 20. The subject of drunkenness relates to both *McTeague* and *Vandover and the Brute*, but this character and the setting, like the people and the area adjacent to the Lick House of *Vandover and the Brute*, suggest a connection with the concluding section of that novel.

42. MY FRIEND TUG WILSON
April 26, 1895

My friend Tug Wilson is a messenger-boy, and at the office they call him simply "thirty eight." Sometimes I hear him going past my house late at night playing on his mouth-organ, now it is "Tommy Atkins"

STUDENT THEMES

and again it will be "Her Golden Hair." He plays very
well indeed, making a sounding box out of the hollow
of his hands, by opening and shutting one hand over
the other he evolves quite a creditable tremulo. Sometimes he will take the organ from his mouth and make
admirable cat-noises to terribly excited dogs under the
fences.

Reader's comment: "Simply expressed."

• The character mentioned in Theme 31, seven weeks earlier,
now reappears as a messenger boy. His new occupation is as well
suited for a figure who might appear along Polk Street as was
his former calling of a plumber's apprentice, but no such person
is named in the final text of *McTeague*.

43. INSTANTANEOUS PHOTOGRAPHS
April 30, 1895

I

The crockery store was on the ground floor. Above
were cheap family suites, dentist's offices, and a pho-
tographer's parlor. A faded and cracked signboard that
read *"Photograph's"* ran along under three windows.
One of these windows was open; two women in spotted
calico gowns leaned out of it, resting on their folded
arms. They were laughing and very intently watching
another woman on the side-walk who had halted her
baby-carriage by the crockery wares spread out in front
of the store. She was chaffering with the sales-man,
a young fellow, who had a pencil behind his ear and
who wore a linen blouse. Near by, a dog, a kind of
mongrel water-spaniel, too big to be of good stock, sat

99

in the sun on the warm asphalt, beyond the shadow of the awning gravely waiting until the woman should finish.

II

Three workmen in dirty blue overalls were repairing the street between the car tracks, readjusting the cobbles; their coats and tin pails upon a big wooden box by the side of the street. The box was full of picks and long handled shovels, together with two un-lit lanterns wrapped in red flannel.

There was a general notion store close by, a cigar Indian, without his hatchet standing in front. In the window were cigarette pictures, tin fire engines and de- livery wagons and jars of candy. The proprietress, a woman on crutches wearing a blue worsted vest over the waist of her dress stood in the doorway watching the men at work.

Reader's comment: "Rapidly and distinctly sketched."

• This text does not appear in *McTeague*, yet it obviously illus- trates the novel's Polk Street setting. Although not especially focused on, here is the first mention in the themes of an upstairs dental parlor; in fact, uncertainty occasioned by Norris' often wandering apostrophe suggests the reference may be to more than one dentist. With that exception, the two "snapshots" are effective in presenting succinctly and with the objectivity and clarity of a photograph just as much but no more than a camera could discern, although Norris neglects to show how one knows what is inside the upstairs windows. Like a photograph, the theme cannot see into buildings or people, but it can describe their exterior appearance vividly and precisely, with emphasis on such distinguishing details as the clothing of the proprietress, cramped by Norris onto the margin of the manuscript as a last- minute addition. Of course, one has to assume from her place in the picture and from her garb that she is the store owner. All the imagery is visual except for the "warm" sidewalk, to be inferred from the sunny day and the place the dog has chosen to rest.

44. MARSEILLES EXPRESS TRAIN

April 30, 1895

It was very early in the morning, perhaps near five o'clock, and the lanterns about the huge arched depot had begun to lose their brilliancy, fading like sickly flowers in the growing daylight.

It was very still and very cold and a keen frosty rime was upon everything metal, like a gray mould. All at once the Marseilles special charged into the depot filling it on the instant with bellowing echoes and whirlpools of white smoke, galloping on like a stampeded bull, reeking with steam and hot oil, blazing with its one flaming red eye bloodshot from the effort of speed, shrieking and clanging splitting the air with its hideous noise, shaking the earth with the thunder of its iron hoofs. All at once the emergency air brakes went down with a hiss and a crash, the wheels grew rigid like braced fore-feet, and the cyclops slid along the slippery rails still at top speed. But the shriek that followed was not all the shriek of steam. The man seemed to be nothing more than a bundle of old clothes as he spun into the air; the engine struck him, tossed him as a bull would have done, ran him down again and swallowed him up beneath its sliding drivers, in a cloud of dust and smoke and steam.

The train stopped at length, the engine's heart beating fast, its one great eye staring wildly as though terrified. After the body had been taken away, the engineer got down from the cab and poked curiously with a splinter of firewood at something sticking to the tire of one of the enormous drive-wheels. It was the man's shoe, the foot and ankle still buttoned into it.

Reader's comment: "Vivid."

• The setting of this gruesome vignette is similar to that at the opening of *Vandover and the Brute*, and some of the text is identical, but the description of a person killed by a train with a cyclopean eye is derived from Zola's *La Bête humaine*, which was probably so much in Norris' mind that he even placed his train on a French railroad line. This scene also summons up Norris' later treatment of the railroad engine in *The Octopus*, particularly as it slaughters sheep on the track. This is the last of Norris' themes to survive, although English 22 continued for another month with twelve more class meetings, for which Norris, like other students, probably wrote six long themes. If, as is probable, these pieces related closely to *McTeague* or *Vandover and the Brute*, Norris may have used them in his final work on those novels, which would explain their disappearance from the packet of compositions.

BLIX

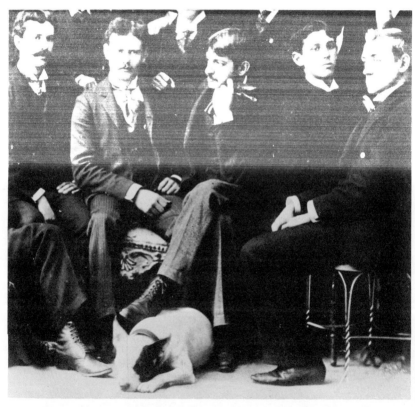

Frank Norris (center) and fraternity brothers at the University of California, 1893

CHAPTER I

It HAD just struck nine from the cuckoo clock that hung over the mantelpiece in the dining room, when Victorine brought in the halved watermelon and set it in front of Mr. Bessemer's plate. Then she went down to the front door for the damp, twisted roll of the Sunday morning's paper, and came back and rang the breakfast-bell for the second time.[1]

As the family still hesitated to appear, she went to the bay window at the end of the room, and stood there for a moment looking out. The view was wonderful. The Bessemers lived upon the Washington Street hill, almost at its very summit, in a flat in the third story of the building. The contractor had been clever enough to reverse the position of kitchen and dining room, so that the latter room was at the rear of the house. From its windows one could command a sweep of San Francisco Bay and the Contra Costa shore, from Mount Diablo, along past Oakland, Berkeley, Saucelito,[2] and Mount Tamalpais, out to the Golden Gate, the Presidio, the ocean, and even—on very clear days—to the Farrallone islands.

For some time Victorine stood looking down at the great expanse of land and sea, then faced about with an impatient exclamation.

On Sundays all the week-day *régime* of the family was deranged, and breakfast was a movable feast, to be had any time after seven or before half-past nine. As Victorine was pouring the ice-water, Mr. Bessemer himself came in, and addressed himself at once to his meal, without so much as a thought of waiting for the others.

He was a little round man. He wore a skull-cap to keep his bald spot warm, and read his paper through a reading-glass. The expression of his face, wrinkled and bearded, the eyes shadowed by enormous gray eyebrows, was that of an amiable gorilla.

Bessemer was one of those men who seem entirely disassociated from their families. Only on rare and intense occasions did his paternal spirit or instincts assert themselves. At table he talked but little. Though devotedly fond of his eldest daughter, she was a puzzle and a stranger to him. His interests and hers were absolutely dissimilar. The children he seldom spoke to but to reprove; while Howard, the son, the ten-year-old and terrible infant of the household, he always referred to as "that boy."

He was an abstracted, self-centred old man, with but two hobbies—homœopathy and the mechanism of clocks. But he had a strange way of talking to himself in a low voice, keeping up a running, half-whispered comment upon his own doings and actions; as, for instance, upon this occasion: "Nine o'clock—the clock's a little fast. I think I'll wind my watch. No, I've forgotten my watch. Watermelon this morning, eh? Where's a knife? I'll have a little salt. Victorine's forgot the spoons—ah, here's a spoon! No, it's a knife I want."

After he had finished his watermelon, and while Victorine was pouring his coffee, the two children came in, scrambling to their places, and drumming on the table with their knife-handles.

The son and heir, Howard, was very much a boy. He played baseball too well to be a very good boy, and for the sake of his own self-respect maintained an at-

titude of perpetual revolt against his older sister, who,
as much as possible, took the place of the mother, long
since dead. Under her supervision, Howard blacked
his own shoes every morning before breakfast, changed
his underclothes twice a week, and was dissuaded from
playing with the dentist's son who lived three doors
below and who had St. Vitus's dance.

His little sister was much more tractable. She had
been christened Alberta, and was called Snooky. She
promised to be pretty when she grew up, but was at
this time in that distressing transitional stage between
twelve and fifteen; was long-legged, and endowed with
all the awkwardness of a colt. Her shoes were still innocent of heels; but on those occasions when she was
allowed to wear her tiny first pair of corsets she was
exalted to an almost celestial pitch of silent ecstasy.
The clasp of the miniature stays around her small body
was like the embrace of a little lover, and awoke in her
ideas that were as vague, as immature and unformed,
as the straight little figure itself.

When Snooky and Howard had seated themselves,
but one chair—at the end of the breakfast-table, opposite Mr. Bessemer—remained vacant.

"Is your sister—is Miss Travis going to have her
breakfast now? Is she got up yet?" inquired Victorine
of Howard and Snooky, as she pushed the cream pitcher
out of Howard's reach. It was significant of Mr. Bessemer's relations with his family that Victorine did not
address her question to him.

"Yes, yes, she's coming," said both the children,
speaking together; and Howard added: "Here she comes
now."

Travis Bessemer came in. Even in San Francisco,
where all women are more or less beautiful, Travis
passed for a beautiful girl. She was young, but tall
as most men, and solidly, almost heavily built. Her

shoulders were broad, her chest was deep, her neck
round and firm. She radiated health; there were exuberance and vitality in the very touch of her foot
upon the carpet, and there was that cleanliness about
her, that freshness, that suggested a recent plunge in
the surf and a "constitutional" along the beach. One
felt that here were stamina, good physical force, and fine
animal vigour. Her arms were large, her wrists were large,
and her fingers did not taper. Her hair was of a brown
so light as to be almost yellow. In fact, it would be safer
to call it yellow from the start—not golden nor flaxen,
but plain, honest yellow. The skin of her face was clean
and white, except where it flushed to a most charming
pink upon her smooth, cool cheeks. Her lips were full
and red, her chin very round and a little salient. Curiously enough, her eyes were small—small, but of the
deepest, deepest brown, and always twinkling and
alight, as though she were just ready to smile or had
just done smiling, one could not say which. And nothing could have been more delightful than those sloe-
brown, glinting little eyes of hers set off by her white
skin and yellow hair.

She impressed one as being a very normal girl: nothing morbid about her, nothing nervous or false or overwrought. You did not expect to find her introspective.
You felt sure that her mental life was not at all the
result of thoughts and reflections germinating from
within, but rather of impressions and sensations that
came to her from without. There was nothing extraordinary about Travis. She never had her vagaries,
was not moody—depressed one day and exalted the
next. She was just a good, sweet, natural, healthy-
minded, healthy-bodied girl, honest, strong, self-reliant, and good-tempered.

Though she was not yet dressed for church, there was
style in her to the pointed tips of her patent-leather

slippers. She wore a heavy black overskirt that rustled in delicious fashion over the coloured silk skirt beneath, and a white shirt-waist, striped black, and starched to a rattling stiffness. Her neck was swathed tight and high with a broad ribbon of white satin, while around her waist, in place of a belt, she wore the huge dog-collar of a St. Bernard—a chic little idea which was all her own, and of which she was very proud.

She was as trig and trim and crisp as a crack yacht: not a pin was loose, not a seam that did not fall in its precise right line; and with every movement there emanated from her a barely perceptible delicious feminine odour—an odour that was in part perfume, but mostly a subtle, vague smell, charming beyond words, that came from her hair, her neck, her arms—her whole sweet personality. She was nineteen years old.

She sat down to breakfast and ate heartily, though with her attention divided between Howard—who was atrociously bad, as usual of a Sunday morning—and her father's plate. Mr. Bessemer was as like as not to leave the table without any breakfast at all unless his fruit, chops, and coffee were actually thrust under his nose.

"Papum," she called, speaking clear and distinct, as though to the deaf, "there's your coffee there at your elbow; be careful, you'll tip it over. Victorine, push his cup farther on the table. Is it strong enough for you, Papum?"

"Eh? Ah, yes—yes—yes," murmured the old man, looking vaguely about him, "coffee, to be sure"—and he emptied the cup at a single draught, hardly knowing whether it was coffee or tea. "Now, I'll take a roll," he continued, in a monotonous murmur. "Where are the rolls? Here they are. Hot rolls are bad for my digestion—I ought to eat bread. I think I eat too much. Where's my place in the paper?—always lose my place in the paper. Clever editorials this fellow Eastman writes, unbiassed by party prejudice—unbiassed—unbiassed." His voice died to a whisper.

The breakfast proceeded, Travis supervising everything that went forward, even giving directions to Victorine as to the hour for serving dinner. It was while she was talking to Victorine as to this matter that Snooky began to whine.

"Stop!"

"And tell Maggie," pursued Travis, "to fricassee her chicken, and not to have it too well done——"

"Sto-o-op!" whined Snooky again.

"And leave the heart out for Papum. He likes the heart——"

"Sto-o-op!"

"Unbiassed by prejudice," murmured Mr. Bessemer, "vigorous and to the point. I'll have another roll."

"Pa, make Howard stop!"

"Howard!" exclaimed Travis; "what is it now?"

"Howard's squirting watermelon-seeds at me," whined Snooky, "and Pa won't make him stop."

"Oh, I didn't so!" vociferated Howard. "I only held one between my fingers, and it just kind of shot out."

"You'll come upstairs with me in just five minutes," announced Travis, "and get ready for Sunday-school."

Howard knew that his older sister's decisions were as the laws of the Persians, and found means to finish his breakfast within the specified time, though not without protest. Once upstairs, however, the usual Sunday-morning drama of despatching him to Sunday-school in presentable condition was enacted. At every moment his voice could be heard uplifted in shrill expostulation and debate. No, his hands were clean enough, and he didn't see why he had to wear that little old pink tie; and, oh! his new shoes were too tight and hurt his sore toe; and he wouldn't, he wouldn't—no, not if he were killed for it, change his shirt. Not for a moment did Travis lose her temper with him. But "very well," she declared at length, "the next time she saw that little Miner girl she would tell her that he had said she was his beau-heart. *Now* would he hold still while she brushed his hair?"

At a few minutes before eleven Travis and her father went to church. They were Episcopalians, and for time out of mind had rented a half-pew in the church of their denomination on California Street, not far from Chinatown. By noon the family reassembled at dinner-table, where Mr. Bessemer ate his chicken-heart—after Travis had thrice reminded him of it—and expressed himself as to the sermon and the minister's theology: sometimes to his daughter and sometimes to himself.

After dinner Howard and Snooky foregathered in the nursery with their beloved lead soldiers; Travis went to her room to write letters; and Mr. Bessemer sat in the bay window of the dining room reading the paper from end to end.

At five Travis bestirred herself. It was Victorine's afternoon out. Travis set the table, spreading a cover of blue denim edged with white braid, which showed off the silver and the set of delft—her great and never-ending joy—to great effect. Then she tied her apron about her, and went into the kitchen to make the mayonnaise dressing for the potato salad, to slice the ham, and to help the cook (a most inefficient Irish person, taken on only for that month during the absence of the family's beloved and venerated Sing Wo) in the matter of preparing the Sunday-evening tea.

Tea was had at half-past five. Never in the history of the family had its *menu* varied: cold ham, potato salad, pork and beans, canned fruit, chocolate, and the inevitable pitcher of ice-water.

In the absence of Victorine, Maggie waited on the table, very uncomfortable in her one good dress and stiff white apron. She stood off from the table, making awkward dabs at it from time to time. In her excess of deference she developed a clumsiness that was beyond all expression. She passed the plates upon the wrong side, and remembered herself with a broken apology at inopportune moments. She dropped a spoon, she spilt the ice-water. She handled the delft cups and platters with an exaggerated solicitude, as though they were glass bombs. She brushed the crumbs into their laps instead of into the crumb-tray, and at last, when she had set even Travis's placid nerves in a jangle, was dismissed to the kitchen, and retired with a gasp of unspeakable relief.

Suddenly there came a prolonged trilling of the electric bell, and Howard flashed a grin at Travis. Snooky jumped up and pushed back, crying out: "I'll go! I'll go!"

Mr. Bessemer glanced nervously at Travis. "That's Mr. Rivers, isn't it, daughter?" Travis smiled. "Well, I think I'll—I think I'd better——" he began.

"No," said Travis, "I don't want you to, Papum; you sit right where you are. How absurd!"

The old man dropped obediently back into his seat.

"That's all right, Maggie," said Travis as the cook reappeared from the pantry. "Snooky went."

"Huh!" exclaimed Howard, his grin widening. "Huh!"

"And remember one thing, Howard," remarked Travis calmly; "don't you ever again ask Mr. Rivers for a nickel to put in your bank."

Mr. Bessemer roused up. "Did that boy do that?" he inquired sharply of Travis.

"Well, well, he won't do it again," said Travis soothingly. The old man glared for an instant at Howard, who shifted uneasily in his seat. But meanwhile Snooky had clamoured down to the outside door, and before anything further could be said young Rivers came into the dining room.

CHAPTER II

FOR some reason, never made sufficiently clear, Rivers's parents had handicapped him from the baptismal font with the prænomen of Condé, which, however, upon Anglo-Saxon tongues, had been promptly modified to Condy, or even, amongst his familiar and intimate friends, to Conny. Asked as to his birthplace—for no Californian assumes that his neighbour is born in the State—Condy was wont to reply that he was "bawn 'n' rais'" in Chicago; "but," he always added, "I couldn't help that, you know." His people had come West in the early 'eighties, just in time to bury the father in alien soil. Condy was an only child. He was educated at the State University, had a finishing year at Yale, and a few months after his return home was taken on the staff of the San Francisco *Daily Times* as an associate editor of its Sunday supplement. For Condy had developed a taste and talent in the matter of writing. Short stories were his mania. He had begun by an inoculation of the Kipling virus, had suffered an almost fatal attack of Harding Davis, and had even been affected by Maupassant. He "went in" for accuracy of detail; held that if one wrote a story involving firemen one should have, or seem to have, every detail of the department at his fingers' ends, and should "bring in" to the tale all manner of technical names and cant phrases.

Much of his work on the Sunday supplements of the *Times* was of the hack order—special articles, write-ups, and interviews. About once a month, however, he wrote a short story, and of late, now that he was convalescing from Maupassant and had begun to be somewhat himself, these stories had improved in quality, and one or two had even been copied in the Eastern journals. He earned $100 a month.

When Snooky had let him in, Rivers dashed up the stairs of the Bessemers' flat, two at a time, tossed his stick into a porcelain cane-rack in the hall, wrenched off his overcoat with a single movement, and precipitated himself, panting, into the dining room, tugging at his gloves.

He was twenty-eight years old—nearly ten years older than Travis; tall and somewhat lean; his face smooth-shaven and pink all over, as if he had just given it a violent rubbing with a crash towel. Unlike most writing folk, he dressed himself according to prevailing custom. But Condy overdid the matter. His scarfs and cravats were too bright, his coloured shirt-bosoms were too broadly barred, his waistcoats too extreme. Even Travis, as she rose to his abrupt entrance, told herself that of a Sunday evening a pink shirt and scarlet tie were a combination hardly to be forgiven.

Condy shook her hand in both of his, then rushed over to Mr. Bessemer, exclaiming between breaths: "Don't get up, sir—don't *think* of it! Heavens! I'm disgustingly late. You're all through. My watch—this beastly watch of mine—I can't imagine how I came to be so late. You did quite right not to wait."

Then as his morbidly keen observation caught a certain look of blankness on Travis's face, and his rapid glance noted no vacant chair at table, he gave a quick gasp of dismay.

"Heavens and earth! didn't you *expect* me?" he cried. "I thought you said—I thought—I must have forgotten—I must have got it mixed up somehow. What a hideous mistake, what a blunder! What a fool I am!"

He dropped into a chair against the wall and mopped his forehead with a blue-bordered handkerchief.

"Well, what difference does it make, Condy?" said Travis quietly. "I'll put another place for you."

"No, no!" he vociferated, jumping up. "I won't hear of it, I won't permit it! You'll think I did it on purpose!"

Travis ignored his interference, and made a place for him opposite the children, and had Maggie make some more chocolate.

Condy meanwhile covered himself with opprobrium.

"And all this trouble—I always make trouble everywhere I go. Always a round man in a square hole, or a square man in a round hole."

He got up and sat down again, crossed and recrossed his legs, picked up little ornaments from the mantelpiece, and replaced them without consciousness of what they were, and finally broke the crystal of his watch as he was resetting it by the cuckoo clock.

"Hello!" he exclaimed suddenly; "where did you get that clock? Where did you get that clock? That's new to me. Where did that come from?"

"That cuckoo clock?" inquired Travis, with a stare. "Condy Rivers, you've been here and in this room at least twice a week for the last year and a half, and that clock, and no other, has always hung there."

But already Condy had forgotten or lost interest in the clock.

"Is that so? is that so?" he murmured absent-mindedly, seating himself at the table.

Mr. Bessemer was murmuring: "That clock's a little fast. I cannot make that clock keep time. Victorine has lost the key. I have to wind it with a monkey-wrench. Now I'll try some more beans. Maggie has put in too much pepper. I'll have to have a new key made tomorrow."

"Hey? Yes—yes. Is that so?" answered Condy Rivers, bewildered, wishing to be polite, yet unable to follow the old man's mutterings.

"He's not talking to you," remarked Travis, without lowering her voice. "You know how Papum goes on. He won't hear a word you say. Well, I read your story in this morning's *Times*."

A few moments later, while Travis and Condy were still discussing this story, Mr. Bessemer rose. "Well, Mr. Rivers," he announced, "I guess I'll say good-night. Come, Snooky."

"Yes, take her with you, Papum," said Travis. "She'll go to sleep on the lounge here if you don't. Howard, have you got your lessons for to-morrow?"

It appeared that he had not. Snooky whined to stay up a little longer, but at last consented to go with her father. They all bade Condy good-night and took themselves away, Howard lingering a moment in the door in the hope of the nickel he dared not ask for. Maggie reappeared to clear away the table.

"Let's go in the parlour," suggested Travis, rising. "Don't you want to?"

The parlour was the front room overlooking the street, and was reached by the long hall that ran the whole length of the flat, passing by the door of each one of its eight rooms in turn.

Travis preceded Condy, and turned up one of the burners in a coloured globe of the little brass chandelier.

The parlour was a small affair, peopled by a family of chairs and sofas robed in white druggets. A gold-and-white effect had been striven for throughout the room. The walls had been tinted instead of papered, and bunches of hand-painted pink flowers tied up with blue ribbons straggled from one corner of the ceiling. Across one angle of the room straddled a brass easel upholding a crayon portrait of Travis at the age of nine, "enlarged from a photograph." A yellow drape ornamented one corner of the frame, while another drape of blue depended from one end of the mantel-piece.

The piano, upon which nobody ever played, balanced the easel in an opposite corner. Over the mantelpiece hung in a gilded frame a steel engraving of Priscilla and John Alden; and on the mantel itself two bisque figures of an Italian fisher boy and girl kept company with the clock, a huge timepiece, set in a red plush palette, that never was known to go. But at the right of the fireplace, and balancing the tuft of pampa-grass, to the left, was an inverted section of a sewer-pipe painted blue and decorated with daisies. Into it was thrust a sheaf of cat-tails, gilded, and tied with a pink ribbon.

Travis dropped upon the shrouded sofa, and Condy set himself carefully down on one of the frail chairs with its spindling golden legs, and they began to talk.

Condy had taken her to the theatre the Monday night of that week, as had been his custom ever since he had known her well, and there was something left for them to say on that subject. But in ten minutes they had exhausted it. An engagement of a girl known to both of them had just been announced. Condy brought that up, and kept conversation going for another twenty minutes, and then filled in what threatened to be a gap by telling her stories of the society reporters, and how they got inside news by listening to telephone party wires for days at a time. Travis's condemnation of this occupied another five or ten minutes; and so what with this and with that they reached nine o'clock. Then decidedly the evening began to drag. It was too early to go. Condy could find no good excuse for taking himself away, and, though Travis was good-natured enough, and met him more than halfway, their talk lapsed, and lapsed, and lapsed. The breaks became more numerous and lasted longer.

Condy began to wonder if he was boring her. No sooner had the suspicion entered his head than it hardened into a certainty, and at once what little fluency and freshness he yet retained forsook him on the spot. What made matters worse was his recollection of other evenings that of late he had failed in precisely the same manner. Even while he struggled to save the situation Condy was wondering if they two were talked out—if they had lost charm for each other. Did he not know Travis through and through by now—her opinions, her ideas, her convictions? Was there any more freshness in her for him? Was their little flirtation of the last eighteen months, charming as it had been, about to end? Had they played out the play, had they come to the end of each other's resources? He had never considered the possibility of this before; but all at once as he looked at Travis—looked fairly into her little brown-black eyes—it was borne in upon him that she was thinking precisely the same thing.

Condy Rivers had met Travis at a dance a year and a half before this, and, because she was so very pretty, so unaffected, and so good-natured, had found means to see her three or four times a week ever since. They two "went out" not a little in San Francisco society, and had been in a measure identified with what was known as the Younger Set; though Travis was too young to come out, and Rivers too old to feel very much at home with girls of twenty and boys of eighteen.

They had known each other in the conventional way (as conventionality goes in San Francisco); during the season Rivers took her to the theatres Monday nights, and called regularly Wednesdays and Sundays. Then they met at dances, and managed to be invited to the same houses for teas and dinners. They had flirted rather desperately, and at times Condy even told himself that he loved this girl so much younger than he

—this girl with the smiling eyes and robust figure and yellow hair, who was so frank, so straightforward, and so wonderfully pretty.

But evidently they had come to the last move in the game; and as Condy reflected that after all he had never known the real Travis, that the girl whom he told himself he knew through and through was only the Travis of dinner parties and afternoon functions, he was surprised to experience a sudden qualm of deep and genuine regret. He had never been *near* to her, after all. They were as far apart as when they had first met. And yet he knew enough of her to know that she was "worth while." He had had experience—all the experience he wanted—with other older women and girls of society. They were sophisticated, they were all a little tired, they had run the gamut of amusements—in a word, they were jaded. But Travis, this girl of nineteen, who was not yet even a *débutante*, had been fresh and unspoiled, had been new and strong and young.

"Of course you may call it what you like. He was nothing more nor less than intoxicated—yes, drunk."

"Hah! who—what—wh—what are you talking about?" gasped Condy, sitting bolt upright.

"Jack Carter," answered Travis. "No," she added, shaking her head at him helplessly, "he hasn't been listening to a word. I'm talking about Jack Carter and the 'Saturday Evening' last night."

"No, no, I haven't heard. Forgive me; I was think-ing—thinking of something else. Who was drunk?"

Travis paused a moment, settling her side-combs in her hair; then:

"If you will try to listen, I'll tell it all over again, because it's serious with me, and I'm going to take a very decided stand about it. You know," she went on —"you know what the 'Saturday Evening' is. Plenty of the girls who are not 'out' belong, and a good many of last year's *débutantes* come, as well as the older girls of three or four seasons' standing. You could call it representative, couldn't you? Well, they always serve punch; and you know yourself that you have seen men there who have taken more than they should."

"Yes, yes," admitted Condy. "I know Carter and the two Catlin boys always do."

"It gets pretty bad sometimes, doesn't it?" she said.

"It does, it does—and it's shameful. But most of the girls—*most* of them—don't seem to mind."

Miss Bessemer stiffened a bit. "There are one or two girls that do," she said quietly. "Frank Catlin had the decency to go home last night," she continued; "and his brother wasn't any worse than usual. But Jack Carter must have been drinking before he came. He was very bad indeed—as bad," she said between her teeth, "as he could be and yet walk straight. As you say, most of the girls don't mind. They say, 'It's only Johnnie Carter; what do you expect?' But one of the girls—you know her, Laurie Flagg—cut a dance with him last night and told him exactly why. Of course Carter was furious. He was sober enough to think he had been insulted; and what do you suppose he did?"

"What? what?" exclaimed Condy, breathless, leaning toward her.

"Went about the halls and dressing rooms circulating some dirty little lie about Laurie. Actually trying to —to"—Travis hesitated—"to make a scandal about her."

Condy bounded in his seat. "Beast, cad, swine!" he exclaimed.

"I didn't think," said Travis, "that Carter would so much as dare to ask me to dance with him——"

"Did he? did—did——"

"Wait," she interrupted. "So I wasn't at all prepared for what happened. During the german, before I knew it, there he was in front of me. It was a break, and he wanted it. I hadn't time to think. The only idea I had was that if I refused him he might tell some dirty little lie about me. I was all confused—mixed up. I felt just as though it were a snake that I had to humour to get rid of. I gave him the break."

Condy sat speechless. Suddenly he arose.

"Well, now, let's see," he began, speaking rapidly, his hands twisting and untwisting till the knuckles cracked. "Now, let's see. You leave it to me. I know Carter. He's going to be at a stag dinner where I am invited to-morrow night, and I—I——"

"No, you won't, Condy," said Travis placidly. "You'll pay no attention to it, and I'll tell you why. Suppose you should make a scene with Mr. Carter— I don't know how men settle these things. Well, it would be told in all the clubs and in all the newspaper offices that two men had quarrelled over a girl; and my name is mentioned, discussed, and handed around from one crowd of men to another, from one club to another; and then, of course, the papers take it up. By that time Mr. Carter will have told his side of the story and invented another dirty little lie, and I'm the one who suffers the most in the end. And remember, Condy, that I haven't any mother in such an affair, not even an older sister. No, we'll just let the matter drop. It would be more dignified, anyhow. Only I have made up my mind what I am going to do."

"What's that?"

"I'm not coming out. If that's the sort of thing one has to put up with in society"—Travis drew a little line on the sofa at her side with her finger-tip—"I am going to—stop—right—there. It's not"—Miss Bessemer stiffened again—"that I'm afraid of Jack Carter and his dirty stories; I simply don't want to know the kind of people who have made Jack Carter possible. The other girls don't mind it, nor many men besides you, Condy; and I'm not going to be associated with people who take it as a joke for a man to come to a function drunk. And as for having a good time, I'll find my amusements somewhere else. I'll ride a wheel, take long walks, study something. But as for leading the life of a society girl—no! And whether I have a good time or not, I'll keep my own self-respect. At least I'll never have to dance with a drunken man. I won't have to humiliate myself like that a second time."

"But I presume you will still continue to go out somewhere," protested Condy Rivers.

She shook her head.

"I have thought it all over, and I've talked about it with Papum. There's no halfway about it. The only way to stop is to stop short. Just this afternoon I've regretted three functions for next week, and I shall resign from the 'Saturday Evening.' Oh, it's not the Jack Carter affair alone!" she exclaimed; "the whole thing tires me. Mind, Condy," she concluded, "I'm not going to break with it because I have any 'purpose in life,' or that sort of thing. I want to have a good time, and I'm going to see if I can't have it in my own way. If the kind of thing that makes Jack Carter possible is conventionality, then I'm done with conventionality for good. I am going to try, from this time on, to be just as true to myself as I can be. I am going to be sincere, and not pretend to like people and things that I don't like; and I'm going to do the things that I like to do—just so long as they are the things a good girl can do. See, Condy?"

"You're fine," murmured Condy, breathless. "You're fine as gold, Travis, and I—I love you all the better for it."

"Ah, *now*," exclaimed Travis, with a brusque

movement, "there's another thing we must talk about.
No more foolishness between us. We've had a jolly
little flirtation, I know, and it's been good fun while
it lasted. I know you like me, and you know that I
like you; but as for loving each other, you know we
don't. Yes, you say that you love me and that I'm the
only girl. That's part of the game. I can play it"—her
little eyes began to dance—"quite as well as you. But
it's playing with something that's quite too serious to
be played with—after all, isn't it, now? It's insincere,
and, as I tell you, from now on I'm going to be as
true and as sincere and as honest as I can."

"But I tell you that I *do* love you," protested Condy,
trying to make the words ring true.

Travis looked about the room an instant as if in
deliberation; then abruptly: "Ah! what am I going to
do with such a boy as you are, after all—a great, big,
overgrown boy? Condy Rivers, look at me straight in
the eye. Tell me, do you honestly love me? You know
what I mean when I say 'love.' Do you love me?"

"No, I don't!" he exclaimed blankly, as though he
had just discovered the fact.

"There!" declared Travis—"and I don't love you."
They both began to laugh.

"Now," added Travis, "we don't need to have the
burden and trouble of keeping up the pretences any
more. We understand each other, don't we?"

"This is queer enough," said Condy drolly.

"But isn't it an improvement?"

Condy scoured his head.

"Tell me the truth," she insisted; "*you* be sincere."

"I do believe it is. Why—why—Travis—by Jingo!
Travis, I think I'm going to like you better than ever
now."

"Never mind. Is it an agreement?"

"What is?"

"That we don't pretend to love each other any more?"

"All right—yes—you're right; because the moment I began to love you I should like you so much less."

She put out her hand. "That's an agreement, then."

Condy took her hand in his. "Yes, it's an agreement." But when, as had been his custom, he made as though to kiss her hand, Travis drew it quickly away.

"No! no!" she said firmly, smiling for all that—"no more foolishness."

"But—but," he protested, "it's not so radical as that, is it? You're not going to overturn such time-worn, time-honoured customs as that? Why, this is a regular rebellion."

"No, sire," quoted Travis, trying not to laugh, "it **is a revolution.**"

CHAPTER III

ALTHOUGH Monday was practically a holiday for the Sunday-supplement staff of the *Times*, Condy Rivers made a point to get down to the office betimes the next morning. There were reasons why a certain article descriptive of a great whaleback steamer taking on grain for famine-stricken India should be written that day, and Rivers wanted his afternoon free in order to go to Laurie Flagg's coming-out tea.

But as he came into his room at the *Times* office, which he shared with the exchange and sporting editors, and settled himself at his desk, he suddenly remembered that, under the new order of things, he need not expect to see Travis at the Flaggs'.

"Well," he muttered, "maybe it doesn't make so much difference, after all. She was a corking fine girl, but—might as well admit it—the play is played out. Of course I don't love her—any more than she loves me. I'll see less and less of her now. It's inevitable, and after a while we'll hardly even meet. In a way, it's a pity; but of course one has to be sensible about these things. . . . Well, this whaleback now."

He rang up the Chamber of Commerce, and found out that the *City of Everett*, which was the whaleback's name, was at the Mission Street wharf. This made it possible for him to write the article in two ways. He either could fake his copy from a clipping on the subject which the exchange editor had laid on his desk, or he could go down in person to the wharf, interview the captain, and inspect the craft for him-

126

self. The former was the short and easy method. The latter was more troublesome, but would result in a far more interesting article.

Condy debated the subject a few minutes, then decided to go down to the wharf. San Francisco's waterfront was always interesting, and he might get hold of a photograph of the whaleback. All at once the "idea" of the article struck him, the certain underlying notion that would give importance and weight to the mere details and descriptions. Condy's enthusiasm flared up in an instant.

"By Jove!" he exclaimed; "by Jove!"

He clapped on his hat wrong side foremost, crammed a sheaf of copy-paper into his pocket, and was on the street again in another moment. Then it occurred to him that he had forgotten to call at his club that morning for his mail, as was his custom, on the way to the office. He looked at his watch. It was early yet, and his club was but two blocks' distance. He decided that he would get his letters at the club, and read them on the way down to the wharf.

For Condy had joined a certain San Francisco club of artists, journalists, musicians, and professional men that is one of the institutions of the city, and, in fact, famous throughout the United States. He was one of the younger members, but was popular and well liked, and on more than one occasion had materially contributed to the fun of the club's "low jinks."

In his box this morning he found one letter that he told himself he must read upon the instant. It bore upon the envelope the name of a New York publishing house to whom Condy had sent a collection of his short stories about a month before. He took the letter into the "round window" of the club, overlooking the street, and tore it open excitedly. The fact that he had received a letter from the firm without the return of his manuscript seemed a good omen. This was what he read:

Condé Rivers, Esq., Bohemian Club,
   San Francisco, Cal.

Dear Sir: We return to you by this mail the manuscript of your stories, which we do not consider as available for publication at the present moment. We would say, however, that we find in several of them indications of a quite unusual order of merit. The best-selling book just now is the short novel—say thirty thousand words —of action and adventure. Judging from the stories of your collection, we suspect that your talent lies in this direction, and we would suggest that you write such a novel and submit the same to us.

Very respectfully,
The Centennial Co.
New York.

Condy shoved the letter into his pocket and collapsed limply into his chair.

"What's the good of trying to do anything anyhow!" he muttered, looking gloomily down into the street. "My level is just the hack-work of a local Sunday supplement, and I am a fool to think of anything else."

His enthusiasm in the matter of the *City of Everett* was cold and dead in a moment. He could see no possibilities in the subject whatever. His "idea" of a few minutes previous seemed ridiculous and overwrought. He would go back to the office and grind out his copy from the exchange editor's clipping.

Just then his eye was caught by a familiar figure in trim, well-fitting black halted on the opposite corner waiting for the passage of a cable-car. It was Travis Bessemer. No one but she could carry off such rigorous simplicity in the matter of dress so well: black skirt, black Russian blouse, tiny black bonnet and black veil, white kids with black stitching. Simplicity itself. Yet the style of her, as Condy Rivers told himself, flew up and hit you in the face; and her figure—was there anything more perfect? and the soft pretty effect of her yellow hair seen through the veil—could anything be more fetching? and her smart carriage and the fling of her fine broad shoulders, and—no, it was no use; Condy had to run down to speak to her.

"Come, come," she said as he pretended to jostle against her on the curbstone without noticing her; "*you* had best go to work. Loafing at ten o'clock on the street-corners—the idea!"

"It *is* not—it cannot be—and yet it is—it is *she*," he burlesqued; "and after all these years!" Then in his natural voice: "Hello, T. B."

"Hello, C. R."

"Where are you going?"

"Home. I've just run down for half an hour to have the head of my banjo tightened."

"If I put you on the car, will you expect me to pay your car-fare?"

"Condy Rivers, I've long since got over the idea of ever expecting you to have any change concealed about your person."

"Huh! no, it all goes for theatre-tickets, and flowers and boxes of candy for a certain girl I know. But"—and he glared at her significantly—"no more foolishness."

She laughed. "What are you 'on' this morning, Condy?"

Condy told her as they started to walk toward Kearney Street.[3]

"But why *don't* you go to the dock and see the vessel, if you can make a better article that way?"

"Oh, what's the good! The Centennial people have turned down my stories."

She commiserated him for this; then suddenly exclaimed:

"No, you must go down to the dock! You ought to, Condy. Oh, I tell you, let me go down with you!"

In an instant Condy leaped to the notion. "Splendid!

129

splendid! no reason why you shouldn't!" he exclaimed.
And within fifteen minutes the two were treading the
wharfs and quays of the city's water-front.

Ships innumerable nuzzled at the endless line of
docks, mast overspiring mast, and bowsprit over-
lapping bowsprit, till the eye was bewildered, as if by
the confusion of branches in a leafless forest. In the
distance the mass of rigging resolved itself into a solid
gray blur against the sky. The great hulks, green and
black and slate gray, laid themselves along the docks,
straining leisurely at their mammoth chains, their
flanks opened, their cargoes, as it were their entrails,
spewed out in a wild disarray of crate and bale and box.
Sailors and stevedores swarmed them like vermin.
Trucks rolled along the wharfs like peals of ordnance,
the horse-hoofs beating the boards like heavy drum-
taps. Chains clanked, a ship's dog barked incessantly
from a companionway, ropes creaked in complaining
pulleys, blocks rattled, hoisting-engines coughed and
strangled, while all the air was redolent of oakum, of
pitch, of paint, of spices, of ripe fruit, of clean cool
lumber, of coffee, of tar, of bilge, and the brisk, nimble
odour of the sea.

Travis was delighted, her little brown eyes snapping,
her cheeks flushing, as she drank in the scene.

"To think," she cried, "where all these ships have
come from! Look at their names; aren't they perfect?
Just the names, see: the *Mary Baker*, Hull; and the
Anandale, Liverpool; and the *Two Sisters*, Calcutta;
and see that one they're calking, the *Montevideo*, Callao; and there, look! look! the very one you're looking
for, the *City of Everett*, San Francisco."

The whaleback, an immense tube of steel plates, lay
at her wharf, sucking in entire harvests of wheat from
the San Joaquin valley—harvests that were to feed
strangely clad skeletons on the southern slopes of the

Himalaya foot-hills. Travis and Condy edged their way among piles of wheat-bags, dodging drays and rumbling trucks, and finally brought up at the after gangplank, where a sailor halted them. Condy exhibited his reporter's badge.

"I represent the *Times*," he said, with profound solemnity, "and I want to see the officer in charge."

The sailor fell back upon the instant.

"Power of the press," whispered Condy to Travis as the two gained the deck.

A second sailor directed them to the mate, whom they found in the chart-room, engaged, singularly enough, in trimming the leaves of a scraggly geranium.

Condy explained his mission with flattering allusions to the whaleback and the novelty of the construction. The mate—an old man with a patriarchal beard—softened at once, asked them into his own cabin aft, and even brought out a camp-stool for Travis, brushing it with his sleeve before setting it down.

While Condy was interviewing the old fellow, Travis was examining, with the interest of a child, the details of the cabin: the rack-like bunk, the wash-stand, ingeniously constructed so as to shut into the bulkhead when not in use, the alarm-clock screwed to the wall, and the array of photographs thrust into the mirror between frame and glass. One, an old daguerreotype, particularly caught her fancy. It was the portrait of a very beautiful girl, wearing the old-fashioned side curls and high comb of a half-century previous. The old mate noticed the attention she paid to it, and, as soon as he had done giving information to Condy, turned and nodded to Travis, and said quietly: "She was pretty, wasn't she?"

"Oh, very!" answered Travis, without looking away.

There was a silence. Then the mate, his eyes wide and thoughtful, said with a long breath:

"And she was just about your age, miss, when I saw her; and you favour her, too."

Condy and Travis held their breaths in attention. There in the cabin of that curious nondescript whale-back they had come suddenly to the edge of a romance —a romance that had been lived through before they were born. Then Travis said in a low voice, and sweetly: "She died?"

"Before I ever set eyes on her, miss. That is, *maybe* she died. I sometimes think—fact is, I really believe she's alive yet, and waiting for me." He hesitated awkwardly. "I dunno," he said, pulling his beard. "I don't usually tell that story to strange folk; but you remind me so of her that I guess I will."

Condy sat down on the edge of the bunk, and the mate seated himself on the plush settle opposite the door, his elbows on his knees, his eyes fixed on a patch of sunlight upon the deck outside.

"I began life," he said, "as a deep-sea diver—began pretty young, too. I first put on the armour when I was twenty, nothing but a lad; but I could take the pressure up to seventy pounds even then. One of my first dives was off Trincomalee, on the coast of Ceylon. A mail packet had gone down in a squall with all on board. Six of the bodies had come up and had been recovered, but the seventh hadn't. It was the body of the daughter of the governor of the island—a beautiful young girl of nineteen, whom everybody loved. I was sent for to go down and bring the body up. Well, I went down. The packet lay in a hundred feet of water, and that's a wonderful deep dive. I had to go down twice. The first time I couldn't find anything, though I went all through the berth-deck. I came up to the wrecking-float and reported that I had seen nothing. There were a lot of men there belonging to the wrecking gang, and some correspondents of London papers. But they would

have it that she was below, and had me go down again.
I did, and this time I found her."

The mate paused a moment.

"I'll have to tell you," he went on, "that when a
body don't come to the surface it will stand or sit in
a perfectly natural position until a current or movement
of the water around touches it. When that happens
—well, you'd say the body was alive; and old divers
have a superstition—no, it *ain't* just a superstition, I
believe it's so—that drowned people really don't die
till they come to the surface, and the air touches them.
We say that the drowned who don't come up still have
some sort of life of their own, way down there in all
that green water . . . some kind of life . . . surely . . .
surely. When I went down the second time, I came
across the door of what I thought at first was the linen-
closet. But it turned out to be a little stateroom. I
opened it. There was the girl. She was sitting on the
sofa opposite the door, with a little hat on her head, and
holding a satchel in her lap, just as if she was ready to
go ashore. Her eyes were wide open, and she was looking
right at me and smiling. It didn't seem terrible or
ghastly in the least. She seemed very sweet. When I
opened the door it set the water in motion, and she
got up and dropped the satchel, and came toward me
smiling and holding out her arms.

"I stepped back quick and shut the door, and sat
down in one of the saloon chairs to fetch my breath,
for it had given me a start. The next thing to do was
to send her up. But I began to think. She seemed so
pretty as she was. What was the use of bringing her
up—up there on the wrecking-float with that crowd
of men—up where the air would get at her, and where
they would put her in the ground along o' the worms?
If I left her there she'd always be sweet and pretty—
always be nineteen; and I remembered what old divers

said about drowned people living just so long as they stayed below. You see, I was only a lad then, and things like that impress you when you're young. Well, I signalled to be hauled up. They asked me on the float if I'd seen anything, and I said no. That was all there was to the affair. They never raised the ship, and in a little while it was all forgotten.

"But I never forgot it, and I always remembered her, 'way down there in all that still green water, waiting there in that little stateroom for me to come back and open the door. And I've growed to be an old man remembering her; but she's always stayed just as she was the first day I saw her, when she came toward me smiling and holding out her arms. She's always stayed young and fresh and pretty. I never saw her but that once. Only afterward I got her picture from a native woman of Trincomalee who was housekeeper at the Residency where the governor of the island lived. Somehow I never could care for other women after that, and I ain't never married for that reason."

"No, no, of course not!" exclaimed Travis, in a low voice, as the old fellow paused.

"Fine, fine; oh, fine as gold!" murmured Condy, under his breath.

"Well," said the mate, getting up and rubbing his knee, "that's the story. Now you know all about that picture. Will you have a glass of Madeira, miss?"

He got out a bottle of wine bearing the genuine Funchal label and filled three tiny glasses. Travis pushed up her veil, and she and Condy rose.

"This is to *her*," said Travis gravely.

"Thank you, miss," answered the mate, and the three drank in silence.

As Travis and Condy were going down the gang-plank they met the captain of the whaleback coming up.

"I saw you in there talking to old McPherson," he explained. "Did you get what you wanted from him?"

"More, more!" exclaimed Condy.

"My hand in the fire, he told you that yarn about the girl who was drowned off Trincomalee. Of course, I knew it. The old boy's wits are turned on that subject. He *will* have it that the body hasn't decomposed in all this time. Good seaman enough, and a first-class navigator, but he's soft in that one spot."

OH, but the *story* of it!" exclaimed Condy as he and Travis regained the wharf—"the story of it! Isn't it a ripper! Isn't it a corker! His leaving her that way, and never caring for any other girl afterward."

"And so original!" she commented, quite as enthusiastic as he.

"Original?—why, it's new as paint! It's—it's—Travis, I'll make a story out of this that will be copied in every paper between the two oceans."

They were so interested in the mate's story that they forgot to take a car, and walked up Clay Street talking it over, suggesting, rearranging, and embellishing; and Condy was astonished and delighted to note that she "caught on" to the idea as quickly as he, and knew the telling points and what details to leave out. "And I'll make a bang-up article out of the whaleback herself," declared Condy. The "idea" of the article had returned to him, and all his enthusiasm with it.

"And look here," he said, showing her the letter from the Centennial Company. "They turned down my book, but see what they say."

"Quite an unusual order of merit!" cried Travis. "Why, that's fine! Why didn't you show this to me before?—and asking you like this to write them a novel of adventure! What *more* can you want? Oh!" she exclaimed impatiently, "that's so like you; you would tell everybody about your reverses, and carry on about them yourself, but never say a word when you get a little boom. Have you an idea for a thirty-thousand-word novel? Wouldn't that diver's story do?"

"No, there's not enough in that for thirty thousand words. I haven't any idea at all—never wrote a story of adventure—never wrote anything longer than six thousand words. But I'll keep my eye open for something that will do. By the way—by Jove! Travis, where are we?"

They looked swiftly around them, and the bustling, breezy water-front faded from their recollections. They were in a world of narrow streets, of galleries and overhanging balconies. Craziest structures, riddled and honeycombed with stairways and passages, shut out the sky, though here and there rose a building of extraordinary richness and most elaborate ornamentation. Colour was everywhere. A thousand little notes of green and yellow, of vermilion and sky-blue, assaulted the eye. Here it was a doorway, here a vivid glint of cloth or hanging, here a huge scarlet sign lettered with gold, and here a kaleidoscopic effect in the garments of a passer-by. Directly opposite, and two stories above their heads, a sort of huge "loggia", one blaze of gilding and crude vermilions, opened in the gray cement of a crumbling façade, like a sudden burst of flame. Gigantic pot-bellied lanterns of red and gold swung from its ceiling, while along its railing stood a row of pots—brass, ruddy bronze, and blue porcelain —from which were growing red, saffron, purple, pink, and golden tulips without number. The air was vibrant with unfamiliar noises. From one of the balconies near at hand, though unseen, a gong, a pipe, and some kind of stringed instrument wailed and thundered in unison. There was a vast shuffling of padded soles and a continuous interchange of singsong monosyllables, high-pitched and staccato, while from every hand rose the strange aromas of the East—sandalwood, punk, incense, oil, and the smell of mysterious cookery.

"Chinatown!" exclaimed Travis. "I hadn't the

faintest idea we had come up so far. Condy Rivers, do you know what time it is?" She pointed a white kid finger through the doorway of a drug-store, where, amid lacquer boxes and bronze urns of herbs and dried seeds, a round Seth Thomas marked half-past two.

"And your lunch?" cried Condy. "Great heavens! I never thought."

"It's too late to get any at home. Never mind; I'll go somewhere and have a cup of tea."

"Why not get a package of Chinese tea, now that you're down here, and take it home with you?"

"Or drink it here."

"Where?"

"In one of the restaurants. There wouldn't be a soul there at this hour. I know they serve tea any time. Condy, let's try it. Wouldn't it be fun?"

Condy smote his thigh. "Fun!" he vociferated; "fun! It is—by Jove—it would be *heavenly!* Wait a moment. I'll tell you what we will do. Tea won't be enough. We'll go down to Kearney Street, or to the market, and get some crackers to go with it."

They hurried back to the California market, a few blocks distant, and bought some crackers and a wedge of new cheese. On the way back to Chinatown Travis stopped at a music-store on Kearney Street to get her banjo, which she had left to have its head tightened; and thus burdened they regained the "town," Condy grieving audibly at having to carry "brown-paper bundles through the street."

"First catch your restuarant," said Travis as they turned into Dupont Street with its thronging coolies and swarming, gayly clad children. But they had not far to seek.

"Here you are!" suddenly exclaimed Condy, halting in front of a wholesale tea-house bearing a sign in Chinese and English. "Come on, Travis!"

They ascended two flights of a broad, brass-bound
staircase leading up from the ground floor, and gained
the restaurant on the top story of the building. As
Travis had foretold, it was deserted. She clasped her
gloved hands gayly, crying: "Isn't it delightful! We've
the whole place to ourselves."

The restaurant ran the whole depth of the building,
and was finished off at either extremity with a gilded
balcony, one overlooking Dupont Street and the other
the old Plaza. Enormous screens of gilded ebony, in-
tricately carved and set with coloured glass panes, divided the room into three, and one of these divisions,
in the rear part, from which they could step out upon
the balcony that commanded the view of the Plaza,
they elected as their own.

It was charming. At their backs they had the huge,
fantastic screen, brave and fine with its coat of gold.
In front, through the glass-paved valves of a pair of
folding doors, they could see the roofs of the houses
beyond the Plaza and, beyond these the blue of the bay
with its anchored ships, and even beyond this the faint
purple of the Oakland shore. On either side of these
doors, in deep alcoves, were divans with mattings and
head-rests for opium-smokers. The walls were painted
blue and hung with vertical Cantonese legends in red
and silver, while all around the sides of the room small
ebony tables alternated with ebony stools, each inlaid
with a slab of mottled marble. A chandelier, all a-glitter
with tinsel, swung from the centre of the ceiling over
a huge round table of mahogany.

And not a soul was there to disturb them. Below
them, out there around the old Plaza, the city drummed
through its work with a lazy, soothing rumble. Nearer
at hand, Chinatown sent up the vague murmur of the
life of the Orient. In the direction of the Mexican quarter, the bell of the cathedral knolled at intervals. The

sky was without a cloud and the afternoon was warm.

Condy was inarticulate with the joy of what he called their "discovery." He got up and sat down. He went out into the other room and came back again. He dragged up a couple of the marble-seated stools to the table. He took off his hat, lit a cigarette, let it go out, lit it again, and burned his fingers. He opened and closed the folding doors, pushed the table into a better light, and finally brought Travis out upon the balcony to show her the "points of historical interest" in and around the Plaza.

"There's the Stevenson memorial ship in the centre, see; and right there, where the flagstaff is, General Baker made the funeral oration over the body of Terry. Broderick killed him in a duel—or was it Terry killed Broderick? [4] I forget which. Anyhow, right opposite, where that pawnshop is, is where the Overland stages used to start in '49. And every other building that fronts on the Plaza, even this one we're in now, used to be a gambling-house in bonanza times; and, see, over yonder is the Morgue and the City Prison."

They turned back into the room, and a great, fat Chinaman brought them tea on Condy's order. But besides tea, he brought dried almonds, pickled watermelon rinds, candied quince, and "China nuts."

Travis cut the cheese into cubes with Condy's penknife, and arranged the cubes in geometric figures upon the crackers.

"But, Condy," she complained, "why in the world did you get so many crackers? There's hundreds of them here—enough to feed a regiment. Why didn't you ask me?"

"Huh! what? what? I don't know. What's the matter with the crackers? You were dickering with the cheese, and the man said, 'How many crackers?' I didn't know. I said, 'Oh, give me a quarter's worth!'"

"And we couldn't possibly have eaten ten cents' worth! Oh, Condy, you are—you are—— But never mind, here's your tea. I wonder if this green, pasty stuff is good."

They found that it was, but so sweet that it made their tea taste bitter. The watermelon rinds were flat to the Western palates, but the dried almonds were a great success. Then Condy promptly got the hiccoughs from drinking his tea too fast, and fretted up and down the room like a chicken with the pip till Travis grew faint and weak with laughter.

"Oh, well," he exclaimed aggrievedly, "laugh, that's right! *I* don't laugh. It isn't such fun when you've got 'em yoursel—*hulp*."

"But sit down, for goodness' sake! You make me so nervous. You can't walk them off. Sit down and hold your breath while you count nine. Condy, I'm going to take off my gloves and veil. What do you think?"

"Sure, of course; and I'll have a cigarette. Do you mind if I smoke?"

"Well, what's that in your hand now?"

"By Jove, I have been smoking! I—I beg your pardon. I'm a regular stable boy. I'll throw it away."

Travis caught his wrist. "What nonsense! I would have told you before if I'd minded."

"But it's gone out!" he exclaimed. "I'll have another."

As he reached into his pocket for his case, his hand encountered a paper-covered volume, and he drew it out in some perplexity.

"Now, how in the wide world did that book come in my pocket?" he muttered, frowning. "What have I been carrying it around for? I've forgotten. I declare I have."

"What book is it?"

141

"Hey? book? . . . h'm," he murmured, staring.

Travis pounded on the table. "Wake up, Condy, I'm talking to you," she called.

"It's *Life's Handicap*," he answered, with a start; "but why and but why have I——"[5]

"What's it about? I never heard of it," she declared.

"You never heard of *Life's Handicap*?" he shouted; "you never heard—you never—you mean to say you never heard—but here, this won't do. Sit right still, and I'll read you one of these yarns before you're another minute older. Any one of them—open the book at random. Here we are—'The Strange Ride of Morrowbie Jukes'; and it's a stem-winder, too."

And then for the first time in her life, there in that airy, golden Chinese restaurant, in the city from which he hasted to flee, Travis Bessemer fell under the charm of the little spectacled colonial, to whose song we all must listen and to whose pipe we all must dance.

There was one "point" in the story of Jukes' strange ride that Condy prided himself upon having discovered. So far as he knew, all critics had overlooked it. It is where Jukes is describing the man-trap of the City of the Dead, who are alive, and mentions that the slope of the enclosing sandhills was "about forty-five degrees." Jukes was a civil engineer, and Condy held that it was a capital bit of realism on the part of the author to have him speak of the pitch of the hills in just such technical terms. At first he thought he would call Travis's attention to this bit of cleverness; but as he read he abruptly changed his mind. He would see if she would find it out for herself. It would be a test of her quickness, he told himself; almost an unfair test, because the point was extremely subtle and could easily be ignored by the most experienced of fiction readers. He read steadily on, working himself into a positive excitement as he approached the passage. He came to it and read it through without any emphasis, almost slurring over it in his eagerness to be perfectly fair. But as he began to read the next paragraph, Travis, her little eyes sparkling with interest and attention, exclaimed:

"Just as an engineer would describe it. Isn't that good!"

"Glory hallelujah!" cried Condy, slamming down the book joyfully. "Travis, you are one in a thousand!"

"What—what is it?" she inquired blankly.

"Never mind, never mind; you're a wonder, that's all,"—and he finished the tale without further explanation. Then, while he smoked another cigarette and she drank another cup of tea, he read to her "The Return of Imri" and the "Incarnation of Krishna Mulvaney." He found her an easy and enrapt convert to the little Englishman's creed, and for himself tasted the intense delight of revealing to another an appreciation of a literature hitherto ignored.

"Isn't he strong!" cried Travis. "Just a *little* better than Marie Corelli and the Duchess!" [6]

"And to think of having all those stories to read! You haven't read any of them yet?"

"Not a one. I've been reading only the novels we take up in the Wednesday class."

"Lord!" muttered Condy.

Condy's spirits had been steadily rising since the incident aboard the whaleback. The exhilaration of the water-front, his delight over the story he was to make out of the old mate's yarn, Chinatown, the charming unconventionality of their lunch in the Chinese restaurant, the sparkling serenity of the afternoon, and the joy of discovering Travis's appreciation of his adored and venerated author, had put him into a mood bordering close upon hilarity.

"The next event upon our interesting programme,"

he announced, "will be a banjosephine obligato in A-sia minor, by that justly renowned impresario, Signor Conde Tin-pani Rivers, specially engaged for this performance; with a pleasing and pan-hellenic song-and-dance turn by Miss Travis Bessemer, the infant phenomenon, otherwise known as 'Babby Bessie.'"

"You're not going to play that banjo here?" said Travis, as he stripped away the canvas covering.

"Order in the gallery!" cried Condy, beginning to tune up. Then in a rapid, professional monotone: "Ladies-and-gentlemen-with-your-kind-permission-I will-endeavour-to-give-you-an-imitation-of-a-Carolina-coon-song,"—and without more ado, singing the words to a rattling, catchy accompaniment, swung off into—

> "F—or *my* gal's a high-born lady,
> *She's* black, but not too shady."

He did not sing loud, and the clack and snarl of the banjo carried hardly farther than the adjoining room; but there was no one to hear, and, as he went along, even Travis began to hum the words. But at that, Condy stopped abruptly, laid the instrument across his knees with exaggerated solicitude, and said deliberately:

"Travis, you are a good, sweet girl, and what you lack in beauty you make up in amiability, and I've no doubt you are kind to your aged father; but you—can—not—sing."

Travis was cross in a moment, all the more so because Condy had spoken the exact truth. It was quite impossible for her to carry a tune half-a-dozen bars without entangling herself in as many different keys. What voice she had was not absolutely bad; but as she persisted in singing in spite of Condy's guying, he put back his head and began a mournful and lugubrious howling.

"Ho!" she exclaimed, grabbing the banjo from his

knees, "if I can't sing, I can play better than some smart people."

"Yes, by note," railed Condy, as Travis executed a banjo "piece" of no little intricacy. "That's just like a machine—like a hand-piano."

"Order in the gallery!" she retorted, without pausing in her playing. She finished with a great flourish and gazed at him in triumph, only to find him pretending a profound slumber. "O—o—o!" she remarked between her teeth, "I just hate you, Condy Rivers."

"There are others," he returned airily.

"Talk about slang."

"*Now* what will we do?" he cried. "Let's *do* something. Suppose we break something—just for fun."

Then suddenly the gayety went out of his face, and he started up and clapped his hand to his head with a gasp of dismay. "Great Heavens!" he exclaimed.

"Condy," cried Travis in alarm, "what is it?"

"The Tea!" he vociferated. "Laurie Flagg's Tea. I ought to be there—right this minute."

Travis fetched a sigh of relief. "Is that all?"

"All!" he retorted. "All! Why, it's past four now—and I'd forgotten every last thing." Then suddenly falling calm again, and quietly resuming his seat: "I don't see as it makes any difference. I won't go, that's all. Push those almonds here, will you, Miss Lady?—But we aren't *doing* anything," he exclaimed, with a brusque return of exuberance. "Let's do things. What'll we do? Think of something. Is there anything we can break?" Then, without any transition, he vaulted upon the table and began to declaim, with tremendous gestures:

"There once was a beast called an Ounce,
Who went with a spring and a bounce.
His head was as flat
As the head of a cat,

This quadrupetantical **Ounce,**
      —tical Ounce,
This quadrupetantical **Ounce.**

"You'd think from his name he was small,
But that was not like him at all.
    He weighed, I'll be bound,
    Three or four hundred pound,
And he looked most uncommonly tall,
      monly—tall,
And he looked most uncommonly tall."[7]

"Bravo! bravo!" cried Travis, pounding on the table. "Hear, hear—none, Brutus, none."

Condy sat down on the table and swung his legs. But during the next few moments, while they were eating the last of their cheese, his good spirits fell rapidly away from him. He heaved a sigh, and thrust both hands gloomily into his pockets.

"Cheese, Condy?" asked Travis.

He shook his head with a dark frown, muttering: "No cheese, no cheese."

"What's wrong, Condy, what's the matter?" asked Travis, with concern.

For some time he would not tell her, answering all her inquiries by closing his eyes and putting his chin in the air, nodding his head in knowing fashion.

"But what is it?"

"You don't respect me," he muttered; and for a long time this was all that could be got from him. No, no, she did not respect him; no, she did not take him seriously.

"But of course I do. Why don't I? Condy Rivers, what's got into you *now?*"

"No, no; I know it. I can tell. You don't take me seriously. You don't respect me."

"But why?"

"Make a blooming buffoon of myself," he mumbled tragically.

In great distress Travis laboured to contradict him. Why, they had just been having a good time, that was all. Why, she had been just as silly as he. Condy caught at the word.

"Silly! There, I knew it. I told you. I'm silly. I'm a buffoon. But haven't we had a great afternoon?" he added, with a sudden grin.

"I never remember," announced Travis emphatically, "when I've had a better time than I've had to-day; and I know just why it's been such a success."

"Why, then?"

"Because we've had no foolishness. We've just been ourselves, and haven't pretended we were in love with each other when we are not. Condy, let's do this lots."

"Do what?"

"Go round to queer little, interesting little places. We've had a glorious time to-day, haven't we?—and we haven't been talked out once."

"As we were last night, for instance," he hazarded.

"I *thought* you felt it, the same as I did. It *was* a bit awful, wasn't it?"

"It was."

"From now on, let's make a resolution. I know you've had a good time to-day. Haven't you had a better time than if you had gone to the Tea?"

"Well, *rather*. I don't know when I've had a better, jollier afternoon."

"Well, now, we're going to try to have lots more good times, but just as chums. We've tried the other, and it failed. Now be sincere; didn't it fail?"

"It worked out. It *did* work out."

"Now from this time on, no more foolishness. We'll just be chums."

"Chums it is. No more foolishness."

"The moment you begin to pretend you're in love with me, it will spoil everything. It's funny," said

Travis, drawing on her gloves. "We're doing a funny thing, Condy. With ninety-nine people out of one hundred, this little affair would have been all ended after our 'explanation' of last night—confessing, as we did, that we didn't love each other. Most couples would have 'drifted apart'; but here we are, planning to be chums, and have good times in our own original, unconventional way—and we can do it, too. There, there, he's a thousand miles away. He's not heard a single word I've said. Condy, are you listening to me?"

"Blix," he murmured, staring at her vaguely. "Blix —you look that way; I don't know, look kind of blix. Don't you feel sort of blix?" he inquired anxiously.

"Blix?"

He smote the table with his palm. "Capital!" he cried; "sounds bully, and snappy, and crisp, and bright, and sort of sudden. Sounds—don't you know, *this* way?"—and he snapped his fingers. "Don't you see what I mean? Blix, that's who you are. You've always been Blix, and I've just found it out. Blix," he added, listening to the sound of the name. "Blix, Blix. Yes, yes; that's your name."

"Blix?" she repeated; "but why Blix?'

"Why not?"

"I don't know why not."

"Well, then," he declared, as though that settled the question. They made ready to go, as it was growing late.

"Will you tie that for me, Condy," she asked, rising and turning the back of her head toward him, the ends of the veil held under her fingers. "Not too tight. Condy, don't pull it so tight. There, there, that will do. Have you everything that belongs to you? I know you'll go away and leave something here. There's your cigarette-case, and your book, and of course the banjo."

As if warned by a mysterious instinct, the fat China-man made his appearance in the outer room. Condy put his fingers into his vest pocket, then dropped back upon his stool with a suppressed exclamation of horror.

"Condy!" exclaimed Blix in alarm, "are you sick?"—for he had turned a positive white.

"I haven't a cent of money," he murmured faintly. "I spent my last quarter for those beastly crackers. What's to be done? What *is* to be done? I'll—I'll leave him my watch. Yes, that's the only thing."

Blix calmly took out her purse. "I expected it," she said resignedly. "I knew this would happen sooner or later, and I always have been prepared. How much is it, John?" she asked of the Chinaman.

"Hefadollah."

"I'll never be able to look you in the face again," protested Condy. "I'll pay you back to-night. I will! I'll send it up by a messenger boy."

"Then you *would* be a buffoon."

"Don't!" he exclaimed. "Don't, it humiliates me to the dust."

"Oh, come along and don't be so absurd! It must be after five."

Halfway down the brass-bound stairs, he clapped his hand to his head with a start.

"And *now* what is it?" she inquired meekly.

"Forgotten, forgotten!" he exclaimed. "I knew I would forget something."

"*I* knew it, you mean."

He ran back, and returned with the great bag of crackers, and thrust it into her hands. "Here, here, take these. We mustn't leave these," he declared earnestly. "It would be a shameful waste of money"; and in spite of all her protests, he insisted upon taking the crackers along.

"I wonder," said Blix, as the two skirted the Plaza, going down to Kearney Street; "I wonder if I ought to ask him to supper?"

"Ask who—me?—how funny to——"

"I wonder if we are talked out—if it would spoil the day?"

"Anyhow, I'm going to have supper at the Club; and I've got to write my article some time to-night."

Blix fixed him with a swift glance of genuine concern. "Don't play to-night, Condy," she said, with a sudden gravity.

"Fat lot *I* can play! What money have I got to play with?"

"You might get some somewhere. But, anyhow, promise me you won't play."

"Well, of course I'll promise. How can I, if I haven't any money? And besides, I've got my whaleback stuff to write. I'll have supper at the Club, and go up in the library and grind out copy for a while."

"Condy," said Blix, "I think that diver's story is almost too good for the *Times*. Why don't you write it and send it East? Send it to the Centennial Company, why don't you? They've paid some attention to you now, and it would keep your name in their minds if you sent the story to them, even if they didn't publish it. Why don't you think of that?"

"Fine—great idea! I'll do that. Only I'll have to write it out of business hours. It will be extra work."

"Never mind, you do it; and," she added, as he put her on the cable car, "keep your mind on that thirty-thousand-word story of adventure. Good-bye, Condy; haven't we had the jolliest day that ever was?"

"Couldn't have been better. Good-bye, Blix."

Condy returned to his club. It was about six o'clock. In response to his question, the hall-boy told him that Tracy Sargeant had arrived a few moments previously, and had been asking for him.

The Saturday of the week before, Condy had made an engagement with young Sargeant to have supper together that night, and perhaps go to the theatre afterward. And now at the sight of Sargeant in the "round window" of the main room, buried in the file of the *Gil Blas*, Condy was pleased to note that neither of them had forgotten the matter.

Sargeant greeted him with extreme cordiality as he came up, and at once proposed a drink. Sargeant was a sleek, well-groomed, well-looking fellow of thirty, just beginning to show the effects of a certain amount of dissipation in the little puffs under the eyes and the faint blueness of the temples. The sudden death of his father, for which event Sargeant was still mourning, had left him in such position that his monthly income was about five times as large as Condy's salary. The two had supper together, and Sargeant proposed the theatre.

"No, no; I've got to work to-night," asserted Condy.

After dinner, while they were smoking their cigars in a window of the main room, one of the hall-boys came up and touched Condy on the arm.

"Mr. Eckert, and Mr. Hendricks, and Mr. George Hands, and several other of those gentlemen are up in the card-room, and are asking for you and Mr. Sargeant."

"Why, I didn't know the boys were here! They've got a game going, Condy. Let's go up and get in. Shall we?"

Condy remembered that he had no money. "I'm flat broke, Tracy," he announced, for he knew Sargeant well enough to make the confession without wincing. "No, I'll not get in; but I'll go up and watch you a few minutes."

They ascended to the card-room, where the air was heavy and acrid with cigar smoke, and where the silence was broken only by the click of poker-chips. At the end of twenty minutes Condy was playing, having

151

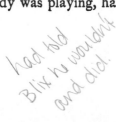
had told
Blix he wouldnt
and did.

borrowed enough money of Sargeant to start him in the game.

Unusually talkative and restless, he had suddenly hardened and stiffened to a repressed, tense calm; speechless, almost rigid in his chair. Excitable under even ordinary circumstances, his every faculty was now keyed to its highest pitch. The nervous strain upon him was like the stretching and tightening of harp-strings, too taut to quiver. The colour left his face, and the moisture fled his lips. His projected article, his promise to Blix, all the jollity of the afternoon, all thought of time or place, faded away as the one indomitable, evil passion of the man leaped into life within him, and lashed and rowelled him with excitement. His world resolved itself to a round green table, columns of tri-coloured chips, and five ever-changing cards that came and went and came again before his tired eyes like the changing, weaving colours of the kaleidoscope. Midnight struck, then one o'clock, then two, three, and four. Still his passion rode him like a hag, spurring the jaded body, rousing up the wearied brain.

Finally, at half-past four, at a time when Condy was precisely where he had started, neither winner nor loser by so much as a dime, a round of Jack-pots was declared, and the game broke up. Condy walked home to the uptown hotel where he lived with his mother, and went to bed as the first milk-wagons began to make their appearance and the news-boys to cry the morning papers.

Then, as his tired eyes closed at last, occurred that strange trick of picture-making that the overtaxed brain plays upon the retina. A swift series of pictures of the day's doings began to whirl *through* rather than *before* the pupils of his shut eyes. Condy saw again a brief vision of the street, and Blix upon the corner waiting to cross; then it was the gay, brisk confusion of the water-front, the old mate's cabin aboard the whaleback, Chinatown, and a loop of vermilion cloth over a gallery rail, the golden balcony, the glint of the Stevenson ship upon the green Plaza, Blix playing the banjo, the delightful and picturesque confusion of the deserted Chinese restaurant; Blix again, turning her head for him to fasten her veil, holding the ends with her white-kid fingers; Blix once more, walking at his side with her trim black skirt, her round little turban hat, her yellow hair, and her small dark, dancing eyes.

Then, suddenly, he remembered the promise he had made her in the matter of playing that night. He winced sharply at this, and the remembrance of his fault harried and harassed him. In spite of himself, he felt contemptible. Yet he had broken his promises to her in this very matter of playing before—before that day of their visit to the Chinese restaurant—and had felt no great qualm of self-reproach. Had their relations changed? Rather the reverse, for they had done with "foolishness."

"Never worried me before," muttered Condy, as he punched up his pillow—"never worried me before. Why should it worry me now—worry me like the devil; and she caught on to that 'point' about the slope of forty-five degrees."

CHAPTER V

CONDY began his week's work for the supplement behindhand. Naturally he overslept himself Tuesday morning, and, not having any change in his pockets, was obliged to walk down to the office. He arrived late, to find the compositors already fretting for copy. His editor promptly asked for the whaleback stuff, and Condy was forced into promising it within a half-hour. It was out of the question to write the article according to his own idea in so short a time; so Condy faked the stuff from the exchange clipping, after all. His description of the boat and his comments upon her mission—taken largely at second hand—served only to fill space in the paper. They were lacking both in interest and in point. There were no illustrations. The article was a failure.

But Condy redeemed himself by a witty interview later in the week with an emotional actress, and by a solemn article—compiled after an hour's reading in Lafcadio Hearn and the Encyclopædia—on the "Industrial Renaissance in Japan."

But the idea of the diver's story came back to him again and again, and Thursday night after supper he went down to his club, and hid himself at a corner desk in the library, and, in a burst of enthusiasm, wrote out some two thousand words of it. In order to get the "technical details," upon which he set such store, he consulted the Encyclopædias again, and "worked in" a number of unfamiliar phrases and odd-sounding names. He was so proud of the result that he felt he could not wait until the tale was finished and in print

154

to try its effect. He wanted appreciation and encouragement upon the instant. He thought of Blix.

"She saw the point in Morrowbie Jukes's description of the slope of the sandhill," he told himself; and the next moment had resolved to go up and see her the next evening, and read to her what he had written.

This was on Thursday. All through that week Blix had kept much to herself, and for the first time in two years had begun to spend every evening at home. In the morning of each day she helped Victorine with the upstairs work, making the beds, putting the rooms to rights; or consulted with the butcher's and grocer's boys at the head of the back stairs, or chaffered with urbane and smiling Chinamen with their balanced vegetable baskets. She knew the house and its management at her fingers' ends, and supervised everything that went forward. Laurie Flagg coming to call upon her, on Wednesday afternoon, to remonstrate upon her sudden defection, found her in the act of tacking up a curtain across the pantry window.

But Blix had the afternoons and evenings almost entirely to herself. These hours, heretofore taken up with functions and the discharge of obligations, dragged not a little during the week that followed upon her declaration of independence. Wednesday afternoon, however, was warm and fine, and she went to the Park with Snooky. Without looking for it or even expecting it, Blix came across a little Japanese tea-house, or rather a tiny Japanese garden, set with almost toy Japanese houses and pavilions, where tea was served and thin sweetish wafers for five cents. Blix and Snooky went in. There was nobody about but the Japanese serving woman. Snooky was in raptures, and Blix spent a delightful half-hour there, drinking Japanese tea, and feeding the wafers to the carp and gold-fish in the tiny pond immediately below where she sat. A Chinaman, evidently of the merchant class, came in, with a Chinese woman following. As he took his place and the Japanese girl came up to get his order, Blix overheard him say in English: "Bring tea for-um leddy."

"He had to speak in English to her," she whispered; "isn't that splendid! Did you notice that, Snooky?"

On the way home Blix was wondering how she should pass her evening. She was to have made one of a theatre party where Jack Carter was to be present. Then she suddenly remembered "Morrowbie Jukes," "The Return of Imri," and "Krishna Mulvaney." She continued on past her home, downtown, and returned late for supper with *Plain Tales* and *Many Inventions*.[8]

Toward half-past eight there came a titter of the electric bell. At the moment Blix was in the upper chamber of the house of Suddhoo, quaking with exquisite horror at the Seal-cutter's magic. She looked up quickly as the bell rang. It was not Condy Rivers's touch. She swiftly reflected that it was Wednesday night, and that she might probably expect Frank Catlin. He was a fair specimen of the Younger Set, a sort of modified Jack Carter, and called upon her about once a fortnight. No doubt he would hint darkly as to his riotous living during the past few days and refer to his diet of bromoseltzers. He would be slangy, familiar, call her by her first name as many times as he dared, discuss the last dance of the Saturday cotillion, and try to make her laugh over Carter's drunkenness. Blix knew the type. Catlin was hardly out of college; but the older girls, even the young women of twenty-five or -six, encouraged and petted these youngsters, driven to the alternative by the absolute dearth of older men.

"I'm not at home, Victorine," announced Blix, intercepting the maid in the hall. It chanced that it was not Frank Catlin, but another boy of precisely the same **breed**; and Blix returned to Suddhoo, Mrs. Hawksbee, and Mulvaney with a little cuddling movement of satisfaction.

"There is only one thing I regret about this," she said to Condy Rivers on the Friday night of that week; "that is, that I never thought of doing it before." Then suddenly she put up her hand to shield her eyes, as though from an intense light, turning away her head abruptly.

"I say, what is it? What—what's the matter?" he exclaimed.

Blix peeped at him fearfully from between her fingers. "He's got it on," she whispered—"that awful crimson scarf."

"Huh!" said Condy, touching his scarf nervously, "it's—it's very swell. Is it too loud?" he asked uneasily.

Blix put her fingers in her ears; then:

"Condy, you're a nice, amiable young man, and, if you're not brilliant, you're good and kind to your aged mother; but your scarfs and neckties are simply impossible."

"Well, look at this room!" he shouted—they were in the parlour. "You needn't talk about bad taste. Those drapes—oh-h! those drapes!! Yellow, s'help me! And those bisque figures that you get with every pound of tea you buy; and this, this, *this*," he whimpered, waving his hands at the decorated sewer-pipe with its gilded cat-tails. "Oh, speak to me of this; speak to me of art; speak to me of æsthetics. Cat-tails, *gilded*. Of course, why not, *gilded!*" He wrung his hands. "'Somewhere people are happy. Somewhere little children are at play——'" [9]

"Oh, hush!" she interrupted. "I know it's bad; but we've always had it so, and I won't have it abused. Let's go into the dining room anyway. We'll sit in there after this. We've always been stiff and constrained in here."

They went out into the dining room, and drew up

a couple of arm-chairs into the bay window, and sat there looking out. Blix had not yet lit the gas—it was hardly dark enough for that; and for upward of ten minutes they sat and watched the evening dropping into night.

Below them the hill fell away so abruptly that the roofs of the nearest houses were almost at their feet; and beyond these the city tumbled raggedly down to meet the bay in a confused, vague mass of roofs, cornices, cupolas, and chimneys, blurred and indistinct in the twilight, but here and there pierced by a new-lit street lamp. Then came the bay. To the east they could see Goat Island, and the fleet of sailing-ships anchored off the water-front; while directly in their line of vision the island of Alcatraz, with its triple crown of forts, started from the surface of the water. Beyond was the Contra Costa shore, a vast streak of purple against the sky. The eye followed its sky-line westward till it climbed, climbed, climbed up a long slope that suddenly leaped heavenward with the crest of Tamalpais, purple and still, looking always to the sunset like a great watching sphinx. Then, farther on, the slope seemed to break like the breaking of an advancing billow, and go tumbling, crumbling downward to meet the Golden Gate— the narrow inlet of green tide-water with its flanking Presidio. But, farther than this, the eye was stayed. Farther than this there was nothing, nothing but a vast, illimitable plain of green—the open Pacific. But at this hour the colour of the scene was its greatest charm. It glowed with all the sombre radiance of a cathedral. Everything was seen through a haze of purple—from the low green hills in the Presidio reservation to the faint red mass of Mount Diablo shrugging its rugged shoulder over the Contra Costa foothills. As the evening faded, the west burned down to a dull red glow that overlaid the blue of the bay with a sheen of ruddy gold.

The foothills of the opposite shore, Diablo, and at last even Tamalpais, resolved themselves in the velvet gray of the sky. Outlines were lost. Only the masses remained, and these soon began to blend into one another. The sky, and land, and the city's huddled roofs were one. Only the sheen of dull gold remained, piercing the single vast mass of purple like the blade of a golden sword.

"There's a ship!" said Blix in a low tone.

A four-master was dropping quietly through the Golden Gate, swimming on that sheen of gold, a mere shadow, specked with lights, red and green. In a few moments her bows were shut from sight by the old fort at the Gate. Then her red light vanished, then the main-mast. She was gone. By midnight she would be out of sight of land, rolling on the swell of the lonely ocean under the moon's white eye.

Condy and Blix sat quiet and without speech, not caring to break the charm of the evening. For quite five minutes they sat, thus watching the stars light one by one, and the immense gray night settle and broaden and widen from mountain-top to horizon. They did not feel the necessity of making conversation. There was no constraint in their silence now.

Gently, and a little at a time, Condy turned his head and looked at Blix. There was just light enough to see. She was leaning back in her chair, her hands fallen into her lap, her head back and a little to one side. As usual, she was in black; but now it was some sort of dinner-gown that left her arms and neck bare. The line of the chin and the throat and the sweet round curve of the shoulder had in them something indescribable —something that was related to music, and that eluded speech. Her hair was nothing more than a warm coloured mist without form or outline. The sloe-brown of her little eyes and the flush of her cheek were mere infer-ences—like the faintest stars that are never visible

when looked at directly; and it seemed to him that
there was disengaged from her something for which
there was no name; something that appealed to a
mysterious sixth sense—a sense that only stirred at
such quiet moments as this; something that was now a
dim, sweet radiance, now a faint aroma, and now again
a mere essence, an influence, an impression—nothing
more. It seemed to him as if her sweet, clean purity
and womanliness took a form of *their* own which his accustomed senses were too gross to perceive. Only a certain vague tenderness in him went out to meet and receive this impalpable presence; a tenderness not for
her only, but for all the good things of the world. Often
he had experienced the same feeling when listening to
music. Her sweetness, her goodness, appealed to what
he guessed must be the noblest in him. And she was
only nineteen. Suddenly his heart swelled, the ache
came to his throat and the smart to his eyes.

"Blixy," he said, just above a whisper; "Blixy, wish
I was a better sort of chap."

"That's the beginning of being better, isn't it,
Condy?" she answered, turning toward him, her chin
on her hand.

"It does seem a pity," he went on, "that when you
want to do the right, straight thing, and be clean and
fine, that you can't just *be* it, and have it over with.
It's the keeping it up that's the grind."

"But it's the keeping it up, Condy, that makes you
worth being good when you finally get to be good; don't
you think? It's the keeping it up that makes you strong;
and then when you get to be good you can make your
goodness count. What's a good man if he's weak?—
if his goodness is better than he is himself? It's the good
man who is strong—as strong as his goodness and who
can make his goodness count—who is the right kind
of man. That's what I think."

"There's something in that, there's something in that." Then, after a pause: "I played Monday night after all, Blix, after promising I wouldn't."

For a time she did not answer, and when she spoke, she spoke quietly: "Well—I'm glad you told me"; and after a little she added, "Can't you stop, Condy?"

"Why, yes—yes, of course—I—oh, Blix, sometimes I don't know! You can't understand! How could a girl understand the power of it? Other things, I don't say; but when it comes to gambling, there seems to be another *me* that does precisely as he chooses, whether *I* will or not. But I'm going to do my best. I haven't played since, although there was plenty of chance. You see, this card business is only a part of this club life, this city life—like drinking and—other vices of men. If I didn't have to lead the life, or if I didn't go with that crowd—Sargeant and the rest of those men —it would be different; easier, maybe."

"But a man ought to be strong enough to be himself and master of himself anywhere. Condy, *is* there anything in the world better or finer than a strong man?"

"Not unless it is a good woman, Blix."

"I suppose I look at it from a woman's point of view; but for me, a *strong* man—strong in everything—is the grandest thing in the world. Women love strong men, Condy. They can forgive a strong man almost anything."

Condy did not immediately answer, and in the interval an idea occurred to Blix that at once hardened into a determination. But she said nothing at the moment. The spell of the sunset was gone, and they had evidently reached the end of that subject of their talk. Blix rose to light the gas. "Will you promise me one thing, Condy?" she said. "Don't, if you don't want to. But will you promise me that you will tell me whenever you do play?"

161

"That I'll promise you!" exclaimed Condy; "and I'll keep that, too."

"And now, let's hear the story—or what you've done of it."

They drew up to the dining-room table with its cover of blue denim edged with white cord, and Condy unrolled his manuscript and read through what he had written. She approved, and, as he had foreseen, "caught on" to every one of his points. He was almost ready to burst into cheers when she said:

"Any one reading that would almost believe you had been a diver yourself, or at least had lived with divers. Those little details count, don't they? Condy, I've an idea. See what you think of it. Instead of having the story end with his leaving her down there and going away, do it this way. Let him leave her there, and then go back after a long time when he gets to be an old man. Fix it up some way to make it natural. Have him go down to see her and never come up again, see? And leave the reader in doubt as to whether it was an accident or whether he did it on purpose."

Condy choked back a whoop and smote his knee. "Blix, you're the eighth wonder! Magnificent—glorious! Say!"—he fixed her with a glance of curiosity— "you ought to take to story-writing yourself."

"No, no," she retorted significantly. "I'll just stay with my singing and be content with that. But remember that story don't go to the *Times* supplement. At least not until you have tried it East—with the centennial Company, at any rate."

"Well, I guess *not!*" snorted Condy. "Why, this is going to be one of the best yarns I ever wrote."

A little later on, he inquired with sudden concern: "Have you got anything to eat in the house?"

"I never saw such a man!" declared Blix; "you are always hungry."

"I love to eat," he protested.

"Well, we'll make some creamed oysters; how would that do?" suggested Blix.

Condy rolled his eyes. "Oh, speak to me of creamed oysters!" Then, with abrupt solemnity: "Blix, I never in my life had as many oysters as I could eat."

She made the creamed oysters in the kitchen over the gas-stove, and they ate them there—Condy sitting on the wash-board of the sink, his plate in his lap.

Condy had a way of catching up in his hands whatever happened to be nearest him, and while still continuing to talk, examining it with apparent deep interest. Just now it happened to be the morning's paper that Victorine had left on the table. For five minutes Condy had been picking it up and laying it down, frowning abstractedly at it during the pauses in the conversation. Suddenly he became aware of what it was, and instantly read aloud the first item that caught his glance.

"'Personal.—Young woman, thirty-one, good housekeeper, desires acquaintance respectable middle-aged gentleman. Object, matrimony. Address K. D. B., this office.'—Hum!" he commented, "nothing equivocal about K. D. B.; has the heroism to call herself young at thirty-one. I'll bet she *is* a good housekeeper. Right to the point. If K. D. B. don't see what she wants, she asks for it."

"I wonder," mused Blix, "what kind of people they are who put personals in the papers. K. D. B., for instance; who is she, and what is she like?"

"They're not tough," Condy assured her. "I see 'em often down at the *Times* office. They are usually a plain, matter-of-fact sort, quite conscientious, you know; generally middle-aged—or thirty-one; outgrown their youthful follies and illusions, and want to settle down."

"Read some more," urged Blix. Condy went on:

"'Bachelor, good habits, twenty-five, affectionate disposition, accomplishments, money, desires acquaintance pretty, refined girl. Object, matrimony. McB. this office.'"

"No, I don't like McB.," said Blix. "He's too—ornamental, somehow."

"He wouldn't do for K. D. B., would he?"

"Oh, my, no! He'd make her very unhappy."

"'Widower, two children, home-loving disposition, desires introduction to good, honest woman to make home for his children. Matrimony, if suitable. B. P. T., Box A, this office.'"

"He's not for K. D. B., that's flat," declared Blix; "the idea, 'matrimony if suitable,'—patronizing enough! I know just what kind of an old man B. P. T. is. I know he would want K. D. B. to warm his slippers, and would be fretful and grumpy. B. P. T., just an abbreviation of 'bumptious.' No, he can't have her."

Condy read the next two or three to himself, despite her protests.

"Condy, don't be mean! Read them to——"

"Ah!" he exclaimed, "here's one for K. D. B. Behold, the bridegroom cometh! Listen.

"'Bachelor, thirty-nine, sober and industrious, retired sea captain, desires acquaintance respectable young woman, good housekeeper, and manager. Object, matrimony. Address Captain Jack, office this paper.'"

"I know he's got a wooden leg!" cried Blix. "Can't you just see it sticking out between the lines? And he lives all alone somewhere down near the bay with a parrot——"

"And makes a glass of grog every night."

"And smokes a long clay pipe."

"But he chews tobacco."

"Yes, isn't it a pity he will chew that nasty, smelly tobacco? But K. D. B. will break him of that."

"Oh, is he for K. D. B.?"

"Sent by Providence!" declared Blix. "They were born for each other. Just see, K. D. B. is a good house-keeper and wants a respectable middle-aged gentleman. Captain Jack is a respectable middle-aged gentleman, and wants a good housekeeper. Oh, and besides, I can read between the lines! I just feel they would be congenial. If they know what's best for themselves, they would write to each other right away."

"But wouldn't you love to be there and see them meet!" exclaimed Condy.

"Can't we fix it up some way," said Blix, "to bring these two together—to help them out in some way?"

Condy smote the table, and jumped to his feet.

"Write to 'em!" he shouted. "Write to K. D. B. and sign it Captain Jack, and write to Captain Jack——"

"And sign it K. D. B.," she interrupted, catching his idea.

"And have him tell her, and her tell him," he added, "to meet at some place; and then we can go to that place and hide, and watch."

"But how will we know them? How would they know each other? They've never met."

"We'll tell them both to wear a kind of flower. Then we can know them, and they can know each other. Of course, as soon as they began to talk they would find out they hadn't written."

"But they wouldn't care."

"No—they *want* to meet each other. They would be thankful to us for bringing them together."

"Won't it be the greatest fun?"

"Fun! Why, it will be a regular drama. Only we are running the show, and everything is real. Let's get at it!"

Blix ran into her room and returned with writing

material. Condy looked at the note-paper critically. "This kind's too swell. K. D. B. wouldn't use Irish linen—never! Here, this is better, glazed with blue lines and a flying bird stamped in the corner. Now I'll write for the Captain, and you write for K. D. B."

"But where will we have them meet?"

This was a point. They considered the Chinese restaurant, the Plaza, Lotta's fountain, the Mechanics' Library, and even the cathedral over in the Mexican quarter, but arrived at no decision.

"Did you ever hear of Luna's restaurant?" said Condy. "By Jove, it's just the place! It's the restaurant where you get Mexican dinners; right in the heart of the Latin quarter; quiet little old-fashioned place, below the level of the street, respectable as a tomb. I was there just once. We'll have 'em meet there at seven in the evening. No one is there at that hour. The place isn't patronized much, and it shuts up at eight. You and I can go there and have dinner at six, say, and watch for them to come."

Then they set to work at their letters.

"Now," said Condy, "we must have these sound perfectly natural, because if either of these people smell the smallest kind of a rat, you won't catch 'em. You must write not as *you* would write, but as you think *they* would. This is an art, a kind of fiction, don't you see? We must imagine a certain character, and write a letter consistent with that character. Then it'll sound natural. Now, K. D. B. Well, K. D. B., she's prim. Let's have her prim, and proud of using correct, precise, 'elegant' language. I guess she wears mits, and believes in cremation. Let's have her believe in cremation. And Captain Jack; oh! he's got a terrible voice, like this, *row-row-row*, see? and whiskers, very fierce; and he says, 'Belay there!' and 'Avast!' and is very grandiloquent and orotund and gallant when it comes to women. Oh, he's the devil of a man when it comes to women, is Captain Jack!"

After countless trials and failures, they evolved the two following missives, which Condy posted that night:

CAPTAIN JACK

SIR: I have perused with entire satisfaction your personal in the *Times*. I should like to know more of you. I read between the lines, and my perception ineradicably convinces me that you are honest and respectable. I do not believe I should compromise my self-esteem at all in granting you an interview. I shall be at Luna's restaurant at seven precisely, next Monday eve, and will bear a bunch of white marguerites. Will you likewise, and wear a marguerite in your lapel?

Trusting this will find you in health, I am

Respectfully yours,
K. D. B.

MISS K. D. B.

DEAR MISS: From the modest and retiring description of your qualities and character, I am led to believe that I will find in you an agreeable life companion. Will you not accord me the great favour of a personal interview? I shall esteem it a high honour. I will be at Luna's Mexican restaurant at seven of the clock P.M. on Monday evening next. May I express the fervent hope that you also will be there? I name the locality because it is quiet and respectable. I shall wear a white marguerite in my buttonhole. Will you also carry a bunch of the same flower?

Yours to command,
CAPTAIN JACK.

So great was her interest in the affair that Blix even went out with Condy while he mailed the letters in the nearest box, for he was quite capable of forgetting the whole matter as soon as he was out of the house.

"Now let it work!" she exclaimed as the iron flap clanked down upon the disappearing envelopes. But Condy was suddenly smitten with nameless misgiving. "Now we've done it! now we've done it!" he cried, aghast. "I wish we hadn't. We're in a fine fix now."

Still uneasy, he saw Blix back to the flat, and bade her good-bye at the door.

167

But before she went to bed that night, Blix sought out her father, who was still sitting up tinkering with the cuckoo clock, which he had taken all to pieces under the pretext that it was out of order and went too fast.

"Papum," said Blix, sitting down on the rug before him, "did you ever—when you were a pioneer, when you first came out here in the 'fifties—did you ever play poker?"

"I—oh, well! it was the only amusement the miners had for a long time."

"I want you to teach me."

The old man let the clock fall into his lap and stared. But Blix explained her reasons.

CHAPTER VI

T HE next day was Saturday, and Blix had planned a walk out to the Presidio. But at breakfast, while she was debating whether she should take with her Howard and Snooky, or *Many Inventions*, she received a note from Condy, sent by special messenger.

All our fun is spoiled [he wrote]. I've got ptomaine poisoning from eating the creamed oysters last night, and am in for a solid fortnight spent in bed. Have passed a horrible night. Can't you look in at the hotel this afternoon? My mother will be here at the time.

"Ptomaine poisoning!" The name had an ugly sound, and Condy's use of the term implied the doctor's visit. Blix decided that she would put off her walk until the afternoon, and call on Mrs. Rivers at once, and ask how Condy did.

She got away from the flat about ten o'clock, but on the steps outside met Condy dressed as if for bicycling, and smoking a cigarette.

"I've got eleven dollars!" he announced cheerily.

"But I thought it was ptomaine poisoning!" she cried with a sudden vexation.

"Pshaw! that's what the doctor says. He's a flap-doodle; nothing but a kind of a sort of a pain. It's all gone now. I'm as fit as a fiddle—and I've got eleven dollars. Let's go somewhere and do something."

"But your work?"

"They don't expect me. When I thought I was going to be sick, I telephoned the office, and they said all right, that they didn't need me. Now I've got eleven dollars, and there are three holidays of perfect weather before us: to-day, to-morrow, and Monday. What will we do?

169

What must we do to be saved? Our matrimonial objects don't materialize till Monday night. In the meanwhile, what? Shall we go down to Chinatown—to the restaurant, or to the water-front again? Maybe the mate on the whaleback would invite us to lunch. Or," added Condy, his eye caught by a fresh-fish peddler who had just turned into the street, "we can go fishing."

"For oysters, perhaps."

But the idea had caught Condy's fancy.

"Blix!" he exclaimed, "let's go fishing."

"Where?"

"I don't know. Where *do* people fish around here? Where there's water, I presume."

"No, is it possible?" she asked with deep concern. "I thought they fished in their backyards, or in their front parlours perhaps."

"Oh, you be quiet! you're all the time guying me," he answered. "Let me think—let me think," he went on, frowning heavily, scouring at his hair. Suddenly he slapped a thigh.

"Come on," he cried, "I've an idea!" He was already halfway down the steps, when Blix called him back.

"Leave it all to me," he assured her; "trust me *implicitly*. Don't you want to go?" he demanded with abrupt disappointment.

"Want to!" she exclaimed. "Why, it would be the very best kind of fun, but——"

"Well, then, come along."

They took a downtown car.

"I've got a couple of split bamboo rods," he explained as the car slid down the terrific grade of the Washington Street hill. "I haven't used 'em in years—not since we lived East; but they're hand-made, and are tip-top. I haven't any other kind of tackle; but it's just as well, because the tackle will all depend upon where we are going to fish."

"Where's that?"

"Don't know yet; am going down now to find out."

He took her down to the principal dealer in sporting goods on Market Street. It was a delicious world, whose atmosphere and charm were not to be resisted. There were shot-guns in rows, their gray barrels looking like so many organ-pipes; sheaves of fishing-rods, from the four-ounce wisp of the brook-trout up to the rigid eighteen-ounce lance of the king-salmon and sea-bass; show-cases of wicked revolvers, swelling by calibres into the thirty-eight and forty-four man-killers of the plainsmen and Arizona cavalry; hunting knives and dirks, and the slender steel whips of the fencers; files of Winchesters, sleeping quietly in their racks, waiting patiently for the signal to speak the one grim word they knew; swarms of artificial flies of every conceivable shade, brown, gray, black, gray-brown, gray-black, with here and there a brisk vermilion note; coils of line, from the thickness of a pencil, spun to hold the sullen plunges of a jew-fish off the Catalina Islands, down to the sea-green gossamers that a vigorous fingerling might snap; hooks, snells, guts, leaders, gaffs, cartridges, shells, and all the entrancing munitions of the sportsman, that savoured of lonely cañons, deer-licks, mountain streams, quail uplands, and the still reaches of inlet and marsh grounds, gray and cool in the early autumn dawn.

Condy and Blix got the attention of a clerk, and Condy explained.

"I want to go fishing—*we* want to go fishing. We want some place where we can go and come in the same day, and we want to catch fair-sized fish—no minnows."

The following half-hour was charming. Never was there a clerk more delightful. It would appear that his one object in life was that Condy and Blix should catch fish. The affairs of the nation stood still while he pondered, suggested, advised, and deliberated. He told them where to go, how to get there, what train to take coming back, and who to ask for when they arrived. They would have to wait till Monday before going, but could return long before the fated hour of 7 P.M.

"Ask for Richardson," said the clerk; "and here, give him my card. He'll put you on to the good spots: some places are A-1 to-day, and to-morrow in the same place you can't kill a single fish."

Condy nudged Blix as the Mentor turned away to get his card.

"Notice that," he whispered: "*kill* a fish. You don't say 'catch', you say 'kill'—technical detail."

Then they bought their tackle: a couple of cheap reels, lines, leaders, sinkers, a book of assorted flies that the delightful clerk suggested, and a beautiful little tin box painted green, and stencilled with a gorgeous gold trout upon the lid, in which they were to keep the pint of salted shrimps to be used as bait in addition to the flies. Blix would get these shrimps at a little market near her home.

"But," said the clerk, "you got to get a permit to fish in that lake. Have you got a pull with the Water Company? Are you a stockholder?"

Condy's face fell, and Blix gave a little gasp of dismay. They looked at each other. Here was a check, indeed.

"Well," said the sublime being in shirt sleeves from behind the counter, "see what you can do; and if you can't make it, come back here an' lemmeno, and we'll fix you up in some other place. But Lake San Andreas has been bang-up this last week—been some great kills there; hope to the deuce you can make it." [10]

Everything now hinged upon this permit. It was not until their expedition had been in doubt that Condy and Blix realized how alluring had been its prospects.

"Oh, I guess you can get a permit," said the clerk soothingly. "An' if you make any good kills, lemmeno and I'll put it in the paper. I'm the editor of the 'Sport-with-Gun-and-Rod' column in the *Press*," he added with a flush of pride.

Toward the middle of the afternoon, Blix, who was waiting at home, in great suspense, for that very purpose, received another telegram from Condy:

Tension of situation relieved. Unconditional permission obtained. Don't forget the shrimps.

It had been understood that Condy was to come to the flat on Sunday afternoon to talk over final arrangements with Blix. But as it was, Saturday evening saw him again at the Bessemers'.

He had been down at his club in the library, writing the last paragraphs of his diver's story, when, just as he finished, Sargeant discovered him.

"Why, Conny, old man, all alone here? Let's go downstairs and have a cigar. Hendricks and George Hands are coming around in half an hour. They told me not to let you get away."

Condy stirred nervously in his chair. He knew what that meant. He had enough money in his pockets to play that night, and in an instant the enemy was all awake. The rowel was in his flank again, and the scourge at his back. Sargeant stood there, the well-groomed clubman of thirty; a little cynical perhaps, but a really good fellow for all that, and undeniably fond of Condy. But somewhere with the eyes of some second self Condy saw the girl of nineteen, part child and part woman; saw her goodness, her fine, sweet feminine strength as it were a dim radiance; "What's a good man worth, Condy," she had said, "if he's not a strong man?"

"I suppose we'll have a game going before midnight,"

admitted Sargeant resignedly, smiling good-humouredly nevertheless.

Condy set his teeth. "I'll join you later. Wait a few moments," he said. He hurried to the office of the club, and sent a despatch to Blix—the third, since morning:

Can I come up right away? It's urgent. Send answer by this messenger.

He got his answer within three-quarters of an hour, and left the club as Hendricks and George Hands arrived by the elevator entrance.

Sitting in the bay window of the dining room, he told Blix why he had come.

"Oh, you were right!" she told him. "Always, *always* come, when—when you feel you must."

"It gets so bad sometimes, Blix," he confessed with abject self-contempt, "that when I can't get someone to play against, I'll sit down and deal dummy hands, and bet on them. Just the touch of the cards—just the *feel* of the chips. Faugh! it's shameful."

The day following, Sunday, Condy came to tea as usual; and after the meal, as soon as the family and Victorine had left the pair alone in the dining room, they set about preparing for their morrow's excursion. Blix put up their lunch—sandwiches of what Condy called "devilish" ham, hard-boiled eggs, stuffed olives, and a bottle of claret.

Condy took off his coat and made a great show of stringing the tackle: winding the lines from the spools on to the reels, and attaching the sinkers and flies to the leaders, smoking the while, and scowling fiercely. He got the lines fearfully and wonderfully snarled, he caught the hooks in the tablecloth, he lost the almost invisible gut leaders on the floor and looped the sinkers on the lines when they should have gone on the leaders. In the end, Blix had to help him out, disentangling the lines foot by foot with a patience that seemed to Condy little short of superhuman.

At nine o'clock she said decisively:

"Do you know what time we must get up in the morning if we are to have breakfast and get the seven-forty train? Quarter of six by the latest, and *you* must get up earlier than that, because you're at the hotel and have farther to go. Come here for breakfast, and — listen—be here by half-past six—are you *listening*, Condy?—and we'll go down to the depot from here. Don't forget to bring the rods."

"I'll wear my bicycle suit," he said, "and one of those golf scarfs that wrap around your neck."

"No," she declared, "I won't have it. Wear the oldest clothes you've got, but look fairly respectable, because we're to go to Luna's when we get back, remember. And now go home; you need all the sleep you can get if you are to get up at six o'clock."

Instead of being late, as Blix had feared, Condy was absurdly ahead of time the next morning. For a wonder, he had not forgotten the rods; but he was one tremor of nervousness. He would eat no breakfast.

"We're going to miss that train," he would announce from time to time; "I just know it. Blix, look what time it is. We ought to be on the way to the depot now. Come on; you don't want any more coffee. Have you got everything? Did you put the reels in the lunch-basket?— and the fly-book? Lord, if we should forget the fly-book!"

He managed to get her to the depot over half an hour ahead of time. The train had not even backed in, nor the ticket office opened.

"I told you, Condy, I told you," complained Blix, sinking helplessly upon a bench in the waiting room.

"No—no—no," he answered vaguely, looking nervously about, his head in the air. "We're none too soon

175

—have more time to rest now. I wonder what track the train leaves from. I wonder if it stops at San Bruno. I wonder how far it is from San Bruno to Lake San Andreas. I'm afraid it's going to rain. Heavens and earth, Blix, we forgot the shrimps!"

"No, *no!* Sit down, I've got the shrimps. Condy, you make me so nervous I shall scream in a minute."

Some three quarters of an hour later the train had set them down at San Bruno—nothing more than a road-house, the headquarters for duck-shooters and fishermen from the city. However, Blix and Condy were the only visitors. Everybody seemed to be especially nice to them on that wonderful morning. Even the supercilious ticket-seller at the San Francisco depot had unbent, and wished them good luck. The conductor of the train had shown himself affable. The very brakeman had gone out of his way to apprize them, quite five minutes ahead of time, that "the next stop was their place." And at San Bruno the proprietor of the road-house himself hitched up to drive them over to the lake, announcing that he would call for them at "Richardson's" in time for the evening train.

"And he only asked me four bits for both trips," whispered Condy to Blix, as they jogged along.

The country was beautiful. It was hardly eight o'clock, and the morning still retained much of the brisk effervescence of the early dawn. Great, bare, rolling hills of gray-green, thinly scattered with live oak, bore back from the road on either hand. The sky was pale blue. There was a smell of cows in the air, and twice they heard an unseen lark singing. It was very still. The old buggy and complacent horse were embalmed in a pungent aroma of old leather and of stables that was entrancing; and a sweet smell of grass and sap came to them in occasional long whiffs. There was exhilaration in the very thought of being alive on that odorous, still morning. The young blood went spanking in the veins. Blix's cheeks were ruddy, her little dark-brown eyes fairly coruscating with pleasure.

"Condy, isn't it all splendid!" she suddenly burst out.

"I feel regularly bigger," he declared solemnly. "I could do anything a morning like this."

Then they came to the lake, and to Richardson's, where the farmer lived who was also the custodian of the lake. The complacent horse jogged back, and Condy and Blix set about the serious business of the day. Condy had no need to show Richardson the delightful sporting clerk's card. The old Yankee—his twang and dry humour singularly incongruous on that royal morning—was solicitude itself. He picked out the best boat on the beach for them, loaned them his own anchor of railroad iron, indicated minutely the point on the opposite shore off which the last big trout had been "killed," and wetted himself to his ankles as he pushed off the boat.

Condy took the oars. Blix sat in the stern, jointing the rods and running the lines through the guides. She even baited the hooks with the salt shrimp, herself, and by nine o'clock they were at anchor some forty feet off-shore, and fishing, according to Richardson's advice, "a leetle mite off the edge o' the weeds."

"If we don't get a bite the whole blessed day," said Condy, as he paid out his line to the ratchet music of the reel, "we'll have fun, just the same. Look around —isn't this great?"

They were absolutely alone. The day was young as yet. The lake, smooth and still as gray silk, widened to the west and south without so much as a wrinkle to roughen the surface. Only to the east, where the sun looked over a shoulder of a higher hill, it flamed up into a blinding diamond iridescence. The surrounding

land lay between sky and water, hushed to a Sunday
stillness. Far off across the lake by Richardson's they
heard a dog bark, and the sound came fine and small
and delicate. At long intervals the boat stirred with a
gentle clap-clapping of the water along its sides. From
the near-by shore in the growth of manzanita bushes
quail called and clucked comfortably to each other;
a bewildered yellow butterfly danced by over their
heads, and slim blue dragon-flies came and poised on
their lines and fishing-rods, bowing their backs.

From his seat in the bow, Condy cast a glance at
Blix. She was holding her rod in both hands, absorbed,
watchful, very intent. She was as trim as ever, even
in the old clothes she had worn for the occasion. Her
round, strong neck was as usual swathed high and
tight in white, and the huge dog-collar girdled her
waist according to her custom. She had taken off her
hat. Her yellow hair rolled back from her round forehead and cool pink cheeks like a veritable nimbus,
and for the fiftieth time Condy remarked the charming
contrast of her small, deep-brown eyes in the midst of
this white satin, yellow hair, white skin, and exquisite
pink cheeks.

An hour passed. Then two.

"No fish," murmured Condy, drawing in his line
to examine the bait. But, as he was fumbling with
the flies he was startled by a sharp exclamation from
Blix.

"Oh-Condy-I've-got-a-bite!"

He looked up just in time to see the tip of her rod
twitch, twitch, twitch. Then the whole rod arched suddenly, the reel sang, the line tautened and cut diagon-
ally through the water.

"You got him! you got him!" he shouted, palpitating
with excitement. "And he's a good one!"

Blix rose, reeling in as rapidly as was possible, the

butt of the twitching, living rod braced against her belt.
All at once the rod straightened out again, the strain
was released, and the line began to slant rapidly away
from the boat.

"He's off!" she cried.

"Off, nothing! *He's going to jump*. Look out for him,
now!"

And then the two watching from the boat, tense
and quivering with the drama of the moment, saw that
most inspiriting of sights—the "break" of a salmon-
trout. Up he went, from a brusque explosion of ripples
and foam—up into the gray of the morning from out the
gray of the water: scales all gleaming, hackles all a-
bristle; a sudden flash of silver, a sweep as of a scimitar
in gray smoke, with a splash, a turmoil, an abrupt burst
of troubled sound that stabbed through the silence of
the morning, and in a single instant dissipated all the
placid calm of the previous hours.

"Keep the line taut," whispered Condy, gritting his
teeth. "When he comes toward you, reel him in; an'
if he pulls too hard, give him his head."

Blix was breathing fast, her cheeks blazing, her eyes
all alight.

"Oh," she gasped, "I'm so afraid I'll lose him!
Oh, look at that!" she cried, as the trout darted straight
for the bottom, bending the rod till the tip was sub-
merged. "Condy, I'll lose him—I know I shall; you,
you take the rod!"

"Not for a thousand dollars! Steady, there; he's
away again! Oh, talk about *sport!*"

Yard by yard Blix reeled in until they began to see
the silver glint of the trout's flanks through the green
water. She brought him nearer. Swimming parallel
with the boat, he was plainly visible from his wide-
open mouth—the hook and fly protruding from his
lower jaw—to the red, quivering flanges of the tail.

His sides were faintly speckled, his belly white as chalk. He was almost as long as Condy's forearm.

"Oh, he's a beauty! Oh, *isn't* he a beauty!" murmured Condy. "Now, careful, careful; bring him up to the boat where I can reach him; e-easy, Blix. If he bolts again, let him run."

Twice the trout shied from the boat's shadow, and twice, as Blix gave him his head, the reel sang and hummed like a watchman's rattle. But the third time he came to the surface and turned slowly on his side, the white belly and one red fin out of the water, the gills opening and shutting. He was tired out. A third time Blix drew him gently to the boat's side. Condy reached out and down into the water till his very shoulder was wet, hooked two fingers under the distended gills, and with a long, easy movement of the arm swung him into the boat.

Their exultation was that of veritable children. Condy whooped like an Apache, throwing his hat into the air; Blix was hardly articulate, her hands clasped, her hair in disarray, her eyes swimming with tears of sheer excitement. They shook each other's hands; they talked wildly at the same time; they pounded on the boat's thwarts with their fists; they laughed at their own absurdity; they looked at the trout again and again, guessed at his weight, and recalled to each other details of the struggle.

"When he broke that time, wasn't it grand?"

"And when I first felt him bite! It was so sudden— why, it actually frightened me. I never—no, never in my life!" exclaimed Blix, "was so happy as I am at this moment. Oh, Condy, to think—just to *think!*"

"Isn't it glory hallelujah?"

"Isn't it better than teas, and dancing, and functions?"

"Blix—how old are we?"

"I don't care how old we are; I think that trout will weigh two pounds."

When they were calm again, they returned to their fishing. The morning passed, and it was noon before they were aware of it. By half-past twelve Blix had caught three trout, though the first was by far the heaviest. Condy had not had so much as a bite. At one o'clock they rowed ashore and had lunch under a huge live oak in a little amphitheatre of manzanita.

Never had a lunch tasted so delicious. What if the wine was warm and the stuffed olives oily? What if the pepper for the hard-boiled eggs had sifted all over the "devilish" ham sandwiches? What if the eggs themselves had not been sufficiently cooked, and the corkscrew forgotten? They *could* not be anything else but inordinately happy, sublimely gay. Nothing short of actual tragedy could have marred the joy of that day.

But after they were done eating, and Blix had put away the forks and spoons, and while Condy was stretched upon his back smoking a cigar, she said to him:

"Now, Condy, what do you say to a little game of cards with me?"

The cigar dropped from Condy's lips, and he sat suddenly upright, brushing the fallen leaves from his hair. Blix had taken a deck of cards from the lunch-basket, and four rolls of chips wrapped in tissue paper. He stared at her in speechless amazement.

"What do you say?" she repeated, looking at him and smiling.

"Why, Blix!" he exclaimed in amazement, "what do you mean?"

"Just what I say. I want you to play cards with me."

"I'll not do it," he declared, almost coldly.

"Listen to me, Condy," answered Blix; and for quite five minutes, while he interrupted and protested and pshawed and argued, she talked to him calmly and quietly.

"I don't ask you to stop playing, Condy," she said, as she finished; "I just ask you that when you feel you must play—or—I mean, when you want to very bad, you will come and play with *me*, instead of playing at your club."

"But it's absurd, it's preposterous. I hate to see a girl gambling—and you of all girls!"

"It's no worse for me than it is for you and—well, do you suppose I would play with anyone else? Maybe you think I can't play well enough to make it interesting for you," she said gaily. "Is that it? I can soon show you, Condy Rivers—never mind when I learned how."

"But, Blix, you don't know how often we play, those men and I. Why, it is almost every—you don't know how often we play."

"Condy, whenever you want to play, and will play with *me*, no matter what I've got in hand, I'll stop everything and play with you."

"But why?"

"Because I think, Condy, that *this* way perhaps you won't play quite so often at first; and then little by little perhaps—perhaps—well, never mind that now. *I* want to play; put it that way. But I want you to promise me never to play with anyone else—say for six months."

And in the end, whipped by a sense of shame, Condy made her the promise. They became very gay upon the instant.

"Hoh!" exclaimed Condy; "what do *you* know of poker? I think we had best play old sledge or cassino."

Blix had dealt a hand and partitioned the chips.

"Straights and flushes *before* the draw," she announced calmly.

Condy started and stared. Then looking at her askance, picked up his hand.

"It's up to you."

"I'll make it five to play."

"Five? Very well. How many cards?"

"Three."

"I'll take two."

"Bet you five more."

Blix looked at her hand. Then, without trace of expression in her voice or face, said:

"There's your five, and I'll raise you five."

"Five better."

"And five better than that."

"Call you."

"Full house. Aces on tens," said Blix, throwing down her cards.

"Heavens! they're good as gold," muttered Condy as Blix gathered in the chips.

An hour later she had won all the chips but five.

"Now we'll stop and get to fishing again; don't you want to?"

He agreed, and she counted the chips.

"Condy, you owe me seven dollars and a half," she announced.

Condy began to smile. "Well," he said jocosely, "I'll send you around a check to-morrow."

But at this Blix was cross upon the instant. "You wouldn't do that—wouldn't talk that way with one of your friends at the club!" she exclaimed; "and it's not right to do it with me. Condy, give me seven dollars and a half. When you play cards with me it's just as though it were with another man. I would have paid you if *you* had won."

"But I haven't got more than nine dollars. Who'll pay for the supper to-night at Luna's, and our railroad fare, going home?"

"I'll pay."

"But I—I can't afford to lose money this way."

"Shouldn't have played then; I took the same chances as you. Condy, I want my money."

"You—you—why, you've regularly flimflammed me."

"Will you give me my money?"

"Oh, take your money then!"

Blix shut the money in her purse, and rose, dusting her dress.

"Now," she said, "now that the pastime of card-playing is over, we will return to the serious business of life, which is the catching—no, *killing* of lake trout."

At five o'clock in the afternoon, Condy pulled up the anchor of railroad iron and rowed back to Richardson's. Blix had six trout to her credit, but Condy's ill-luck had been actually ludicrous.

"I can hold a string in the water as long as anybody," he complained, "but I'd like to have the satisfaction of merely changing the bait *occasionally*. I've not had a single bite—not a nibble, y'know, all day. Never mind, you got the big trout, Blix; that first one. That five minutes was worth the whole day. It's been glorious, the whole thing. We'll come down here once a week right along now."

But the one incident that completed the happiness of that wonderful day occurred just as they were getting out of the boat on the shore by Richardson's. In a mud-hole between two rocks they discovered a tiny striped snake, hardly bigger than a lead-pencil, in the act of swallowing a little green frog, and they passed a rapt ten minutes in witnessing the progress of this miniature drama, which culminated happily in the victim's escape, and triumph of virtue.

"That," declared Blix as they climbed into the old buggy which was to take them to the train, "was the one thing necessary. That made the day perfect."

They reached the city at dusk, and sent their fish, lunch-basket, and rods up to the Bessemers' flat by a messenger boy with an explanatory note for Blix's father.

"Now," said Condy, "for Luna's and the matrimonial objects."

LUNA'S Mexican restaurant has no address. It is on no particular street, at no particular corner; even its habitués, its most enthusiastic devotees, are unable to locate it upon demand. It is "over there in the quarter," "not far from the cathedral there." One could find it if one started out with that intent; but to direct another there—no, that is out of the question. It *can* be reached by following the alleys of Chinatown. You will come out of the last alley—the one where the slave girls are—upon the edge of the Mexican quarter, and by going straight forward a block or two, and by keeping a sharp lookout to right and left you will hit upon it. It is always to be searched for. Always to be discovered.[11]

On that particular Monday evening Blix and Condy arrived at Luna's some fifteen minutes before seven. Condy had lost himself and all sense of direction in the strange streets of the quarter, and they were on the very brink of despair when Blix discovered the sign upon an opposite corner.

As Condy had foretold, they had the place to themselves. They went into the back room with its one mirror, six tables, and astonishing curtains of Nottingham lace; and the waiter, whose name was Richard or Riccardo, according to taste, began to officiate at the solemn rites of the "supper Mexican." Condy and Blix ate with their eyes continually wandering to the door; and as the *frijoles* were being served, started simultaneously and exchanged glances.

A man wearing two marguerites in the lapel of his coat had entered abruptly, and sat down to a table close at hand.

Condy drew a breath of suppressed excitement.

"There he is," he whispered—"Captain Jack!"

They looked at the newcomer with furtive anxiety, and told themselves that they were disappointed. For a retired sea captain he was desperately commonplace. His hair was red, he was younger than they had expected, and, worst of all, he did look tough.

"Oh, poor K. D. B.!" sighed Blix, shaking her head. "He'll never do, I'm afraid. Perhaps he has a good heart, though; red-headed people are *sometimes* affectionate."

"They are impulsive," hazarded Condy.

As he spoke the words, a second man entered the little room. He, too, sat down at a near-by table. He, too, ordered the "supper Mexican." He, too, wore marguerites in his buttonhole.

"Death and destruction!" gasped Condy, turning pale.

Blix collapsed helplessly in her chair, her hands dropping in her lap. They stared at each other in utter confusion.

"Here's a how-do-you-do," murmured Condy, pretending to strip a *tamale* that Richard had just set before him. But Blix had pushed hers aside.

"What does it mean?" whispered Condy across the table. "In Heaven's name, what does it mean?"

"It can only mean one thing," Blix declared; "one of them is the captain, and one is a coincidence. Anybody might wear a marguerite; we ought to have though of that."

"But which is which?"

"If K. D. B. should come now!"

"But the last man looks more like the captain."

The last man was a sturdy, broad-shouldered fellow, who might have been forty. His heavy moustache was just touched with gray, and he did have a certain vaguely "sober and industrious" appearance. But the difference between the two men was slight, after all; the red-headed man could easily have been a sea captain, and he certainly was over thirty-five.

"Which? which? which?—how can we tell? We might think of some way to get rid of the coincidence, if we could only tell which the coincidence was. We owe it to K. D. B. In a way, Condy, it's our duty. We brought her here, or we are going to, and we ought to help her all we can; and she may be here at any moment. What time is it now?"

"Five minutes after seven. But, Blix, I should think the right one—the captain—would be all put out himself by seeing another chap here wearing marguerites. Does either one of 'em seem put out to you? Look. I should think the captain, whichever one he is, would kind of *glare* at the coincidence."

Stealthily they studied the two men for a moment.

"No, no," murmured Blix, "you can't tell. Neither of them seems to glare much. Oh, Condy"—her voice dropped to a faint whisper. "The red-headed one has put his hat on a chair, just behind him, notice? Do you suppose if you stood up you could see inside?"

"What good would that do?"

"He might have his initials inside the crown, or his whole name even; and you could see if he had a 'captain' before it."

Condy made a pretence of rising to get a match in a ribbed, truncated cone of china that stood upon an adjacent table, and Blix held her breath as he glanced down into the depths of the hat. He resumed his seat.

"Only initials," he breathed—"W. J. A. It might be Jack, that J., and it might be Joe, or Jeremiah, or Joshua; and even if he was a captain he might not use the title. We're no better off than we were before."

"And K. D. B. may come at any moment. Maybe she

has come already and looked through the windows, and saw *two* men with marguerites and went away. She'd be just that timid. What can we do?"

"Wait a minute, look here," murmured Condy. "I've an idea. *I'll* find out which the captain is. You see that picture, that chromo, on the wall opposite?"

Blix looked as he indicated. The picture was a gorgeously coloured lithograph of a pilot-boat, schooner-rigged, all sails set, dashing bravely through seas of emerald-green colour.

"You mean that schooner?" asked Blix.

"That schooner, exactly. Now listen. You ask me in a loud voice what kind of a boat that is; and when I answer, you keep your eye on the two men."

"Why, what are you going to do?"

"You'll see. Try it now; we've no time to lose."

Blix shifted in her seat and cleared her throat. Then:

"What a pretty boat that is up there, that picture on the wall. See over there, on the wall opposite? Do you notice it? Isn't she pretty? Condy, tell me what kind of a boat is that?"

Condy turned about in his place with great deliberation, fixed the picture with a judicial eye, and announced decisively:

"That?—why, that's a *barkentine*."

Condy had no need to wait for Blix's report. The demonstration came far too quickly for that. The red-headed man at his loud declaration merely glanced in the direction of the chromo and returned to his *enchellados*. But he of the black moustache followed Condy's glance, noted the picture of which he spoke, and snorted contemptuously. They even heard him mutter beneath his moustache:

"*Barkentine* your eye!"

"No doubt as to which is the captain now," whispered Condy so soon as the other had removed from him a glance of withering scorn.

They could hardly restrain their gaiety; but their gravity promptly returned when Blix kicked Condy's foot under the table and murmured: "He's looking at his watch, the captain is. K. D. B. isn't here yet, and the red-headed man, the coincidence, is. We *must* get rid of him. Condy, can't you think of something?"

"Well, he won't go till he's through his supper, you can depend upon that. If he's here when K. D. B. arrives, it will spoil everything. She wouldn't stay a moment. She wouldn't even come in."

"Isn't it disappointing? And I had so counted upon bringing these two together! And Captain Jack *is* a nice man!"

"You can see that with one hand tied behind you," whispered Condy. "The other chap's tough."

"Looks just like the kind of man to get into jail sooner or later."

"Maybe he's into some mischief now; you never can tell. And the Mexican quarter of San Francisco is just the place for 'affairs.' I'll warrant he's got *pals*."

"Well, here he is—that's the main point—just keeping those people apart, spoiling a whole romance. Maybe ruining their lives. It's *quite* possible; really it is. Just stop and think. This is a positive crisis we're looking at now."

"Can't we get rid of him *somehow?*"

"O-oh!" whispered Blix, all at once, in a quiver of excitement. "There *is* a way, if we'd ever have the courage to do it. It might work; and if it didn't, he'd never know the difference, never would suspect us. Oh! but we wouldn't dare."

"What? what? In Heaven's name what is it, Blix?"

"We wouldn't dare—we couldn't. Oh! but it would be such——"

"K. D. B. may come in that door at any second."

"I'm half afraid, but all the same——— Condy, let me have a pencil." She dashed off a couple of lines on the back of the bill of fare, and her hand trembled like a leaf as she handed him what she had written.

"Send him the red-headed man—that telegram. There's an office just two doors below here, next the drug-store. I saw it as we came by. You know his initials; remember, you saw them in his hat. W. J. A., Luna's restaurant. That's all you want."

"Lord," muttered Condy, as he gazed upon what Blix had written.

"Do you dare?" she whispered, with a little hysterical shudder.

"If it failed we've nothing to lose."

"And K. D. B. is coming nearer every instant!"

"But would he go—that is, at once?"

"We can only try. You won't be gone a hundred seconds. You can leave me here that length of time. Quick, Condy; decide one way or the other. It's getting desperate."

Condy reached for his hat.

"Give me some money, then," he said. "You won all of mine."

A few moments later he was back again; and the two sat, pretending to eat their chili peppers, their hearts in their throats, hardly daring to raise their eyes from their plates. Condy was actually sick with excitement, and all but tipped the seltzer bottle to the floor when a messenger boy appeared in the outer room. The boy and the proprietor held a conference over the counter. Then Richard appeared between the portières of Nottingham lace, the telegram in his hand and the boy at his heels.

Evidently Richard knew the red-headed man, for he crossed over to him at once with the words:

"I guess this is for you, Mr. Atkins?"

He handed him the despatch and retired. The red-headed man signed the receipt; the boy departed. Blix and Condy heard the sound of torn paper as the red-headed man opened the telegram.

Ten seconds passed, then fifteen, then twenty. There was a silence. Condy dared to steal a glance at the red-headed man's reflection in the mirror. He was studying the despatch, frowning horribly. He put it away in his pocket, took it out again with a fierce movement of impatience, and consulted it a second time. His "supper Mexican" remained untasted before him; Condy and Blix heard him breathing loud through his nose. That he was profoundly agitated, they could not doubt for a single moment. All at once a little panic terror seemed to take possession of him. He rose, seized his hat, jammed it over his ears, slapped a half-dollar upon the table, and strode from the restaurant.

This is what the red-headed man had read in the despatch; this is what Blix had written:

All is discovered. Fly at once.

And never in all their subsequent rambles about the city did Blix or Condy set eyes upon the red-headed man again, nor did Luna's restaurant, where he seemed to have been a habitué, ever afterward know his presence. He disappeared; he was swallowed up. He had left the restaurant, true. Had he also left that neighbourhood? Had he fled the city, the State, the country even? What skeleton in the red-headed man's closet had those six words called to life and the light of day? Had they frightened him forth to spend the rest of his days fleeing from an unnamed, unknown avenger— a veritable wandering Jew? What mystery had they touched upon there in the bald, bare back room of the Quarter's restaurant? What dark door had they opened, what red-headed phantom had they evoked? Had they broken up a plot, thwarted a conspiracy, prevented a crime? They never knew. One thing only was certain. The red-headed man had had a past.

Meanwhile the minutes were passing, and K. D. B. still failed to appear. Captain Jack was visibly growing impatient, anxious. By now he had come to the fiery liqueur called *mescal*. He was nearly through his supper. At every moment he consulted his watch and fixed the outside door with a scowl. It was already twenty minutes after seven.

"I know the red-headed man spoiled it, after all," murmured Blix. "K. D. B. saw the two of them in here and was frightened."

"We could send Captain Jack a telegram from her," suggested Condy. "I'm ready for anything now."

"What could you say?"

"Oh, that she couldn't come. Make another appointment."

"He'd be offended with her. He'd never make another appointment. Sea captains are always so punctilious, y' know."

Richard brought them their coffee and kirsch, and Condy showed Blix how to burn a lump of sugar and sweeten the coffee with syrup. But they were disappointed. Captain Jack was getting ready to leave. K. D. B. had evidently broken the appointment.

Then all at once she appeared.

They knew it upon the instant by a brisk opening and shutting of the street door, and by a sudden alertness on the part of Captain Jack, which he immediately followed by a quite inexplicable move. The street door in the outside room had hardly closed before his hand shot to his coat lapel and tore out the two marguerites.

The action was instinctive; Blix knew it for such immediately. The retired captain had not premeditated

193

it. He had not seen the face of the newcomer. She had
not time to come into the back room, or even to close
the street door. But the instant that the captain had
recognized a bunch of white marguerites in her belt
he had, without knowing why, been moved to conceal
his identity.

"He's afraid," whispered Blix. "Positively, I believe
he's afraid. How absolutely stupid men are!"

But meanwhile, K. D. B., the looked-for, the planned-
for and intrigued-for; the object of so much diplomacy,
such delicate manœuvring; the pivot upon which all
plans were to turn, the storm-centre round which so
many conflicting currents revolved, and for whose
benefit the peace of mind of the red-headed man had
been forever broken up—had entered the room.

"Why, she's *pretty!*" was Blix's first smothered exclamation, as if she had expected a harridan.

K. D. B. looked like a servant-girl of the better sort,
and was really very neatly dressed. She was small, little
even. She had snappy black eyes, a resolute mouth,
and a general air of being very quiet, very matter-of-
fact and complacent. She would be disturbed at nothing,
excited at nothing; Blix was sure of that. She was placid,
but it was the placidity not of the absence of emotion,
but of emotion disdained. Not the placidity of the mol-
lusk, but that of a mature and contemplative cat.

Quietly she sat down at a corner table, quietly she
removed her veil and gloves, and quietly she took in
the room and its three occupants.

Condy and Blix glued their eyes upon their coffee
cups like guilty conspirators; but a crash of falling
crockery called their attention to the captain's table.

Captain Jack was in a tremor. Hitherto he had acted
the rôle of a sane and sensible gentleman of middle age,
master of himself and of the situation. The entrance of
K. D. B. had evidently reduced him to a semi-idiotic

BLIX

condition. He enlarged himself; he eased his neck in his
collar with a rotary movement of head and shoulders.
He frowned terribly at trifling objects in corners of the
room. He cleared his throat till the glassware jingled.
He pulled at his moustache. He perspired, fumed,
fretted, and was suddenly seized with an insane desire to
laugh. Once only he caught the eye of K. D. B., calmly
sitting in her corner picking daintily at her fish, where-
upon he immediately overturned the vinegar and pepper
casters upon the floor. Just so might have behaved an
overgrown puppy in the presence of a sleepy, unper-
turbed chessy-cat, dozing by the fire.

"He ought to be shaken," murmured Blix at the end
of her patience. "Does he think *she* is going to make the
first move?"

"Ha, ah'm!" thundered the captain, clearing his
throat for the twentieth time, twirling his moustache,
and burying his scarlet face in an enormous pocket
handkerchief.

Five minutes passed and he was still in his place.
From time to time K. D. B. fixed him with a quiet,
deliberate look, and resumed her delicate picking.

"Do you think she knows it's he, now that he's taken
off his marguerites?" whispered Condy.

"Know it?—of course she does! Do you think women
are absolutely *blind*, or so imbecile as men are? And,
then, if she didn't think it was he, she'd go away. And
she's so really pretty, too. He ought to thank his stars
alive. Think what a fright she might have been! She
doesn't *look* thirty-one."

"Huh!" returned Condy. "As long as she *said* she
was thirty-one you can bet everything you have that
she *is*; that's as true as revealed religion."

"Well, it's something to have seen the kind of people
who write the personals," said Blix. "I had always
imagined that they were kind of tough."

195

"You see they are not," he answered. "I told you they were not. Maybe, however, we have been exceptionally fortunate. At any rate, these are respectable enough."

"Not the least doubt about that. But why won't he do something, that captain?" mourned Blix. "Why *will* he act like such a ninny?"

"He's waiting for us to go," said Condy; "I'm sure of it. They'll never meet so long as we're here. Let's go and give 'em a chance. If you leave the two alone here, one or the other will *have* to speak. The suspense would become too terrible. It would be as though they were on a desert island."

"But I wanted to *see* them meet," she protested.

"You wouldn't hear what they said."

"But we'd never know if they did meet, and oh—and *who* spoke first."

"She'll speak first," declared Condy.

"Never!" returned Blix, in an indignant whisper.

"I tell you what. We could go and then come back in five minutes. I'll forget my stick here. Savvy?"

"You would probably do it anyhow," she told him.

They decided this would be the better course. They got together their things, and Condy neglected his stick, hanging upon a hook on the wall.

At the counter in the outside room, Blix, to the stupefaction of Richard, the waiter, paid the bill. But as she was moving toward the door, Condy called her back.

"Remember the waiter," he said severely, while Richard grinned and bobbed. "Fifty cents is the very least you could tip him." Richard actually protested, but Condy was firm, and insisted upon a half-dollar tip.

"*Noblesse oblige,*" he declared with vast solemnity.

They walked as far as the cathedral, listened for a moment to the bell striking the hour of eight; then as

196

they remembered that the restaurant closed at that time, hurried back and entered the outside room in feigned perturbation.

"Did I, could I possibly have left my stick here!" exclaimed Condy to Richard, who was untying his apron behind the counter. But Richard had not noticed.

"I think I must have left it back here where we were sitting."

Condy stepped into the back room, Blix following. They got his stick and returned to the outside room.

"Yes, yes, I did leave it," he said, as he showed it to Richard. "I'm always leaving that stick wherever I go."

"Come again," said Richard, as he bowed them out of the door.

On the curb outside Condy and Blix shook hands and congratulated each other on the success of all their labours. In the back room, seated at the same table, a bunch of wilting marguerites between them, they had seen their "matrimonial objects" conferring earnestly together, absorbed in the business of getting acquainted.

Blix heaved a great sigh of relief and satisfaction, exclaiming:

"At last K. D. B. and Captain Jack have met!"

Bᴜᴛ," she added, as they started to walk, "we will never know which one spoke first."

But Condy was already worrying.

"I don't know, I don't know," he murmured anxiously. "Perhaps we've done an awful thing. Suppose they aren't happy together after they're married? I wish we hadn't; I wish we hadn't now. We've been playing a game of checkers with human souls. We've an awful responsibility. Suppose he kills her some time?"

"Fiddlesticks, Condy! And, besides, if we've done wrong with our matrimonial objects, we've offset it by doing well with our red-headed coincidence. How do you know, you may have 'foiled a villain' with that telegram—prevented a crime?"

Condy grinned at the recollection of the incident.

"'Fly at once,'" he repeated. "I guess he's flying yet. 'All is discovered.' I'd give a dollar and a half——"

"If you had it?"

"Oh, well, if I had it, to know just what it was we have discovered."

Suddenly Blix caught his arm.

"Condy, here they come!"

"Who? Who?"

"Our objects, Captain Jack and K. D. B."

"Of course, of course. They couldn't stay. The restaurant shuts up at eight."

Blix and Condy had been walking slowly in the direction of Pacific Street, and K. D. B. and her escort

198

soon overtook them going in the same direction. As they passed, the captain was saying:

"—jumped on my hatches, and says we'll make it an international affair. That didn't——"

A passing wagon drowned the sound of his voice.

"He was telling her of his adventures!" cried Blix. "Splendid! Othello and Desdemona. They're getting on."

"Let's follow them!" exclaimed Condy.

"Should we? Wouldn't it be—indiscreet?"

"No. We are the arbiters of their fate; we *must* take an interest."

They allowed their objects to get ahead some half a block and then fell in behind. There was little danger of their being detected. The captain and K. D. B. were absorbed in each other. She had even taken his arm.

"They make a fine-looking couple, really," said Blix. "Where do you suppose they are going? To another restaurant?"

But this was not the case. Blix and Condy followed them as far as Washington Square, where the Geodetic Survey stone stands,[12] and the enormous flagstaff; and there in front of a commonplace little house, two doors above the Russian church with its minarets like inverted balloons, K. D. B. and the captain halted. For a few moments they conversed in low tones at the gate, then said good-night, K. D. B. entering the house, the captain bowing with great deference, his hat in his hand. Then he turned about, glanced once or twice at the house, set his hat at an angle, and disappeared across the square, whistling a tune, his chin in the air.

"Very good, excellent, highly respectable," approved Blix; and Condy himself fetched a sigh of relief.

"Yes, yes, it might have been worse."

"We'll never see them again, our 'Matrimonial Objects,'" said Blix, "and they'll never know about us;

but we have brought them together. We've started a romance. Yes, I think we've done a good day's work. And now, Condy, I think we had best be thinking of home ourselves. I'm just beginning to get most awfully sleepy. What a day we've had!"

A sea fog, or rather *the* sea fog—San Francisco's old and inseparable companion—had gathered by the time they reached the top of the Washington Street hill. Everything was wet with it. The asphalt was like varnished ebony. Indistinct masses and huge dim shadows stood for the houses on either side. From the eucalyptus trees and the palms the water dripped like rain. Far off, oceanward, the fog-horn was lowing like a lost gigantic bull. The gray bulk of a policeman—the light from the street lamp reflected in his star—loomed up on the corner as they descended from the car.

.   .   .   .   .   .

Condy had intended to call his diver's story "A Submarine Romance," but Blix had disapproved.

"It's too 'Twenty Thousand Leagues Under the Sea,'" she had said. "You want something much more dignified. There *is* that about you, Condy, you like to be too showy; you don't know when to stop. But you have left off red-and-white scarfs, and I am very glad to see you wearing white shirt-fronts instead of pink ones."

"Yes, yes, I thought it would be quieter," he had answered, as though the idea had come from him. Blix allowed him to think so.

But "A Victory Over Death," as the story was finally called, was a success. Condy was too much of a born story-teller not to know when he had done something distinctly good. When the story came back from the typewriter's, with the additional strength that print lends to fiction, and he had read it over, he could not repress a sense of jubilation. The story rang true.

"Bully, bully!" he muttered between his teeth as he finished the last paragraph. "It's a corker! If it's rejected everywhere, it's an out-of-sight yarn just the same."

And there Condy's enthusiasm in the matter began to dwindle. The fine fire which had sustained him during the story's composition had died out. He was satisfied with his work. He had written a good story, and that was the end of it. No doubt he would send it East—to the Centennial Company—to-morrow or the day after—some time that week. To mail the manuscript meant quite half an hour's effort. He would have to buy stamps for return postage; a letter would have to be written, a large envelope procured, the accurate address ascertained. For the moment his supplement work demanded his attention. He put off sending the story from day to day. His interest in it abated. And for the matter he soon discovered he had other things to think of.

It had been easy to promise Blix that he would no longer gamble at his club with the other men of his acquaintance; but it was "death and the devil," as he told himself, to abide by that promise. More than once in the fortnight following upon his resolution he had come up to the little flat on the Washington Street hill as to a place of refuge; and Blix, always pretending that it was all a huge joke and part of their good times, had brought out the cards and played with him. But she knew very well the fight he was making against the enemy, and how hard it was for him to keep from the round green tables and group of silent shirt-sleeved men in the card-rooms of his club. She looked forward to the time when Condy would cease to play even with her. But she was too sensible and practical a girl to expect him to break a habit of years' standing in a couple of weeks. The thing would have to be accomplished little by little. At times she had misgivings as to the honesty of the course she had adopted. But nowadays, playing as he did with her only, Condy gambled but two or three evenings in the week, and then not for more than two hours at a time. Heretofore hardly an evening that had not seen him at the round table in his club's card-room, whence he had not risen until long after midnight.

Condy had told young Sargeant that he had "reformed" in the matter of gambling, and intended to swear off for a few months. Sargeant, like the thoroughbred he was, never urged to play after that, and never spoke of the previous night's game when Condy was about. The other men of his "set" were no less thoughtful, and, though they rallied him a little at first upon his defection, soon let the matter drop. Condy told himself that there were plenty of good people in the world, after all. Everyone seemed conspiring to make it easy for him, and he swore at himself for a weak-kneed cad.

On a certain Tuesday, about a week after the fishing excursion and the affair of the "Matrimonial Objects," toward half-past six in the evening, Condy was in his room, dressing for a dinner engagement. Young Sargeant's sister had invited him to be one of a party who were to dine at the University Club and later on fill a box at a charity play, given by amateurs at one of the downtown theatres. But as he was washing his linen shirt-studs with his tooth-brush, his eye feel upon a note, in Laurie Flagg's handwriting, that lay on his writing-desk, and that he had received some ten days previous. Condy turned cold upon the instant, hurled the tooth-brush across the room, and dropped into a chair with a groan of despair. Miss Flagg was giving a theatre party for the same affair, and he remembered now that he had promised to join her party as well, forgetting all about the engagement he had made with

Miss Sargeant. It was impossible at this late hour to accept either one of the young women's invitations without offending the other.

"Well, I won't go to *either*, that's all," he vociferated aloud to the opposite wall. "I'll send 'em each a wire, and say that I'm sick or have got to go down to the office, and—and, by George! I'll go up and see Blix, and we'll read and make things to eat."

And no sooner had this alternative occurred to him than it appeared too fascinating to be resisted. A weight seemed removed from his mind. When it came to that, what amusement would he have at either affair?

"Sit up there with your shirt-front starched like a board," he blustered, "and your collar throttling you, and smile till your face is sore, and reel off small talk to a girl whose last name you can't remember! Do I have any fun, does it do me any good, do I get ideas for yarns! What do I do it for? I don't know."

While speaking he had been kicking off his tight shoes and such of his full dress as he had already put on, and with a feeling of enormous relief turned again to his sack suit of tweed. "Lord, these feel better!" he exclaimed, as he substituted the loose business suit for the formal rigidity of his evening dress. It was with a sensation of positive luxury that he put on a "soft" shirt of blue cheviot and his tan walking-shoes.

"But no more red scarfs," he declared, as he knotted his black satin "club" before the mirror. "She *was* right there." He put his cigarettes in his pocket, caught up his gloves and stick, clapped on his hat, and started for the Bessemers' flat with a feeling of joyous expectancy he had not known for days.

Evidently Blix had seen him coming, for she opened the door herself; and it suited her humour for the moment to treat him as a peddler or book-agent.

"No, no," she said airily, her head in the air as she held the door. "No, we don't want any to-day. We *have* the biography of Abraham Lincoln. Don't want to subscribe to any Home Book of Art. We're not artistic; we use drapes in our parlours. Don't want 'The Wives and Mothers of Great Men.'"

But Condy had noticed a couple of young women on the lower steps of the adjacent flat, quite within ear-shot, and at once he began in a loud, harsh voice:

"Well, y' know, we can't wait for our rent forever; I'm only the collector, and I've nothing to do with repairs. Pay your rent that's three months overdue, and then——"

But Blix pulled him within the house and clapped to the door.

"Condy *Rivers!*" she exclaimed, her cheeks flaming, "those are our neighbours. They heard every word. What *do* you suppose they think?"

"Huh! I'd rather have 'em think I was a rent-collector than a book-agent. *You* began it. 'Evenin', Miss Lady.'"

"'Evenin', Mister Man.'"

But Condy's visit, begun thus gaily, soon developed along much more serious lines. After supper, while the light still lasted, Blix read stories to him while he smoked cigarettes in the bay window of the dining room. But as soon as the light began to go she put the book aside, and the two took their accustomed places in the window, and watched the evening burning itself out over the Golden Gate.

It was just warm enough to have one of the windows opened, and for a long time after the dusk they sat listening to the vague clamour of the city, lapsing by degrees, till it settled into a measured, soothing murmur, like the breathing of some vast monster asleep. Condy's cigarette was a mere red point in the half-darkness.

The smoke drifted out of the open window in long blue strata. At his elbow Blix was leaning forward, looking down upon the darkening, drowsing city, her round, strong chin propped upon her hand. She was just close enough for Condy to catch the sweet, delicious feminine perfume that came indefinitely from her clothes, her hair, her neck. From where Condy sat he could see the silhouette of her head and shoulders against the dull golden blur of the open window; her round, high forehead, with the thick yellow hair rolling back from her temples and ears, her pink clean cheeks, her little dark-brown, scintillating eyes, and her firm red mouth, made all the firmer by the position of her chin upon her hand. As ever, her round, strong neck was swathed high and tight in white satin; but between the topmost fold of the satin and the rose of one small ear-lobe was a little triangle of white skin, that was partly her neck and partly her cheek, and that Condy knew should be softer than down, smoother than satin, warm and sweet and redolent as new apples. Condy imagined himself having the right to lean toward her there and kiss that little spot upon her neck or her cheek; and as he fancied it, was surprised to find his breath come suddenly quick, and a barely perceptible qualm, as of a certain faintness, thrill him to his finger-tips; and then, he thought, how would it be if he could, without fear of rebuff, reach out his arm and put it about her trim, firm waist, and draw her very close to him, till he should feel the satiny coolness of her smooth cheek against his; till he could sink his face in the delicious, fragrant confusion of her hair, then turn that face to his—that face with its strong, calm mouth and sweet, full lips— the face of this dear young girl of nineteen, and then——

"I say—I—shall we—let's read again. Let's—let's do something."

"Condy, how you frightened me!" exclaimed Blix,

with a great start. "No, listen: I want to talk to you, to tell you something. Papum and I have been having some very long and serious talks since you were last here. What do you think, I may go away."

"The deuce you say!" exclaimed Condy, sitting suddenly upright. "Where to, in Heaven's name?" he added, "and when? and what for?"

"To New York, to study medicine."

There was a silence; then Condy exclaimed, waving his hands at her:

"Oh, go right on! Don't mind me. Little thing like going to New York—to study medicine. Of course, that happens every day, a mere detail. I presume you'll go back and forth for your meals?"

Then Blix began to explain. It appeared that she had two aunts, both sisters of her father—one a widow, the other unmarried. The widow, a certain Mrs. Kihm, lived in New York, and was wealthy, and had views on "women's sphere of usefulness." The other, Miss Bessemer, a little old maid of fifty, Condy had on rare occasions seen at the flat, where everyone called her Aunt Dodd. She lived in that vague region of the city known as the Mission, where she owned a little property.

From what Blix told him that evening Condy learned that Mrs. Kihm had visited the coast a few winters previous and had taken a great fancy to Blix. Even then she had proposed to Mr. Bessemer to take Blix back to New York with her, and educate her to some woman's profession; but at that time the old man would not listen to it. Now it seemed that the opportunity had again presented itself.

"She's a dear old lady," Blix said; "not a bit strongminded, as you would think, and ever so much cleverer than most men. She manages all her property herself. For the last month she's been writing again to Papum for me to come on and stay with her three or four years. She hasn't a chick nor a child, and she don't entertain or go out any, so maybe she feels lonesome. Of course if I studied there, Papum wouldn't think of Aunt Kihm—don't you know—paying for it at all. I wouldn't go if it was that way. But I could stay with her and she could make a home for me while I was there—if I should study—anything—study medicine."

"But why!" he exclaimed. "What do you want to study to be a doctor for? It isn't as though you had to support yourself."

"I know, I know I've not got to support myself. But why shouldn't I have a profession just like a man—just like you, Condy? You stop and think. It seemed strange to me when I first thought of it; but I got thinking about it and talking it over with Papum, and I should *love* it. I'd do it, not because I would have to do it, but because it would interest me. Condy, you know that I'm not a bit strong-minded, and that I hate a masculine, unfeminine girl as much as you do."

"But a medical college, Blix! You don't know what you are talking about."

"Yes, I do. There's a college in New York just for women. Aunt Kihm sent me the prospectus, and it's one of the best in the country. I don't dream of practising, you know; at least, I don't think about that now. But one must have some occupation; and isn't studying medicine, Condy, better than piano-playing, or French courses, or literary classes and Browning circles? [13] Oh, I've no patience with that kind of girl! And look at the chance I have now; and Aunt Kihm is such a dear! Think, she writes, I could go to and from the college in her coupé every day, and I would see New York; and just being in a big city like that is an education."

"You're right, it would be a big thing for you," assented Condy, "and I like the idea of *you* studying something. It would be the making of such a girl as you, Blix."

And then Blix, seeing him thus acquiescent, said:

"Well, it's all settled; Papum and I both wrote last night."

"When are you going?"

"The first week in January."

"Well, that's not so *awfully* soon. But who will take your place here? However in the world would your father get along without you, and Snooky and Howard?"

"Aunt Dodd is going to come."

"Sudden enough," said Condy, "but it *is* a great thing for you, Blix, and I'm mighty glad for you. Your future is all cut out for you now. Of course your aunt, if she's so fond of you and hasn't any children, will leave you everything—maybe settle something on you right away; and you'll marry some one of those New York chaps, and be great big people before you know it."

"The idea, Condy!" she protested. "No; I'm going there to study medicine. Oh, you don't know how enthusiastic I am over the idea! I've bought some of the first-year books already, and have been reading them. Really, Condy, they are even better than *Many Inventions*."

"Wish *I* could get East," muttered Condy gloomily. Blix forgot her own good fortune upon the instant.

"I do so wish you *could*, Condy!" she exclaimed. "You are too good for a Sunday supplement. I know it and *you* know it, and I've heard ever so many people who have read your stories say the same thing. You could spend twenty years working as you are now, and at the end what would you be? Just an assistant editor of a Sunday supplement, and still in the same place; and worse, you'd come to be contented with that, and think you were only good for that and nothing better.

You've got it in you, Condy, to be a great story-teller. I believe in you, and I've every confidence in you. But just so long as you stay here and are willing to do hack work, just so long you will be a hack writer. You *must* break from it; you *must* get away. I know you have a good time here; but there are so many things better than that and more worth while. You ought to make up your mind to get East, and work for that and nothing else. I know you want to go, but wanting isn't enough. Enthusiasm without energy isn't enough. You have enthusiasm, Condy; but you *must* have energy. You must be willing to give up things; you must make up your mind that you will go East, and then set your teeth together and do it. Oh, I *love* a man that can do that—make up his mind to a thing and then put it through!"

Condy watched her as she talked, her brown-black eyes coruscating, her cheeks glowing, her small hands curled into round pink fists.

"Blix, you're splendid!" he exclaimed; "you're fine! You could put life into a dead man. You're the kind of girl that are the making of men. By Jove, you'd back a man up, wouldn't you? You'd stand by him till the last ditch. Of course," he went on after a pause, "of course I ought to go to New York. But, Blix, suppose I went— well, then what? It isn't as though I had any income of my own, or rich aunt. Suppose I didn't find something to do—and the chances are that I wouldn't for three or four months—what would I live on in the meanwhile? 'What would the robin do then, poor thing?' I'm a poor young man, Miss Bessemer, and I've got to eat. No; my only chance is 'to be discovered' by a magazine or a publishing house or somebody, and get a bid of some kind."

"Well, there is the Centennial Company. They have taken an interest in you, Condy. You must follow that right up and keep your name before them all the time. Have you sent them 'A Victory Over Death' yet?"

Condy sat down to his eggs and coffee the next morning in the hotel, harried with a certain sense of depression and disappointment for which he could assign no cause. Nothing seemed to interest him. The newspaper was dull. He could look forward to no pleasure in his day's work; and what was the matter with the sun that morning? As he walked down to the office he noted no cloud in the sky, but the brightness was gone from the day. He sat down to his desk and attacked his work, but "copy" would not come. The sporting editor and his inane jokes harassed him beyond expression. Just the sight of the clipping editor's back was an irritation. The office boy was a mere incentive to profanity. There was no spring in Condy that morning, no elasticity, none of his natural buoyancy. As the day wore on, his ennui increased; his luncheon at the club was tasteless, tobacco had lost its charm. He ordered a cocktail in the wine-room, and put it aside with a wry face.

The afternoon was one long tedium. At every hour he flung his pencil down, utterly unable to formulate the next sentence of his article, and, his hands in his pockets, gazed gloomily out of the window over the wilderness of roofs—grimy, dirty, ugly roofs that spread out below. He craved diversion, amusement, excitement. Something there was that he wanted with all his heart and soul; yet he was quite unable to say what it was. Something was gone from him to-day that he had possessed yesterday, and he knew he would not regain it on the morrow, nor the next day, nor the day after that. What was it? He could not say. For half an hour he imagined he was going to be sick. His mother was not to be at home that evening, and Condy dined at his club in the hopes of finding someone with whom he could go to the theatre later on in the evening. Sargeant joined him over his coffee and cigarette, but declined to go with him to the theatre.

"Another game on to-night?" asked Condy.

"I suppose so," admitted the other.

"I guess I'll join you to-night," said Condy. "I've had the blue devils since morning, and I've got to have something to drive them off."

"Don't let me urge you, you know," returned Sargeant.

"Oh, that's all right!" Condy assured him. "My time's about up, anyways."

An hour later, just as he, Sargeant, and the other men of their "set" were in the act of going upstairs to the card-rooms, a hall-boy gave Condy a note, at that moment brought by a messenger, who was waiting for an answer. It was from Blix. She wrote:

Don't you want to come up and play cards with me to-night? We haven't had a game in over a week.

"How did she know?" thought Condy to himself—"how could she tell?" Aloud, he said:

"I can't join you fellows, after all. 'Despatch from the managing editor.' Some special detail or other."

For the first time since the previous evening Condy felt his spirits rise as he set off toward the Washington Street hill. But though he and Blix spent as merry an evening as they remembered in a long time, his name-less, formless irritation returned upon him almost as soon as he had bidden her good-night. It stayed with him all through the week, and told upon his work. As a result, three of his articles were thrown out by the editor.

"We can't run such rot as that in the paper," the chief had said. "Can't you give us a story?"

"Oh, I've got a kind of a yarn you can run if you

like," answered Condy, his week's depression at its very lowest.

"A Victory Over Death" was published in the following Sunday's supplement of the *Times*, with illustrations by one of the staff artists. It attracted not the least attention.

Just before he went to bed the Sunday evening of its appearance, Condy read it over again for the last time.

"It's a rotten failure," he muttered gloomily as he cast the paper from him. "Simple drivel. I wonder what Blix will think of it. I wonder if I amount to a hill of beans. I wonder *what* she wants to go East for, anyway."

THE old-fashioned Union Street cable car, with its low, comfortable outside seats, put Blix and Condy down just inside the Presidio Government Reservation. Condy asked a direction of a sentry nursing his Krag-Jörgensen at the terminus of the track, and then with Blix set off down the long board walk through the tunnel of overhanging evergreens.[14]

The day could not have been more desirable. It was a little after ten of a Monday morning, Condy's weekly holiday. The air was neither cool nor warm, effervescent merely, brisk and full of the smell of grass and of the sea. The sky was a speckless sheen of pale blue. To their right, and not far off, was the bay, blue as indigo. Alcatraz seemed close at hand; beyond was the enormous green, red, and purple pyramid of Tamalpais climbing out of the water, head and shoulders above the little foothills, and looking out to the sea and to the west.

The Reservation itself was delightful. There were rows of the officers' houses, all alike, drawn up in lines like an assembly of the staff; there were huge barracks, most like college dormitories; and on their porches enlisted men in shirt sleeves and overalls were cleaning saddles, and polishing the brass of head-stalls and bridles, whistling the while or smoking corn-cob pipes. Here on the parade-ground a soldier, his coat and vest removed, was batting grounders and flies to a half-dozen of his fellows. Over by the stables, strings of horses, all of the same colour, were being curried and cleaned. A young lieutenant upon a bicycle spun silently past. An officer came from his front gate, his coat unbuttoned and a briar in his teeth. The walks and roads were flanked with lines of black-painted cannon-balls; inverted pieces of abandoned ordnance stood at corners. From a distance came the mellow snarling of a bugle.

Blix and Condy had planned a long walk for that day. They were to go out through the Presidio Reservation, past the barracks and officers' quarters, and on to the old fort at the Golden Gate. Here they would turn and follow the shore-line for a way, then strike inland across the hills for a short half mile, and regain the city and the street-car lines by way of the golf-links. Condy had insisted upon wearing his bicycle outfit for the occasion, and, moreover, carried a little satchel, which, he said, contained a pair of shoes.

But Blix was as sweet as a rose that morning, all in tailor-made black but for the inevitable bands of white satin wrapped high and tight about her neck. The St. Bernard's dog-collar did duty as a belt. She had disdained a veil, and her yellow hair was already blowing about her smooth pink cheeks. She walked at his side, her step as firm and solid as his own, her round, strong arms swinging, her little brown eyes shining with good spirits and vigour, and the pure, clean animal joy of being alive on that fine cool Western morning. She talked almost incessantly. She was positively garrulous. She talked about the fine day that it was, about the queer new forage caps of the soldiers, about the bare green hills of the reservation, about the little cemetery they passed just beyond the limits of the barracks, about a rabbit she saw, and about the quail they both heard whistling and calling in the hollows under the bushes.

Condy walked at her side in silence, yet no less happy than she, smoking his pipe and casting occasional glances at a great ship—a four-master that was being

214

towed out toward the Golden Gate. At every moment and at every turn they noted things that interested them, and to which they called each other's attention.

"Look, Blix!"

"Oh, Condy, look at that!"

They were soon out of the miniature city of the Post, and held on down through the low reach of *tules* and sand-dunes that stretch between the barracks and the old red fort.

"Look, Condy!" said Blix. "What's that building down there on the shore of the bay—the one with the flagstaff?"

"I think that must be the life-boat station."

"I wonder if we could go down and visit it. I think it would be good fun."

"Idea!" exclaimed Condy.

The station was close at hand. To reach it they had but to leave the crazy board walk that led on toward the fort, and cross a few hundred yards of sand-dune. Condy opened the gate that broke the line of evergreen hedge around the little two-story house, and promptly unchained a veritable pandemonium of dogs.

Inside, the place was not without a certain charm of its own. A brick walk, bordered with shells, led to the front of the station, which gave directly upon the bay; a little well-kept lawn opened to right and left, and six or eight gaily-painted old row-boats were set about, half filled with loam in which fuchsias, geraniums, and mignonettes were flowering. A cat or two dozed upon the window sills in the sun. Upon a sort of porch overhead, two of the crew paced up and down in a manner that at once suggested the poop. Here and there was a gleam of highly polished red copper or brass trimmings. The bay was within two steps of the front door, while a little farther down the beach was the house where the surf-boat was kept, and the long runway leading down from it to the water. Condy rapped boldly at the front door. It was opened by Captain Jack.

Captain Jack, and no other; only now he wore a blue sweater and a leather-visored cap, with the letters U. S. L. B. S. around the band.

Not an instant was given them for preparation. The thing had happened with the abruptness of a transformation scene at a theatre. Condy's knock had evoked a situation. Speech was stricken from their mouths. For a moment they were bereft even of action, and stood there on the threshold, staring open-mouthed and open-eyed at the sudden reappearance of their "matrimonial object." Condy was literally dumb; in the end it was Blix who tided them over the crisis.

"We were just going by—just taking a walk," she explained, "and we thought we'd like to see the station. Is it all right? Can we look around?"

"Why, of course," assented the Captain with great cordiality. "Come right in. This is visitors' day. You just happened to hit it—only it's mighty few visitors we ever have," he added.

While Condy was registering for himself and Blix, they managed to exchange a lightning glance. It was evident the Captain did not recognize them. The situation readjusted itself, even promised to be of extraordinary interest. And for that matter it made little difference whether the Captain remembered them or not.

"No, we don't get many visitors," the Captain went on, as he led them out of the station and down the small gravel walk to the house where the surf-boat was kept. "This is a quiet station. People don't fetch out this way very often, and we're not called out very often either. We're an inside post, you see, and usually we don't get a call unless the sea's so high that the Cliff House station can't launch their boat. So, you see, we don't go out much; but when we *do*, it means business with a great big B. Now this here, you see," continued the Captain, rolling back the sliding doors of the house, "is the surf-boat. By the way, let's see; I ain't just caught your names yet."

"Well, my name's Rivers," said Condy, "and this is Miss Bessemer. We're both from the city."

"Happy to know you, sir; happy to know you, miss," he returned, pulling off his cap. "My name's Hoskins, but you can just call me Captain Jack. I'm so used to it that I don't kind of answer to the other. Well, now, Miss Bessemer, this here's the surf-boat; she's self-right-in', self-bailin', she can't capsize, and if I was to tell you how many thousands of dollars she cost, you wouldn't believe me."

Condy and Blix spent a delightful half-hour in the boat-house while Captain Jack explained and illustrated and told them anecdotes of wrecks, escapes, and rescues till they held their breaths like ten-year-olds.

It did not take Condy long to know that he had discovered what the story-teller so often tells of but so seldom finds, and what, for want of a better name, he elects to call "a character."

Captain Jack had been everywhere, had seen everything, and had done most of the things worth doing, including a great many things that he had far better have left undone. But on this latter point the Captain seemed to be innocently and completely devoid of a moral sense of right and wrong. It was quite evident that he saw no matter for conscience in the smuggling of Chinamen across the Canadian border at thirty dollars a head—a venture in which he had had the assistance of the prodigal son of an American divine of international renown. The trade to Peruvian insurgents of condemned rifles was to be regretted only because the ring manipulating it was broken up. The appropriation of a schooner in the harbour of Callao was a story in itself; while the robbery of thirty thousand dollars' worth of sea-otter skins from a Russian trading-post in Alaska, accomplished chiefly through the agency of a barrel of rum manufactured from sugar-cane, was a veritable achievement.

He had been born, so he told them, in Winchester, in England, and—Heaven save the mark!—had been brought up with a view of taking orders. For some time he was a choir boy in the great Winchester Cathedral; then, while yet a lad, had gone to sea. He had been boat-steerer on a New Bedford whaler, and struck his first whale when only sixteen. He had filibustered down to Chili; had acted as ice pilot on an Arctic relief expedition; had captained a crew of Chinamen shark-fishing in Magdalena Bay, and had been nearly murdered by his men; had been a deep-sea diver, and had burst his ear-drums at the business, so that now he could blow tobacco smoke out of his ears; he had been shipwrecked in the Gilberts, fought with the Seris on the lower California Islands,[15] sold champagne—made from rock candy, effervescent salts, and Reisling wine—to the Coreans, had dreamed of "holding up" a Cunard liner, and had ridden on the Strand in a hansom with William Ewart Gladstone. But the one thing of which he was proud, the one picture of his life he most delighted to recall, was himself as manager of a negro minstrel troupe, in a hired drum-major's uniform, marching down the streets of Sacramento at the head of the brass band in burnt cork and regimentals.

"The star of the troupe," he told them, "was the lady with the iron jore. We busted in Stockton, and she gave me her diamonds to pawn. I pawned 'em, and kept back something in the hand for myself and hooked it to San Francisco. Strike me straight if she didn't follow me, that iron-jored piece; met me one day in front of the

Bush Street Theatre, and horsewhipped me properly. Now, just think of that,"—and he laughed as though it was the best kind of a joke.

"But," hazarded Blix, "don't you find it rather dull out here—lonesome? I should think you would want to have someone with you to keep you company—to—to do your cooking for you?"

But Condy, ignoring her diplomacy and thinking only of possible stories, blundered off upon another track.

"Yes," he said, "you've led such a life of action, I should think this station would be pretty dull for you. How did you happen to choose it?"

"Well, you see," answered the Captain, leaning against the smooth white flank of the surf-boat, his hands in his pockets, "I'm lying low just now. I got into a scrape down at Libertad, in Mexico, that made talk, and I'm waiting for that to die down some. You see, it was this way."

Mindful of their experience with the mate of the whaleback, Condy and Blix were all attention in an instant. Blix sat down upon an upturned box, her elbows on her knees, leaning forward, her little eyes fixed and shining with interest and expectation; Condy, the story-teller all alive and vibrant in him, stood at her elbow, smoking cigarette after cigarette, his fingers dancing with excitement and animation as the Captain spoke.

And then it was that Condy and Blix, in that isolated station, the bay lapping at the shore within ear-shot, in that atmosphere redolent of paint and oakum and of seaweed decaying upon the beach outside, first heard the story of "In Defiance of Authority."

Captain Jack began it with his experience as a restaurant keeper during the boom days in Seattle, Washington. He told them how he was the cashier of a dining saloon whose daily net profits exceeded eight hundred dollars; how its proprietor suddenly died, and how he,

Captain Jack, continued the management of the restaurant pending a settlement of the proprietor's affairs and an appearance of heirs; how in the confusion and excitement of the boom no settlement was ever made; and how, no heirs appearing, he assumed charge of the establishment himself, paying bills, making contracts, and signing notes, until he came to consider the business and all its enormous profits as his own; and how at last, when the restaurant was burned, he found himself some forty thousand dollars "ahead of the game."

Then he told them of the strange club of the place, called "The Exiles," made up chiefly of "younger sons" of English and British-Canadian families, every member possessed of a "past" more or less disreputable; men who had left their country for their country's good, and for their family's peace of mind—adventurers, wanderers, soldiers of fortune, gentlemen vagabonds, men of hyphenated names and even noble birth, whose appellations were avowedly aliases. He told them of his meeting with Billy Isham, one of the club's directors, and of the happy-go-lucky, reckless, unpractical character of the man; of their acquaintance, intimacy, and subsequent partnership; of how the filibustering project was started with Captain Jack's forty thousand, and the never-to-be-forgotten interview in San Francisco with Señora Estrada, the agent of the insurgents; of the incident of her calling-card—how she tore it in two and gave one-half to Isham; of their outfitting, and the broken sextant that was to cause their ultimate discomfiture and disaster, and of the voyage to the rendezvous on a Panama liner. [16]

"Strike me!" continued Captain Jack, "you should have seen Billy Isham on that Panama dough-dish; a passenger ship she was, and Billy was the life of her from stem to stern-post. There was a church pulpit aboard that they were taking down to Mazatlan for some chapel

or other, and this here pulpit was lashed on deck aft.
Well, Billy had been most kinds of a fool in his life, and
amongst others a play-actor; called hisself Gaston
Maundeville, and was clean daft on his knowledge of
Shakespeare and his own power of interpretin' the
hidden meanin' of the lines. I ain't never going to forgit
the day he gave us Portia's speech. We were just under
the tropic, and the day was a scorcher. There was mostly
men folk aboard, and we lay around the deck in our
pajamas, while Billy—Gaston Maundeville, dressed in
striped red-and-white pajamas—clum up in that bally
pulpit, with the ship's Shakespeare in his hands, an' let
us have—'The quality o' mercy isn't strained; it
droppeth as the genteel dew from heavun.' Laugh, I
tell you I was sore with it. Lord, how we guyed him!
An' the more we guyed and the more we laughed, the
more serious he got and the madder he grew. He
said he was interpretin' the hidden meanin' of the
lines."

And so the Captain ran through that wild, fiery tale
—of fighting and loving, buccaneering and conspiring;
mandolins tinkling, knives clicking; oaths mingling with
sonnets, and spilled wine with spilled blood. He told
them of Isham's knife duel with the Mexican lieutenant,
their left wrists lashed together; of the "battle of the
thirty" in the pitch dark of the Custom-House cellar;
of Señora Estrada's love for Isham; and all the roll and
plunge of action that make up the story of "In Defiance
of Authority."

At the end, Blix's little eyes were snapping like
sparks; Condy's face was flaming, his hands were cold,
and he was shifting his weight from foot to foot, like an
excited thoroughbred horse.

"Heavens and earth, what a yarn!" he exclaimed, almost in a whisper.

Blix drew a long, tremulous breath and sat back upon

the upturned box, looking around her as though she had
but that moment been awakened.

"Yes, sir," said the Captain, rolling a cigarette. "Yes,
sir, those were great days. Get down there around the
line in those little, out-o'-the-way republics along the
South American coast, and things happen to you. You
hold a man's life in the crook of your forefinger, an'
nothing's done by halves. If you hate a man, you lay
awake nights biting your mattress, just thinking how
you hate him; an' if you love a woman, good Lord,
how you do *love* her!"

"But—but!" exclaimed Condy, "I don't see how
you can want to do anything else. Why, you're living
sixty to the minute when you're playing a game like
that!"

"Oh, I ain't dead yet!" answered the Captain. "I got
a few schemes left that I could get fun out of."

"How can you wait a minute!" exclaimed Blix
breathlessly. "Why don't you get a ship right away—
to-morrow—and go right off on some other adventure?"

"Well, I can't just now," returned the Captain, blowing the smoke from his cigarette through his ears.
"There's a good many reasons; one of 'em is that I've
just been married."

CHAPTER X

MUM "MAR—MARRIED!" gasped Condy, swallowing something in his throat.

Blix rose to her feet.

"Just been *married!*" she repeated, a little frightened. 'Why—why—why, how *delightful!*"

"Yes—yes," mumbled Condy. "How delightful. I congratulate you!"

"Come in—come back to the station," said the Captain jovially, "and I'll introduce you to m' wife. We were married only last Sunday."

"Why, yes—yes, of course, we'd be delighted," vociferated the two conspirators a little hysterically.

"She's a mighty fine little woman," declared the Captain, as he rolled the door of the boat-house to its place and preceded them up the gravel walk to the station.

"Of course she is," responded Blix. Behind Captain Jack's back she fixed Condy with a wide-eyed look, and nudged him fiercely with an elbow to recall him to himself; for Condy's wits were scattered like a flock of terrified birds, and he was gazing blankly at the Captain's coat collar with a vacant, maniacal smile.

"For Heaven's sake, Condy!" she had time to whisper before they arrived in the hallway of the station.

But fortunately they were allowed a minute or so to recover themselves and prepare for what was coming. Captain Jack ushered them into what was either the parlour, office, or sitting room of the station, and left them with the words:

"Just make yourselves comfortable here, an' I'll go fetch the little woman."

No sooner had he gone than the two turned to each other.

"Well!"

"*Well!*"

"We're in for it now."

"But we must see it through, Condy; act just as natural as you can, and we're all right."

"But supposing *she* recognizes us?"

"Supposing she does—what then? How *are* they to know that we wrote the letters?"

"Sh, Blix, not so loud! They know by now that *they* didn't."

"But it seems that it hasn't made any difference to them; they are married. And besides, they wouldn't speak about putting 'personals' in the paper to us. They would never let anybody know that."

"Do you suppose they could possibly suspect?"

"I'm sure they couldn't."

"Here they come."

"Keep perfectly calm, and we're saved."

"Suppose it isn't K. D. B., after all?"

But it was, of course, and she recognized them in an instant. She and the Captain—the latter all grins—came in from the direction of the kitchen, K. D. B. wearing a neat blue calico gown and an apron that was really a marvel of cleanliness and starch.

"Kitty!" exclaimed Captain Jack, seized again with an unexplainable mirth, "here's some young folks come out to see the place, an' I want you to know 'em. Mr. Rivers, this is m' wife, Kitty, and—lessee, miss, I don't rightly remember your name."

"Bessemer!" exclaimed Condy and Blix in a breath.

"Oh!" exclaimed K. D. B., "you were in the restaurant the night that the Captain and I—I—that is—yes,

I'm quite sure I've seen you before." She turned from one to the other, beginning to blush furiously.

"Yes, yes, in Luna's restaurant, wasn't it?" said Condy desperately. "It seems to me I do just barely remember."

"And wasn't the Captain there?" Blix ventured.

"I forgot my stick, I remember," continued Condy. "I came back for it; and just as I was going out, it seems to me I saw you two at a table near the door."

He thought it best to allow their "matrimonial objects" to believe he had not seen them before.

"Yes, yes, we were there," answered K. D. B. tactfully. "We dine there almost every Monday night."

Blix guessed that K. D. B. would prefer to have the real facts of the situation ignored, and determined she should have the chance to change the conversation if she wished.

"What a delicious supper one has there!" she said.

"Can't say I like Mexican cooking myself," answered K. D. B., forgetting that they dined there every Monday night. "Plain United States is good enough for me."

Suddenly Captain Jack turned abruptly to Condy, exclaiming: "Oh, *you* was the chap that called the picture of that schooner a barkentine."

"Yes, *wasn't* that a barkentine?" he answered innocently.

"Barkentine your *eye!*" spluttered the Captain. "Why, that was a schooner as plain as a pie plate."

But ten minutes later the ordeal was over, and Blix and Condy, once more breathing easy, were on their walk again. The Captain and K. D. B. had even accompanied them to the gate of the station, and had strenuously urged them to "come in and see them again the next time they were out that way."

"Married!" murmured Condy, putting both hands to his head. "We've done it, we've done it now."

"Well, what of it?" declared Blix, a little defiantly. "I think it's all right. You can see the Captain is in love with her, and she with him. No, we've nothing to reproach ourselves with."

"But—but—but so sudden!" whispered Condy, all aghast. "That's what makes me faint—the suddenness of it."

"It shows how much they are in love, how—how readily they—adapted themselves to each other. No, it's all right."

"They seemed to like us—actually."

"Well, they had better—if they knew the truth. Without us they never would have met."

"They both asked us to come out and see them again, did you notice that? Let's do it, Blix," Condy suddenly exclaimed; "let's get to know them."

"Of course we must. Wouldn't it be fun to call on them—to get regularly acquainted with them!"

"They might ask us to dinner some time."

"And think of the stories he could tell you!"

They enthused immediately upon this subject, both talking excitely at the same time, going over the details of the Captain's yarns, recalling the incidents to each other.

"Fancy!" exclaimed Condy—"fancy Billy Isham in his pajamas, red-and-white stripes, reading Shakespeare from that pulpit on board the ship, and the other men guying him! Isn't that a *scene* for you? Can't you just *see* it?"

"I wonder if the Captain wasn't making all those things up as he went along. He don't seem to have any sense of right and wrong at all. He might have been lying, Condy."

"What difference would that make?"

And so they went along in that fine, clear, Western morning, on the edge of the Continent, both of them young and strong and vigorous, the Pacific under their eyes, the great clean Trades blowing in their faces, the smell of the salt sea coming in long aromatic whiffs to their nostrils. Young and strong and fresh, their imaginations thronging with pictures of vigorous action and adventure, buccaneering, filibustering, and all the swing, the leap, the rush and gallop, the exuberant, strong life of the great, uncharted world of Romance.

And all unknowingly they were a Romance in themselves. Cynicism, old age, and the weariness of all things done had no place in the world in which they walked. They still had their illusions, all the keenness of their sensations, all the vividness of their impressions. The simple things of the world, the great, broad, primal emotions of the race stirred in them. As they swung along, going toward the ocean, their brains were almost as empty of thought or of reflection as those of two fine, clean animals. They were all for the immediate sensation; they did not think—they *felt*. The intellect was dormant; they looked at things, they heard things, they smelt the smell of the sea, and of the seaweed, of the fat, rank growth of cresses in the salt marshes; they turned their cheeks to the passing wind, and filled their mouths and breasts with it. Their life was sweet to them; every hour was one glad effervescence. The fact that the ocean was blue was a matter for rejoicing. It was good to be alive on that royal morning. Just to be young was an exhilaration; and everything was young with them—the day was young, the country was young, and the civilization to which they belonged, teeming there upon the green, Western fringe of the continent, was young and heady and tumultuous with the boisterous, red blood of a new race.

Condy even forgot, or rather disdained on such a morning as that, to piece together and rearrange Captain Jack's yarns into story form. To look at the sea and the green hills, to watch the pink on Blix's cheek and her yellow hair blowing across her eyes and lips, was better than thinking. Life was better than literature. To live was better than to read; one live human being was better than ten thousand Shakespeares; an act was better than a thought. Why, just to love Blix, to be with her, to see the sweet, clean flush of her cheek, to know that she was there at his side, and to have the touch of her elbow as they walked, was better than the best story, the greatest novel he could ever hope to write. Life was better than literature, and love was the best thing in life. To love Blix and to be near her—what else was worth while? Could he ever think of finding anything in life sweeter and finer than this dear young girl of nineteen?

Suddenly Condy came to himself with an abrupt start. What was this he was thinking—what was this he was telling himself? Love Blix! He loved Blix! Why, of *course* he loved her—loved her so, that with the thought of it there came a great, sudden clutch at the heart and a strange sense of tenderness, so vague and yet so great that it eluded speech and all expression. Love her! Of course he loved her! He had, all unknowing, loved her even before this wonderful morning; had loved her that day at the lake, and that never-to-be-forgotten, delicious afternoon in the Chinese restaurant; all those long, quiet evenings spent in the window of the little dining room, looking down upon the darkening city, he had loved her. Why, all his days for the last few months had been full of the love of her.

How else had he been so happy? how else did it come about that little by little he was withdrawing from the society and influence of his artificial world, as represented by such men as Sargeant? how else was he slowly loosening the grip of the one evil and vicious habit that had clutched him so long? how else was his ambition stirring? how else was his hitherto aimless enthusiasm hardening to energy and determination? She had not always so influenced him. In the days when they had just known each other, and met each other in the weekly course of their formal life, it had not been so, even though they pretended a certain amount of affection. He remembered the evening when Blix had brought those days to an abrupt end, and how at the moment he had told himself that after all he had never known the real Blix. Since then, in the charming, unconventional life they had led, everything had been changed. He had come to know her for what she was, to know her genuine goodness, her sincerity, her contempt of affectations, her comradeship, her calm, fine strength and unbroken good nature; and day by day, here a little and there a little, his love for her had grown so quietly, so evenly, that he had never known it, until now, behold! it was suddenly come to flower, full and strong—a flower whose fragrance had suddenly filled all his life and all his world with its sweetness.

Half an hour after leaving the life-boat station, Condy and Blix reached the old, red-brick fort, deserted, abandoned, and rime-encrusted, at the entrance of the Golden Gate. They turned its angle, and there rolled the Pacific, a blue floor of shifting water, stretching out there forever and forever over the curve of the earth, over the shoulder of the world, with never a sail in view and never a break from horizon to horizon.

They followed down the shore, sometimes upon the old and broken flume that runs along the seaward face of the hills that rise from the beach, or sometimes upon the beach itself, stepping from boulder to boulder, or holding along at the edge of the water upon reaches of white, hard sand.

The beach was solitary; not a soul was in sight. Close at hand, to landward, great hills, bare and green, shut

off the sky; and here and there the land came tumbling
down into the sea in great, jagged, craggy rocks, knee-
deep in swirling foam, and all black with wet. The air
was full of the prolonged thunder of the surf, and at
intervals sea-birds passed overhead with an occasional,
piping cry. Wreckage was tumbled about here and there;
and innumerable cocoanut shards, huge, brown cups
of fuzzy bark, lay under foot and in the crevices of the
rocks. They found a jelly-fish—a pulpy, translucent
mass; and once even caught a sight of a seal in the hollow of a breaker, with sleek and shining head, his bar-
bels bristling, and heard his hoarse croaking bark as he
hunted the off-shore fish.

Blix refused to allow Condy to help her in the least.
She was quite as active and strong as he, and clambered
from rock to rock and over the shattered scantling of the
flume with the vigour and agility of a young boy. She
muddied her shoes to the very tops, scratched her hands,
tore her skirt, and even twisted her ankle; but her little
eyes were never so bright, nor was the pink flush of her
cheeks ever more adorable. And she was never done
talking—a veritable chatterbox. She saw everything
and talked about everything she saw, quite indifferent
as to whether or no Condy listened. Now it was a queer
bit of seaweed, now it was a group of gulls clamouring
over a dead fish, now a purple star-fish, now a breaker
of unusual size. Her splendid vitality carried her away.
She was excited, alive to her very finger-tips, vibrant to
the least sensation, quivering to the least impression.

"Let's get up here and sit down somewhere," said
Condy, at length.

They left the beach and climbed up the slope of the
hills, near a point where a long arm of land thrust out
into the sea and shut off the wind; a path was there, and
they followed it for a few yards, till they had come to a
little amphitheatre surrounded with blackberry bushes.

Here they sat down, Blix settling herself on an old log
with a little sigh of contentment, Condy stretching himself out, a new-lit pipe in his teeth, his head resting on
the little handbag he had persistently carried ever since
morning. Then Blix fell suddenly silent, and for a long
time the two sat there without speaking, absorbed in
the enjoyment of looking at the enormous green hills
rolling down to the sea, the breakers thundering at the
beach, the gashed pinnacles of rock, the vast reach of the
Pacific, and the distant prospect of the old fort at the
entrance of the Golden Gate.

"We might be a thousand miles away from the city,
for all the looks of it, mightn't we, Condy?" said Blix,
after a while. "And I'm that *hungry !* It must be nearly
noon."

For answer, Condy sat up with profound gravity, and
with a great air of nonchalance opened the handbag,
and, instead of shoes, took out, first, a pint bottle of
claret, then "devilish" ham sandwiches in oiled paper,
a bottle of stuffed olives, a great bag of salted almonds,
two little tumblers, a paper-covered novel, and a mouth
organ.

Blix fairly crowed with delight, clasping her hands
upon her knees, and rocking to and fro where she sat
upon the log.

"Oh, Condy, and you thought of a *lunch*—you said
it was shoes—and you remembered I loved stuffed
olives, too; and a book to read. What is it—*The Seven
Seas?* [17] No, I never *was* so happy. But the mouth organ
—what's that for?"

"To play on. What did you think—think it was a can-
opener?"

Blix choked with merriment over his foolery, and
Condy added proudly:

"Look there! *I* made those sandwiches!"

They looked as though he had—great, fat chunks of

bread, the crust still on; the "devilish" ham in thick strata between; and, positively, he had *buttered* the bread. But it was all one with them; they ate as though at a banquet, and Blix even took off her hat and hung it upon one of the near-by bushes. Of course Condy had forgotten a corkscrew. He tried to dig out the cork of the claret bottle with his knife, until he had broken both blades and was about to give up in despair, when Blix, at the end of her patience, took the bottle from him and pushed in the cork with her finger.

"Wine, music, literature, and feasting," observed Condy. "We're getting regularly luxurious, just like Sardineapalus."

But Condy himself had suddenly entered into an atmosphere of happiness, the like of which he had never known or dreamed of before. He loved Blix—he had just discovered it. He loved her because she was so genuine, so radiantly fresh and strong; loved her because she liked the things that he liked, because they two looked at the world from precisely the same point of view, hating shams and affectations, happy in the things that were simple and honest and natural. He loved her because she liked his books, appreciating the things therein that he appreciated, liking what he liked, disapproving of what he condemned. He loved her because she was nineteen, and because she was so young and unspoiled and was happy just because the ocean was blue and the morning fine. He loved her because she was so pretty, because of the softness of her yellow hair, because of her round, white forehead and pink cheeks, because of her little, dark-brown eyes, with that look in them as if she were just done smiling or just about to smile, one could not say which; loved her because of her good, firm mouth and chin, because of her full neck and its high, tight bands of white satin. And he loved her because her arms were strong and round, and because she

232

wore the great dog-collar around her trim, firm-corseted waist, and because there emanated from her with every movement a barely perceptible, delicious, feminine odour, that was in part perfume, but mostly a subtle, vague aroma, charming beyond words, that came from her mouth, her hair, her neck, her arms, her whole sweet personality. And he loved her because she was herself, because she was Blix, because of that strange, sweet influence that was disengaged from her in those quiet moments when she seemed so close to him, when some unnamed, mysterious, sixth sense in him stirred and woke and told him of her goodness, of her clean purity and womanliness; and that certain, vague tenderness in him went out toward her, a tenderness not for her only, but for all the good things of the world; and he felt his nobler side rousing up and the awakening of the desire to be his better self.

Covertly he looked at her, as she sat near him, her yellow hair rolling and blowing back from her forehead, her hands clasped over her knee, looking out over the ocean, thoughtful, her eyes wide.

She had told him she did not love him. Condy remembered that perfectly well. She was sincere in the matter; she did not love him. That subject had been once and for all banished from their intercourse. And it was because of that very reason that their companion-ship of the last three or four months had been so charm-ing. She looked upon him merely as a chum. She had not changed in the least from that time until now, whereas he—why, all his world was new for him that morning! Why, he loved her so, she had become so dear to him, that the very thought of her made his heart swell and leap.

But he must keep all this to himself. If he spoke to her, told her of how he loved her, it would spoil and end their companionship upon the instant. They had both agreed upon that; they had tried the other, and it had worked out. As lovers they had wearied of each other; as chums they had been perfectly congenial, thoroughly and completely happy.

Condy set his teeth. It was a hard situation. He must choose between bringing an end to this charming comradeship of theirs, or else fight back all show of love for her, keep it down and under hand, and that at a time when every nerve of him quivered like a smitten harpstring. It was not in him or in his temperament to love her calmly, quietly, or at a distance; he wanted the touch of her hand, the touch of her cool, smooth cheek, the delicious aroma of her breath in his nostrils, her lips against his, her hair and all its fragrance in his face.

"Condy, what's the matter?" Blix was looking at him with an expression of no little concern. "What are you frowning so about, and clinching your fists? And you're pale, too. What's gone wrong?"

He shot a glance at her, and bestirred himself sharply.

"Isn't this a jolly little corner?" he said. "Blix, how long is it before you go?"

"Six weeks from to-morrow."

"And you're going to be gone four years—four years! Maybe you never will come back. Can't tell what will happen in four years. Where's the blooming mouth organ?"

But the mouth organ was full of crumbs. Condy could not play on it. To all his efforts it responded only by gasps, mournfullest death-rattles, and lamentable wails. Condy hurled it into the sea.

"Well, where's the blooming book, then?" he demanded. "You're sitting on it, Blix. Here, read something in it. Open it anywhere."

"No; you read to me."

"I will not. Haven't I done enough! Didn't I *buy* the book and get the lunch, and make the sandwiches, and pay the car fare. I think this expedition will cost me pretty near three dollars before we're through with the day. No; the least you can do is to read to me. Here, we'll match for it."

Condy drew a dime from his pocket, and Blix a quarter from her purse.

"You're matching *me*," she said.

Condy tossed the coin and lost, and Blix said, as he picked up the book:

"For a man that has such unvarying bad luck as you, gambling is just simple madness. You and I have never played a game of poker yet that I've not won every cent of money you had."

"Yes; and what are you doing with it all?"

"Spending it," she returned loftily; "gloves and veils and lace pins—all kinds of things."

But Condy knew the way she spoke that this was not true.

For the next hour or so he read to her from *The Seven Seas*, while the afternoon passed, the wind stirring the chaparral and blackberry bushes in the hollows of the huge, bare hills, the surf rolling and grumbling on the beach below, the sea-birds wheeling overhead. Blix listened intently, but Condy could not have told of what he was reading. Living was better than reading, life was better than literature, and his new-found love for her was poetry enough for him. He read so that he might not talk to her or look at her, for it seemed to him at times as though some second self in him would speak and betray him in spite of his best efforts. Never before in all his life had he been so happy; never before had he been so troubled. He began to jumble the lines and words as he read, overrunning periods, even turning two pages at once.

"What a splendid line!" Blix exclaimed.

"What line—what—what are you talking about?

Blix, let's always remember to-day. Let's make a promise, no matter what happens or where we are, let's always write to each other on the anniversary of to-day.
What do you say?"

"Yes; I'll promise—and you——"

"I'll promise faithfully. Oh, I'll never forget to-day
nor—yes, yes; I'll promise—why, to-day—Blix—where's
that damn book gone?"

"Condy!"

"Well, I can't find the book. You're sitting on it
again. Confound the book, anyway! Let's walk some
more."

"We've a long ways to go if we're to get home in time
for supper. Let's go to Luna's for supper."

"I never saw such a girl as you to think of ways for
spending money. What kind of a purse-proud plutocrat
do you think I am? I've only seventy-five cents left.
How much have you got?"

Blix had fifty-five cents in her purse, and they had a
grave council over their finances. They had just enough
for carfare and two "suppers Mexican," with ten cents
left over.

"That's for Richard's tip," said Blix.

"That's for my *cigar*," he retorted.

"You made *me* give him fifty cents. You said it was
the least I could offer him—*noblesse oblige*."

"Well, then, I *couldn't* offer him a dime, don't you
see? I'll tell him we are broke this time."

They started home, not as they had come, but climbing the hill and going on across a breezy open down,
radiant with blue iris, wild heliotrope, yellow poppies,
and even a violet here and there. A little farther on they
gained one of the roads of the Reservation, red earth
smooth as a billiard table; and just at an angle where
the road made a sharp elbow and trended cityward, they
paused for a moment and looked down and back at the

superb view of the ocean, the vast half-moon of land, and the rolling hills in the foreground tumbling down toward the beach and all spangled with wild flowers.

Some fifteen minutes later they reached the golf links.

"We can go across the links," said Condy, "and strike any number of car lines on the other side."

They left the road and struck across the links, Condy smoking his new-lit pipe. But as they came around the edge of a long line of eucalyptus trees near the teeing ground, a warning voice suddenly called out:

"Fore!"

Condy and Blix looked up sharply, and there in a group not twenty feet away, in tweeds and "knickers," in smart, short golfing skirts and plaid cloaks, they saw young Sargeant and his sister, two other girls whom they knew as members of the fashionable "set," and Jack Carter in the act of swinging his driving iron.

CHAPTER XI

AS THE clock in the library of the club struck midnight, Condy laid down his pen, shoved the closely written sheets of paper from him, and leaned back in his chair, his fingers to his tired eyes. He was sitting at a desk in one of the farther corners of the room and shut off by a great Japanese screen. He was in his shirtsleeves, his hair was tumbled, his fingers ink-stained, and his face a little pale.

Since late in the evening he had been steadily writing. Three chapters of *In Defiance of Authority* were done, and he was now at work on the fourth. The day after the excursion to the Presidio—that wonderful event which seemed to Condy to mark the birthday of some new man within him—the idea had suddenly occurred to him that Captain Jack's story of the club of the exiles, the boom restaurant, and the filibustering expedition was precisely the novel of adventure of which the Centennial Company had spoken. At once he had set to work upon it, with an enthusiasm that, with shut teeth, he declared would not be lacking in energy. The story would have to be written out of his business hours. That meant he would have to give up his evenings to it. But he had done this, and for nearly a week had settled himself to his task in the quiet corner of the club at eight o'clock, and held to it resolutely until twelve.

The first two chapters had run off his pen with delightful ease. The third came harder; the events and incidents of the story became confused and contradictory; the character of Billy Isham obstinately refused to take the prominent place which Condy had designed for him; and with the beginning of the fourth chapter, Condy had finally come to know the enormous difficulties, the exasperating complications, the discouragements that begin anew with every paragraph, the obstacles that refuse to be surmounted, and all the pain, the labour, the downright mental travail and anguish that fall to the lot of the writer of novels.

To write a short story with the end in plain sight from the beginning was an easy matter compared to the upbuilding, grain by grain, atom by atom, of the fabric of *In Defiance of Authority*. Condy soon found that there was but one way to go about the business. He must shut his eyes to the end of his novel—that far-off, divine event—and take his task chapter by chapter, even paragraph by paragraph; grinding out the tale, as it were, by main strength, driving his pen from line to line, hating the effort, happy only with the termination of each chapter, and working away, hour by hour, minute by minute, with the dogged, sullen, hammer-and-tongs obstinacy of the galley-slave, scourged to his daily toil.

At times the tale, apparently out of sheer perversity, would come to a full stop. To write another word seemed beyond the power of human ingenuity, and for an hour or more Condy would sit scowling at the half-written page, gnawing his nails, scouring his hair, dipping his pen into the ink-well, and squaring himself to the sheet of paper, all to no purpose.

There was no pleasure in it for him. A character once fixed in his mind, a scene once pictured in his imagination, and even before he had written a word the character lost the charm of its novelty, the scene the freshness of its original conception. Then, with infinite painstaking and with a patience little short of miraculous, he must slowly build up, brick by brick, the plan his brain had outlined in a single instant. It was all work—hard, disagreeable, laborious work; and no juggling with phrases, no false notions as to the "delight of creation," could make it appear otherwise. "And for what," he muttered as he rose, rolled up his sheaf of manuscript, and put on his coat; "what do I do it for, *I* don't know."

It was beyond question that, had he begun his novel three months before this time, Condy would have long since abandoned the hateful task. But Blix had changed all that. A sudden male force had begun to develop in Condy. A master-emotion had shaken him, and he had commenced to see and to feel the serious, more abiding, and perhaps the sterner side of life. Blix had steadied him, there was no denying that. He was not quite the same boyish, harebrained fellow who had made "a buffoon of himself" in the Chinese restaurant, three months before.

The cars had stopped running by the time Condy reached the street. He walked home and flung himself to bed, his mind tired, his nerves unstrung, and all the blood of his body apparently concentrated in his brain. Working at night after writing all day long was telling upon him, and he knew it.

What with his work and his companionship with Blix, Condy soon began to drop out of his wonted place in his "set." He was obliged to decline one invitation after another that would take him out in the evening, and instead of lunching at his club with Sargeant or George Hands, as he had been accustomed to do at one time, he fell into another habit of lunching with Blix at the flat on Washington Street, and spending the two hours allowed to him in the middle of the day in her company.

Condy's desertion of them was often spoken of by the men of his club with whom he had been at one time so intimate, and the subject happened to be brought up again one noon when Jack Carter was in the club as

George Hands's guest.. Hands, Carter, and Eckert were at one of the windows over their after-dinner cigars and liqueurs.

"I say," said Eckert suddenly, "who's that girl across the street there—the one in black, just going by that furrier's sign? I've seen her somewhere before. Know who it is?"

"That's Miss Bessemer, isn't it?" said George Hands, leaning forward. "Rather a stunning-looking girl."

"Yes, that's Travis Bessemer," assented Jack Carter; adding, a moment later, "It's too bad about that girl."

"What's the matter?" asked Eckert.

Carter lifted a shoulder. "Isn't *anything* the matter as far as I know, only somehow the best people have dropped her. She *used* to be received everywhere."

"Come to think, I *haven't* seen her out much this season," said Eckert. "But I heard she had bolted from 'Society' with the big S, and was going East— going to study medicine, I believe."

"I've always noticed," said Carter, with a smile, "that so soon as a girl is *déclassée*, she develops a purpose in life, and gets earnest, and all that sort of thing."

"Oh, well, come," growled George Hands. "Travis Bessemer is not *déclassée*."

"I didn't say she was," answered Carter; "but she has made herself talked about a good deal lately. Going around with Rivers, as she does, isn't the most discreet thing in the world. Of course it's all right, but it all makes talk; and I came across them by a grove of trees out on the links the other day——"

"Yes" observed Sargeant, leaning on the back of Carter's armchair; "yes; and I noticed, too, that she cut you dead. You fellows should have been there," he went on, in perfect good humour, turning to the others. "You missed a good little scene. Rivers and Miss Bessemer had been taking a tramp over the Reservation

—and, by the way, it's a great place to walk, so my sister tells me; she and Dick Forsythe take a constitutional out there every Saturday morning—well, as I was saying, Rivers and Miss Bessemer came upon our party rather unexpectedly. We were all togged out in our golfing bags, and I presume we looked more like tailors' models, posing for the gallery, than people who were taking an outing; but Rivers and Miss Bessemer had been regularly exercising; looked as though they had done their fifteen miles since morning. They had their old clothes on, and they were dusty and muddy.

"You would have thought that a young girl such as Miss Bessemer is—for she's very young—would have been a little embarrassed at running up against such a spick-and-span lot as we were. Not a bit of it; didn't lose her poise for a moment. She bowed to my sister and to me, as though from the top of a drag, by Jove! and as though she were fresh from Redfern and Virot.[18] You know a girl that can manage herself that way is a thoroughbred. She even remembered to cut little Johnnie Carter here, because Johnnie forced himself upon her one night at a dance when he was drunk; didn't she, Johnnie? Johnnie came up to her there, out on the links, fresh as a daisy, and put out his hand, with, 'Why, how do you do, Miss Bessemer?' and 'wherever did you come from?' and 'I haven't seen you in so long'; and she says, 'No, not since our last dance, I believe, Mr. Carter,' and looked at his hand as though it was something funny.

"Little Johnnie mumbled and flushed and stammered and backed off; and it was well that he did, because Rivers had begun to get red around the wattles. *I* say the little girl is a thoroughbred, and my sister wants to give her a dinner as soon as she comes out. But Johnnie says she's *déclassée*, so maybe my sister had better think it over."

"I didn't say she was *déclassée*," exclaimed Carter. "I only said she would do well to be more careful."

Sargeant shifted his cigar to the other corner of his mouth, one eye shut to avoid the smoke.

"One might say as much of lots of people," he answered.

"I don't like your tone!" Carter flared out.

"Oh, go to the devil, Johnnie! Shall we all have a drink?"

On the Friday evening of that week, Condy set himself to his work at his accustomed hour. But he had had a hard day on the *Times* Supplement, and his brain, like an overdriven horse, refused to work. In half an hour he had not written a paragraph.

"I thought it would be better, in the end, to loaf for one evening," he explained to Blix, some twenty minutes later, as they settled themselves in the little dining room. "I can go at it better to-morrow. See how you like this last chapter."

Blix was enthusiastic over *In Defiance of Authority*. Condy had told her the outline of the story, and had read to her each chapter as he finished it.

"It's the best thing you have ever done, Condy, and you know it. I suppose it has faults, but I don't care anything about them. It's the story itself that's so interesting. After that first chapter of the boom restaurant and the exiles' club, nobody would want to lay the book down. You're doing the best work of your life so far, and you stick to it."

"It's grinding out copy for the Supplement at the same time that takes all the starch out of me. You've no idea what it means to write all day, and then sit down and write all evening."

"I *wish* you could get off the *Times*," said Blix. "You're just giving the best part of your life to hack work, and *now* it's interfering with your novel. I know you could do better work on your novel if you didn't have to work on the *Times*, couldn't you?"

"Oh, if you come to that, of course I could," he answered. "But they won't give me a vacation. I was sounding the editor on it day before yesterday. No; I'll have to manage somehow to swing the two together.

"Well, let's not talk shop now, Condy. You need a rest. Do you want to play poker?"

They played for upward of an hour that evening, and Condy, as usual, lost. His ill-luck was positively astonishing. During the last two months he had played poker with Blix on an average of three or four evenings in the week, and at the close of every game it was Blix who had all the chips.

Blix had come to know the game quite as well, if not better, than he. She could almost invariably tell when Condy held a good hand, but on her part could assume an air of indifference absolutely inscrutable.

"Cards?" said Condy, picking up the deck after the deal.

"I'll stand pat, Condy."

"The deuce you say," he answered, with a stare. "I'll take three."

"I'll pass it up to you," continued Blix gravely.

"Well—well, I'll bet you five chips."

"Raise you twenty."

Condy studied his hand, laid down the cards, picked them up again, scratched his head, and moved uneasily in his place. Then he threw down two high pairs.

"No," he said; "I won't see you. What did you have? Let's see, just for the fun of it."

Blix spread her cards on the table.

"Not a blessed thing!" exclaimed Condy. "I might have known it. There's my last dollar gone, too. Lend me fifty cents, Blix."

Blix shook her head.

"Why, what a little niggard!" he exclaimed aggrievedly. "I'll pay them all back to you."

"Now, why should I lend you money to play against me? I'll not give you a chip; and, besides, I don't want to play any more. Let's stop."

"I've a mind to stop for good; stop playing even with you."

Blix gave a little cry of joy.

"Oh, Condy, will you, could you? and never, never touch a card again? never play for money? I'd be so happy—but don't, unless you know you would keep your promise. I would much rather have you play every night, down there at your club, than break your promise."

Condy fell silent, biting thoughtfully at the knuckle of a forefinger.

"Think twice about it, Condy," urged Blix; "because this would be for always."

Condy hesitated; then, abstractedly and as though speaking to himself:

"It's different now. Before we took that—three months ago, I don't say. It was harder for me to quit then, but now—well, everything is different now; and it would please you, Blixy!"

"More than anything else I can think of, Condy."

He gave her his hand.

"That settles it," he said quietly. "I'll never gamble again, Blix."

Blix gripped his hand hard, then jumped up, and, with a quick breath of satisfaction, gathered up the cards and chips and flung them into the fireplace.

"Oh, I'm so glad that's over with," she exclaimed, her little eyes dancing. "I've pretended to like it, but I've hated it all the time. You don't know *how* I've hated it! What men can see in it to make them sit up all night long is beyond me. And you truly mean, Condy, that you never will gamble again? Yes, I know you mean it this time. Oh, I'm so happy I could sing!"

"Good Heavens, don't do that!" he cried quickly. "You're a nice, amiable girl, Blix, even if you're not pretty, and you——"

"Oh, bother you!" she retorted; "but you promise?"

"On my honour."

"That's enough," she said quietly.

But even when "loafing," as he was this evening, Condy could not rid himself of the thought and recollection of his novel; resting or writing, it haunted him. Otherwise he would not have been the story-writer that he was. From now on until he should set down the last sentence, the "thing" was never to let him alone, never to allow him a moment's peace. He could think of nothing else, could talk of nothing else; every faculty of his brain, every sense of observation or imagination incessantly concentrated themselves upon this one point.

As they sat in the bay window watching the moon rise, his mind was still busy with it, and he suddenly broke out:

"I ought to work some kind of a *treasure* into the yarn. What's a story of adventure without a treasure? By Jove, Blix, I wish I could give my whole time to this stuff! It's ripping good material, and it ought to be handled as carefully as glass. Ought to be worked up, you know."

"Condy," said Blix, looking at him intently, "what is it stands in your way of leaving the *Times?* Would they take you back if you left them long enough to write your novel? You could write it in a month, couldn't you, if you had nothing else to do? Suppose you left them for a month—would they hold your place for you?"

"Yes—yes, I think they would; but in the meanwhile, Blix—there's the rub. I've never saved a cent out of my salary. When I stop, my pay stops, and wherewithal would I be fed? What are you looking for in that drawer—matches? Here, I've got a match."

Blix faced about at the sideboard, shutting the drawer by leaning against it. In both hands she held one of the delft sugar-bowls. She came up to the table, and emptied its contents upon the blue denim tablecover—two or three gold pieces, some fifteen silver dollars, and a handful of small change.

Disregarding all Condy's inquiries, she counted it, making little piles of the gold and silver and nickel pieces.

"Thirty-five and seven is forty-two," she murmured, counting off on her fingers, "and six is forty-eight, and ten is fifty-eight, and ten is sixty-eight; and here is ten, twenty, thirty, fifty-five cents in change." She thrust it all toward him, across the table. "There," she said, "is your wherewithal."

Condy stared. "My wherewithal!" he muttered.

"It ought to be enough for over a month."

"Where did you get all that? Whose is it?"

"It's your money, Condy. You loaned it to me, and now it has come in very handy."

"I *loaned* it to you?"

"It's the money I won from you during the time you've been playing poker with me. You didn't know it would amount to so much, did you?"

"Pshaw, I'll not touch it!" he exclaimed, drawing back from the money as though it was red-hot.

"Yes, you will," she told him. "I've been saving it up for you, Condy, every penny of it, from the first day we played down there at the lake; and I always told myself that the moment you made up your mind to quit playing, I would give it back to you."

"Why, the very idea!" he vociferated, his hands deep

man's woman

X

BLIX

in his pockets, his face scarlet. "It's—it's preposterous, Blix! I won't let you *talk* about it even—I won't touch a nickel of that money. But, Blix, you're—you're—the finest woman I ever knew. You're a *man's* woman, that's what you are." He set his teeth. "If you loved a man, you'd be a regular pal to him; you'd back him up, you'd stand by him till the last gun was fired. I could do *anything* if a *woman* like you cared for me. Why, Blix, I —you haven't any idea——" He cleared his throat, stopping abruptly.

"But you must take this money," she answered; "*your* money. If you didn't, Condy, it would make me out nothing more nor less than a gambler. I wouldn't have dreamed of playing cards with you if I had ever intended to keep one penny of your money. From the very start I intended to keep it for you, and give it back to you so soon as you would stop; and now you have a chance to put this money to a good use. You don't have to stay on the *Times* now. You can't do your novel justice while you are doing your hack work at the same time, and I do so want *In Defiance of Authority* to be a success. I've faith in you, Condy. I know if you got the opportunity you would make a success."

"But you and I have played like two men playing," exclaimed Condy. "How would it look if Sargeant, say, should give me back the money he had won from me? What a cad I would be to take it!"

"That's just it—we've not played like two men. Then I *would* have been a gambler. I've played with you because I thought it would make a way for you to break off with the habit; and knowing as I did how fond you were of playing cards and how bad it was for you, how wicked it would have been for me to have played with you in any other spirit! Don't you see? And as it has turned out, you've given up playing, and you've enough money to make it possible for you to

248

write your novel. The Centennial Company have asked you to try a story of adventure for them, you've found one that is splendid, you're just the man who could handle it, and now you've got the money to make it possible. Condy," she exclaimed suddenly, "don't you see your *chance?* Aren't you a big enough man to see your chance when it comes? And, besides, do you think I would take *money* from you? Can't you understand? If you don't take this money that belongs to you, you would insult me. That is just the way I would feel about it. You must see that. If you care for me at all, you'll take it."

.   .   .   .

The editor of the Sunday Supplement put his tooth-pick behind his ear and fixed Condy with his eyeglasses.

"Well, it's like this, Rivers," he said. "Of course you know your own business best. If you stay on here with us, it will be all right. But I may as well tell you that I don't believe I can hold your place for a month. I can't get a man in here to do your work for just a month, and then fire him out at the end of that time. I don't like to lose you, but if you have an opportunity to get in on another paper during this vacation of yours, you're at liberty to do so, for all of me."

"Then you think my chance of coming back here would be pretty slim if I leave for a month now?"

"That's right."

There was a silence. Condy hesitated; then he rose.

"I'll take the chance," he announced.

To Blix that evening, as he told her of the affair, he said:

"It's neck or nothing now, Blix."

CHAPTER XII

Bur did Blix care for him?

In the retired corner of his club, shut off by the Japanese screen, or going up and down the city to and from his work, or sitting with her in the bay window of the little dining room looking down upon the city, blurred in the twilight or radiant with the sunset, Condy asked himself the question. A score of times each day he came to a final, definite, negative decision; and a score of times reopened the whole subject. Beyond the fact that Blix had enjoyed herself in his company during the last months, Condy could find no sign or trace of encouragement; and for that matter he told himself that the indications pointed rather in the other direction. She had no compunction in leaving him to go away to New York, perhaps never to return. In less than a month now all their companionship was to end, and he would probably see the last of her.

He dared not let her know that at last he had really come to love her—that it was no pretence now; for he knew that with such declaration their "good times" would end even before she should go away. But every day, every hour that they were together made it harder for him to keep himself within bounds.

What with this trouble on his mind and the grim determination with which he held to his work, Condy changed rapidly. Blix had steadied him, and a certain earnestness and seriousness of purpose, a certain *strength* he had not known before, came swiftly into being.

Was Blix to go away, leave him, perhaps for all time,

250

and not know how much he cared? Would he speak
before she went? Condy did not know. It was a question
that circumstances would help him to decide. He would
not speak, so he resolved, unless he was sure that she
cared herself; and if she did, she herself would give him
a cue, a hint whereon to speak. But days went by, the
time set for Blix's departure drew nearer and nearer,
and yet she gave him not the slightest sign.

These two interests had now absorbed his entire life
for the moment—his love for Blix, and his novel. Little
by little *In Defiance of Authority* took shape. The
boom restaurant and the club of the exiles were disposed of, Billy Isham began to come to the front, the
filibustering expedition and Señora Estrada (with
her torn calling card) had been introduced, and the
expedition was ready to put to sea. But here a new
difficulty was encountered.

"What do I know about ships?" Condy confessed to
Blix. "If Billy Isham is going to command a filibustering schooner, I've got to know something about a
schooner—appear to, anyhow. I've got to know nautical
lingo, the *real* thing, you know. I don't believe a *real*
sailor ever in his life said 'belay there,' or 'avast.' We'll
have to go out and see Captain Jack; get some more
technical detail."

This move was productive of the most delightful
results. Captain Jack was all on fire with interest the
moment that Condy and Blix told him of the idea.

"An' you're going to put Billy Isham in a book.
Well, strike me straight, that's a snorkin' good idea!
I've always said that all Billy needed was a ticket
seller an' an advance agent, an' he was a whole show in
himself."

"We're going to send it East," said Blix, "as soon as
it's finished, and have it published."

"Well, it ought to make prime readin', miss; an'"

BLIX

that's a good fetchin' title, *In Defiance of Authority*."

Regularly Wednesday and Sunday afternoons, Blix and Condy came out to the life-boat station. Captain Jack received them in sweater and visored cap, and ushered them into the front room.

"Well, how's the yarn getting on?" Captain Jack would ask.

Then Condy would read the last chapter while the Captain paced the floor, frowning heavily, smoking cigars, listening to every word. Condy told the story in the first person, as if Billy Isham's partner were narrating scenes and events in which he himself had moved. Condy called this protagonist "Burke Cassowan," and was rather proud of the name. But the Captain would none of it. Cassowan, the protagonist, was simply "Our Mug."

"Now," Condy would say, notebook in hand, "now, Cap., we've got down to Mazatlan. Now I want to sort of organize the expedition in this next chapter."

"I see, I see," Captain Jack would exclaim, interested at once. "Wait a bit till I take off my shoes. I can think better with my shoes off"; and having removed his shoes, he would begin to pace the room in his stocking feet, puffing fiercely on his cigar as he warmed to the tale, blowing the smoke out through either ear, gesturing savagely, his face flushed and his eyes kindling.

"Well, now, lessee. First thing Our Mug does when he gets to Mazatlan is to communicate his arrival to Señora Estrada—telegraphs, you know; and, by the way, have him use a cipher."

"What kind of cipher?"

"Count three letters on from the right letter, see. If you were spelling 'boat,' for instance, you would begin with an *e*, the third letter after *b*; then *r* for the *o*, *r* being the third letter from *o*. So you'd spell 'boat,' *erdw;* and Señora Estrada knows when she gets that

252

dispatch that she must count three letters *back* from each letter to get the right ones. Take now such a cipher word as *ulioh*. That means *rifle*. Count three letters back from each letter of *ulioh*, and it'll spell *rifle*. You can make up a lot of dispatches like that, just to have the thing look natural; savvy?"

"Out of sight!" muttered Condy, making a note.

"Then Our Mug and Billy Isham start getting a crew. And Our Mug, he buys the sextant there in Mazatlan—the sextant, that got out of order and spoiled everything. Or, no; don't have it a sextant; have it a quadrant—an old-fashioned, ebony quadrant. Have Billy Isham buy it because it was cheap."

"How did it get out of order, Captain Jack?" inquired Blix. "That would be a good technical detail, wouldn't it, Condy?"

"Well, it's like this. Our Mug an' Billy get a schooner that's so bally small that they have to do their cooking in the cabin; quadrant's on a rack over the stove, and the heat warps the joints, so when Our Mug takes his observation he gets fifty miles off his course and raises the land where the government forces are watching for him."

"And here's another point, Cap.," said Condy. "We ought to work some kind of a treasure into this yarn; can't you think up something new and original in the way of a treasure? I don't want the old game of a buried chest of money. Let's have him get track of something that's worth a fortune—something novel."

"Yes, yes; I see the idea," answered the Captain, striding over the floor with great thuds of his stockinged feet. "Now, lessee; let me think." He began, rubbing all his hair the wrong way. "We want something new and queer, something that ain't ever been written up before. I tell you what! Here it is! Have Our Mug get wind of a little river schooner that sunk fifty years before his time in one of the big South American rivers, during a flood—I heard of this myself. Schooner went down and was buried twenty feet under mud and sand; and since that time—you know how the big rivers act— the whole blessed course of the river has changed at that point, and that schooner is on dry land, or rather twenty feet under it, and as sound as the day she chartered."

"Well?"

"Well, have it that when she sank she had aboard of her a cargo of five hundred cases of whiskey, prime stuff, seven thousand quart bottles, sealed up tight as drums. Now Our Mug—nor Billy Isham, either—they ain't born yesterday. No, sir; they're right next to themselves! They figure this way. This here whiskey's been kept fifty years without being moved. Now, what do you suppose seven thousand quart bottles of fifty-year-old whiskey would be worth? Why, twenty dollars a quart wouldn't be too fancy. So there you are; there's your treasure. Our Mug and Billy Isham have only got to dig through twenty feet of sand to pick up a hundred thousand dollars, *if they can find the schooner.*"

Blix clapped her hands with a little cry of delight, and Condy smote a knee, exclaiming:

"By Jove! that's as good as Loudon Dodds' opium ship! [19] Why Cap., you're a treasure in yourself for a fellow looking for stories."

Then after the notes were taken and the story talked over, Captain Jack, especially if the day happened to be Sunday, would insist upon their staying to dinner— boiled beef and cabbage, smoking coffee and pickles— that K. D. B. served in the little, brick-paved kitchen in the back of the station. The crew messed in their quarters overhead.

K. D. B. herself was not uninteresting. Her respectability encased her like armour plate, and she never laughed without putting three fingers to her lips. She told them that she had at one time been a "costume reader."

"A costume reader?"

"Yes; reading extracts from celebrated authors in the appropriate costume of the character. It used to pay very well, and it was very refined. I used to do 'In a Balcony,' by Mister Browning, and 'Laska,' the same evening, and it always made a hit. I'd do 'In a Balcony,' first, and I'd put on a Louis-Quinze-the-fifteenth gown and wig-to-match over a female cowboy outfit. When I'd finished 'In a Balcony,' I'd do an exit, and shunt the gown and wig-to-match, and come on as 'Laska,' with thunder noises off. It was one of the strongest effects in my repertoire, and it always got me a curtain call." [20]

And Captain Jack would wag his head and murmur: "Extraordinary! extraordinary!"

Blix and Condy soon noted that upon the occasion of each one of their visits, K. D. B. found means to entertain them at great length with long discussions upon certain subjects of curiously diversified character. Upon their first visit she elected to talk upon the Alps mountains. The Sunday following it was bacteriology; on the next Wednesday it was crystals; while for two hours during their next visit to the station, Condy and Blix were obliged to listen to K. D. B.'s interminable discourse on the origin, history, and development of the kingdom of Denmark. Condy was dumbfounded.

"I never met such a person, man or woman, in all my life. Talk about education! Why, I think she knows everything!"

In Defiance of Authority soon began to make good progress, but Condy, once launched upon technical navigation, must have Captain Jack at his elbow continually, to keep him from foundering. In some sea novel he remembered to have come across the expression "garboard streak," and from the context guessed it was to be applied to a detail of a vessel's construction. In an unguarded moment he had written that his schooner's name "was painted in showy gilt letters upon her garboard streak."

"What's the garboard streak, Condy?" Blix had asked, when he had read the chapter to her.

"That's where they paint her name," he declared promptly. "I don't know exactly, but I like the sound of it."

But the next day, when he was reading this same chapter to Captain Jack, the latter suddenly interrupted with an exclamation as of acute physical anguish.

"What's that? Read that last over again," he demanded.

"'When they had come within a few boats' lengths,'" read Condy, "'they were able to read the schooner's name, painted in showy gilt letters upon her garboard streak.'"

"My God!" gasped the Captain, clasping his head. Then, with a shout: "Garboard streak! garboard streak! Don't you know that the garboard streak is the last plank next the keel? You mean *counter*, not garboard streak. That regularly gravelled me, that did!"

They stayed to dinner with the couple that afternoon, and for half an hour afterward K. D. B. told them of the wonders of the caves of Elephanta. One would have believed that she had actually been at the place. But when she changed the subject to the science of fortification, Blix could no longer restrain herself.

"But it is really wonderful that you should know all these things! Where *did* you find time to study so much?"

"One must have an education," returned K. D. B. primly.

But Condy had caught sight of a half-filled book-
shelf against the opposite wall, and had been suddenly
smitten with an inspiration. On a leaf of his notebook
he wrote: "Try her on the G's and H's," and found
means to show it furtively to Blix. But Blix was puzzled,
and at the earliest opportunity Condy himself said to
the retired costume reader:

"Speaking of fortifications, Mrs. Hoskins, Gibraltar
now—that's a wonderful rock, isn't it?"

"Rock!" she queried. "I thought it was an island."

"Oh, no; it's a fortress. They have a castle there—a
castle, something like—well, like the old Schloss at
Heidelberg. Did you ever hear about or read about
Heidelberg University?"

But K. D. B. was all abroad now. Gibraltar and
Heidelberg were unknown subjects to her as were also
inoculation, Japan, and Kosciusko. Above the H's
she was sound; below that point her ignorance was
benighted.

"But what is it, Condy?" demanded Blix, as soon as
they were alone.

"I've the idea," he answered, chuckling. "Wait till
after Sunday to see if I'm right; then I'll tell you. It's a
dollar to a paper dime, K. D. B. will have something for
us by Sunday, beginning with an I."

And she had. It was Internal Revenue.

"Right! right!" Condy shouted gleefully, as he and
Blix were on their way home. "I knew it. She's done
with Ash—Bol, Bol—Car, and all those, and has
worked through Cod—Dem, and Dem—Eve. She's
down to Hor—Kin now, and she'll go through the whole
lot before she's done: Kin—Mag, Mag—Mot, Mot—
Pal, and all the rest."

"The Encyclopædia?"

"Don't you see it? No wonder she didn't know beans

about Gibraltar! She hadn't come to the G's by then."

"She's reading the Encyclopædia."

"And she gets the volumes on the instalment plan, don't you see? Reads the heading articles, and then springs 'em on us. To know things and talk about 'em, that's her idea of being cultured. 'One must have an education.' Do you remember her saying that? Oh, our matrimonial objects are panning out beyond all expectation!"

What a delicious, never-to-be-forgotten month it was for those two! There in the midst of life they were as much alone as upon a tropic island. Blix had deliberately freed herself from a world that had grown distasteful to her; Condy little by little had dropped away from his place among the men and the women of his acquaintance, and the two came and went together, living in a little world of their own creation, happy in each other's society, living only in the present, and asking nothing better than to be left alone and to their own devices.

They saw each other every day. In the morning from nine till twelve, and in the afternoon until three, Condy worked away upon his novel; but not an evening passed that did not see him and Blix in the dining room of the little flat. Thursdays and Sunday afternoons they visited the life-boat station, and at other times prowled about the unfrequented corners of the city, now passing an afternoon along the water-front, watching the departure of a China steamer or the loading of the great, steel wheat-ships; now climbing the ladder-like streets of Telegraph Hill, or revisiting the Plaza, Chinatown, and the restaurant; or taking long walks in the Presidio Reservation, watching cavalry and artillery drills; or sitting for hours on the rocks by the seashore, watching the ceaseless roll and plunge of the surf, the wheeling sea-birds, and the sleek-headed seals hunting the off-shore fish, happy for a half-hour when they surprised one with his prey in his teeth.

One day, some three weeks before the end of the year, toward two in the afternoon, Condy sat in his usual corner of the club, behind the screen, writing rapidly. His coat was off and the stump of a cigar was between his teeth. At his elbow was the rectangular block of his manuscript. During the last week the story had run from him with a facility that had surprised and delighted him; words came to him without effort, ranging themselves into line with the promptitude of well-drilled soldiery; sentences and paragraphs marched down the clean-swept spaces of his paper like companies and platoons defiling upon review; his chapters were brigades that he marshalled at will, falling them in one behind the other, each preceded by its chapter head, like an officer in the space between two divisions. In the guise of a commander-in-chief sitting his horse upon an eminence that overlooked the field of operations, Condy at last took in the entire situation at a glance, and, with the force and precision of a machine, marched his forces straight to the goal he had set for himself so long a time before.

Then at length he took a fresh penful of ink, squared his elbows, drew closer to the desk, and with a single swift spurt of the pen wrote the last line of his novel, dropping the pen upon the instant and pressing the blotter over the words as though setting a seal of approval upon the completed task.

"There!" he muttered, between his teeth; "I've done for *you!*"

That same afternoon he read the last chapter to Blix, and she helped him to prepare the manuscript for expressage. She insisted that it should go off that very day, and herself wrote the directions upon the outside wrapper. Then the two went down together to the Wells

Fargo office, and *In Defiance of Authority* was sent on its journey across the continent.

"Now," she said, as they came out of the express office and stood for a moment upon the steps, "now there's nothing to do but wait for the Centennial Company. I do so hope we'll get their answer before I go away. They *ought* to take it. It's just what they asked for. Don't you think they'll take it, Condy?"

"Oh, bother that!" answered Condy. "I don't care whether they take it or not. How long now is it before you go, Blix?"

A WEEK passed; then another. The year was coming to a close. In ten days Blix would be gone. Letters had been received from Aunt Kihm, and also an exquisite black leather travelling-case, a present to her niece, full of cut-glass bottles, ebony-backed brushes, and shell combs. Blix was to leave on the second day of January. In the meanwhile she had been reading far into her first-year text-books, underscoring and annotating, studying for hours upon such subjects as she did not understand, so that she might get hold of her work the readier when it came to classroom routine and lectures. Hers was a temperament admirably suited to the study she had chosen—self-reliant, cool, and robust.

But it was not easy for her to go. Never before had Blix been away from her home; never for longer than a week had she been separated from her father, nor from Howard and Snooky. That huge city upon the Atlantic seaboard, with its vast, fierce life, where beat the heart of the nation, and where beyond Aunt Kihm she knew no friend, filled Blix with a vague sense of terror and of oppression. She was going out into a new life, a life of work and of study, a harsher life than she had yet known. Her father, her friends, her home—all these were to be left behind. It was not surprising that Blix should be daunted at the prospect of so great a change in her life, now so close at hand. But if the tears did start at times, no one ever saw them fall, and with a courage that was all her own Blix watched the last days of the year trooping past, and the approach of the New Year that was to begin the new life.

But Condy was thoroughly unhappy. Those wonderful three months were at an end. Blix was going. In less than a week now she would be gone. He would see the last of her. Then what? He pictured himself—when he had said good-bye to her and the train had lessened to a smoky blur in the distance—facing about, facing the life that must then begin for him, returning to the city alone, picking up the routine again. There would be nothing to look forward to then; he would not see Blix in the afternoon; would not sit with her in the evening in the little dining room of the flat overlooking the city and the bay; would not wake in the morning with the consciousness that before the sun would set he would see her again, be with her, and hear the sound of her voice. The months that were to follow would be one long ache, one long, harsh, colourless grind without her. How was he to get through that first evening that he must pass alone? And she did not care for him. Condy at last knew this to be so. Even the poor solace of knowing that she, too, was unhappy was denied him. She had never loved him, and never would. He was a chum to her, nothing more. Condy was too clear-headed to deceive himself upon this point. The time was come for her to go away, and she had given him no sign, no cue.

The last days passed; Blix's trunk was packed, her half section engaged, her ticket bought. They said good-bye to the old places they had come to know so well —Chinatown, the Golden Balcony, the water-front, the lake of San Andreas, Telegraph Hill, and Luna's— and had bidden farewell to Ricardo and to old Richardson. They had left K. D. B. and Captain Jack until the last day. Blix was to go on the second of January. On New Year's Day she and Condy were to take their last walk, were to go out to the life-boat station, and then on around the shore to the little amphitheatre of blackberry bushes—where they had promised always to write one another on the anniversary of their first visit—and then for the last time climb the hill, and go across the breezy downs to the city.

Then came the last day of the old year, the last day but one that they would be together. They spent it in a long ramble along the water-front, following the line of the shipping even as far as Meiggs's wharf. They had come back to the flat for supper, and afterward, as soon as the family had left them alone, had settled themselves in the bay window to watch the New Year in.

The little dining room was dark but for the indistinct blur of light that came in through the window—a light that was a mingling of the afterglow, the new-risen moon, and the faint haze that the city threw off into the sky from its street lamps and electrics. From where they sat they could look down, almost as from a tower, into the city's streets. Here a corner came into view; farther on a great puff of green foliage—palms and pines side by side—overlooked a wall. Here a street was visible for almost its entire length, like a stream of asphalt flowing down the pitch of the hill, dammed on either side by rows upon rows of houses; while farther on the vague confusion of roofs and façades opened out around a patch of green lawn, the garden of some larger residence.

As they looked and watched, the afterglow caught window after window, till all that quarter of the city seemed to stare up at them from a thousand ruddy eyes. The windows seemed infinite in number, the streets endless in their complications; yet everything was deserted. At this hour the streets were empty, and would remain so until daylight. Not a soul was stirring; no face looked from any of those myriads of glowing windows; no footfall disturbed the silence of those asphalt streets. There, almost within call behind those windows, shut off from those empty streets, a thousand human lives were teeming, each the centre of its own circle of thoughts and words and actions; and yet the solitude was profound, the desolation complete, the stillness unbroken by a single echo.

The night—the last night of the old year—was fine; the white, clear light from a moon they could not see grew wide and clear over the city, as the last gleam of the sunset faded. It was just warm enough for the window to be open, and for nearly three hours Condy and Blix sat looking down upon the city in these last moments of the passing year, feeling upon their faces an occasional touch of the breeze, that carried with it the smell of trees and flowers from the gardens below them, and the faint, fine taint of the ocean from far out beyond the Heads. But the scene was not in reality silent. At times when they listened intently, especially when they closed their eyes, there came to them a subdued, steady bourdon, profound, unceasing, a vast, numb murmur, like no other sound in all the gamut of nature—the sound of a city at night, the hum of a great, conglomerate life, wrought out there from moment to moment under the stars and under the moon, while the last hours of the old year dropped quietly away.

A star fell.

Sitting in the window, the two noticed it at once, and Condy stirred for the first time in fifteen minutes.

"That was a very long one," he said, in a low voice. "Blix, you must write to me—we must write each other often."

"Oh, yes," she answered. "We must not forget each other; we have had too good a time for that."

"Four years is a long time," he went on. "Lots can happen in four years. Wonder what I'll be doing at the end of four years? We've had a pleasant time while it lasted, Blix."

"Haven't we?" she said, her chin on her hand, the moonlight shining in her little, dark-brown eyes.

Well, he was going to lose her. He had found out that he loved her only in time to feel the wrench of parting from her all the more keenly. What was he to do with himself after she was gone? What could he turn to in order to fill up the great emptiness that her going would leave in his daily life? And was she never to know how dear she was to him? Why not speak to her, why not tell her that he loved her? But Condy knew that Blix did not love him, and the knowledge of that must keep him silent; he must hug his secret to him, like the Spartan boy with his stolen fox, no matter how grievously it hurt him to do so. He and Blix had lived through two months [21] of rarest, most untroubled happiness, with hardly more self-consciousness than two young and healthy boys. To bring that troublous, disquieting element of love between them—unrequited love, of all things—would be a folly. She would tell him—must in all honesty tell him that she did not love him, and all their delicious *camaraderie* would end in a "scene." Condy, above everything, wished to look back on those two months, after she had gone, without being able to remember therein one single note that jarred. If the memory of her was all that he was to have, he resolved that at least that memory should be perfect.

And the love of her had made a man of him—he could not forget that; had given to him just the strength that made it possible for him to keep that resolute, grim silence now. In those two months he had grown five years; he was more masculine, more virile. The very set of his mouth was different; between the eyebrows the cleft had deepened; his voice itself vibrated to a heavier note. No, no; so long as he should live, he, man grown as he was, could never forget this girl of nineteen who had come into his life so quietly, so unexpectedly, who had influenced it so irresistibly and so unmistakably for its betterment, and who had passed out of it with the passing of the year.

For a few moments Condy had been absent-mindedly snapping the lid of his cigarette case, while he thought; now he selected a cigarette, returned the case to his pocket, and fumbled for a match. But the little gun-metal safe he carried was empty. Blix rose and groped for a moment upon the mantel-shelf, then returned and handed him a match, and stood over him while he scraped it under the arm of the chair wherein he sat. Even when his cigarette was lit she still stood there, looking at him, the fingers of her hands clasped in front of her, her hair, one side of her cheek, her chin, and sweet, round neck outlined by the faint blur of light that came from the open window. Then quietly she said:

"Well, Condy?"

"Well, Blix?"

"Just 'well'?" she repeated. "Is that all? Is that all you have to say to me?"

He gave a great start.

"Blix!" he exclaimed.

"Is that all? And you are going to let me go away from you for so long, and say nothing more than that to me? You think you have been so careful, think you have kept your secret so close! Condy, don't you suppose I know? Do you suppose women are so blind? No, you don't need to tell me; I know, I've known it— oh, for weeks!"

"You know—know—know what?" he exclaimed, breathless.

"That you have been pretending that you did not love me. I know that you do love me—I know you have been trying to keep it from me for fear it would spoil our good times, and because we had made up our minds to be chums, and have 'no more foolishness.'

266

Once—in those days when we first knew each other—I knew you did not love me when you said you did; but now, since—oh, since that afternoon in the Chinese restaurant, remember?—I've known that you did love me, although you pretended you didn't. It was the pretence I wanted to be rid of; I wanted to be rid of it when you said you loved me and didn't, and I want to be rid of it now when you pretend *not* to love me and I *know* you do," and Blix leaned back her head as she spoke that "know," looking at him from under her lids, a smile upon her lips. "It's the pretence that I won't have," she added. "We must be sincere with each other, you and I."

"Blix, do *you* love *me?*"

Condy had risen to his feet, his breath was coming quick, his cigarette was flung away, and his hands opened and shut swiftly.

"Oh, Blixy, little girl, do *you* love *me?*"

They stood there for a moment in the half dark, facing one another, their hearts beating, their breath failing them in the tension of the instant. There in that room, high above the city, a little climax had come swiftly to a head, a crisis in two lives had suddenly developed. The moment that had been in preparation for the last few months, the last few years, the last few centuries, behold! it had arrived.

"Blix, do you love me?"

Suddenly it was the New Year. Somewhere close at hand a chorus of chiming church bells sang together. Far off in the direction of the wharves, where the great ocean steamships lay, came the glad, sonorous shouting of a whistle; from a near-by street a bugle called aloud. And then from point to point, from street to roof top, and from roof to spire, the vague murmur of many sounds grew and spread and widened, slowly, grandly; that profound and steady bourdon, as of an invisible

267

organ swelling, deepening, and expanding to the full
male diapason of the city aroused and signalling the
advent of another year.

And they heard it, they two heard it, standing there
face to face, looking into each other's eyes, that un-
answered question yet between them, the question that
had come to them with the turning of the year. It was
the old year yet when Condy had asked that question.
In that moment's pause, while Blix hesitated to answer
him, the New Year had come. And while the huge, vast
note of the city swelled and vibrated, she still kept silent. But only for a moment. Then she came closer to
him, and put a hand on each of his shoulders.

"Happy New Year, dear," she said.

On New Year's Day, the last day they were to be
together, Blix and Condy took "their walk," as they
had come to call it—the walk that included the life-boat
station, the Golden Gate, the ocean beach beyond the
old fort, the green, bare, flower-starred hills and downs,
and the smooth levels of the golf links. Blix had been
busy with the last details of her packing, and they did
not get started until toward two in the afternoon.

"Strike me!" exclaimed Captain Jack, as Blix informed him that she had come to say good-bye. "Why,
ain't this very sudden-like, Miss Bessemer? Hey, Kitty,
come in here. Here's Miss Bessemer come to say good-
bye; going to New York to-morrow."

"We'll regularly be lonesome without you, miss," said
K. D. B., as she came into the front room, bringing with
her a brisk, pungent odour of boiled vegetables. "New
York—such a town as it must be! It was called Man-
hattan at first, you know, and was settled by the Dutch."

Evidently K. D. B. had reached the N's.

With such deftness as she possessed, Blix tried to turn
the conversation upon the first meeting of the retired
sea captain and the one-time costume reader, but all to

no purpose. The "Matrimonial Objects" were perhaps a little ashamed of their "personals" by now, and neither Blix nor Condy was ever to hear their version of the meeting in the back dining room of Luna's Mexican restaurant. Captain Jack was, in fact, anxious to change the subject.

"Any news of the yarn yet?" he suddenly inquired of Condy. "What do those Eastern publishin' people think of Our Mug and Billy Isham and the whiskey schooner?"

Condy had received the rejected manuscript of *In Defiance of Authority* that morning, accompanied by a letter from the Centennial Company.

"Well," he said in answer, "they're not, as you might say, falling over themselves trying to see who'll be the first to print it. It's been returned."

"The devil you say!" responded the Captain. "Well, that's kind of disappointin' to you, ain't it?"

"But," Blix hastened to add, "we're not at all discouraged. We're going to send it off again right away."

Then she said good-bye to them.

"I dunno as you'll see me here when you come back, miss," said the Captain, at the gate, his arm around K. D. B. "I've got to schemin' again. Do you know," he added, in a low, confidential tone, "that all the mines in California send their clean-ups and gold bricks down to the Selby smeltin' works once every week? They send 'em to San Francisco first, and they are taken up to Selby's Wednesday afternoons on a little stern-wheel steamer called the *Monticello*. All them bricks are in a box—dumped in like so much coal—and that box sets just under the wheel-house, for'ard. How much money do you suppose them bricks represent? Well, I'll tell you; last week they represented seven hundred and eithty thousand dollars. Well, now, I got a chart of the bay near Vallejo; the channel's all right, but there are mud-flats that ran out from shore three miles. Enough water for a whitehall,[22] but not enough for—well, for the patrol boat, for instance. Two or three slick boys, of a foggy night—of course, I'm not in that kind of game, but strike! it would be a deal now, wouldn't it?"

"Don't you believe him, miss," put in K. D. B. "He's just talking to show off."

"I think your scheme of holding up a Cunard liner," said Condy, with great earnestness, "is more feasible. You could lay across her course and fly a distress signal. She'd have to heave to."

"Yes, I been thinkin' o' that; but look here—what's to prevent the liner taking right after your schooner after you've got the stuff aboard—just followin' you right around an' findin' out where you land?"

"She'd be under contract to carry government mails," contradicted Condy. "She couldn't do that. You'd leave her mails aboard for just that reason. You wouldn't rob her of her mails; just so long as she was carrying government mails she couldn't stop."

The Captain clapped his palm down upon the gate-post.

"Strike me straight! I never thought of that."

BLIX and Condy went on; on along the narrow road upon the edge of the salt marshes and *tules* that lay between the station and the Golden Gate; on to the Golden Gate itself, and around the old rime-encrusted fort to the ocean shore, with its reaches of hard, white sand, where the boulders lay tumbled and the surf grumbled incessantly.

The world seemed very far away from them there on the shores of the Pacific, on that first afternoon of the New Year. They were supremely happy, and they sufficed to themselves. Condy had forgotten all about the next day, when he must say good-bye to Blix. It did not seem possible, it was not within the bounds of possibility, that she was to go away—that they two were to be separated. And for that matter, to-morrow was to-morrow. It was twenty-four hours away. The present moment was sufficient.

The persistence with which they clung to the immediate moment, their happiness in living only in the the present, had brought about a rather curious condition of things between them.

In their love for each other there was no thought of marriage; they were too much occupied with the joy of being together at that particular instant to think of the future. They loved each other, and that was enough. They did not look ahead further than the following day and then but furtively, and only in order that their morrow's parting might intensify their happiness of to-day. That New Year's Day was to be the end of everything. Blix was going; she and Condy would never see each other again. The thought of marriage—with its certain responsibilities, its duties, its gravity, its vague, troublous seriousness, its inevitable disappointments—was even a little distasteful to them. Their romance had been hitherto without a flaw; they had been genuinely happy in little things. It was as well that it should end that day, in all its pristine sweetness, unsullied by a single bitter moment, undimmed by the cloud of a single disillusion or disappointment. Whatever chanced to them in later years, they could at least cherish this one memory of a pure, unselfish affection, young and unstained and almost without thought of sex, come and gone on the very threshold of their lives. This was the end, they both understood. They were glad that it was to be so. They did not even speak again of writing to each other.

They found once more the little semicircle of blackberry bushes and the fallen log, halfway up the hill above the shore, and sat there awhile, looking down upon the long green rollers, marching incessantly toward the beach, and there breaking in a prolonged explosion of solid green water and flying spume. And their glance followed their succeeding ranks farther and farther out to sea, till the multitude blended into the mass—the vast, green, shifting mass that drew the eye on and on, to the abrupt, fine line of the horizon.

There was no detail in the scene. There was nothing but the great reach of the ocean floor, the unbroken plane of blue sky, and the bare green slope of land— three immensities, gigantic, vast, primordial. It was no place for trivial ideas and thoughts of little things. The mind harked back unconsciously to the broad, simpler, basic emotions, the fundamental instincts of the race. The huge spaces of earth and air and water carried with them a feeling of kindly but enormous force—elemental force, fresh, untutored, new, and young. There was buoyancy in it; a fine, breathless sense of uplifting and exhilaration; a sensation as of bigness and a return to the homely, human, natural life, to the primitive old impulses, irresistible, changeless, and unhampered; old as the ocean, stable as the hills, vast as the unplumbed depths of the sky.

Condy and Blix sat still, listening, looking, and watching—the intellect drowsy and numb; the emotions, the senses, all alive and brimming to the surface. Vaguely they felt the influence of the moment. Something was preparing for them. From the lowest, untouched depths in the hearts of each of them something was rising steadily to consciousness and the light of day. There is no name for such things, no name for the mystery that spans the interval between man and woman—the mystery that bears no relation to their love for each other, but that is something better than love, and whose coming savours of the miraculous.

The afternoon had waned and the sun had begun to set when Blix rose.

"We should be going, Condy," she told him.

They started up the hill, and Condy said: "I feel as though I had been somehow asleep with my eyes wide open. What a glorious sunset! It seems to me as though I were living double every minute; and, oh! Blix, isn't it the greatest thing in the world to love each other as we do?"

They had come to the top of the hill by now, and went on across the open, breezy downs, all starred with blue iris and wild heliotrope. Blix drew his arm about her waist, and laid her cheek upon his shoulder with a little caressing motion.

"And I do love you, dear," she said,—"love you with all my heart. And it's for always, too; I know that. I've been a girl until within the last three or four days—just a girl, dearest; not very serious, I'm afraid, and not caring for anything else beyond what was happening

273

close around me—don't you understand? But since I've found out how much I loved you and knew that you loved me—why, everything is changed for me. I'm not the same, I enjoy things that I never thought of enjoying before, and I feel so—oh, *larger*, don't you know?—and stronger, and so much more serious. Just a little while ago I was only nineteen, but I think, dear, that by loving you I have become—all of a sudden and without knowing it—a woman."

A little trembling ran through her with the words. She stopped and put both arms around his neck, her head tipped back, her eyes half closed, her sweet yellow hair rolling from her forehead. Her whole dear being radiated with that sweet, clean perfume that seemed to come alike from her clothes, her neck, her arms, her hair, and mouth—the delicious, almost divine, feminine aroma that was part of herself.

"You do love me, Condy, don't you, just as I love you?"

Such words as he could think of seemed pitifully inadequate. For answer he could only hold her the closer. She understood. Her eyes closed slowly, and her face drew nearer to his. Just above a whisper, she said:

"I love you, dear!"

"I love you, Blix!"

And they kissed each other then upon the mouth.

Meanwhile the sun had been setting. Such a sunset! The whole world, the three great spaces of sea and land and sky, were incarnadined with the glory of it. The ocean floor was a blinding red radiance, the hills were amethyst, the sky one gigantic opal, and they two seemed poised in the midst of all the chaotic glory of a primitive world. It was New Year's Day; the earth was new, the year was new, and their love was new and strong. Everything was before them. There was no longer any past, no longer any present. Regrets and

memories had no place in their new world. It was Hope,
Hope, Hope, that sang to them and called to them and
smote into life the new keen blood of them.

Then suddenly came the miracle, like the flashing out
of a new star, whose radiance they felt but could not see,
like a burst of music whose harmony they felt but could
not hear. And as they stood there alone in all that simple
glory of sky and earth and sea, they knew all in an instant that *they were for each other*, forever and forever,
for better or for worse, till death should them part. Into
their romance, into their world of little things, their
joys of the moment, their happiness of the hour, had
suddenly descended a great and lasting joy, the happiness of the great, grave issues of life—a happiness so
deep, so intense, as to thrill them with a sense of solemnity and wonder. Instead of being the end, that New
Year's Day was but the beginning—the beginning of
their real romance. All the fine, virile, masculine energy
of him was aroused and rampant. All her sweet, strong
womanliness had been suddenly deepened and broad-
ened. In fine, he had become a man, and she a woman.
Youth, life, and the love of man and woman, the
strength of the hills, the depth of the ocean, and the
beauty of the sky at sunset; that was what the New
Year had brought to them

.   .   .   .

"It's good-bye, dear, isn't it?" said Blix.

But Condy would not have it so.

"No, no," he told her; "no, Blix; no matter how
often we separate after this wonderful New Year's Day,
no matter how far we are apart, *we* two shall never,
never say good-bye."

"Oh, you're right, you're right!" she answered, the
tears beginning to shine in her little dark-brown eyes.
"No; so long as we love each other, nothing matters.
There's no such thing as distance for us, is there? Just

think, you will be here on the shores of the Pacific, and I on the shores of the Atlantic, but the whole continent can't come between us."

"And we'll be together again, Blix," he said; "and it won't be very long now. Just give me time—a few years now."

"But so long as we love each other, *time* won't matter, either."

"What are the tears for, Blixy?" he asked, pressing his handkerchief to her cheek.

"Because this is the saddest and happiest day of my life," she answered. Then she pulled from him with a little laugh, adding: "Look, Condy, you've dropped your letter. You pulled it out just now with your handkerchief."

As Condy picked it up, she noted the name of the Centennial Company upon the corner.

"It's the letter I got with the manuscript of the novel when they sent it back," he explained.

"What did they say?"

"Oh, the usual thing. I haven't read it yet. Here's what they say." He opened it and read:

We return to you herewith the MS. of your novel, *In Defiance of Authority*, and regret that our reader does not recommend it as available for publication at present. We have, however, followed your work with considerable interest, and have read a story by you, copied in one of our exchanges, under the title, "A Victory Over Death," which we would have been glad to publish ourselves, had you given us the chance.

Would you consider the offer of the assistant editorship of our *Quarterly*, a literary and critical pamphlet, that we publish in New York, and with which we presume you are familiar? We do not believe there would be any difficulty in the matter of financial arrangements. In case you should decide to come on, we enclose R. R. passes *via* the A. T. & S. F. C., & A., and New York Central.

Very truly,

THE CENTENNIAL PUBLISHING CO.

NEW YORK.

276

The two exchanged glances. But Blix was too excited to speak, and could only give vent to a little, quivering, choking sigh. The letter was a veritable god from the machine, the one thing lacking to complete their happiness.

"I don't know how this looks to *you*," Condy began, trying to be calm, "but it seems to me that this is—that this—this——"

But what they said then, they could never afterward remember. The golden haze of the sunset somehow got into their recollection of the moment, and they could only recall the fact that they had been gayer in that moment than ever before in all their lives.

Perhaps as gay as they ever were to be again. They began to know the difference between gayety and happiness. That New Year's Day, that sunset, marked for them an end and a beginning. It was the end of their gay, irresponsible, hour-to-hour life of the past three months; and it was the beginning of a new life, whose possibilities of sorrow and of trouble, of pleasure and of happiness, were greater than aught they had yet experienced. They knew this—they felt it instinctively, as with a common impulse they turned and looked back upon the glowing earth and sea and sky, the breaking surf, the beach, the distant, rime-encrusted, ancient fort—all that scene that to their eyes stood for the dear, free, careless companionship of those last few months. Their new-found happiness was not without its sadness already. All was over now; their solitary walks, the long, still evenings in the little dining room overlooking the sleeping city, their excursions to Luna's, their afternoons spent in the golden Chinese balcony, their mornings on the lake, calm and still and hot. Forever and forever they had said good-bye to that life. Already the sunset was losing its glory.

Then, with one last look, they turned about and set

their faces from it to the new life, to the East, where lay the Nation. Out beyond the purple bulwarks of the Sierras, far off, the great, grim world went clashing through its grooves—the world that now they were to know, the world that called to them, and woke them and roused them. Their little gayeties were done; the life of little things was all behind. Now for the future. The sterner note had struck—work was to be done; that, too, the New Year had brought to them—work for each of them, work and the world of men.

For a moment they shrank from it, loath to take the first step beyond the confines of the garden wherein they had lived so joyously and learned to love each other; and as they stood there, facing the gray and darkening Eastern sky, their backs forever turned to the sunset, Blix drew closer to him, putting her hand in his, looking a little timidly into his eyes. But his arm was around her, and the strong young force that looked into her eyes from his gave her courage.

"A happy New Year, dear," she said.

"A very, very happy New Year, Blix," he answered.

VANDOVER AND THE BRUTE

Notes by Norris for an uncompleted revision of *Vandover and the Brute*

IT WAS always a matter of wonder to Vandover that he was able to recall so little of his past life. With the exception of the most recent events he could remember nothing connectedly. What he at first imagined to be the story of his life, on closer inspection turned out to be but a few disconnected incidents that his memory had preserved with the greatest capriciousness, absolutely independent of their importance. One of these incidents might be a great sorrow, a tragedy, a death in his family; and another, recalled with the same vividness, the same accuracy of detail, might be a matter of the least moment.

A certain one of these wilful fillips of memory would always bring before him a particular scene during the migration of his family from Boston to their new home in San Francisco, at a time when Vandover was about eight years old.

It was in the depot of one of the larger towns in western New York. The day had been hot and after the long ride on the crowded day coach the cool shadow under the curved roof of the immense iron vaulted depot seemed very pleasant. The porter, the brakeman, and Vandover's father very carefully lifted his mother from the car. She was lying back on pillows in a long steamer chair. The three men let the chair slowly down, the brakeman went away, but the porter remained, taking off his cap and wiping his forehead with the back of his left hand, which in turn he wiped against the pink palm of his right. The other train, the train to which they were to change, had not yet arrived. It was rather still; at the far end of the depot a locomotive, sitting back on its motionless drivers like some huge sphinx crouching along the rails, was steaming quietly, drawing long breaths. The repair gang in greasy caps and spotted blue overalls were inspecting the train, pottering about the trucks, opening and closing the journal-boxes, striking clear notes on the wheels with long-handled hammers.

Vandover stood close to his father, his thin legs wide apart, holding in both his hands the satchel he had been permitted to carry. He looked about him continually, rolling his big eyes vaguely, watching now the repair-gang, now a huge white cat dozing on an empty baggage truck.

Several passengers were walking up and down the platform, staring curiously at the invalid lying back in the steamer chair.

The journey was too much for her. She was very weak and very pale, her eyelids were heavy, the skin of her forehead looked blue and tightly drawn, and tiny beads of perspiration gathered around the corners of her mouth. Vandover's father put his hand and arm along the back of the chair and his sick wife rested against him, leaning her head on his waistcoat over the pocket where he kept his cigars and pocket-comb. They were all silent.

By and by she drew a long sigh, her face became the face of an imbecile, stupid, without expression, her eyes half-closed, her mouth half-open. Her head rolled forward as though she were nodding in her sleep, while a long drip of saliva trailed from her lower lip. Vandover's father bent over her quickly, crying out sharply, "Hallie!—what is it?" All at once the train for which they were waiting charged into the depot, filling the place with a hideous clangour and with the smell of steam and of hot oil.

This scene of her death was the only thing that Vandover could remember of his mother.

As he looked back over his life he could recall nothing after this for nearly five years. Even after that lapse of time the only scene he could picture with any degree of clearness was one of the greatest triviality in which he saw himself, a rank thirteen-year-old boy, sitting on a bit of carpet in the back yard of the San Francisco house playing with his guinea-pigs.

In order to get at his life during his teens, Vandover would have been obliged to collect these scattered memory pictures as best he could, rearrange them in some more orderly sequence, piece out what he could imperfectly recall and fill in the many gaps by mere guesswork and conjecture.

It was the summer of 1880 that they had come to San Francisco. Once settled there, Vandover's father began to build small residence houses and cheap flats which he rented at various prices, the cheapest at ten dollars, the more expensive at thirty-five and forty. He had closed out his business in the East, coming out to California on account of his wife's ill health. He had made his money in Boston and had intended to retire.

But he soon found that he could not do this. At this time he was an old man, nearly sixty. He had given his entire life to his business to the exclusion of everything else, and now when his fortune had been made and when he could afford to enjoy it, discovered that he had lost the capacity for enjoying anything but the business itself. Nothing else could interest him. He was not what would be called in America a rich man, but he had made money enough to travel, to allow himself any reasonable relaxation, to cultivate a taste for art, music, literature, or the drama, to indulge in any harmless fad, such as collecting etchings, china, or bric-à-brac, or even to permit himself the luxury of horses. In the place of all these he found himself, at nearly sixty years of age, forced again into the sordid round of business as the only escape from the mortal *ennui* and weariness of the spirit that preyed upon him during every leisure hour of the day.

Early and late he went about the city, personally superintending the building of his little houses and cheap flats, sitting on saw-horses and piles of lumber, watching the carpenters at work. In the evening he came home to a later supper, completely fagged, bringing with him the smell of mortar and of pine shavings.

On the first of each month when his agents turned over the rents to him he was in great spirits. He would bring home the little canvas sack of coin with him before banking it, and call his son's attention to the amount, never failing to stick a twenty-dollar gold-piece in each eye, monocle fashion, exclaiming, "Good for the masses," a meaningless jest that had been one of the family's household words for years.

His plan of building was peculiar. His credit was good, and having chosen his lot he would find out from the banks how much they would loan him upon it in case he should become the owner. If this amount suited him, he would buy the lot, making one large payment outright and giving his note for the balance. The lot once his, the banks loaned him the desired amount. With this money and with money of his own he would make the final payment on the lot and would begin the building itself, paying his labour on the nail, but getting his material, lumber, brick, and fittings on time. When the building was halfway up he would negotiate a second loan from the banks in order to complete it and in order to meet the notes he had given to his contractors for material.

He believed this to be a shrewd business operation, since the rents as they returned to him were equal to the interest on a far larger sum than that which he had originally invested. He said little about the double mortgage on each piece of property "improved" after this fashion and which often represented a full two-thirds of its entire value. The interest on each loan was far more than covered by the rents; he chose his neighbourhoods with great discrimination; real estate was flourishing in the rapidly growing city, and the new houses, although built so cheaply that they were mere shells of lath and plaster, were nevertheless made gay and brave with varnish and cheap mill-work. They rented well at first, scarcely a one was ever vacant. People spoke of the Old Gentleman as one of the most successful realty owners in the city. So pleased did he become with the success of his new venture that in course of time all his money was reinvested after this fashion.

At the time of his father's greatest prosperity Vandover himself began to draw toward his fifteenth year, entering upon that period of change when the first raw elements of character began to assert themselves and when, if ever, there was a crying need for the influence of his mother. Any feminine influence would have been well for him at this time: that of an older sister, even that of a hired governess. The housekeeper looked after him a little, mended his clothes, saw that he took his bath Saturday nights, and that he did not dig tunnels under the garden walks. But her influence was entirely negative and prohibitory and the two were constantly at war. Vandover grew in a haphazard way and after school hours ran about the streets almost at will.

At fifteen he put on long trousers, and the fall of the

same year entered the High School. He had grown too fast and at this time was tall and very lean; his limbs were straight, angular, out of all proportion, with huge articulations at the elbows and knees. His neck was long and thin and his head large, his face was sallow and covered with pimples, his ears were big, red, and stuck out stiff from either side of his head. His hair he wore "pompadour."

Within a month after his entry of the High School he had a nickname. The boys called him "Skinny-seldom-fed," to his infinite humiliation.

Little by little the crude virility of the young man began to develop in him. It was a distressing, uncanny period. Had Vandover been a girl he would at this time have been subject to all sorts of abnormal vagaries, such as eating his slate pencil, nibbling bits of chalk, wishing he were dead, and drifting into states of unreasoned melancholy. As it was, his voice began to change, a little golden down appeared on his cheeks and upon the nape of his neck, while his first summer vacation was altogether spoiled by a long spell of mumps.

His appetite was enormous. He ate heavy meat three times a day, but took little or no exercise. The pimples on his face became worse and worse. He grew peevish and nervous. He hated girls, and when in their society was a very bull-calf for bashfulness and awkward self-consciousness. At times the strangest and most morbid fancies took possession of him, chief of which was that everyone was looking at him while he was walking in the street.

Vandover was a good little boy. Every night he said his prayers, going down upon his huge knees at the side of his bed. To the Lord's Prayer he added various petitions of his own. He prayed that he might be a good boy and live a long time and go to Heaven when he died and see his mother; that the next Saturday might be sunny all day long, and that the end of the world might not come while he was alive.

It was during Vandover's first year at the High School that his eyes were opened and that he acquired the knowledge of good and evil. Till very late he kept his innocence, the crude raw innocence of the boy, like that of a young animal, at once charming and absurd. But by and by he became very curious, stirred with a blind unreasoned instinct. In the Bible which he read Sunday afternoons, because his father gave him a quarter for doing so, he came across a great many things that filled him with vague and strange ideas; and one Sunday at church, when the minister was intoning the Litany, he remarked for the first time the words, "all women in the perils of child-birth."

He puzzled over this for a long time, smelling out a mystery beneath the words, feeling the presence of something hidden, with the instinct of a young brute. He could get no satisfaction from his father and by and by began to be ashamed to ask him; why, he did not know. Although he could not help hearing the abominable talk of the High School boys, he at first refused to believe that part of it which he could understand. For all that he was ashamed of his innocence and ignorance and affected to appreciate their stories nevertheless.

At length one day he heard the terse and brutal truth. In an instant he believed it, some lower, animal intuition in him reiterating and confirming the fact. But even then he hated to think that people were so low, so vile. One day, however, he was looking through the volumes of the old Encyclopædia Britannica in his father's library, hoping that he might find a dollar bill which the Old Gentleman told him had been at one time misplaced between the leaves of some one of the great tomes. All at once he came upon the long article "Obstetrics," profusely illustrated with old-fashioned plates and steel engravings. He read it from beginning to end.

It was the end of all his childish ideals, the destruction of all his first illusions. The whole of his rude little standard of morality was lowered immediately. Even his mother, whom he had always believed to be some kind of an angel, fell at once in his estimation. She could never be the same to him after this, never so sweet, so good and so pure as he had hitherto imagined her.

It was very cruel, the whole thing was a grief to him, a blow, a great shock; he hated to think of it. Then little by little the first taint crept in, the innate vice stirred in him, the brute began to make itself felt, and a multitude of perverse and vicious ideas commenced to buzz about him like a swarm of nasty flies.

A certain word, the blunt Anglo-Saxon name for a lost woman, that he heard on one occasion among the boys at school, opened to him a vista of incredible wickedness, but now after the first moment of revolt the thing began to seem less horrible. There was even a certain attraction about it. Vandover soon became filled with an overwhelming curiosity, the eager evil curiosity of the schoolboy, the perverse craving for the knowledge of vice. He listened with all his ears to everything that was said and went about through the great city with eyes open only to its foulness. He even looked up in the dictionary the meanings of the new words, finding in the cold, scientific definitions some strange sort of satisfaction.

There was no feminine influence about Vandover at this critical time to help him see the world in the right light and to gauge things correctly, and he might have been totally corrupted while in his earliest teens had it not been for another side of his character that began to develop about the same time.

This was his artistic side. He seemed to be a born

artist. At first he only showed bent for all general art. He drew well, he made curious little modellings in clayey mud; he had a capital ear for music and managed in some unknown way of his own to pick out certain tunes on the piano. At one time he gave evidence of a genuine talent for the stage. For days he would pretend to be some dreadful sort of character, he did not know whom, talking to himself, stamping and shaking his fists; then he would dress himself in an old smoking-cap, a red tablecloth, and one of his father's discarded Templar swords, and pose before the long mirrors ranting and scowling. At another time he would devote his attention to literature, making up endless stories with which he terrified himself, telling them to himself in a low voice for hours after he had got into bed. Sometimes he would write out these stories and read them to his father after supper, standing up between the folding doors of the library, acting out the whole narrative with furious gestures. Once he even wrote a little poem which seriously disturbed the Old Gentleman, filling him with formless ideas and vague hopes for the future.

In a suitable environment Vandover might easily have become an author, actor, or musician, since it was evident that he possessed the fundamental *afflatus* that underlies all branches of art. As it was, the merest chance decided his career.

In the same library where he had found the famous encyclopædia article was "A Home Book of Art," one of those showily bound gift books one sees lying about conspicuously on parlour centre tables. It was an English publication calculated to meet popular and general demand. There were a great many full-page pictures of lonely women, called Reveries or Idylls, ideal "Heads" of gipsy girls, of coquettes, and heads of little girls crowned with cherries and illustrative of such titles as Spring, Youth, Innocence. Besides these

were sentimental pictures, as, for instance, one entitled
It Might Have Been, a sad-eyed girl, with long hair,
musing over a miniature portrait, and another especially
impressive which represented a handsomely dressed
woman flung upon a *Louis Quinze* sofa, weeping, her
hands clasped over her head. She was alone; it was twilight; on the floor was a heap of opened letters. The
picture was called "Memories."

Vandover thought this last a wonderful work of art
and made a hideous copy of it with very soft pencils.
He was so pleased with it that he copied another one
of the pictures and then another. By and by he had
copied almost all of them. His father gave him a dollar
and Vandover began to add to his usual evening petition
the prayer that he might become a great artist. Thus it
was that his career was decided upon.

He was allowed to have a drawing teacher. This was
an elderly German, an immense old fellow, who wore a
wig and breathed loudly through his nose. His voice was
like a trumpet and he walked with a great striding gait
like a colonel of cavalry. Besides drawing he taught
ornamental writing and engrossing. With a dozen
curved and flowing strokes of an ordinary writing pen
he could draw upon a calling card a conventionalized
outline-picture of some kind of dove or bird of paradise,
all curves and curlicues, flying very gracefully and carrying in its beak a half-open scroll upon which could be
inscribed such sentiments as "From a Friend" or
"With Fond Regards," or even one's own name.

His system of drawing was of his own invention. Over
the picture to be copied he would paste a great sheet of
paper, ruling off the same into spaces of about an inch
square. He would cut out one of these squares and Vandover would copy the portion of the picture thus disclosed. When he had copied the whole picture in this
fashion the teacher would go over it himself, retouching

it here and there, labouring to obviate the checker-board effect which the process invariably produced.

At other times Vandover copied into his sketch-book, with hard crayons, those lithographed studies on buff paper which are published by the firm in Berlin. He began with ladders, wheel-barrows and water barrels, working up in course of time to rustic buildings set in a bit of landscape; stone bridges and rural mills, overhung by some sort of linden tree, with ends of broken fences in a corner of the foreground to complete the composition. From these he went on to bunches of grapes, vases of fruit, and at length to more "Ideal heads." The climax was reached with a life-sized Head, crowned with honeysuckles and entitled "*Flora.*" He was three weeks upon it. It was an achievement, a veritable *chef-d'œuvre.* Vandover gave it to his father upon Christmas morning, having signed his name to it with a great ornamental flourish. The Old Gentleman was astounded, the housekeeper was called in and exclaimed over it, raising her hands to Heaven. Vandover's father gave him a five-dollar gold-piece, fresh from the mint, had the picture framed in gilt, and hung it up in his smoking room over the clock.

Never for a moment did the Old Gentleman oppose Vandover's wish to become an artist and it was he himself who first spoke about Paris to the young man. Vandover was delighted; the Latin Quarter became his dream. Between the two it was arranged that he should go over as soon as he had finished his course at the High School. The Old Gentleman was to take him across, returning only when he was well established in some suitable studio.

At length Vandover graduated, and within three weeks of that event was on his way to Europe with his father. He never got farther than Boston.

At the last moment the Old Gentleman wavered.

Vandover was still very young and would be entirely alone in Paris, ignorant of the language, exposed to every temptation. Besides this, his education would stop where it was. Somehow he could not make it seem right to him to cut the young man adrift in this fashion. On the other hand, the Old Gentleman had a great many old-time friends and business acquaintances in Boston who could be trusted with a nominal supervision of his son for four years. He had no college education himself, but in some vague way he felt convinced that Vandover would be a better artist for a four years' course at Harvard.

Vandover took his father's decision hardly. He had never thought of being a college-man and nothing in that life appealed to him. He urged upon his father the loss of time that the course would entail, but his father met this objection by offering to pay for any artistic tuition that would not interfere with the regular college work.

Little by little the idea of college life became more attractive to Vandover; at the worst, it was only postponing the Paris trip, not abandoning it. Besides this, two of his chums from the High School were expecting to enter Harvard that fall, and he could look forward to a very pleasant four years spent in their company.

Out at Cambridge the term was just closing. The Old Gentleman's friends procured him tickets to several of the more important functions. From the gallery of Memorial Hall, Vandover and his father saw some of the great dinners; they went up to New London for the boat-race; they gained admittance to the historic Yard on Class-day, and saw the strange football rush for flowers around the "Tree." They heard the seniors sing "Fair Harvard" for the last time, and later saw them receive their diplomas at Sanders Theatre.[1]

The great ceremonies of the place, the picturesqueness of the elm-shaded Yard, the old red dormitories covered with ivy, the associations and traditions of the buildings, the venerable pump, Longfellow's room, the lecture hall where the minute-men had barracked, all of these things, in the end, appealed strongly to Vandover's imagination. Instead of passing the summer months in an ocean voyage and a continental journey, he at last became content to settle down to work under a tutor, "boning up" for the examinations. His father returned to San Francisco in July.

Vandover matriculated the September of the same year; on the first of October he signed the college rolls and became a Harvard freshman. At that time he was eighteen years old.

CHAPTER II

THERE was little of the stubborn or unyielding about Vandover, his personality was not strong, his nature pliable, and he rearranged himself to suit his new environment at Harvard very rapidly. Before the end of the first semester he had become to all outward appearances a typical Harvardian. He wore corduroy vests and a grey felt hat, the brim turned down over his eyes. He smoked a pipe and bought himself a brindled bull-terrior. He cut his lectures as often as he dared, "ragged" signs and barber-poles, and was in continual evidence about Foster's and among Leavitt and Pierce's billiard-tables. When the great football games came off he worked himself into a frenzy of excitement over them and even tried to make several of his class teams, though without success.

He chummed with Charlie Geary and with young Dolliver Haight, the two San Francisco boys. The three were continually together. They took the same courses, dined at the same table in Memorial Hall, and would have shared the same room if it had been possible. Vandover and Charlie Geary were fortunate enough to get a room in Matthews on the lower floor looking out upon the Yard; young Haight was obliged to put up with an outside room in a boarding house.

Vandover had grown up with these fellows and during all his life was thrown in their company. Haight was a well-bred young boy of good family, very quiet; almost every morning he went to Chapel. He was always polite, even to his two friends. He invariably tried to be pleasant and agreeable and had a way of making people like him. Otherwise, his character was not strongly marked.

Geary was quite different. He never could forget himself. He was incessantly talking about what he had done or was going to do. In the morning he would inform Vandover of how many hours he had slept and of the dreams he had dreamed. In the evening he would tell him everything he had done that day; the things he had said, how many lectures he had cut, what brilliant recitations he had made, and even what food he had eaten at Memorial. He was pushing, self-confident, very shrewd and clever, devoured with an inordinate ambition, and particularly pleased when he could get the better of anybody, even of Vandover or of young Haight. He delighted to assume the management of things. Vandover, he made his protégé, taking over the charge of such business as the two had in common. It was he who had found the room in Matthews, getting it away from all other applicants, securing it at the eleventh hour. He put Vandover's name on the waiting list at Memorial, saw that he filled out his blanks at the proper time, helped him balance his accounts, guided him in the choice of his courses and in the making out of his study-card.

"Look here, Charlie," Vandover would exclaim, throwing down the Announcement of Courses, "I can't make this thing out. It's all in a tangle. See here, I've got to fill up my hours some way or other; *you* straighten this thing out for me. Find me some nice little course, two hours a week, say, that comes late in the morning, a good hour after breakfast; something easy, all lectures, no outside reading, nice instructor and all that." And Geary would glance over the complicated schedule, cleverly untangling it at once, and would find two or three such courses as Vandover desired.

Vandover's yielding disposition led him to submit to

Geary's dictatorship and he thus early began to contract
easy, irresponsible habits, becoming indolent, shirking
his duty whenever he could, sure that Geary would
think for the two and pull him out of any difficulty into
which he might drift.

Otherwise the three freshmen were very much alike.
They were hardly more than boys and full of boyish
spirits and activity. They began to see "college life."
Vandover was already smoking; pretty soon he began
to drink. He affected beer, whisky he loathed, and such
wine as was not too expensive was either too sweet or
too sour. It became a custom for the three to go into
town two or three nights in the week and have beer and
Welsh rabbits at Billy Park's. On these occasions, however, young Haight drank only beer, he never touched
wine or spirits.

It was in Billy Park's the evening after the football
game between the Yale and Harvard freshmen that
Vandover was drunk for the first time. He was not so
drunk but that he knew he was, and the knowledge of
the fact so terrified him that it kept him from getting
very bad. The first sensation soon wore off, and by the
time that Geary took charge of him and brought him
back to Cambridge he was disposed to treat the affair
less seriously. Nevertheless, when he got to his room he
looked at himself in the mirror a long time, saying to
himself over and over again, "I'm drunk—just regularly
drunk. Good Heavens! what *would* the governor say to
this?"

In the morning he was surprised to find that he felt
so little ashamed. Geary and young Haight treated the
matter as a huge joke and told him of certain funny
things he had said and done and which he had entirely
forgotten. It was impossible for him to take the matter
seriously even if he had wished to, and within a few
weeks he was drunk again. He found that he was not an

exception; Geary was often drunk with him, fully a third of all the Harvard men he knew were intoxicated at different times. It was out of the question for Vandover to consider them as drunkards. Certainly, neither he nor any of the others drank because they liked the beer; after the fifth or sixth glass it was all they could do to force down another. Such being the case, Vandover often asked himself why he got drunk at all. This question he was never able to answer.

It was the same with gambling. At first the idea of playing cards for money shocked him beyond all expression. But soon he found that a great many of the fellows, fellows like young Haight, beyond question steady, sensible, and even worthy of emulation in other ways, "went in for that sort of thing." Every now and then Vandover's "crowd" got together in his room in Matthews, and played Van John [2] "for keeps," as they said, until far into the night. Vandover joined them. The stakes were small, he lost as often as he won, but the habit of the cards never grew upon him. It was like the beer, he "went in for it" because the others did, without knowing why. Geary, however, drew his line at gambling; he never talked against it or tried to influence Vandover, but he never could be induced to play "for keeps" himself.

One very warm Sunday afternoon in the first days of April, when the last snows were melting, Vandover and Geary were in their room, sitting at opposite ends of their window-seat, Geary translating his Monday's "Horace" by the help of a Bohn's translation, Vandover making a pen and ink drawing for the next *Lampoon*. A couple of young women passed down the walk, going across the Yard toward the Square. They were cheaply and showily dressed. One of them wore a mannish shirt-waist, with a high collar and scarf. The other had taken off her gloves and was swinging a bright red cape in one of her bare hands. As the couple passed they stared calmly at the two young fellows in the window; Vandover lowered his eyes over his work, blushing, he could not tell why. Geary stared back at them, following them with his eyes until they had gone by.

All at once he began laughing and pounding on the window.

"Oh, for goodness' sake, quit!" exclaimed Vandover in great alarm, twisting off the window-seat and shrinking back out of sight into the room. "Quit, Charlie; you don't want to insult a girl that way." Geary looked at him over his shoulder in some surprise, and was about to answer when he turned to the window again and exclaimed, grinning and waving his hand:

"Oh, just come here, Skinny; get on to this, will you? Ah, come here and look, you old chump! Do you think they're nice girls? Just take a *look* at them." Vandover peered timidly around Geary's head and saw that the two girls were looking back and laughing, and that the one with the red cape was waving it at them.

At supper that night they saw the girls in the gallery of Memorial. They pointed them out to young Haight, and Geary at length managed to attract their attention. After supper the three freshmen, together with two of their sophomore acquaintances, strolled slowly over toward the Yard, lighting their pipes and cigarettes. All at once, as they turned into the lower gate, they came full upon the same pair of girls. They were walking fast, talking and laughing very loudly.

"Track!" called out one of the sophomores, and the group of young fellows parted to let them pass. The sophomore exclaimed in a tone of regret, "Don't be in such a hurry, girls." Vandover became scarlet and turned his face away, but the girls looked back and laughed good-naturedly. "Come on," said the sophomore. The group closed around the girls and brought them to a standstill; they were not in the least embarrassed at this, but laughed more than ever. Neither of them was pretty, but there was a certain attraction about them that pleased Vandover immensely. He was very excited.

Then there was a very embarrassing pause. No one knew what to say. Geary alone regained his assurance at length, and began a lively interchange of chaff with one of them. The others could only stand about and smile.

"*Well*," cried the other girl after a while, "I ain't going to stand here in the snow all *night*. Let's take a walk; come along. I choose *you*." Before Vandover knew it she had taken his arm. The sophomore managed in some way to pair off with the other girl; Haight had already left the group; the two couples started off, while Geary and the other sophomore who were left out followed awkwardly in the rear for a little way and then disappeared.

Vandover was so excited that he could scarcely speak. This was a new experience. At first it attracted him, but the hopeless vulgarity of the girl at his side, her tawdry clothes, her sordid, petty talk, her slang, her miserable profanity, soon began to revolt him. He felt that he could not keep his self-respect while such a girl hung upon his arm.

"Say," said the girl at length, "didn't I see you in town the other afternoon on Washington Street?"

"Maybe you did," answered Vandover, trying to be polite. "I'm down there pretty often."

"Well, I guess yes," she answered. "You Harvard sports make a regular promenade out o' Washington Street Saturday afternoons. I suppose I've seen you down there pretty often, but didn't notice. Do you stand or walk?"

Vandover's gorge rose with disgust. He stopped

abruptly and pulled away from the girl. Not only did
she disgust him, but he felt sorry for her; he felt ashamed
and pitiful for a woman who had fallen so low. Still he
tried to be polite to her; he did not know how to be rude
with any kind of woman.

"You'll have to excuse me," he said, taking off his hat.
"I don't believe I can take a walk with you to-night.
I—you see—I've got a good deal of work to do; I think
I'll have to leave you." Then he bowed to her with his
hat in his hand, hurrying away before she could answer
him a word.

He found Geary alone in their room, cribbing "Horace" again.

"Ah, you bet," Geary said. "I shook those chippies.
I sized them up right away. I was clever enough for
that. They were no good. I thought you would get
enough of it."

"Oh, I don't know," said Vandover after a while, as
he settled to his drawing. "She was pretty common, but
anyhow I don't want to help bring down a poor girl like
that any lower than she is already." This saying struck
Vandover as being very good and noble, and he found
occasion to repeat it to young Haight the next day.

But within three days of this, at the time when Vandover would have fancied himself farthest from such a
thing, he underwent a curious reaction. On a certain
evening, moved by an unreasoned instinct, he sought
out the girl who had just filled him with such deep pity
and such violent disgust, and that night did not come
back to the room in Matthew's. The thing was done
almost before he knew it. He could not tell why he had
acted as he did, and he certainly would not have believed
himself capable of it.

He passed the next few days in a veritable agony of
repentance, overwhelmed by a sense of shame and dishonour that were almost feminine in their bitterness and

intensity. He felt himself lost, unworthy, and as if he
could never again look a pure woman in the eyes unless
with an abominable hypocrisy. He was ashamed even
before Geary and young Haight, and went so far as to
send a long letter to his father acknowledging and de-
ploring what he had done, asking for his forgiveness and
reiterating his resolve to shun such a thing forever after.

What had been bashfulness in the boy developed in
the young man to a profound respect and an instinctive
regard for women. This stood him in good stead throughout all his four years of Harvard life. In general, he kept
himself pretty straight. There were plenty of fast girls
and lost women about Cambridge, but Vandover found
that he could not associate with them to any degree of
satisfaction. He never knew how to take them, never
could rid himself of the idea that they were to be treated
as ladies. They, on their part, did not like him; he was
too diffident, too courteous, too "slow." They preferred
the rough self-assertion and easy confidence of Geary,
who never took "no" as an answer and who could chaff
with them on their own ground.

Vandover did poor work at Harvard and only graduated, as Geary said, "by a squeak." Besides his regular
studies he took time to pass three afternoons a week in
the studio of a Boston artist, where he studied anatomy
and composition and drew figures from the nude. In the
summer vacations he did not return home, but accompanied this artist on sketching tours along the coast of
Maine. His style improved immensely the moment he
abandoned flat studies and began to work directly from
Nature. He drew figures well, showed a feeling for deso-
late landscapes, and even gave promise of a good eye
for colour. But he allowed his fondness for art to interfere constantly with his college work. By the middle of
his senior year he was so loaded with conditions that

it was only Geary's unwearied coaching that pulled him through at all—as Vandover knew it would, for that matter.

Vandover returned to San Francisco when he was twenty-two. It was astonishing; he had gone away a pimply, overgrown boy, raw and callow as a fledgling, constrained in society, diffident, awkward. Now he returned, a tall, well-formed Harvardian, as careful as a woman in the matter of dress, very refined in his manners. Besides, he was a delightful conversationalist. His father was rejoiced; everyone declared he was a charming fellow.

They were right. Vandover was at his best at this time; it was undeniable that he had great talent, but he was so modest about it that few knew how clever he really was.

He went out to dinners and receptions and began to move a little in society. He became very popular: the men liked him because he was so unaffected, so straightforward, and the women because he was so respectful and so deferential.

He had no vices. He had gone through the ordeal of college life and had come out without contracting any habit more serious than a vague distaste for responsibility, and an inclination to shirk disagreeable duties. Cards he never thought of. It was rare that he drank so much as a glass of beer.

However, he had come back to a great disappointment. Business in San Francisco had entered upon a long period of decline, and values were decreasing; for ten years rents had been sagging lower and lower. At the same time the interest on loans and insurances had increased, and real estate was brought to a standstill; one spoke bitterly of a certain great monopoly that was ruining both the city and state. Vandover's father had suffered with the rest, and now told his son that he could not at this time afford to send him to Paris. He would have to wait for better times.

At first this was a sharp grief to Vandover; for years he had looked forward to an artist's life in the Quarter. For a time he was inconsolable, then at length readjusted himself good-naturedly to suit the new order of things with as little compunction as before, when he had entered Harvard. He found that he could be contented in almost any environment, the weakness, the certain pliability of his character easily fitting itself into new grooves, reshaping itself to suit new circumstances. He prevailed upon his father to allow him to have a downtown studio. In a little while he was perfectly happy again.

Vandover's love for his art was keen. On the whole, he kept pretty steadily to his work, spending a good six hours at his easel every day, very absorbed over the picture in hand. He was working up into large canvases the sketches he had made along the Maine coast, great, empty expanses of sea, sky, and sand-dune, full of wind and sun. They were really admirable. He even sold one of them. The Old Gentleman was delighted, signed him a check for twenty dollars, and told him that in three years he could afford to send him abroad.

In the meanwhile, Vandover set himself to enjoy the new life. Little by little his "set" formed around him; Geary and young Haight, of course, and some half-dozen young men of the city: young lawyers, medical students, and clerks in insurance offices. As Vandover thus began to see the different phases of that life which lay beyond the limits of the college, he perceived more and more clearly that he was an exception among men for his temperance, his purity, and his clean living.

At their clubs and in their smoking rooms he heard certain practices, which he had always believed to be degrading and abominable, discussed with shouts of laughter. Those matters which until now he had regarded with an almost sacred veneration were subjects for immense jokes. A few years ago he would have been horrified at it all, but the fine quality of this first sensitiveness had been blunted since his experience at college. He tolerated these things in his friends now.

Gradually Vandover allowed his ideas and tastes to be moulded by this new order of things. He assumed the manners of these young men of the city, very curious to see for himself the other lower side of their life that began after midnight in the private rooms of fast cafés and that was continued in the heavy musk-laden air of certain parlours amid the rustle of heavy silks.

Slowly the fascination of this thing grew upon him until it mounted to a veritable passion. His strong artist's imagination began to be filled with a world of charming sensuous pictures.

He commenced to chafe under his innate respect and deference for women, to resent and to despise it. As the desire of vice, the blind, reckless desire of the male, grew upon him, he set himself to destroy this barrier that had so long stood in his way. He knew that it was the wilful and deliberate corruption of part of that which was best in him; he was sorry for it, but persevered, nevertheless, ashamed of his old-time timidity, his ignorance, his boyish purity.

For a second time the animal in him, the perverse evil brute, awoke and stirred. The idea of resistance hardly occurred to Vandover; it would be hard, it would be disagreeable to resist, and Vandover had not accustomed himself to the performance of hard, disagreeable duties. They were among the unpleasant things that he shirked. He told himself that later on, when he had grown older and steadier and had profited by experience and knowledge of the world, when he was stronger, in a word, he would curb the thing and restrain it. He saw no danger in such a course. It was what other men did with impunity.

In company with Geary and young Haight he had come to frequent a certain one of the fast cafés of the city. Here he met and became acquainted with a girl called Flossie. It was the opportunity for which he was waiting, and he seized it at once.

This time there was no recoil of conscience, no shame, no remorse; he even felt a better estimation of himself, that self-respect that comes with wider experiences and with larger views of life. He told himself that all men should at one time see certain phases of the world; it rounded out one's life. After all, one had to be a man of the world. Those men only were perverted who allowed themselves to be corrupted by such vice.

Thus it was that Vandover, by degrees, drifted into the life of a certain class of the young men of the city. Vice had no hold on him. The brute had grown larger in him, but he knew that he had the creature in hand. He was its master, and only on rare occasions did he permit himself to gratify its demands, feeding its abominable hunger from that part of him which he knew to be the purest, the cleanest, and the best.

Three years passed in this fashion.

CHAPTER III

VANDOVER had decided at lunch that day that he
would not go back to work at his studio in the afternoon,
but would stay at home instead and read a very interesting story about two men who had bought a wrecked
opium ship for fifty thousand dollars, and had afterward
discovered that she contained only a few tins of the
drug. He was curious to see how it turned out; the studio
was a long way downtown, the day was a little cold, and
he felt that he would enjoy a little relaxation. Anyhow,
he meant to stay at home and put in the whole afternoon
on a good novel.

But even when he had made up his mind to do this he
did not immediately get out his book and settle down
to it. After lunch he loitered about the house while his
meal digested, feeling very comfortable and contented.
He strummed his banjo a little and played over upon the
piano the three pieces he had picked up: two were polkas
and the third, the air of a topical song; he always played
the three together and in the same sequence. Then he
strolled up to his room, and brushed his hair for a while,
trying to make it lie very flat and smooth. After this he
went out to look at Mr. Corkle, the terrier, and let him
run a bit in the garden; then he felt as though he must
have a smoke, and so went back to his room and filled
his pipe. When it was going well, he took down his book
and threw himself into a deep leather chair, only to jump
up again to put on his smoking-jacket. All at once he
became convinced that he must have something to eat
while he read, and so went to the kitchen and got himself some apples and a huge slice of fresh bread. Ever

since Vandover was a little boy he had loved fresh bread and apples. Through the windows of the dining room he saw Mr. Corkle digging up great holes in the geranium beds. He went out and abused him and finally let him come back into the house and took him upstairs with him.

Then at last he settled down to his novel, in the very comfortable leather chair, before a little fire, for the last half of August is cold in San Francisco. The room was warm and snug, the fresh bread and apples were delicious, the good tobacco in his pipe purred like a sleeping kitten, and his novel was interesting and well written. He felt calm and soothed and perfectly content, and took in the pleasure of the occasion with the lazy complacency of a drowsing cat.

Vandover was self-indulgent—he loved these sensuous pleasures, he loved to eat good things, he loved to be warm, he loved to sleep. He hated to be bored and worried—he liked to have a good time.

At about half-past four o'clock he came to a good stopping-place in his book; the two men had got to quarrelling, and his interest flagged a little. He pushed Mr. Corkle off his lap and got up yawning and went to the window.

Vandover's home was on California Street not far from Franklin. It was a large frame house of two stories; all the windows in the front were bay. The front door was directly in the middle between the windows of the parlour and those of the library, while over the vestibule was a sort of balcony that no one ever thought of using. The house was set in a large well-kept yard. The lawn was pretty; an enormous eucalyptus tree grew at one corner. Nearer to the house were magnolia and banana trees growing side by side with pines and firs. Humming-birds built in these, and one could hear their curious little warbling mingling with the hoarse chirp of the English sparrows which nested under the eaves. The back yard was separated from the lawn by a high fence of green latticework. The hens and chickens were kept here and two roosters, one of which crowed every time a cable-car passed the house. On the door cut through the lattice-fence was a sign, "Look Out for the Dog." Close to the unused barn stood an immense windmill with enormous arms; when the wind blew in the afternoon the sails whirled about at a surprising speed, pumping up water from the artesian well sunk beneath. There was a small conservatory where the orchids were kept. Altogether, it was a charming place. However, adjoining it was a huge vacant lot with cows in it. It was full of dry weeds and heaps of ashes, while around it was an enormous fence painted with signs of cigars, patent bitters, and soap.

Vandover stood at a front window and looked out on a rather dreary prospect. The inevitable afternoon trades had been blowing hard since three, strong and brisk from the ocean, driving hard through the Golden Gate and filling the city with a taint of salt. Now the fog was coming in; Vandover could see great patches of it sweeping along between him and the opposite houses. All the eucalyptus trees were dripping, and occasionally there came the faint moan of the fog-horn out at the heads. He could see up the street for nearly two miles as it climbed over Nob Hill. It was almost deserted; a cable-car now and then crawled up and down its length, and at times a delivery wagon rattled across it; but that was about all. On the opposite sidewalk two boys and a girl were coasting downhill on their roller-skates and their brake-wagons. The cable in its slot kept up an incessant burr and clack. The whole view was rather forlorn, and Vandover turned his back on it, taking up his book again.

About five o'clock his father came home from his

office. "Hello!" said he, looking into the room; "aren't you home a little early to-day? Ah, I thought you weren't going to bring that dog into the house any more. I wish you wouldn't, son; he gets hair and fleas about everywhere."

"All right, governor," answered Vandover. "I'll take him out. Come along, Cork."

"But aren't you home earlier than usual to-day?" persisted his father as Vandover got up.

"Yes," said Vandover, "I guess I am, a little."

After supper the same evening when Vandover came downstairs, drawing on his gloves, his father looked over his paper, saying pleasantly:

"Well, where are you going to-night?"

"I'm going to see my girl," said Vandover, smiling; then foreseeing the usual question, he added, "I'll be home about eleven, I guess."

"Got your latch-key?" asked the Old Gentleman, as he always did when Vandover went out.

"Yep," called back Vandover as he opened the door. "I'll not forget it again. Good-night, governor."

Vandover used to call on Turner Ravis about twice a week; people said they were engaged. This was not so.

Vandover had met Miss Ravis some two years before. For a time the two had been sincerely in love with each other, and though there was never any talk of marriage between them, they seemed to have some sort of tacit understanding. But by this time Vandover had some-how outgrown the idea of marrying Turner. He still kept up the fiction, persuaded that Turner must understand the way things had come to be. However, he was still very fond of her; she was a frank, sweet-tempered girl and very pretty, and it was delightful to have her care for him.

Vandover could not shut his eyes to the fact that young Haight was very seriously in love with Turner.

But he was sure that Turner preferred him to his chum. She was too sincere, too frank, too conscientious to practise any deception on him.

There was quite a party at the Ravises' house that evening when Vandover arrived. Young Haight was there, of course, and Charlie Geary. Besides Turner herself there was Henrietta Vance, a stout, pretty girl, with pop eyes and a little nose, who laughed all the time and who was very popular. These were all part of Vandover's set; they called each other by their first names and went everywhere together. Almost every Saturday evening they got together at Turner's house and played whist, or euchre, or sometimes even poker. "Just for love," as Turner said.

When Vandover came in they were all talking at the same time, disputing about a little earthquake that had occurred the night before. Henrietta Vance declared that it had happened early in the morning.

"*Wasn't* it just about midnight, Van?" cried Turner.

"I don't know," answered Vandover. "It didn't wake me up. I didn't even know there was one."

"Well, I know I heard our clock strike two just about half an hour afterward," protested young Haight.

"Oh, it was almost five o'clock when it came," cried Henrietta Vance.

"Well, now, you're *all* off," said Charlie Geary. "I know just when she quaked to the fraction of a minute, because it stopped our hall clock at just a little after three."

They were silent. It was an argument which was hard to contradict. By and by, young Haight declared, "There must have been two of them then, because——"

"How about whist or euchre or whatever it is to be?" said Charlie Geary, addressing Turner and interrupting in an annoying way that was peculiar to him. "Can't we start in now that Van has come?" They played euchre for a while, but Geary did not like the game, and by and by suggested poker.

"Well—if it's only just for love," said Turner, "because, you know, Mamma doesn't like it any other way."

At ten o'clock Geary said, "Let's quit after this hand round—what do you say?" The rest were willing and so they all took account of their chips after the next deal. Geary was protesting against his poor luck. Honestly he hadn't held better than three tens more than twice during the evening. It was Henrietta Vance who took in everything; did one ever *see* anything to beat her luck? "the funniest thing!"

They began to do tricks with the cards. Young Haight showed them a very good trick by which he could make the pack break every time at the ace of clubs. Vandover exclaimed: "Lend me a silk hat and ninety dollars and I'll show you the queerest trick you ever saw," which sent Henrietta Vance off into shrieks of laughter. Then Geary took the cards out of young Haight's hands, asking them if they knew *this* trick.

Turner said yes, she knew it, but the others did not, and Geary showed it to them. It was interminable. Henrietta Vance chose a card and put it back into the deck. Then the deck was shuffled and divided into three piles. After this Geary made a mental calculation, selected one of these piles, shuffled it, and gave it back to her, asking her if she saw her card in it; then more shuffling and dividing until their interest and patience were quite exhausted. When Geary finally produced a jack of hearts and demanded triumphantly if that was her card, Henrietta began to laugh and declared she had forgotten *what* card she chose. Geary said he would do the trick all over for her. At this, however, they all cried out, and he had to give it up, very irritated at Henrietta's stupidity.

Vexed at the ill success of this first trick he retired a

little from their conversation, puzzling over the cards, thinking out new tricks. Every now and then he came back among them, going about from one to another, holding out the deck and exclaiming, "Choose any card —choose any card."

After a while they all adjourned to the dining room and Turner and Vandover went out into the kitchen, foraging among the drawers and shelves. They came back bringing with them a box of sardines, a tin of *paté*, three quart bottles of blue-ribbon beer, and what Vandover called "devilish-ham" sandwiches.

"Now do we want *tamales* to go with these?" said Turner, as she spread the lunch on the table. Henrietta Vance cried out joyfully at this, and young Haight volunteered to go out to get them. "Get six," Turner cried out after him. "Henrietta can always eat two. Hurry up, and we won't eat till you get back."

While he was gone Turner got out some half-dozen glasses for their beer. "Do you know," she said as she set the glasses on the table, "the funniest thing happened this morning to Mamma. It was at breakfast; she had just drunk a glass of water and was holding the glass in her hand like this"—Turner took one of the thin beer glasses in her hand to show them how—"and was talking to Pa, when all at once the glass broke right straight around a ring, just below the brim, you know, and fell all——" On a sudden Turner uttered a shrill exclamation; the others started up; the very glass she held in her hand at the moment cracked and broke in precisely the manner she was describing. A narrow ring snapped from the top, dropping on the floor, breaking into a hundred bits.

Turner drew in a long breath, open-mouthed, her hand in the air still holding the body of the glass that remained in her fingers. They all began to exclaim over the wonder.

"Well, did you ever in all your *life?*" shouted Miss Vance, breaking into a peal of laughter. Geary cried out, "Cæsar's ghost!" and Vandover swore under his breath.

"If that isn't the strangest thing I ever saw!" cried Turner. "*Isn't* that funny—why—oh! I'm going *to try it with another glass!*" But the second glass remained intact. Geary recovered from his surprise and tried to explain how it could happen.

"It was the heat from your fingers and the glass was cold, you know," he said again and again.

But the strangeness of the thing still held them. Turner set down the glass with the others and dropped into a chair, letting her hands fall in her lap, looking into their faces, nodding her head and shutting her lips.

"Ah, *no*," she said after a while. "That *is* funny. It kind of scares one." She was actually pale.

"Oh, there's Dolly Haight!" cried Henrietta Vance as the door bell rang. They all rushed to the door, running and scrambling, eager to tell the news. Young Haight stood bewildered on the door mat in the vestibule, his arms full of brown-paper packages, while they recounted the marvel. They all spoke at once, holding imaginary beer glasses toward him in their outstretched hands. Geary, however, refused to be carried away by their excitement, and one heard him from time to time repeating, between their ejaculations: "It was the heat from her fingers, you know, and the glass was cold."

Young Haight was confused, incredulous; he could not at first make out what *had* happened.

"Well, just come and *look* at the broken *glass* on the *floor*," shouted Turner decisively, dragging him into the dining room. They waited, breathless, to hear what he would say. He looked at the broken glass and then into their faces. Then he suddenly exclaimed:

313

"Ah, you're joking me."

"No, honestly," protested Vandover, "that was just the way it happened."

It was some little time before they could get over their impression of queerness, but by and by Geary cried out that the *tamales* were getting cold. They settled down to their lunch, and the first thing young Haight did was to cut his lip on the edge of the broken glass. Turner had set it down with the others and he had inadvertently filled it for himself.

It was a trifling cut. Turner fetched some court-plaster, and his lip was patched up. For all that, it bled quite a little. He was very embarrassed; he kept his handkerchief to his mouth and told them repeatedly to go on with their lunch and not to mind him.

As soon as they were eating and drinking they began to be very jolly, and Vandover was especially good-humoured and entertaining. He made Henrietta Vance shout with laughter by pretending that the olive in his *tamale* was a green hen's egg.

About half-past ten young Haight rose from the table saying he thought it was about time to say good-night. "Don't be in a hurry," said Turner. "It's early yet." After that, however, they broke up very quickly.

Before he left Vandover saw Turner in the dining room alone for a minute.

"Will I see you at church to-morrow?" he asked, as she held his overcoat for him.

"I don't know, Van," she answered. "You know Henrietta is going to stay all night with me, and I think she will want me to go home with her to-morrow morning and then stay to dinner with her. But I'm going to early communion to-morrow morning; why can't you meet me there?"

"Why, I can," answered Vandover, settling his collar. "I should like to very much."

"Well, then," she replied, "you can meet me in front of the church at half-past seven o'clock."

"Hey, break away there!" cried Geary from the front door. "Come along, Van, if you are going with us."

Turner let Vandover kiss her before they joined the others. "I'll see you at seven-thirty to-morrow morning," he said as he went away.

The three young men went off down the street, arm in arm, smoking their cigars and cigarettes. As soon as they were alone, Charlie Geary began to tell the other two of everything he had been doing since he had last seen them.

"Well, sir," he said as he took an arm of each, "well, sir, I had a fine sleep last night; went to bed at ten and never woke up till half-past eight this morning. Ah, you bet I needed it, though. I've been working like a slave this week. You know I take my law-examinations in about ten days. I'll pass all right. I'm right up to the handle in everything. I don't believe the judge could stick me anywhere in the subject of torts."

"Say, boys," said Vandover, pausing and looking at his watch, "it isn't very late; let's go downtown and have some oysters."

"That's a good idea," answered young Haight. "How about you, Charlie?"

Geary said he was willing. "Ah," he added, "you ought to have seen the beefsteak I had this evening at the Grillroom." And as they rode downtown he told them of the steak in question. "I had a little mug of ale with it, too, and a dish of salad. Ah, it went great."

They decided after some discussion that they would go to the Imperial.

THE Imperial was a resort not far from the corner of Sutter and Kearney streets, a few doors below a certain well-known drug store, in one window of which was a showcase full of live snakes.

The front of the Imperial was painted white, and there was a cigar-stand in the vestibule of the main entrance. At the right of this main entrance was another smaller one, a ladies' entrance, on the frosted pane of which one read, "Oyster Café."

The main entrance opened directly into the barroom. It was a handsome room, paved with marble flags. To the left was the bar, whose counter was a single slab of polished redwood. Behind it was a huge, plate-glass mirror, balanced on one side by the cash-register and on the other by a statuette of the Diving Girl in tinted bisque. Between the two were pyramids of glasses and bottles, liqueur flasks in wicker cases, and a great bouquet of sweet-peas.

The three bartenders, in clean linen coats and aprons, moved about here and there, opening bottles, mixing drinks, and occasionally turning to punch the indicator of the register.

On the other side of the room, facing the bar, hung a large copy of a French picture representing a *Sabbath*, witches, goats, and naked girls whirling through the air. Underneath it was the lunch counter, where clam-fritters, the specialty of the place, could be had four afternoons in the week.

Elsewhere were nickel-in-the-slot machines, cigar-lighters, a vase of wax flowers under glass, and a racing chart setting forth the day's odds, weights, and entries. On the end wall over the pantry-slides was a second "barroom" picture, representing the ladies of a harem at their bath.

But its "private rooms" were the chief attraction of the Imperial. These were reached by going in through the smaller door to the right of the main vestibule. Anyone coming in through this entrance found himself in a long and narrow passage. On the right of this passage were eight private rooms, very small, and open at the top as the law required. Halfway down its length the passage grew wider. Here the rooms were on both sides and were much larger than those in front.

It was this part of the Imperial that was most frequented, and that had made its reputation. In the smaller rooms in front one had beer and Welsh rabbits; in the larger rooms, champagne and terrapin.

Vandover, Haight, and Geary came in through the ladies' entrance of the Imperial at about eleven o'clock, going slowly down the passage, looking into each of the little rooms, searching for one that was empty. All at once Vandover, who was in the lead, cried out:

"Well, if here isn't that man Ellis, drinking whisky by himself. Bah! a man that will drink whisky all *alone*! Glad to see you just the same, Bandy; move along, will you—give a man some room."

"Hello, hello, Bandy!" cried Geary and young Haight, hitting him in the back, while Geary added: "How long have you been down here? *I've* just come from making a call with the boys. Had a fine time; what are you drinking, whisky? *I'm* going to have something to eat. Didn't have much of a lunch to-day, but you ought to have seen the steak I had at the Grillroom—as thick as that, and tender! Oh, it went great! Here, hang my coat up there on that side, will you?"

317

Bancroft Ellis was one of the young men of the city with whom the three fellows had become acquainted just after their return from college. For the most part, they met him at downtown restaurants, in the foyers and vestibules of the theatres, on Kearney Street of a Saturday afternoon, or, as now, in the little rooms of the Imperial, where he was a recognized habitué and where he invariably called for whisky, finishing from three to five "ponies" at every sitting. On very rare occasions they saw him in society, at the houses where their "set" was received. At these functions Ellis could never be persuaded to remain in the parlours; he slipped up to the gentlemen's dressing-rooms at the earliest opportunity, and spent the evening silently smoking the cigars and cigarettes furnished by the host. When Vandover and his friends came up between dances, to brush their hair or to rearrange their neckties, they found him enveloped in a blue haze of smoke, his feet on a chair, his shirt bosom broken, and his waistcoat unbuttoned. He would tell them that he was bored and thirsty and ask how much longer they were going to stay. He knew but few of their friends; his home was in a little town in the interior and he prided himself on being a "Native Son of the Golden West." He was a clerk in an insurance office on California Street, and had never been out of the state.

For the rest he was a good enough fellow and the three others liked him very much. He had a curious passion for facts and statistics, and his pockets were full of little books and cards to which he was constantly referring. He had one of those impossible pocket-diaries, the first half-dozen pages loaded with information of every kind printed in blinding type, postal rates to every country in the world, statistics as to population and rates of death, weights and measures, the highest mountains in the world, the greatest depths of the ocean.

He kept a little book in his left-hand vest pocket that gave the plan and seating capacity of every theatre in the city, while in the right-hand pocket was a tiny Webster's dictionary which was his especial pride. The calendar for the current year was pasted in the lining of his hat, together with the means to be employed in the resuscitation of a half-drowned person. He also carried about a "Vest Pocket Edition of Popular Information," which had never been of the slightest use to him.

The room in which they were now seated was very small and opened directly upon the passage. On either side of the table was a seat that would hold two, and on the wall opposite the door hung a mirror, its gilt frame enclosed in pink netting. The table itself was covered with a tolerably clean cloth, though it was of coarse linen and rather damp.

There were the usual bottles of olives and pepper sauce, a plate of broken crackers, and a ribbed match-safe of china. The sugar bowl was of plated ware and on it were scratched numberless dates together with the first names of a great many girls, "Nannie," "Ida," "Flossie."

Between the castor bottles was the bill of fare, held by a thin string between two immense leather covers which were stamped with wine merchants' advertisements. Geary reached for this before any of the others, saying at the same time, "Well, what are you going to have? *I'm* going to have a Welsh rabbit and a pint of ale." He looked from one to the other as if demanding whether or no they approved of his choice. He assumed the management of what was going on, advising the others what to have, telling Vandover not to order certain dishes that he liked because it took so long to cook them. He had young Haight ring for the waiter, and when he had come Geary read off the entire order to him twice over, making sure that he had taken it correctly. "That's what we want all right, all right—isn't it?" he said, looking around at the rest.

The waiter, whose eyes were red from lack of sleep, put down before them a plate of limp, soft shrimps.[3]

"Hello, Toby!" said Vandover.

"Good evening, gentlemen," answered Toby. "Why, good evening, Mr. Vandover; haven't seen you 'round here for some time." He took their order, and as he was going away, Vandover called him back:

"Say, Toby," said he, "has Flossie been around to-night?"

"No," answered Toby, "she hasn't shown up yet. Her running-mate was in about nine, but she went out again right away."

"Well," said Vandover, smiling, "if Flossie comes 'round show her in here, will you?"

The others laughed, and joked him about this, and Vandover settled back in his seat, easing his position.

"Ah," he exclaimed, "I like it in here. It's always pleasant and warm and quiet and the service is good and you get such good things to eat."

Now that the young fellows were by themselves, and could relax that restraint, that good breeding and delicacy which had been natural to them in the early part of the evening at the Ravises', their manners changed: they lounged clumsily upon their seats, their legs stretched out, their waistcoats unbuttoned, caring only to be at their ease. Their talk and manners became blunt, rude, unconstrained, the coarser masculine fibre reasserting itself. With the exception of young Haight they were all profane enough, and it was not very long before their conversation became obscene.

Geary told them how he had spent the afternoon promenading Kearney and Market streets and just where he had gone to get his cocktail and his cigar. "Ah," he added, "you ought to have seen Ida Wade and Bessie Laguna. Oh, Ida was rigged up to beat the band; honestly her *hat* was as broad across as that. You know there's no use talking, she's an awfully handsome girl."

A discussion arose over the girl's virtue. Ellis, Geary, and young Haight maintained that Ida was only fast; Vandover, however, had his doubts.

"For that matter," said Ellis after a while, "I like Bessie Laguna a good deal better than I do Ida."

"Ah, yes," retorted young Haight, "you like Bessie Laguna too much anyhow."

Young Haight had a theory that one should never care in any way for that kind of a girl nor become at all intimate with her.

"The matter of liking her or not liking her," he said, "ought not to enter into the question at all. You are both of you out for a good time and that's all; you have a jolly flirtation with her for an hour or two, and you never see her again. That's the way it ought to be! This idea of getting intimate with that sort of a piece, and trying to get her to care for you, is all wrong."

"Oh," said Vandover deprecatingly, "you take all the pleasure out of it; where does your good time come in if you don't at least pretend that you like the girl and try to make her like you?"

"But don't you see," answered Haight, "what a dreadful thing it would be if a girl like that came to care for you seriously? It isn't the same as if it were a girl of your own class."

"Ah, Dolly, you've got a bean," muttered Ellis, sipping his whisky.

Meanwhile, the Imperial had been filling up; at about eleven the theatres were over, and now the barroom was full of men. They came in by twos and threes and sometimes even by noisy parties of a half dozen or more. The white swing doors of the main entrance flapped back and forth continually, letting out into the street puffs of tepid air tainted with the smell of alcohol. The men entered and ordered their drinks, and leaning their elbows upon the bar continued the conversation they had begun outside. Afterward they passed over to the lunch counter and helped themselves to a plate of stewed tripe or potato salad, eating it in a secluded corner, leaning over so as not to stain their coats. There was a continual clinking of glasses and popping of corks, and at every instant the cash-register clucked and rang its bell.

Between the barroom and the other part of the house was a door hung with blue plush curtains, looped back; the waiters constantly passed back and forth through this, carrying plates of oysters, smoking rarebits, tiny glasses of liqueurs, and goblets of cigars.

All the private rooms opening from either passage were full; the men came in, walking slowly, looking for their friends; but more often, the women and girls passed up and down with a chatter of conversation, a rattle of stiff skirts and petticoats, and a heavy whiff of musk. There was a continual going and coming, a monotonous shuffle of feet and hum of talk. A heavy odorous warmth in which were mingled the smells of sweetened whisky, tobacco, the fumes of cooking, and the scent of perfume, exhaled into the air. A gay and noisy party developed in one of the large back rooms; at every moment one could hear gales of laughter, the rattle of chairs and glassware, mingled with the sounds of men's voices and the little screams and cries of women. Every time the waiter opened the door to deliver an order he let out a momentary torrent of noises.

Girls, habitués of the place, continued to pass the door of the room where Vandover and his friends were seated. Each time a particularly handsome one went by, the four looked out after her, shutting their lips and eyes and nodding their heads.

Young Haight had called for more drinks, ordering, however, mineral water for himself, and Vandover was just telling about posing the female models in a certain life-class to which he belonged, when he looked up and broke off, exclaiming:

"Well, well, here we are at last! How are you, Flossie? Come right in."

Flossie stood in the doorway smiling good-humouredly at them, without a trace of embarrassment or of confusion in her manner. She was an immense girl, quite six feet tall, broad and well-made, in proportion. She was very handsome, full-throated, heavy-eyed, and slow in her movements. Her eyes and mouth, like everything about her, were large, but each time she spoke or smiled, she disclosed her teeth, which were as white, as well-set, and as regular as the rows of kernels on an ear of green corn. In her ears were small yellow diamonds, the only jewellery she wore. There was no perceptible cosmetic on her face, which had a clean and healthy look as though she had just given it a vigorous washing.

She wore a black hat with a great flare to the brim on one side. It was trimmed very dashingly with black feathers, imitation jet, and a little puff of plush—robin's egg blue. Her dress was of rough, black camel's hair, tailor-made, and but for the immense balloon sleeves, absolutely plain. It was cut in such a way that from neck to waist there was no break, the buttons being on the shoulder and under the arm. The skirt was full and stiff, and without the least trimming. Everything was black—hat, dress, gloves—and the effect was of a simplicity and severity so pronounced as to be very striking.

However, around her waist she wore as a belt a thick rope of oxidized silver, while her shoes, or rather walking slippers, were of white canvas.

She belonged to that class of women who are not to know one's last name or address, and whose hate and love are equally to be dreaded. There was upon her face the unmistakable traces of a ruined virtue and a vanished innocence. Her slightest action suggested her profession; as soon as she removed her veil and gloves it was as though she were partially undressed, and her uncovered face and hands seemed to be only portions of her nudity.

The general conception of women of her class is a painted and broken wreck. Flossie radiated health; her eyes were clear, her nerves steady, her flesh hard and even as a child's. There hung about her an air of cleanliness, of freshness, of good nature, of fine, high spirits, while with every movement she exhaled a delicious perfume that was not only musk, but that seemed to come alike from her dress, her hair, her neck, her very flesh and body.

Vandover was no longer the same as he had been during his college days. He was familiar now with this odour of abandoned women, this foul sweet savour of the great city's vice, that quickened his breath and that sent his heart knocking at his throat. It was the sensitive artist nature in him that responded instantly to anything sensuously attractive. Each kind and class of beautiful women could arouse in Vandover passions of equal force, though of far different kind. Turner Ravis influenced him upon his best side, calling out in him all that was cleanest, finest, and most delicate. Flossie appealed only to the animal and the beast in him, the evil, hideous brute that made instant answer.

"What will you take, Flossie?" asked Vandover, as she settled herself among them. "We are all drinking beer except Ellis. *He's* filling up with whisky." But Flossie never drank. It was one of the peculiarities for which she was well known.

324

"I don't want either," she answered, and turning to the waiter, she added, "You can bring me some Apollinaris water, Toby."

Flossie betrayed herself as soon as she spoke, the effect of her appearance was spoiled. Her voice was hoarse, a low-pitched rasp, husky, throaty, and full of brutal, vulgar modulations.

"Smoke, Flossie?" said Geary, pushing his cigarette case across to her. Flossie took a cigarette, rolled it to make it loose, and smoked it while she told them how she had once tried to draw up the smoke through her nose as it came out between her lips.

"And honestly, boys," she growled, "it made me that sick that I just had to go to bed."

"Who is the crowd out back?" asked Geary for the sake of saying something. Flossie embarrassed them all a little, and conversation with girls of her class was difficult.

"Oh, that's May and Nannie with some men from a banquet at the Palace Hotel," she answered.

The talk dragged along little by little and Flossie began badgering young Haight. "Say, you over there," she exclaimed, "what's the matter with you? You don't say anything."

Young Haight blushed and answered very much embarrassed: "Oh, I'm just listening." He was anxious to get away. He got up and reached for his hat and coat, saying with a good-natured smile: "Well, boys and girls, I think I shall have to leave you."

"Don't let me frighten you away," said Flossie, laughing.

"Oh, no," he answered, trying to hide his embarrassment, "I have to go anyhow."

While the others were saying good-night to him and asking when they should see him again, Flossie leaned over to him, crying out, "Good-night!" All at once, and before he knew what she was about, she kissed him full on the mouth. He started sharply at this, but was not angry, simply pulling away from her, blushing, very embarrassed, and more and more anxious to get away. Toby, the waiter, appeared at their door.

"The last was on me, you know," said young Haight, intercepting Vandover and settling for the round of drinks.

"Hello!" exclaimed Toby, "what's the matter with your lip?"

"I cut it a little while ago on a broken glass," answered young Haight. "Is it bleeding again?" he added, putting two fingers on his lips.

"It is sure enough," said Geary. "Here," he went on, wetting the corner of a napkin from the water bottle, "hold that on it."

The others began to laugh. "Flossie did that," Vandover explained to Toby. Ellis was hastily looking through his pockets, fumbling about among his little books.

"I had something here," he kept muttering, "if I can only *find* it, that told just what to do when you cut yourself with glass. There may be glass *in* it, you know."

"Oh, that's all right, that's all right," exclaimed young Haight, now altogether disconcerted. "It don't amount to anything."

"I tell you what," observed Geary: "get some court-plaster at the snake doctor's just above here."

"No, no, that's all right," returned young Haight, moving off. "Good-night. I'll see you again pretty soon."

He went away. Ellis, who was still searching through his little books, suddenly uttered an exclamation. He leaned out into the passage, crying: "The half of a hot onion; tie it right on the cut." But Haight had already gone. "You see," explained Ellis, "that draws out any little particles of glass. Look at this," he added, reading an item just below the one he had found. "You can use cigar ashes for eczema."

Flossie nodded her head at him, smiling and saying: "Well, the next time I have eczema I will remember that."

Flossie left them a little after this, joining Nannie and May in the larger room that held the noisy party. The three fellows had another round of drinks.

All the evening Ellis had been drinking whisky. Now he astonished the others by suddenly calling for beer. He persisted in drinking it out of the celery glass, which he emptied at a single pull. Then Vandover had claret-punches all round, protesting that his mouth felt dry as a dust-bin. Geary at length declared that he felt pretty far gone, adding that he was in the humour for having "a high old time."

"Say, boys," he exclaimed, bringing his hand down on the table, "what do you say that we all go to every joint in town, and wind up at the Turkish baths? We'll have a regular *time*. Let's see now how much money I have."

Thereat they all took account of their money. Vandover had fourteen dollars, but he owed for materials at his art dealer's, and so put away eight of it in an inside pocket. The others followed his example, each one reserving five dollars for immediate use.

"That will be one dollar for the Hammam," said Geary, "and four dollars apiece for drinks. You can get all we want on four dollars." They had a last claret-punch and, having settled with Toby, went out.

Coming out into the cold night air from the warm interior of the Imperial affected Vandover and Geary in a few minutes. But apparently nothing could affect Ellis, neither whisky, claret-punch, nor beer. He walked steadily between Vandover and Geary, linking an arm in each of theirs.

These two became very drunk almost at once. At every minute Vandover would cry out, "Yee-ee-*ow!* Thash way I feel, jush like that." Geary made a "Josh" that was a masterpiece, the success of the occasion. It consisted in exclaiming from time to time, "Cherries are ripe!" This was funny. It seemed to have some ludicrous, hidden double-meaning that was irresistible. It stuck to them all the evening; when a girl passed them on Kearney Street and Geary cried out at her that "Cherries were ripe!" it threw them all into spasms of laughter.

They went first to the Palace Garden near the Tivoli Theatre, where Geary and Vandover had beer and Ellis a whisky cocktail. The performance was just finishing and they voted that they were not at all amused at a lean, overworked girl whom they saw performing a song and dance through a blue haze of tobacco smoke; so they all exclaimed, "Cherries are ripe!" and tramped out again to visit the Luxembourg. The beer began to go against Vandover's stomach by this time, but he forced it down his throat, shutting his eyes. Then they said they would go to the toughest place in town, "Steve Casey's"; this was on a side-street. The walls were covered with yellowed photographs of once-famous pugilists and old-time concert-hall singers. There was sand on the floor, and in the dancing room at the back, where nobody danced, a jaded young man was banging out polkas and quick-steps at a cheap piano.

At the Crystal Palace, where they all had shandygaff, they met one of Ellis's friends, a young fellow of about twenty. He was stone deaf, and in consequence had become dumb; but for all that he was very eager to associate with the young men of the city and would not hear of being separated and set apart with the other deaf mutes. He was very pleased to meet them and joined them at once. They all knew him pretty well and called him the "Dummy."

328

In the course of the evening the party was seen at nearly every bar and saloon in the neighbourhood of Market and Kearney streets. Geary and Vandover were very drunk indeed. Vandover was having a glorious time; he was not silent a minute, talking, laughing, and singing, and crying out continually, "Cherries are ripe!" When he could think of nothing else to say he would exclaim, "Yee-ee-*ow*! Thash way I feel."

For two hours they drank steadily. Vandover was in a dreadful condition; the Dummy got so drunk that he could talk, a peculiarity which at times had been known to occur to him. As will sometimes happen, Geary sobered up a little and at the "Grotto" bathed his head and face in the washroom. After this he became pretty steady, he stopped drinking, and tried to assume the management of the party, ordering their drinks for them, and casting up the amount of the check.

About two o'clock they returned toward the Luxembourg, staggering and swaying. The Luxembourg was a sort of German restaurant under a theatre where one could get some very good German dishes. There Vandover had beer and sauerkraut, but Ellis took more whisky. The Dummy continued to make peculiar sounds in his throat, half-noise, half-speech, and Geary gravely informed the waiter that cherries were ripe.

All at once Ellis was drunk, collapsing in a moment. The skin around his eyes was purple and swollen, the pupils themselves were contracted, and their range of vision seemed to stop at about a yard in front of his face. Suddenly he swept glasses, plates, castor, knives, forks, and all from off the table with a single movement of his arm.

They all jumped up, sober in a minute, knowing that a scene was at hand. The waiter rushed at Ellis, but Ellis knocked him down and tried to stamp on his face. Vandover and the Dummy tried to hold his arms and pull him off. He turned on the Dummy in a silent frenzy of rage and brought his knuckles down upon his head again and again. For the moment Ellis could neither hear, nor see, nor speak; he was blind, dumb, fighting drunk, and his fighting was not the fighting of Vandover.

"Get in here and help, will you?" panted Vandover to Geary, as he struggled with Ellis. "He can kill people when he's like this. Oh, damn the whisky, anyhow! Look out—don't let him get that knife! Grab his other arm, there! now, kick his feet from under him! Oh, kick hard! Sit on his legs; there now. Ah! Hell! he's bitten me! Look out! here comes the bouncer!"

The bouncer and three other waiters charged into them while they were struggling on the floor. Vandover was twice knocked down and the Dummy had his lip split. Ellis struggled to his feet again and, still silent, fought them all alike, a fine line of froth gathering at the corners of his lips.

When they were finally ejected, and pulled themselves together in the street outside, Geary had disappeared. He had left them during the struggle with Ellis and had gone home. Ah, you bet he wasn't going to stay any longer with the crowd when they got like that. If Ellis was fool enough to get as drunk as that it was his own lookout. *He* wasn't going to stay and get thrown out of any saloon; ah, no, you bet he was too clever for that. He was sober enough now and would go home to bed and get a good sleep.

The fight in the saloon had completely sobered the rest of them. Ellis was tractable enough again, and very sorry for having got them into such a row. Vandover was horribly sick at his stomach.

The three locked arms and started slowly toward the Turkish baths. On their way they stopped at an all-night drug store and had some seltzer.

Vandover had about three hours' sleep that night.

He was awakened by the attendant shaking his arm and crying:

"Half-past six, sir."

"Huh!" he exclaimed, starting up. "What about half-past six? I don't want to get up."

"Told me to call you, sir, at half-past six; quarter to seven now."

"Oh, all right, very well," answered Vandover. He turned away his face on the pillow, while a wretched feeling of nausea crept over him; every movement of his head made it ache to bursting. Behind his temples the blood throbbed and pumped like the knocking of hammers. His mouth would have been dry but for a thick slime that filled it and that tasted of oil. He felt weak, his hands trembled, his forehead was cold and seemed wet and sticky.

He could recall hardly anything of the previous night. He remembered, however, of going to the Imperial and of seeing Flossie, and he *did* remember at last of leaving word to be called at half-past six.

He got up without waking the other two fellows and took a plunge in the cold tank, dressed very slowly, and went out. The stores were all closed, the streets were almost deserted. He walked to the nearest uptown car-line and took an outside seat, feeling better and steadier for every moment of the sharp morning air.

Van Ness Avenue was very still. It was about half-past seven. The curtains were down in all the houses; here and there a servant could be seen washing down the front steps. In the vestibules of some of the smaller houses were loaves of French bread and glass jars of cream, while near them lay the damp twisted roll of the morning's paper. There was everywhere a great chittering of sparrows, and the cable-cars, as yet empty, trundled down the cross streets, the conductors cleaning the windows and metal work. From far down at one end of the avenue came the bells of the Catholic Cathedral ringing for early mass; and a respectable-looking second girl hurried past him carrying her prayer-book. At the other end of the avenue was a blue vista of the bay, the great bulk of Mount Tamalpais rearing itself out of the water like a waking lion.

In front of the little church Turner was waiting for him. She was dressed very prettily and the cold morning air had given her a fine colour.

"You don't look more than half awake," she said, as Vandover came up. "It was awfully good of you to come. Oh, Van, you look dreadfully. It is too bad to make you get up so early."

"No, no," protested Vandover. "I was only too glad to come. I didn't sleep well last night. I hope I haven't kept you waiting."

"I've only just come," answered Turner. "But I think it is time to go in."

The little organ was muttering softly to itself as they entered. It was very still otherwise. The morning sun struck through the stained windows and made pretty lights about the altar; besides themselves there were some half-dozen other worshippers. The little organ ceased with a long droning sigh, and the minister in his white robes turned about, facing his auditors, and in the midst of a great silence opened the communion service with the words: "Ye who do truly and earnestly repent you of your sins and are in love and charity with your neighbours——"

As Vandover rose with the rest the blood rushed to his head and a feeling of nausea and exhaustion, the dregs of his previous night's debauch, came over him again for a moment, so that he took hold of the back of the pew in front of him to steady himself.

332

In THE afternoons Vandover worked in his studio, which was on Sacramento Street, but in the mornings he was accustomed to study in the life-class at the School of Design.

This was on California Street over the Market, an immense room partitioned by enormous wooden screens into alcoves, where the still-life classes worked, painting carrots, grapes, and dusty brown stone jugs.

All about were a multitude of casts, the fighting gladiator, the discobulus, the Venus of Milo, the hundreds of smaller pieces, masks, torsos, and the heads of the Parthenon horses. Flattened paint-tubes and broken bits of charcoal littered the floor and cluttered the chairs and shelves. A strong odour of turpentine and fixative was in the air, mingled with the stronger odours of linseed oil and sour, stale French bread.

Every afternoon a portrait class of some thirty-odd assembled in one of the larger alcoves near the door. Several of the well-known street characters of the city had posed for this class, and at one time Father Elphick, the white-haired, bareheaded vegetarian, with his crooked stick and white clothes, had sat to it for his head.

Vandover was probably the most promising member of the school. His style was sketchy, conscientious, and full of strength and decision. He worked in large lines, broad surfaces, and masses of light or shade. His colour was good, running to purples, reds, and admirable greens, full of bitumen and raw sienna.

Though he had no idea of composition, he was clever

enough to acknowledge it. His finished pictures were broad reaches of landscape, deserts, shores, and moors in which he placed solitary figures of men or animals in a way that was very effective—as, for instance, a great strip of shore and in the foreground the body of a drowned sailor; a lion drinking in the midst of an immense Sahara; or, one that he called The Remnant of an Army, a dying war horse wandering on an empty plain, the saddle turned under his belly, his mane and tail snarled with burrs.

Some time before there had come to him the idea for a great picture. It was to be his first masterpiece, his salon picture when he should get to Paris. A British cavalryman and his horse, both dying of thirst and wounds, were to be lost on a Soudanese desert, and in the middle distance on a ridge of sand a lion should be drawing in upon them, crouched on his belly, his tail stiff, his lower jaw hanging. The melodrama of the old English "Home Book of Art" still influenced Vandover. He was in love with this idea for a picture and had determined to call it The Last Enemy. The effects he wished to produce were isolation and intense heat; as to the soldier, he was as yet undecided whether to represent him facing death resignedly, calmly, or grasping the barrel of his useless rifle, determined to fight to the last.

Vandover loved to paint and to draw. He was perfectly contented when his picture was "coming right," and when he felt sure he was doing good work. He often did better than he thought he would, but never so well as he thought he *could*.

However, it bored him to work very hard, and when he did not enjoy his work he stopped it at once. He would tell himself on these occasions that one had to be in the mood and that he should wait for the inspiration, although he knew very well how absurd such excuses were, how false and how pernicious.

334

That certain little weakness of Vandover's character, his self-indulgence, had brought him to such a point that he thought he *had* to be amused. If his painting amused him, very good; if not, he found something else that would.

On the following Monday as he worked in the life-class, Vandover was thinking, or, rather, trying not to think, of what he had done the Sunday morning previous when he had gone to communion with Turner Ravis. For a long time he evaded the thought because he knew that if he allowed it to come into his mind it would worry and harass him. But by and by the effort of dodging the enemy became itself too disagreeable, so he gave it up and allowed himself to look the matter squarely in the face.

Ah, yes; it was an ugly thing he had done there, a really awful thing. He must have been still drunk when he had knelt in the chancel. Vandover shuddered as he thought of this, and told himself that one could hardly commit a worse sacrilege, and that some time he would surely be called to account for it. But here he checked himself suddenly, not daring to go further. One would have no peace of mind left if one went on brooding over such things in this fashion. He realized the enormity of what he had done. He had tried to be sorry for it. It was perhaps the worst thing he had ever done, but now he had reached the lowest point. He would take care never to do such a thing again. After this he would be better.

But this was not so. Unconsciously, Vandover had shut a door behind him; he would never again be exactly the same, and the keeping of his appointment with Turner Ravis that Sunday morning was, as it were, a long step onward in his progress of ruin and pollution.

He shook himself as though relieving his shoulders of a weight. The model in the life-class had just been posed for the week, and the others had begun work. The model for that week was a woman, a fact that pleased Vandover, for he drew these nude women better than anyone in the school, perhaps better than anyone in the city. Portrait work and the power to catch subtle intellectual distinctions in a face were sometimes beyond him, but his feeling for the flesh, and for the movement and character of a pose, was admirable.

He set himself to work. Holding his stick of charcoal toward the model at arm's length, he measured off the heads, five in all, and laid off an equal number of spaces upon his paper. After this, by aid of his mirror, he studied the general character of the pose for nearly half an hour. Then, with a few strokes of his charcoal he laid off his larger construction lines with a freedom and a precision that were excellent. Upon these lines he made a second drawing a little more detailed, though as yet everything was blocked in, angularly and roughly. Then, putting a thin flat edge upon his charcoal, he started the careful and finished outline.

By the end of an hour the first sketch of his drawing was complete. It was astonishingly good, vigorous and solid; better than all, it had that feeling for form that makes just the difference between the amateur and the genuine artist.

By this time Vandover's interest began to flag. Four times he had drawn and redrawn the articulation of the model's left shoulder. As she stood, turned sideways to him, one hand on her hip, the deltoid muscle was at once contracted and foreshortened. It was a difficult bit of anatomy to draw. Vandover was annoyed at his ill success—such close attention and continued effort wearied him a little—the room was overheated and close, and the gas stove, which was placed near the throne to warm the model, leaked and filled the room with a nasty brassy smell. Vandover remembered that the previous week

he had been looking over some old bound copies of
l'Art in the Mechanics' Library [4] and had found them of
absorbing interest. There was a pleasant corner and a
huge comfortable chair near where they were in the
reading room, and from the window one could occasionally look out upon the street. It was a quiet spot, and he
would not be disturbed all the morning. The idea was so
attractive that he put away his portfolio and drawing
things and went out.

For an hour he gave himself up to the enjoyment of
l'Art, excusing his indolence by telling himself that it was
all in his profession and was not time lost. A reproduction of a picture by Gérome gave him some suggestions
for the Last Enemy, which he noted very carefully.

He was interrupted by a rustle of starched skirts and
a voice that said:

"Why, hello, Van!"

He looked up quickly to see a young girl of about
twenty dressed in a black close-fitting bolero jacket of
imitation astrakhan with big leg-of-mutton sleeves, a
striped silk skirt, and a very broad hat tilted to one side.
Her hair was very blond, though coarse and dry from
being bleached, and a little flat curl of it lay very low on
her forehead. She was marvellously pretty. Vandover
was delighted.

"Why, *Ida!*" he exclaimed, holding her hand; "*it's*
awfully nice to see you here; won't you sit down?" and
he pushed his chair toward her.

But Ida Wade said no, she had just come in after a
new book, and of course it had to be out. But where had
he kept himself so long? That was the way he threw off
on her; ah, yes, he was going with Miss Ravis now and
wouldn't look at anyone else.

Vandover protested against this, and Ida Wade went
on to ask him why he couldn't come up to call on her
that very night, adding:

"We might go to the Tivoli or somewhere." All at once she interrupted herself, laughing, "Oh, I heard all about you the other night. *'Cherries are ripe!'* You and the boys painted the town red, didn't you? Ah, Van, I'm right on to *you!*"

She would not tell him how she heard, but took herself off, laughing and reminding him to come up early.

Ida Wade belonged to a certain type of young girl that was very common in the city. She was what men, among each other, called "gay," though that was the worst that could be said of her. She was virtuous, but the very fact that it was necessary to say so was enough to cause the statement to be doubted. When she was younger and had been a pupil at the Girls' High School, she had known and had even been the companion of such girls as Turner Ravis and Henrietta Vance, but since that time girls of that class had ignored her. Now, almost all of her acquaintances were men, and to half of these she had never been introduced. They had managed to get acquainted with her on Kearney Street, at theatres, at the Mechanics' Fair, and at baseball games. She loved to have a "gay" time, which for her meant to drink California champagne, to smoke cigarettes, and to kick at the chandelier. She was still virtuous and meant to stay so; there was nothing vicious about her, and she was as far removed from Flossie's class as from that of Turner Ravis.

She was very clever; half of her acquaintances, even the men, did not know how very "gay" she was. Only those—like Vandover—who knew her best, knew her for what she was, for Ida was morbidly careful of appearances, and as jealous of her reputation as only fast girls are.

Bessie Laguna was her counterpart. Bessie was "the girl she went with," just as Henrietta Vance was

Turner's "chum" and Nannie was Flossie's "running-mate."

Ida lived with her people on Golden Gate Avenue not far from Larkin Street. Her father had a three-fourths interest in a carpet-cleaning establishment on Howard Street, and her mother gave lessons in painting on china and on velvet. Ida had just been graduated from the normal school, and often substituted at various kinder-gartens in the city. She hoped soon to get a permanent place.

Vandover arrived at Ida's house that night at about eight o'clock in the midst of a drenching fog. The par-lour and front room on the second floor were furnished with bay windows decorated with some meaningless sort of millwork. The front door stood at the right of the parlour windows. Two Corinthian pillars on either side of the vestibule supported a balcony; these pillars had iron capitals which were painted to imitate the wood of the house, which in its turn was painted to imitate stone. The house was but two stories high, and the roof was topped with an iron cresting. There was a microscopical front yard in which one saw a tiny gravel walk, two steps long, that led to a door under the front steps, where the gas-meter was kept. A few dusty and strag-gling calla-lilies grew about.

Ida opened the door for Vandover almost as soon as he rang, and pulled him into the entry, exclaiming: "Come in out of the wet, as the whale said to Jonah. *Isn't* it a nasty night?" Vandover noticed as he came in that the house smelt of upholstery, cooking, and tur-pentine. He did not take off his overcoat, but went with her into the parlour.

The parlour was a little room with tinted plaster walls shut off from the "back-parlour" by sliding doors. A ply carpet covered the floor, a cheap piano stood across one corner of the room, and a greenish sofa across an-

339

other. The mantelpiece was of white marble with gray spots; on one side of it stood an Alaskan "grass basket" full of photographs, and on the other an inverted section of a sewer-pipe painted with daisies and full of gilded cattails tied with a blue ribbon. Near the piano straddled a huge easel of imitation brass upholding the crayon picture of Ida's baby sister enlarged from a photograph. Across one corner of this picture was a yellow "drape." There were a great many of these "drapes" all about the room, hanging over the corners of the chairs, upon an edge of the mantelpiece, and even twisted about the chandelier. In the exact middle of the mantelpiece itself was the clock, one of the chief ornaments of the room, almost the first thing one saw upon entering; it was a round-faced timepiece perversely set in one corner of an immense red plush palette; the palette itself was tilted to one side, and was upheld by an easel of twisted brass wire. Out of the thumb-hole stuck half a dozen brushes wired together in a round bunch and covered with gilt paint. The clock never was wound. It went so fast that it was useless as a timepiece. Over it, however, hung a large and striking picture, a species of cheap photogravure, a lion lying in his cage, looking mildly at the spectator over his shoulder. In front of the picture were real iron bars, with real straw tucked in behind them.

Ida sat down on the piano stool, twisting back and forth, leaning her elbows on the keys.

"All the folks have gone out to a whist-party, and I'm left all alone in the house with Maggie," she said. Then she added: "Bessie and Bandy Ellis said they would come down to-night, and I thought we could all go downtown to the Tivoli, or somewhere in the open-air boxes, you know, way up at the top." Hardly had she spoken the words when Bessie and Ellis arrived.

Ida went upstairs to get on her hat at once, because it was so late, and Bessie went with her.

Ellis and Vandover laughed as soon as they saw each other, and Ellis exclaimed mockingly, "Ye-e-ow, thash jush way I feel." Vandover grinned.

"That's so," he answered. "I *do* remember now of having made that remark several times. But *you*—oh, you were fearful. Do you remember the row in the Luxembourg? Look there where you bit me."

Ellis was incensed with Geary because he had forsaken their party.

"Oh, that's Charlie Geary, all over," answered Vandover.

As they were speaking there came a sudden outburst of bells in various parts of the city and simultaneously they heard the hoarse croaking of a whistle down by the water-front.

"Fire," said Vandover indifferently.

Ellis was already fumbling in his pockets, keeping count of the strokes.

"That's one," he exclaimed, pulling out and studying his list of alarm-boxes, "and one-two-three, that's three and one-two-three-*four*, one thirty-four. Let's see now! That's Bush and Hyde streets, not very far off," and he returned his card to the inside pocket of his coat as though he had accomplished a duty.

He lit a cigar. "I wonder now," he said, hesitating. "I guess I better not smoke in here. I'll go outside and get a mouthful of smoke before the girls come down." He went out and Vandover sat down to the cheap piano and played his three inevitable pieces, the two polkas and the air of the topical song; but he was interrupted by Ellis, who opened the door, crying out:

"Oh, come out here and see the *fire*, will you? Devil of a blaze!" Vandover ran out and saw a great fan-

341

shaped haze of red through the fog over the roofs of the houses.

"Oh, say, girls," he shouted, jumping back to the foot of the stairs; "Ida, Bessie, there's a fire. Just look out of your windows. Hark, there go the engines."

Bessie came tearing down the stairs and out on the front steps, where the two fellows were standing hatless.

"Where? Oh, show me where! O-o-oh, sure enough! That's a *big* fire. Just *hear* the engines. *Oh, let's go!*"

"Sure; come on, let's go!" exclaimed Vandover. "Tell Ida to hurry up."

"Oh, Ida," cried Bessie up the stairs, "there's an awful big fire right near here, and we're going."

"Oh, wait!" shouted Ida, her mouth full of pins. "I had to change my waist. Oh, *do* wait for me. Where is it *at?* Please wait; I'm coming right down in just a minute."

"Hurry up, hurry up!" cried Vandover. "It will be all out by the time we get there. I'm coming up to help."

"No, no, no!" she screamed. "Don't; you rattle me. I'm all mixed up. Oh, *darn* it, I can't find my czarina!" [5]

But at last she came running down, breathless, shrugging herself into her bolero jacket. They all hurried into the street and turned in the direction of the blaze. Other people were walking rapidly in the same direction, and there was an opening and shutting of windows and front doors. A steamer thundered past, clanging and smoking, followed by a score of half-exhausted boys. It took them longer to reach the fire than they expected, and by the time they had come within two blocks of it they were quite out of breath. Here the excitement was lively; the sidewalks were full of people going in the same direction; on all sides there were guesses as to where the fire was. On the front steps of many houses stood middle-aged gentlemen, still holding their evening papers and cigars, very amused and interested in watching the crowd go past. One heard them from time to time calling to their little sons, who were dancing on the sidewalks, forbidding them to go; in the open windows above could be seen the other members of the family, their faces faintly tinged with the glow, looking and pointing, or calling across the street to their friends in the opposite houses. Everyone was in good humour; it was an event, a fête for the entire neighbourhood.

Vandover and his party came at last to the first engines violently pumping and coughing, the huge grey horses standing near by, already unhitched and blanketed, indifferently feeding in their nosebags. Some of the crowd preferred to watch the engines rather than the fire, and there were even some who were coming away from it, exclaiming "false alarm" or "all out now."

The party had come up quite close; they could smell the burning wood and could see the roofs of the nearer houses beginning to stand out sharp and black against the red glow beyond. It was a barn behind a huge frame house that was afire, the dry hay burning like powder, and by the time they reached it the flames were already dwindling. The hose was lying like a python all about the streets, while upon the neighbouring roofs were groups of firemen with helmets and axes; some were shouting into the street below, and others were holding the spouting nozzles of the hose. "Ah," exclaimed an old man, standing near to Ida and Vandover, "ah, *I* was here when it first broke out; you ought to have seen the flames then! Look, there's a tree catching!"

The crowd became denser; policemen pushed it back and stretched a rope across the street. There was a world of tumbling yellow smoke that made one's eyes smart, and a great crackling and snapping of flames. Terribly excited little boys were about everywhere whistling and calling for each other as the crowd separated them.

They watched the fire for some time, standing on a pile of boards in front of a half-built house, but as it dwindled they wearied of it.

"Want to go?" asked Vandover at last.

"Yes," answered Ida, "we might as well. Oh, where's Bessie and Ellis?" They were nowhere to be seen. Vandover whistled and Ida even called, but in vain. The little boys in the crowd mimicked Ida, crying back, "Hey! Bessie! Oh, *Bes-see*, mommer wants you!" The men who stood near laughed at this, but it annoyed Vandover much more than it did Ida.

"Ah, well, never mind," she said at length. "Let them go. Now shall *we* go?"

It was too late for the theatre, but to return home was out of the question. They started off aimlessly downtown.

While he talked Vandover was perplexed. Ida was gayly dressed and was one of those girls who cannot open their mouths nor raise a finger in the street without attracting attention. Vandover was not at all certain that he cared to be seen on Kearney Street as Ida Wade's escort; one never knew who one was going to meet. Ida was not a bad girl, she was not notorious, but, confound it, it would look queer; and at the same time, while Ida was the kind of girl that one did not want to be seen with, she was not the kind of girl that could be told so. In an upper box at the Tivoli it would have been different—one could keep in the background; but to appear on Kearney Street with a girl who wore a hat like that and who would not put on her gloves—ah, no, it was out of the question.

Ida was talking away endlessly about a kindergarten in which she had substituted the last week.

She told him about the funny little nigger girl, and about the games and songs and how they played birds and hopped around and cried, "Twit, twit," and the

game of the butterflies visiting the flowers. She even
sang part of a song about the waves.

> "Every little wave had its night-cap on;
> Its white-cap, night-cap, white-cap on."

"It's more *fun* than enough," she said.

"Say, Ida," interrupted Vandover at length, "I'm
pretty hungry. Can't we go somewhere and eat something? I'd like a Welsh rabbit."

"All right," she answered. "Where do you want to
go?"

"Well," replied Vandover, running over in his mind
the places he might reach by unfrequented streets.
"There's Marchand's or Tortoni's or the Poodle Dog." [6]

"Suits *me*," she answered, "any one you like. Say,
Van," she added, "weren't you boys at the Imperial
the other night? What kind of a place is that?"

On the instant Vandover wondered what she could
mean. Was it possible that Ida would go to a place like
that with him?

"The Imperial?" he answered. "Oh, I don't know;
the Imperial is a sort of a nice place. It has private
rooms, like all of these places. The cooking is simply out
of sight. I think there is a bar connected with it." Then
he went on to talk indifferently about the kindergarten,
though his pulse was beating fast, and his nerves were
strung taut. By and by Ida said:

"I didn't know there was a bar at the Imperial. I
thought it was just some kind of an oyster joint. Why,
I heard of a very nice girl, a swell girl, going in there."

"Oh, yes," said Vandover, "they do. I say, Ida,"
he went on, "what's the matter with going down
there ?"

"The *Imperial ?*" exclaimed Ida. "Well, I guess
not !"

"Why, it's all right, if I'm with you," retorted Vandover, "but if you don't like it we can go anywhere else."

"Well, I guess we *will* go anywhere else," returned Ida, and for the time the subject was dropped.

They took a Sutter Street car and got off at Grant Avenue, having decided to go to Marchand's.

"That's the Imperial down there, isn't it?" asked Ida as they reached the sidewalk. Vandover made a last attempt:

"I say, Ida, come on, let's go there. It's all right if I'm with you. Ah, come along; what's the odds?"

"*No—no—*NO," she answered decisively. "What kind of a girl do you think I am, anyway?"

"Well, I tell you what," answered Vandover, "just come down *by* the place, and if you don't like the looks of it you needn't go in. I want to get some cigarettes, anyhow. You can walk down with me till I do *that.*"

"I'll walk down with you," replied Ida, "but I shan't go in."

They drew near to the Imperial. The street about was deserted, even the usual hacks that had their stand there were gone.

"You see," explained Vandover as they passed slowly in front of the doors, "this is all quiet enough. If you pulled down your veil no one would know the difference, and here's the ladies' entrance, you see, right at the side."

"All right, come along, let's go in," exclaimed Ida suddenly, and before he knew it they had swung open the little door of the ladies' entrance with its frosted pane of glass and had stepped inside.

It was between nine and ten o'clock, and the Imperial was quiet as yet; a few men were drinking in the bar-room outside, and Toby, the red-eyed waiter, was talking in low tones to a girl under one of the electric lights.

Vandover and Ida went into one of the larger rooms

346

in the rear passage and shut the door. Ida pushed her bolero jacket from her shoulders, saying, "This seems nice and quiet enough."

"Well, of course," answered Vandover, as though dismissing the question for good. "Now, what are we going to have? I say we have champagne and oysters."

"Let's have Cliquot, then," exclaimed Ida, which was the only champagne she had ever heard of besides the California brands.

She was very excited. This was the kind of "gay" time she delighted in, tête-à-tête champagne suppers with men late at night. She had never been in such a place as the Imperial before, and the daring and novelty of what she had done, the whiff of the great city's vice caught in this manner, sent a little tremor of pleasure and excitement over all her nerves.

They did not hurry over their little supper, but ate and drank slowly, and had more oysters to go with the last half of their bottle. Ida's face was ablaze, her eyes flashing, her blond hair disordered and falling about her cheeks.

Vandover put his arm about her neck and drew her toward him, and as she sank down upon him, smiling and complaisant, her hair tumbling upon her shoulders and her head and throat bent back he leaned his cheek against hers, speaking in a low voice.

"No—no," she murmured, smiling; "never—ah, if I hadn't come—no, Van—please——" And then with a long breath she abandoned herself.

About midnight he left her at the door of her house on Golden Gate Avenue. On their way home Ida had grown more serious than he had ever known her to be. Now she began to cry softly to herself. "Oh, Van," she said, putting her head down upon his shoulder, "oh, I am so *sorry*. You don't think any less of me, do you? Oh, Van, you must be true to me now!"

CHAPTER VI

EVERYBODY in San Francisco knew of the Ravises
and always made it a point to speak of them as one of
the best families of the city. They were not new and
they were not particularly rich. They had lived in the
same house on California Street for nearly twenty years
and had always been comfortably well off. As things go
in San Francisco, they were old-fashioned. They had
family traditions and usages and time-worn customs.
Their library had been in process of collection for the
past half century and the pictures on the walls were oil
paintings or steel engravings and genuine old-fashioned
chromos, beyond price to-day.

Their furniture and ornaments were of the preceding
generation, solid, conservative. They were not chosen
with reference to any one style, nor all bought at the
same time. Each separate piece had an individuality of
its own. The Ravises kept their old things, long after the
fashion had gone out, preferring them to the smarter
"art" objects on account of their associations.

There were six in the family, Mr. and Mrs. Ravis,
Turner, and her older brother, Stanley, Yale '88, a very
serious young gentleman of twenty-seven, continually
professing an interest in economics and finance. Besides
these were the two children, Howard, nine years old, and
his sister, aged fourteen, who had been christened
Virginia.

They were a home-loving race. Mr. Ravis, senior,
belonged to the Bohemian Club,[7] but was seldom seen
there. Stanley was absorbed in his law business, and
Turner went out but little. They much preferred each

other's society to that of three fourths of their acquaintances, most of their friends being "friends of the family," who came to dinner three or four times a year.

It was a custom of theirs to spend the evenings in the big dining room at the back of the house, after the table had been cleared away, Mr. Ravis and Stanley reading the papers, the one smoking his cigar, the other his pipe; Mrs. Ravis, with the magazines and Turner with the *Chautauquan.* Howard and Virginia appropriated the table to themselves where they played with their soldiers and backgammon board.

The family kept two servants, June the "China boy," who had been with them since the beginning of things, and Delphine the cook, a more recent acquisition. June was, in a way, butler and second boy combined; he did all the downstairs work and the heavy sweeping, but it was another timeworn custom for Mrs. Ravis and Turner to spend part of every morning in putting the bedrooms to rights, dusting and making up the beds. Besides this, Turner exercised a sort of supervision over Howard and Virginia, who were too old for a nurse but too young to take care of themselves. She had them to bed at nine, mended some of their clothes,. made them take their baths regularly, reëstablished peace between them in their hourly quarrels, and, most arduous task of all, saw that Howard properly washed himself every morning, and on Wednesday and Saturday afternoons that he was suitably dressed in time for dancing school.

It was Sunday afternoon. Mrs. Ravis was reading to her husband, who lay on the sofa in the back-parlour smoking a cigar. Stanley had gone out to make a call, while Howard and Virginia had forgathered in the bathroom to sail their boats and cigar boxes in the tub. Toward half-past three, as Turner was in her room writing letters, the door-bell rang. She stopped, with her pen in the air, wondering if it might be Vandover. It was

June's afternoon out. In a few minutes the bell rang again, and Turner ran down to answer it herself, intercepting Delphine, who took June's place on these occasions, but who was hopelessly stupid.

Mrs. Ravis had peered out through the curtains of the parlour window to see who it was, and Turner met her and Mr. Ravis coming upstairs, abandoning the parlour to Turner's caller.

"Mamma and I are going upstairs to read," explained Mr. Ravis. "It's some one of your young men. You can bring him right in the parlour."

"I think it's Mr. Haight," said Turner's mother. "Ask him to stay to tea."

"Well," said Turner doubtfully, as she paused at the foot of the stairs, "I will, but you know we never have anything to speak of for Sunday evening tea. June is out, and you know how clumsy and stupid Delphine is when she waits on the table."

It *was* young Haight. Turner was very glad to see him, for next to Vandover she liked him better than any of the others. She was never bored by being obliged to entertain him, and he always had something to say and some clever way of saying it.

About half-past five, as they were talking about amateur photography, Mrs. Ravis came in and called them to tea.

Tea with the Ravises was the old-fashioned tea of twenty years ago. One never saw any of the modern "delicacies" on their Sunday evening table, no enticing cold lunch, no spices, not even catsups or pepper sauces. The turkey or chicken they had had for dinner was served cold in slices; there was canned fruit, preserves, tea, crackers, bread and butter, a large dish of cold pork and beans, and a huge glass pitcher of ice-water.

In the absence of June, Victorine the cook went through the agony of waiting on the table, very nervous and embarrassed in her clean calico gown and starched apron. Her hands were red and knotty, smelling of soap, and they touched the chinaware with an over-zealous and constraining tenderness as if the plates and dishes had been delicate glass butterflies. She stood off at a distance from the table making sudden and awkward dabs at it. When it came to passing the plates, she passed them on the wrong side and remembered herself at the wrong moment with a stammering apology. In her excess of politeness she kept up a constant murmur as she attended to their wants. Another fork? Yes, sir. She'd get it right away, sir. Did Mrs. Ravis want another cuppa tea? No? No more tea? Well, she'd pass the bread. Some bread, Master Howard? Nice French bread, he always liked that. Some more preserved pears, Miss Ravis? Yes, miss, she'd get them right away; they were just over here on the sideboard. Yes, here they were. No more? Now she'd go and put them back. And at last when she had set the nerves of all of them in a jangle, was dismissed to the kitchen and retired with a gasp of unspeakable relief.

Somewhat later in the evening young Haight was alone with Turner, and their conversation had taken a very unusual and personal turn. All at once Turner exclaimed:

"I often wonder what good I am in the world to anybody. I don't *know* a thing, I can't *do* a thing. I couldn't cook the plainest kind of a meal to *save* me, and it took me all of two hours yesterday to do just a little button-hole stitching. I'm not good for anything. I'm not a help to anybody."

Young Haight looked into the blue flame of the gas-log, almost the only modern innovation throughout the entire house, and was silent for a moment; then he leaned his elbows on his knees and, still looking at the flame, replied:

"I don't know about that. You have been a considerable help to *me*."

"To *you* !" exclaimed Turner, surprised. "A help to
you ? Why, how do you mean?"

"Well," he answered, still without looking at her,
"one always has one's influence, you know."

"Ah, lots of influence *I* have over anybody," retorted
Turner, incredulously.

"Yes, you have," he insisted. "You have plenty of
influence over the people that care for you. You have
plenty of influence over me."

Turner, very much embarrassed, and not knowing
how to answer, bent down to the side of the mantelpiece
and turned up the flame of the gas-log a little. Young
Haight continued, almost as embarrassed as she:

"I suppose I'm a bad lot, perhaps a little worse than
most others, but I think—I hope—there's some good
in me. I know all this sounds absurd and affected, but
really I'm not posing; you won't mind if I speak just as I
think, for this once. I promise," he went on with a half
smile, "not to do it again. You know my mother died
when I was little and I have lived mostly with men. You
have been to me what the society of women has been to
other fellows. You see, you are the only girl I ever knew
very well—the only one I ever wanted to know. I have
cared for you the way other men have cared for the
different women that come into their lives; as they have
cared for their mothers, their sisters—and their wives.
You have already influenced me as a mother or sister
should have done; what if I should ever ask you to be—
to be the *other* to me, the one that's best of all?"

Young Haight turned toward her as he finished and
looked at her for the first time. Turner was still very
much embarrassed.

"Oh, I'm very glad if I've been a help to—to anybody
—to you," she said, confusedly. "But I never knew that

you cared—that you thought about me—in that way.
But you mustn't, you know, you mustn't care for me in
that way. I ought to tell you right away that I never
could care for you more than—I always have done; I
mean care for you only as a very, very good friend. You
don't know, Dolly," she went on eagerly, "how it hurts
me to tell you so, because I care so much for you in every
other way that I wouldn't hurt your feelings for anything; but then you know at the same time it would
hurt you a great deal more if I *shouldn't* tell you, but
encourage you, and let you go on thinking that perhaps
I liked you more than anyone else, when I *didn't*. Now
wouldn't that be wrong? You don't know how glad it
makes me feel that I have been of some good to you,
and that is just why I want to be sincere *now* and not
make you think any less of me—think any worse of
me."

"Oh, *I* know," answered young Haight. "I know I
shouldn't have said anything about it. I knew before-
hand, or thought I knew, that you didn't care in that
way."

"Maybe I have been wrong," she replied, "in not seeing that you cared so much, and have given you a
wrong impression. I thought you knew how it was all
the time."

"Knew how what was?" he asked, looking up.

"Why," she said, "knew how Van and I were."

"I knew that Van cared for you a great deal."

"Yes, but you know," she went on, hesitating and
confused, "you know we are engaged. We have been engaged for nearly two years."

"But *he* don't consider himself as engaged!" The
words were almost out of Haight's mouth, but he shut
his teeth against them and kept silence—he hardly knew
why.

"Suppose Vandover were out of the question," he

said, getting up and smiling in order not to seem as serious as he really was.

"Ah," she said, smiling back at him. "I don't know; that's a hard question to answer. I've never *asked* myself *that* question."

"Well, I'm saving you the trouble, you see," he answered, still smiling. "I am asking it *for* you."

"But I don't want to answer such a question off-hand like that; how can I tell? It would only be *perhaps*, just now."

Young Haight answered quickly that "just now" he would be contented with that "perhaps"; but Turner did not hear this. She had spoken at the same time as he, exclaiming, "But what is the good of talking of that? Because no matter what happened I feel as though I could not break my promise to Van, even if I should want to. Because I have talked like this, Dolly," she went on more seriously, "you must not be deceived or get a wrong impression. You understand how things are, don't you?"

"Oh, yes," he answered, still trying to carry it off with a laugh. "I know, I know. But now I hope you won't let anything I have said bother you, and that things will go on just as if I hadn't spoken, just as if nothing had happened."

"Why, of course," she said, laughing with him again. "Of *course*, why shouldn't they?"

They were both at their ease again by the time young Haight stood at the door with his hat in his hand ready to go.

He raised his free hand over her head, and said, with burlesque, dramatic effect, trying to keep down a smile:

"Bless you both; go, go marry Vandover and be happy; I forgive you."

"Ah—don't be so *utterly* absurd," she cried, beginning to laugh.

ON A certain evening about four months later Ellis and Vandover had a "date" with Ida Wade and Bessie Laguna at the Mechanics' Fair. Ellis, Bessie, and Ida were to meet Vandover there in the Art Gallery, as he had to make a call with his father, and could not get there until half-past nine. They were all to walk about the Fair until ten, after which the two men proposed to take the girls out to the Cliff House in separate coupés. The whole thing had been arranged by Ellis and Bessie, and Vandover was irritated. Ellis ought to have had more sense; rushing the girls was all very well, but everybody went to the Mechanics' Fair, and he didn't like to have nice girls like Turner or Henrietta Vance see him with chippies like that. It was all very well for Ellis, who had no social position, but for *him*, Vandover, it would look too confounded queer. Of course he was in for it now, and would have to face the music. You can't tell a girl like that that you're ashamed to be seen with her, but very likely he would get himself into a regular box with it all.

When he arrived at the Mechanics' Pavilion, it was about twenty minutes of ten, and as he pushed through the wicket he let himself into a huge amphitheatre full of colour and movement.

There was a vast shuffling of thousands of feet and a subdued roar of conversation like the noise of a great mill; mingled with these were the purring of distant machinery, the splashing of a temporary fountain, and the rhythmic clamour of a brass band, while in the

355

piano exhibit the hired performer was playing a concert-grand with a great flourish. Nearer at hand one could catch ends of conversation and notes of laughter, the creaking of boots, and the rustle of moving dresses and stiff skirts. Here and there groups of school children elbowed their way through the crowd, crying shrilly, their hands full of advertisement pamphlets, fans, picture cards, and toy whips with pewter whistles on the butts, while the air itself was full of the smell of fresh popcorn.

Ellis and Bessie were in the Art Gallery upstairs. Mrs. Wade, Ida's mother, who gave lessons in hand painting, had an exhibit there which they were interested to find: a bunch of yellow poppies painted on velvet and framed in gilt. They stood before it some little time hazarding their opinions and then moved on from one picture to another; Ellis bought a catalogue and made it a duty to find the title of every picture. Bessie professed to be very fond of painting; she had "taken it up" at one time and had abandoned it, only because the oil or turpentine or something was unhealthy for her. "Of course," she said, "I'm no critic, I only know what I like. Now that one over there, I like *that*. I think those ideal heads like that are lovely, don't you, Bandy? Oh, there's Van!"

"Hello!" said Vandover, coming up. "Where's Ida?"

"Hello, Van!" answered Bessie. "Ida wouldn't come. Isn't it too mean? She said she couldn't come because she had a cold, but she was just talking through her face, I know. She's just got kind of a streak on and you can't get anything out of her. You two haven't had a row, have you? Well, I didn't *think* you had. But she's worried about something or other. I don't believe she's been out of the house this week. But isn't it mean of her to throw cold water on the procession like this? She's been giving me a lecture, too, and says she's going to reform."

"Well," said Vandover, greatly relieved, "that's too

bad. We could have had a lot of fun to-night. I'm awfully sorry. Well, what are you two going to do?"

"Oh, I guess we'll follow out our part of the programme," said Ellis. "You are kind of left out, though."

"I don't know," answered Vandover. "Maybe I'll go downtown, and see if I can find some of the boys."

"Oh, Dolly Haight is around here somewheres," said Ellis. "We saw him just now over by the chess machine."

"I guess I'll try and find him, then," responded Vandover. "Well, I hope you two enjoy yourselves." As he was turning away Bessie Laguna came running back, and taking him a little to one side said:

"You'd better go around and see Ida pretty soon if you can. She's all broke up about something, I'm sure. I think she'd like to see you pretty well. Honestly," she said, suddenly very grave, "I never saw Ida so cut up in my life. She's been taking on over something in a dreadful way, and I think she'd like to see you. She won't tell *me* anything. You go around and see her."

"All right," answered Vandover, smiling, "I'll go."

As he was going down the stairs on his way to find young Haight it occurred to him what Ida's trouble might be. He was all at once struck with a great fear, so that for an instant he turned cold and weak, and reached out his hand to steady himself against the railing of the stairs. Ah, what a calamity that would be! What a calamity! What a dreadful responsibility! What a crime! He could not keep the thought out of his mind. He tried to tell himself that Ida had practically given her consent by going into such a place; that he was not the only one, after all; that there was nothing certain as yet. He stood on the stairway, empty for that moment, biting the end of his thumb, saying to himself in a low voice:

"What a calamity, what a horrible calamity that

would be! Ah, you scoundrel! You damned fool, not to have thought!" A couple of girls, the counter girls at one of the candy booths, came down the stairs behind him with a great babble of talk. Vandover gave an irritated shrug of his shoulders as if freeing himself from the disagreeable subject and went on.

He could not find young Haight downstairs and so went up into the gallery again. After a long time he came upon him sitting on an empty bench nursing his cane and watching the crowd go past.

"Hello, old man!" he exclaimed. "Ellis told me I would find you around somewhere. I was just going to give you up." He sat down beside his chum, and the two began to talk about the people as they passed. "Ah, get on to the red hat!" exclaimed Vandover on a sudden. "That's the third time she's passed."

"Has Ellis gone off with Bessie Laguna?" asked young Haight.

"Yes," answered Vandover. "They're going to have a time at the Cliff House."

"That's too bad," young Haight replied. "Ellis has just thrown himself away with that girl. He might have known some very nice people when he first came here. Between that girl and his whisky he has managed to spoil every chance he might have had."

"There's Charlie Geary," Vandover exclaimed suddenly, whistling and beckoning. "Hey, there, Charlie! where you going? Oh," he cried on a sudden as Geary came up, "oh, get on to his new store clothes, will you?" They both pretended to be overwhelmed by the elegance of Geary's new suit.

"O-oh!" cried young Haight. "The bloody, bloomin', bloated swell. Just let me *touch* them!"

Vandover shaded his eyes and turned away as though dazzled. "This is *too* much," he gasped. "Such magnificence, such purple and fine linen." Then suddenly he shouted, "Oh, *oh !* *look* at the crease in those trousers. No; it's too much, I can't stand it."

"Oh, shut up," said Geary, irritated, as they had intended he should be. "Yes," he went on, "I thought I'd blow myself. I've been working like a dog the whole month. I'm trying to get in Beale's office. Beale and Storey, you know. I got the promise of a berth last week, so I thought I'd blow myself for some rags. I've been over to San Rafael all day visiting my cousins: had a great time; went out to row. Oh, and had a great feed: lettuce sandwiches with mayonnaise. Simply out of sight. I came back on the four o'clock boat and held down the 'line' on Kearney Street for an hour or two."

"Yes?" young Haight said perfunctorily, adding after a moment, "Isn't this a gay crowd, a typical San Francisco crowd and——"

"I had a cocktail in the Imperial at about quarter of five," said Geary, "and got a cigar at the Elite; then I went around to get my clothes. Oh, you ought to have heard the blowing up I gave my tailor! I let him have it right straight."

Geary paused a moment, and Vandover said: "Come on, let's walk around a little; don't you want to? We might run on to the red hat again."

"I told him," continued Geary without moving, "that if he wanted to do any more work for me, he'd have to get in front of himself in a hurry, and that *I* wasn't full of bubbles, if *he* was. 'Why,' says he, 'why, Mr. Geary, I've never had a customer talk like this to me before since I've been in the business!' 'Well, Mr. Allen,' says I, 'it's time you *had!*' Oh, sure, I gave it to him straight."

"Vandover has gone daft over a girl in a red hat," said young Haight, as they got up and began to walk. "Have you noticed her up here?"

359

"I went to the Grillroom after I left the tailor's," continued Geary, "and had supper downtown. Ah, you ought to have seen the steak they gave me! Just about as thick as it was wide. I gave the slavey a four-bit tip. Oh, it's just as well, you know, to keep in with them, if you go there often. I lunch there four or five times a week."

They descended to the ground floor and promenaded the central aisle watching for pretty girls. In front of a candy-counter, where there was a soda fountain, they saw the red hat again. Vandover looked her squarely in the face and laughed a little. When he had passed he looked back; the girl caught his eye and turned away with a droll smile. Vandover paused, grinning, and raising his hat. "I guess that's mine," he said.

"You are not going, are you?" exclaimed young Haight, as Vandover stopped. "Oh, for goodness' sake, Van, do leave the girls alone for one hour in the day. Come on! Come on downtown with us."

"No, no," answered Vandover. "I'm going to chase it up. Good-bye. I may see you fellows later," and he turned back and went up to the girl.

"Look at that!" said young Haight, exasperated. "He knows he's liable to meet his acquaintances here, and yet there he goes, almost arm in arm with a girl like that. It's too bad; why *can't* a fellow keep straight when there are such a lot of *nice* girls?"

Geary never liked to see anything done better than he could do it himself. Just now he was vexed because Vandover had got in ahead of him. He looked after the girl a moment and muttered scornfully:

"Cheap meat!" adding, "Ah, you bet *I* wouldn't do that. I flatter myself that I'm a little too clever to cut my own throat in that fashion. I look out after my interests better than that. Well, Dolly," he concluded, "*I've* got a thirst on. Van and Ellis have gone off with their girls; let's you and I go somewhere and have something wet."

"All right. What's the matter with the Luxembourg?" answered young Haight.

"Luxembourg goes, then," assented Geary, and they turned about and started for the door. As they were passing out someone came running up behind them and took an arm of each; it was Vandover.

"Hello," cried Geary, delighted, "your girl shook you, didn't she?"

"Not a bit of it," answered Vandover. "Oh, but say, she is out of sight! Says her name is Grace Irving. No, she didn't shake me. I made a date with her for next Wednesday night. I didn't want to be seen around here with her, you know."

"Of *course* she will keep that date!" said Geary.

"Well, now, I think she will," protested Vandover.

"Well, come along," interrupted young Haight. "We'll all go down to the Luxembourg and have something cold and wet."

"Ah, make it the Imperial instead," objected Vandover. "We may find Flossie."

"Say," cried Geary, "can't you *live* without trailing around after some kind of petticoats?"

"You're right," admitted Vandover, "I can't," but he persuaded them to go to the Imperial for all that.

At the Imperial, Toby, the red-eyed waiter, came to take their order.

"Good evening, gentlemen," he said. "Haven't seen you around here for some time."

"No, no," said Geary. "I've been too busy. I've been working like a dog lately to get into a certain office. You bet I'll make it all right—all right. Bring me a stringy rabbit and a pint of dog's-head.

"You bet I've been working," he continued after they had settled down to their beer and rabbits, "working like a dog. A man's got to rustle if he's going to make a success at law. *I'm* going to make it go, by George, or I'll know the reason why. I'll make my way in this town and my pile. There's money to be made here and *I* might just as well make it as the next man. Every man for himself, that's what *I* say; that's the way to get along. It may be selfish, but you've got to do it. By God! it's human nature. Isn't that right, hey? Isn't that right?"

"Oh, that's right," admitted young Haight, trying to be polite. After this the conversation lagged a little. Young Haight drank his Apollinaris lemonade through a straw, Geary sipped his ale, and Vandover fed himself Welsh rabbit and Spanish olives with the silent enjoyment of a glutton. By and by, when they had finished and had lighted their cigars and cigarettes, they began to talk about the last Cotillon, to which Vandover and Haight belonged.

"Say, Van," said young Haight, tilting his head to one side and shutting one eye to avoid the smoke from his cigar, "say, didn't I see you dancing with Mrs. Doane after supper?"

"Yes," said Vandover, laughing; "all the men were trying to get a dance with her. She had an edge on."

"No?" exclaimed Geary, incredulously.

"That's a fact," admitted young Haight. "Van is right."

"She was opposite to me at table," said Vandover, "and *I* saw her empty a whole bottle of champagne."

"Why, I didn't know they got drunk like that at the Cotillons," said Geary. "I thought they were very swell."

"Well, of course, they don't as a rule," returned Vandover. "Of course there are girls like—like Henrietta Vance who belong to the Cotillon and make it what it is, and what it ought to be. But there are other girls like

Mrs. Doane and Lilly Stannard and the Trafford girls
that like their champagne pretty well now, and don't
you forget it! Oh, you know, I wouldn't call it getting
drunk, though."

"Well, why not?" exclaimed young Haight, impatiently. "Why not call it 'getting drunk'? Why not call
things by their right name? You can see just how bad
they are then; and I think it's shameful that such things
can go on in an organization that is supposed to contain
the very best people in the city. Now, I just want to tell
you what I saw at one of these same Cotillons in the first
part of the season. Lilly Stannard disappeared after
supper and people said she was sick and was going home,
but I knew exactly what was the matter, because I had
seen her at the supper table. Well, I had gone outside
on the steps to get a mouthful of smoke, and my little
cousin, Hetty, who had just come out and who is only
nineteen, was out there with me because it was so warm
inside, and *she* had seen Lilly Stannard filling up with
champagne at supper, and didn't know what to make of
it. Well, we were just talking about it, and I was trying
to make her believe too that Lilly Stannard was sick,
when here comes Lilly herself out to her carriage. Her
maid was supporting her, just about half-carrying her.
Lilly's face was so pale that the powder on it looked like
ashes, her hair was all coming down, and she was hiccoughing. Now," continued young Haight, his eyes
snapping, and his voice raised so as to make itself heard
above the exclamations of his two friends, "now, that's
a *fact;* I give you my word of honour that it actually
happened. It's not hearsay; I saw it myself. It's fine,
isn't it?" he went on, wrathfully. "It sounds well, don't
it, when it's told *just as it happened?* The girl was dead
drunk. Oh, she may have made a mistake; it may have
been the first time; but the fact remains that she always
drinks a lot of champagne at the Cotillons, and other

girls have been drunk there, too. Mrs. Doane, that Van tells about, was *drunk;* that's the word for it. She was dead drunk that night, and there was my little cousin, Hetty, who had never seen even a man the worse for his liquor, standing there and taking it all in. Of course, everyone hushed the thing up or else said the poor girl was sick; but Hetty knew, and what effect do you suppose it had upon a little girl like that, who had always been told what nice, irreproachable people went to the Cotillons? Hetty will never be the same little girl now that she was before. Oh, it makes me damned tired."

"Well, I don't see," said Geary, "why the girls should make such a fuss about the men keeping straight. I daresay now that this Stannard girl would cut us all dead if she knew how drunk we were that night about four months ago—that night that you fellows got thrown out of the Luxembourg."

"No, I don't believe she would at all," said young Haight.

"She'd think better of you for it," put in Vandover. "Look here," he went on, "all this talk of women demanding the same moral standard for men as men do for women is fine on paper, but how does it work in real life? The women don't demand it at all. Take the average society girl in a big city like this. The girls that we meet at teas and receptions and functions—don't you suppose they know the life we men lead? Of course they do. They may not know it in detail, but they know in a general way that we get drunk a good deal and go to disreputable houses and that sort of thing, and do they ever cut us for that? No, sir; not much. Why, I tell you, they even have a little more respect for us. They like a man to know things, to be experienced. A man that keeps himself straight and clean and never goes around with fast women, they think is ridiculous. Of course, a girl don't want to know the particulars of a man's vice;

what they want is that a man should have the knowledge of good and evil, yes, and lots of evil. To a large
extent I really believe it's the women's fault that the
men are what they are. If they demanded a higher moral
standard the men would come up to it; they encourage a
man to go to the devil and then—and then when he's
rotten with disease and ruins his wife and has children
—what is it—'*spotted toads*'—*then* there's a great cry
raised against the men, and women write books and all,
when half the time the woman has only encouraged him
to be what he is."

"Oh, well now," retorted young Haight, "you know
that all the girls are not like that."

"Most of them that you meet in society are."

"But they are the best people, aren't they?" demanded Geary.

"No," answered Vandover and young Haight in a
breath, and young Haight continued:

"No; I believe that very few of what you would call
the 'best people' go out in society—people like the
Ravises, who have good principles, and keep up old-
fashioned virtues and all that. You know," he added,
"they have family prayers down there every morning
after breakfast."

Geary began to smile.

"Well, now, I don't care," retorted young Haight. "I
like that sort of thing."

"So do I," said Vandover. "Up home, now, the governor asks a blessing at each meal, and somehow I
wouldn't like to see him leave it off. But you can't tell
me," he went on, going back to the original subject of
their discussion, "you can't tell me that American society girls, city-bred, and living at the end of the nineteenth century, don't know about things. Why, man
alive, how can they help but know? Look at those that
have brothers—don't you suppose they know, and if

they know, why don't they use their influence to stop it? I tell you if anyone were to write up the lives that we young men of the city lead after dark, people wouldn't believe it. At that party that Henrietta Vance gave last month there were about twenty fellows there and I knew every one, and I was looking around the supper-table and wondering how many of those young fellows had never been inside of a disreputable house, and there was only *one* besides Dolly Haight!"

Young Haight exclaimed at this, laughing good-naturedly, twirling his thumbs, and casting down his eyes with mock-modesty.

"Well, that's the truth just the same," Vandover went on. "We young men of the cities are a fine lot. I'm not doing the baby act. I'm not laying the blame on the girls altogether, but I say that in a measure the girls are responsible. They want a man to be a *man*, to be up to date, to be a man of the world and to go in for that sort of vice, but they don't know, they don't dream, how rotten and disgusting it is. Oh, I'm not preaching. I know I'm just as bad as the rest, and I'm going to have a good time while I can, but sometimes when you stop and think, and as Dolly says 'call things by their right names,' why you feel, don't you know—*queer*."

"I don't believe, Van," responded young Haight, "that it's *quite* as bad as you say. But it's even wrong, I think, that a good girl should know anything about vice at all."

"Oh, that's nonsense," broke in Geary; "you can't expect nowadays that a girl, an American girl, can live twenty years in a city and not know things. Do you think the average modern girl is going to be the absolutely pure and innocent girl of, say, fifty years ago? Not much; they are right on to things to-day. You can't tell them much. And it's all right, too; they know how to look out for themselves, then. It's part of their education; and I think if they haven't the knowledge of evil, and don't know what sort of life the average young man leads, that their mothers ought to tell them."

"Well, I don't agree with you," retorted young Haight. "There's something revolting in the idea that it's necessary a young girl should be instructed in that sort of nastiness."

"Why, not at all," answered Geary. "Without it she might be ruined by the first man that came along. It's a protection to her virtue."

"Oh, pshaw! I don't believe it at all," cried young Haight, impatiently. "I believe that a girl is born with a natural intuitive purity that will lead her to protect her virtue just as instinctively as she would dodge a blow; if she wants to go wrong she will have to make an effort herself to overcome that instinct."

"And if she don't," cried Vandover eagerly, "if she don't—if she don't protect her virtue, I say a man has a right to go as far with her as he can."

"If *he* don't, someone else will," said Geary.

"Ah, you can't get around it that way," answered young Haight, smiling. "It's a man's duty to protect a girl, even if he has to protect her against herself."

When he got home that night Vandover thought over this remark of young Haight's and in its light reviewed what had occurred in the room at the Imperial. He felt aroused, nervous, miserably anxious. At length he tried to dismiss the subject from his mind; he woke up his drowsing grate fire, punching it with the poker, talking to it, saying, "Wake up there, you!" When he was undressed, he sat down before it in his bathrobe, absorbing its heat luxuriously, musing into the coals, scratching himself as was his custom. But for all that he fretted nervously and did not sleep well that night.

Next morning he took his bath. Vandover enjoyed his bath and usually spent two or three hours over it.

When the water was very warm he got into it with his novel on a rack in front of him and a box of chocolates conveniently near. Here he stayed, for over an hour, eating and reading, and occasionally smoking a cigarette, until at length the enervating heat of the steam gradually overcame him and he dropped off to sleep.

On this particular morning between nine and ten Geary called, and as was his custom came right up to Vandover's room. Mr. Corkle, lying on the wolfskin in the bay window, jumped up with a gruff bark, but, recognizing him, came up wiggling his short tail. Geary saw Vandover's clothes thrown about the floor and the closed door of the bathroom.

"Hey, Van!" he called. "It's Charlie Geary. Are you taking a bath?"

"Hello! What? Who is it?" came from behind the door. "Oh, is that you, Charlie? Hello! how are you? Yes, I'm taking a bath. I must have been asleep. Wait a minute; I'll be out."

"No, I can't stop," answered Geary. "I've an appointment downtown; overslept myself, and had to go without my breakfast; makes me feel all broke up. I'll get something at the Grillroom about eleven; a steak, I guess. But that isn't what I came to say. Ida Wade has killed herself! Isn't it fearful? I thought I'd drop in on my way downtown and speak to you about it. It's dreadful! It's all in the morning papers. She must have been out of her head."

"What is it—what has she done?" came back Vandover's voice. "Papers—I haven't seen—what has she done? Tell me—what has she done?"

"Why, she committed suicide last night by taking laudanum," answered Geary, "and nobody knows why. She didn't leave any message or letter or anything of the kind. It's a fearful thing to happen so suddenly, but it seems she has been very despondent and broke up about something or other for a week or two. They found her in her room last night about ten o'clock lying across her table with only her wrapper on. She was unconscious then, and between one and two she died. She was unconscious all the time. Well, I can't stop any longer, Van; I've an appointment downtown. I was just going past the house and I thought I would run up and speak to you about Ida. I'll see you again pretty soon and we'll talk this over."

Mr. Corkle politely attended Geary to the head of the stairs, then went back to Vandover's room, and after blowing under the crack of the bathroom door to see if his master was still there returned to the wolfskin and sat down on his short tail and yawned. He was impatient to see Vandover and thought he stayed in his bath an unnecessarily long time. He went up to the door again and listened. It was very still inside; he could not hear the slightest sound, and he wondered again what could keep Vandover in there so long. He had too much self-respect to whine, so he went back to the wolfskin and curled up in the sun, but did not go to sleep.

By and by, after a very long time, the bathroom door swung open, and Vandover came out. He had not dried himself and was naked and wet. He went directly to the table in the centre of the room and picked up the morning paper, looking for the article of which Geary had spoken. At first he could not find it, and then it suddenly jumped into prominence from out the gray blur of the print on an inside page beside an advertisement of a charity concert for the benefit of a home for incurable children. There was a picture of Ida taken from a photograph like one that she had given him, and which even then was thrust between the frame and glass of his mirror. He read the article through; it sketched her life and character and the circumstances of her death with the relentless terseness of the writer cramped for space.

According to this view, the causes of her death were unknown. It had been remarked that she had of late been despondent and in ill health.

Vandover threw the paper down and straightened up, naked and dripping, putting both hands to his head. In a low voice under his breath he said:

"What have I done? What have I done now?"

Like the sudden unrolling of a great scroll he saw his responsibility for her death and for the ruin of that something in her which was more than life. What would become of her now? And what would become of him? For a single brief instant he tried to persuade himself that Ida had consented after all. But he knew that this was not so. She had consented, but he had forced her consent; he was none the less guilty. And then in that dreadful moment when he saw things in their true light, all the screens of conventionality and sophistry torn away, the words that young Haight had spoken came back to him. No matter if she had consented, it was his duty to have protected her, even against herself.

He walked the floor with great strides, steaming with the warm water, striking his head with his hands and crying out, "Oh, this is fearful, fearful! What have I done now? I have killed her; yes, and worse!"

He could think of nothing worse that could have happened to him. What a weight of responsibility to carry—he who hated responsibility of any kind, who had always tried to escape from anything that was even irksome, who loved his ease, his comfort, his peace of mind!

At every moment now he saw the different consequences of what he had done. Now, it was that his life was ruined, and that all through its course this crime would hang like a millstone about his neck. There could be no more enjoyment of anything for him; all the little pleasures and little self-indulgences which till now had delighted him were spoiled and rendered impossible.

The rest of his life would have to be one long penitence; any pleasure he might take would only make his crime seem more abominable.

Now, it was a furious revolt against his mistake that had led him to such a fearful misunderstanding of Ida; a silent impotent rage against himself and against the brute in him that he had permitted to drag him to this thing.

Now, it was a wave of immense pity for the dead girl that overcame him, and he saw himself as another person, destroying what she most cherished for the sake of gratifying an unclean passion.

Now, it was a terror for himself. What would they do to him? His part in the affair was sure to be found out. He tried to think what the punishment for such crime would be; but would he not be considered a murderer as well? Could he not hang for this? His imagination was never more active; his fear never more keen. At once a thousand plans of concealment or escape were tossed up in his mind.

But worse than all was the thought of that punishment from which there was absolutely no escape, and of that strange other place where his crime would assume right proportions and receive right judgment, no matter how it was palliated or evaded here. Then for an instant it was as if a gulf without bottom had opened under him, and he had to fight himself back from its edge for sheer self-preservation. To look too long in that direction was simple insanity beyond any doubt.

And all this time he threw himself to and fro in his room, his long white arms agitated and shaking, his wet and shining hair streaming far over his face, and the sparse light fell upon his legs and ankles, all straight and trickling with moisture. At times an immense unreasoning terror would come upon him all of a sudden, horrible, crushing, so that he rolled upon the bed groaning and sobbing, digging his nails into his scalp, shutting his teeth against a desire to scream out, writhing in the throes of terrible mental agony.

That day and the next were fearful. To Vandover everything in his world was changed. All that had happened before the morning of Geary's visit appeared to him to have occurred in another phase of his life, years and years ago. He lay awake all night long, listening to the creaking of the house and the drip of the water faucets. He turned from his food with repugnance, told his father that he was sick, and kept indoors as much as he could, reading all the papers to see if he had been found out. To his great surprise and relief, a theory gained ground that Ida was subject to spells of ill health, to long fits of despondency, and that her suicide had occurred during one of these. If Ida's family knew anything of the truth, it was apparent that they were doing their best to cover up their disgrace. Vandover was too thoroughly terrified for his own safety to feel humiliated at this possible explanation of his security. There was as yet not even a guess that implicated him.

He thought that he was bearing up under the strain well enough, but on the evening of the second day, as he was pretending to eat his supper, his father sent the servant out and turning to him, said kindly:

"What is it, Van? Aren't you well nowadays?"

"Not very, sir," answered Vandover. "My throat is troubling me again."

"You look deathly pale," returned his father. "Your eyes are sunken and you don't eat."

"Yes, I know," said Vandover. "I'm not feeling well at all. I think I'll go to bed early to-night. I don't know"—he continued, after a pause, feeling a desire to escape from his father's observation—"I don't know but what I'll go up now. Will you tell the cook to feed Mr. Corkle for me?"

372

His father looked at him as he pushed back from the table.

"What's the matter, Van?" he said. "Is there anything wrong?"

"Oh, I'll be all right in the morning," he replied, nervously. "I feel a little under the weather just now."

"Don't you think you had better tell me what the trouble is?" said his father, kindly.

"There *isn't* any trouble, sir," insisted Vandover. "I just feel a little under the weather."

But as he was starting to undress in his room a sudden impulse took possession of him, an overwhelming childish desire to tell his father all about it. It was beginning to be more than he was able to bear alone. He did not allow himself to stop and reason with this impulse, but slipped on his vest again and went downstairs. He found his father in the smoking room, sitting unoccupied in the huge leather chair before the fireplace.

As Vandover came in the Old Gentleman rose and without a word, as if he had been expecting him, went to the door and shut and locked it. He came back and stood before the fireplace watching Vandover as he approached and took the chair he had just vacated. Vandover told him of the affair in two or three phrases, without choosing his words, repeating the same expressions over and over again, moved only with the desire to have it over and done with.

It was like a burst of thunder. The worst his father had feared was not as bad as this. He had expected some rather serious boyish trouble, but this was the crime of a man. Still watching his son, he put out his hand, groping for the edge of the mantelpiece, and took hold of it with a firm grasp. For a moment he said nothing; then:

"And—and you say you seduced her."

Without looking up, Vandover answered, "Yes, sir,"

373

and then he added: "It is horrible; when I think of it I sometimes feel as though I should go off my head. I——"

But the Old Gentleman interrupted him, putting out his hand:

"Don't," he said, quickly, "don't say anything now—please."

They were both silent for a long time, Vandover gazing stupidly at a little blue and red vase on the table, wondering how his father would take the news, what next he would say; the Old Gentleman drawing his breath short, occasionally clearing his throat, his eyes wandering vaguely about the walls of the room, his fingers dancing upon the edge of the mantelpiece. Then at last he put his hand to his neck as though loosening his collar and said, looking away from Vandover:

"Won't you—won't you please go out—go away for a little while—leave me alone for a little while."

When Vandover closed the door, he shut the edge of a rug between it and the sill; as he reopened it to push the rug out of the way he saw his father sink into the chair and, resting his arm upon the table, bow his head upon it.

He did not see his father again that night, and at breakfast next morning not a word was exchanged between them, but his father did not go downtown to his office that forenoon, as was his custom. Vandover went up to his room immediately after breakfast and sat down before the window that overlooked the little garden in the rear of the house.

He was utterly miserable, his nerves were gone, and at times he would feel again a touch of that hysterical, unreasoning terror that had come upon him so suddenly the other morning.

Now there was a new trouble: the blow he had given his father. He could see that the Old Gentleman was crushed under it, and that he had never imagined that his son could have been so base as this. Vandover wondered what he was going to do. It would seem as if he had destroyed all of his father's affection for him, and he trembled lest the Old Gentleman should cast him off, everything. Even if his father did not disown him, he did not see how they could ever be the same. They might go on living together in the same house, but as far apart from each other as strangers. This, however, did not seem natural; it was much more likely that his father would send him away, anywhere out of his sight, forwarding, perhaps through his lawyer or agents, enough money to keep him alive. The more Vandover thought of this, the more he became convinced that such would be his father's decision. The Old Gentleman had spent the night over it, time enough to make up his mind, and the fact that he had neither spoken to him nor looked at him that morning was only an indication of what Vandover was to expect. He fancied he knew his father well enough to foresee how this decision would be carried out, not with any imprecations or bursts of rage, but calmly, sadly, inevitably.

Toward noon his father came into the room, and Vandover turned to face him and to hear what he had to say as best he could. He knew he should not break down under it, for he felt as though his misery had reached its limit, and that nothing could touch or affect him much now.

His father had a decanter of port in one hand and a glass in the other; he filled the glass and held it toward Vandover, saying gently:

"I think you had better take some of this; you've hardly eaten anything in three days. Do you feel pretty bad, Van?"

Vandover put the glass down and got upon his feet. All at once a great sob shook him.

"Oh, governor!" he cried.

It was as if it had been a mother or a dear sister. The prodigal son put his arms about his father's neck for the first time since he had been a little boy, and clung to him and wept as though his heart were breaking.

CHAPTER VIII

"W E WILL begin all over again, Van," his father said later that same day. "We will start in again and try to forget all this, not as much as we *can*, but as much as we *ought*, and live it down, and from now on we'll try to do the thing that is right and brave and good."

"Just try me, sir!" cried Vandover.

That was it, begin all over again. He had never seen more clearly than now that other life which it was possible for him to live, a life that was above the level of self-indulgence and animal pleasures, a life that was not made up of the society of lost women or fast girls, but yet a life of keen enjoyment.

Whenever he had been deeply moved about anything, the power and desire of art had grown big within him, and he turned to it now, instinctively and ardently.

It was all the better half of him that was aroused—the better half that he had kept in check ever since his college days, the better half that could respond to the influences of his father and of Turner Ravis, that other Vandover whom he felt was his real self, Vandover the true man, Vandover the artist, not Vandover the easy-going, the self-indulgent, not Vandover the lover of women.

From this time forward he was resolved to give up the world that he had hitherto known, and devote himself with all his strength to his art. In the first glow of that resolution he thought that he had never been happier; he wondered how he could have been blind so long; what was all that life worth compared with the life of a

377

great artist, compared even with a life of sturdy, virile effort and patient labour even though barren of achievement?

And then something very curious happened: The little picture of Turner Ravis that hung over his mantelpiece caught his glance, looking out at him with her honest eyes and sweet smile. In an instant he seemed to love her as he had never imagined he could love anyone. All that was best in him went out toward her in a wave of immense tenderness; the tears came to his eyes, he could not tell why. Ah, he was not good enough for her now, but he would love her so well that he would grow better, and between her and his good father and his art, the better Vandover, the real Vandover, would grow so large and strong within him that there should be no room for the other Vandover, the Vandover of Flossie and of the Imperial, the Vandover of the brute.

During the course of talk that day between himself and his father, it was decided that Vandover should go away for a little while. He was in a fair way to be sick from worry and nervous exhaustion, and a sea trip to San Diego and back seemed to be what he stood most in need of. Besides this, his father told him, it was inevitable that his share in Ida's death would soon be known; in any case it would be better for him to be away from the city.

"You take whatever steamer sails next," said his father, "and go down to Coronado and stay there as long as you like, three weeks anyway; stay there until you get well, and when you get back, Van, we'll have a talk about Paris again. Perhaps you would like to get away this winter, maybe as soon as next month. You think it over while you are away, and when you want to go, why, we'll go over together, Van. What do you think? Would you like to have your old governor along for a little while?"

The *Santa Rosa* cast off the company's docks the next day about noon in the midst of a thick, cold mist that was half rain. The Old Gentleman came to see Vandover off.

The steamer, which seemed gigantic, was roped and cabled to the piers, feeling the water occasionally with her screw to keep the hawsers taut. About the forward gangway a band of overworked stevedores were stowing in the last of the cargo, aided by a donkey engine, which every now and then broke out into a spasm of sputtering coughs. At the passenger gangway a great crowd was gathered, laughing and exchanging remarks with the other crowd that leaned over the railings of the decks.

There was a smell of pitch and bilge in the air mingled with the reek of hot oil from the engines. About twelve o'clock an odour of cooking arose, and the steward went about the decks drumming upon a snoring gong for dinner.

Half an hour later the great whistle roared interminably, drowning out the chorus of "good-byes" that rose on all sides. Long before it had ceased, the huge bulk had stirred, almost imperceptibly at first, then, gathering headway, swung out into the stream and headed for the Golden Gate.

Vandover was in the stern upon the hurricane deck, shaking his hat toward his father, who had tied his handkerchief to his cane and was waving it at him as he stood upon an empty packing-case. As the throng of those who were left behind dwindled away, one by one, Vandover could see him standing there, almost the last of all, and long after the figure itself was lost in the blur of the background he still saw the tiny white dot of the handkerchief moving back and forth, as if spelling out a signal to him across the water.

The fog drew a little higher as they passed down the bay. To the left was the city swarming upon its hills, a dull gray mass, cut in parallel furrows by the streets; straggling and uneven where it approached the sand-dunes in the direction of the Presidio. To the right the long slope of Tamalpais climbed up and was lost in the fog, while directly in front of them was the Golden Gate, a bleak prospect of fog-drenched headlands on either side of a narrow strip of yellow, frothy water. Beyond that, the open Pacific.

A brisk cannonade was going on from the Presidio and from Black Point, and both forts were hidden behind a great curtain of tumbling white smoke that rolled up to mingle with the fog. Everybody was on that side of the deck watching and making guesses as to the reason of it. It was perhaps target practice. Ah, it was a good thing that the steamer was not in line with the target. Perhaps, though, that was the safest place to be. Some-one told about a derelict that was anchored as a target off the heads, and shot at for fifteen hours without being touched once. Oh, they were great gunners at the Presidio! But just the same the sound of cannon was a fine thing to hear; it excited one. A noisy party of gentlemen already installed in the smoking room came out on deck for a moment with their cards in their hands, and de-clared laughingly that the whole thing was only a salute in the *Santa Rosa's* honour.

By the middle of the afternoon, Vandover began to see that for him the trip was going to be tedious. He knew no one on board and had come away so hurriedly that he had neglected to get himself any interesting books. He spent an hour or two promenading the upper deck until the cold wind that was blowing drove him to the smoking room, where he tried to interest himself in watching some of the whist games that were in progress.

It surprised him that he could find occasion to be bored so soon after what had happened; but he no longer

380

wished to occupy his mind by brooding over anything
so disagreeable and wanted some sort of amusement to
divert and entertain him. Vandover had so accustomed
himself to that kind of self-indulgence that he could
not go long without it. It had become a simple necessity
for him to be amused, and just now he thought himself
justified in seeking it in order to forget about Ida's death.
He had dwelt upon this now for nearly four days, until
it had come to be some sort of a formless horror that it
was necessary to avoid. He could get little present enjoyment by looking forward to the new life that he was
going to begin and in which his father, his art, and
Turner Ravis were to be the chief influences. The
thought of this prospect did give him pleasure, but he
had for so long a time fed his mind upon the more tan-
gible and concrete enjoyments of the hour and minute
that it demanded them now continually.

He sat for a long time upon the slippery leather cushions of the smoking room trying desperately to become
interested in the whist game, or gazing awestruck at the
man at his elbow who was smoking black Perrique in a
pipe, inhaling the smoke and blowing it out through his
nose. After a while he returned to the deck.

There it was cold and wet and a strong wind was
blowing from the ocean. Four miles to the east an endless procession of brown, bare hills filed slowly past
under the fog. The sky was a dreary brown and the
leagues of shifting water a melancholy desert of grey.
Besides these there was nothing but the bleached hills
and the drifting fog; the wind blew continually, passing
between the immense reaches of sea and sky with prolonged sighs of infinite sadness.

Three seagulls followed the vessel, now in a long line,
now abreast, and now in a triangle. They sailed slowly
about, dipping and rising in the vast hollows between the
waves, turning their heads constantly from side to side.

381

Vandover went to the stern and for a time found amusement in watching the indicator of the patent log, and listening for its bell. But his interest in this was soon exhausted, and he returned to the smoking room again, reflecting that this was only the first afternoon and that there still remained two days that somehow had to be gone through with.

About five o'clock, as he was on his way to get a glass of seltzer, he saw Grace Irving, the girl of the red hat whom he had met at the Mechanics' Fair, sitting on a camp-stool just inside of her stateroom eating a banana. The sight of her startled him out of all composure for the minute. His first impulse was to speak to her, but he reflected that he was done with all that now and that it was better for him to pass on as though he had not seen her, but as he came in front of her she looked up quickly and nodded to him very pleasantly in such a way that it was evident she had already known he was on board. It was impossible for Vandover to ignore her, and though he did not stop, he looked back at her and smiled as he took off his hat.

He went down to supper in considerable agitation, marvelling at the coincidence that had brought them together again. He wondered, too, how she could be so pleasant to him now, for as a matter of course he had not kept the engagement he had made with her at the Fair. At the same time, he felt that she must think him a great fool not to have stopped and spoken to her; either he should have done that or else have ignored her little bow entirely. He was firmly resolved to have nothing to do with her, yet it chafed him to feel that she thought him diffident. It seemed now as though he owed it to himself to speak to her if only for a minute and make some sort of an excuse. By the time he had finished his supper, he had made up his mind to do this, and then to avoid her for the rest of the trip.

As he was leaving the dining saloon he met her coming down the stairs alone, dressed very prettily in a checked travelling ulster with a gray velvet collar, and a little fore and aft cap to match. He stopped her and made his excuses; she did not say much in reply and seemed a little offended, so that Vandover could not refrain from adding that he was very glad to see her on board.

"Ah, you don't seem as if you were, very," she said, putting out her chin at him prettily and passing on. It was an awkward and embarrassing little scene and Vandover was glad that it was over. But the thing had been done now, he had managed to show the girl that he did not wish to keep up the acquaintance begun at the Fair, and from now on she would keep out of his way.

He took a few turns on the upper deck, smoking his pipe, walking about fast, while his dinner digested. The sun went down behind the black horizon in an immense blood-red nebula of mist, the sea turned from gray to dull green and then to a lifeless brown, and the *Santa Rosa's* lights began to glow at her quarters and at her masthead; in her stern the screw drummed and threshed monotonously, a puff of warm air reeking with the smell of hot oil came from the engine hatch, and in an instant Vandover saw again the curved roof of the immense iron-vaulted depot, the passengers on the platform staring curiously at the group around the invalid's chair, the repair gang in spotted blue overalls, and the huge white cat dozing on an empty baggage truck.

The wind freshened and he returned to the smoking room to get warm. The same game of whist was going on, and the man with the Perrique tobacco had filled another pipe and continued to blow the smoke through his nose.

After a while Vandover went back to the main deck and wandered aft, where he stood a long time looking over the stern, interested in watching the receding water. It was dark by this time, the wind had increased and had blown the fog to landward, and the ocean had changed to a deep blue, the blue of the sky at night; here and there a wave broke, leaving a line of white on the sea like the trail of a falling star across the heavens, while the white haze of the steamer's wake wandered vaguely across the intense blue like the milky way across the zenith.

Vandover was horribly bored. There seemed to be absolutely nothing to amuse him, unless, indeed, he should decide to renew his acquaintance with Grace Irving. But this was out of the question now, for he knew what it would lead to. Even if he should yield to the temptation, he did not see how he could take any great pleasure in that sort of thing again, after what had happened.

Of all the consequences of what he had done, the one which had come to afflict him the most poignantly was that his enjoyment of life was spoiled. At first he had thought that he never could take pleasure in anything again so long as he should live, that his good times were gone. But as his pliable character rearranged itself to suit the new environment, he began to see that there would come a time when he would grow accustomed to Ida's death and when his grief would lose its sharpness. He had even commenced to look forward to this time and to long for it as a sort of respite and relief. He believed at first that it would not be for a great many years; but even so soon after the suicide as this, he saw with a little thrill of comfort that it would be but a matter of months. At the same time Vandover was surprised and even troubled at the ease with which he was recovering from the first shock. He wondered at himself, because he knew he had been sincere in his talk with his father. Vandover was not given to self-analysis, but now for a minute he was wondering if this reaction were due to his youth, his good health, and his good spirits, or whether there was something wrong with him. However, he dismissed these thoughts with a shrug of his shoulders as though freeing himself from some disagreeable burden. Ah, he was no worse than the average; one could get accustomed to almost anything; it was only in the books that people had their lives ruined; and to brood over such things was unnatural and morbid. Ah! what a dreadful thing to become morbid! He could not bring Ida back, or mitigate what he had done, or be any more sorry for it by making himself miserable. Well, then! Only he would let that sort of thing alone after this, the lesson had been too terrible; he would try and enjoy himself again, only it should be in other ways.

Later in the evening, about nine o'clock, when nearly all the passengers were in bed, and Vandover was leaning over the side of the boat finishing his pipe before turning in himself, Grace Irving came out of her stateroom and sat down at a little distance from him, looking out over the water, humming a little song. She and Vandover were the only people to be seen on the deserted promenade.

Vandover saw her without moving, only closing his teeth tighter on his pipe. It was evident that Grace expected him to speak to her and had given him a chance for an admirable little tête-à-tête. For a moment Vandover's heart knocked at his throat; he drew his breath once or twice sharply through his nose. In an instant all the old evil instincts were back again, urging and clamouring never so strong, never so insistent. But Vandover set his face against them, honestly, recalling his resolution, telling himself that he was done with that life. As he had said, the lesson had been too terrible.

He turned about resolutely, and walked slowly away

from her. The girl looked after him a moment, surprised, and then called out:

"Oh, Mr. Vandover!"

Vandover paused a moment, looking back.

"Where are you going?" she went on. "Didn't you see me here? Don't you want to come and talk to me?"

"No," answered Vandover, smiling good-humouredly, trying to be as polite as was possible. "No, I don't." Then he took a sudden resolution, and added gravely, "I don't want to have anything to do with you."

In his stateroom, as he sat on the edge of his berth winding his watch before going to bed, he thought over what he had said. "That was a mean way to talk to a girl," he told himself, "but," he added, "it's the only thing to do. I simply couldn't start in again after all that's happened. Oh, yes, that was the right thing to do!"

He felt a glow of self-respect for his firmness and his decision, a pride in the unexpected strength, the fine moral rigour that he had developed at the critical moment. He *could* turn sharp around when he wanted to, after all. Ah, yes, that was the only thing to do if one was to begin all over again and live down what had happened. He wished that the governor might know how well he had acted.

CHAPTER IX

VANDOVER stayed for two weeks at Coronado
Beach and managed to pass the time very pleasantly.
He was fortunate enough to find a party at the hotel
whom he knew very well. In the morning they bathed
or sailed on the bay, and in the afternoon rode out with
a pack of greyhounds and coursed jack-rabbits on the
lower end of the island. Vandover's good spirits began
to come back to him, his appetite returned, his nerves
steadied themselves, he slept eight hours every night.
But for all that he did not think that things were the
same with him. He said to himself that he was a changed
man; that he was older, more serious.

During this time he received several letters from his
father which he answered very promptly. In the course
of their correspondence it was arranged that they should
both leave for Europe on the twenty-fifth of that month,
and that consequently, Vandover should return to the
city not later than the fifteenth. Vandover was having
such a good time, however, that he stayed over the
regular steamer in order to go upon a moonlight picnic
down on the beach. The next afternoon he took passage
for San Francisco on a second-class boat.

This homeward passage turned out to be one long
misery for Vandover. He had never been upon a second-
class boat before and had never imagined that anything
could be so horribly uncomfortable or disagreeable.
The *Mazatlan* was overcrowded, improperly ballasted,
and rolled continually. The table was bad, the accom-
modations inadequate, the passengers hopelessly un-

congenial. Cold and foggy weather accompanied the boat continually. The same endless procession of bleached hills still filed past under the mist, going now in the opposite direction, and the same interminable game of whist was played in the smoking room, only with greasier, second-class cards, amidst the acrid smoke of second-class tobacco. At supper, the first day out, a little Jew who sat next to Vandover, and who invariably wore a plush skull-cap with ear-laps, tried to sell him two flawed and yellow diamonds.

The evening after leaving Port Hartford the *Mazatlan* ran into dirty weather. It was not stormy—simply rough, disagreeable, the wind and sea directly ahead. Half an hour after supper Vandover began to be sick. For a long time he sat on the slippery leather cushions in the nasty smoking room, sucking limes, drinking seltzer, and trying to be interested in the card games. He dozed a little and awoke, feeling wretched, covered with a cold sweat, racked by a pain in the back of his head, and tortured by an abominable nausea. He groped his way out upon the swaying, gusty deck, descended to his cabin, and went to bed.

The *Mazatlan* had booked more passengers than could be accommodated, the steward being obliged to make up beds on the floor of the dining saloon and even upon some of the tables. Vandover had not been able to get a stateroom, and so had put up with a bunk in the common cabin at the stern of the vessel.

About two o'clock in the morning he woke up in this place frightfully sick at the stomach and wretched in body and mind. He had an upper bunk, and for a long time he lay on his back rolling about with the rolling of the steamer, vaguely staring straight above him at the roof of the cabin, hardly a hand's-breadth above his face. The roof was iron, painted with a white paint very thick and shiny, and was studded with innumerable

bolt-heads and enormous nuts. By and by, for no particular reason, he rose on his elbow and, leaning over
the side of his berth, looked about him.

The light streaming from two strong-smelling ship's
lanterns showed the cabin, long and narrow. There were
two cramped passageways, on either side of which the
tiers of bunks, mere open racks filled with bedding, rose
to the roof, those occupied by women hung with spotted
turkey-red calico.

The cabin was two decks below the open air and every
berth was occupied, the only ventilation being through
the door. The air was foul with the stench of bilge, the
reek of the untrimmed lamps, the exhalation of so
many breaths, and the close, stale smell of warm bedding.

A vague murmur rose in the air, the sound of deep
breathing, the moving of restless bodies between the
coarse sheets, the momentary noise of the scratching of
blunt finger-tips, a subdued cough, the moan of a sleeping child. All the while the shaft of the screw, seemingly
close beneath the floor, pounded and rumbled without a
moment's stop.

Immediately underneath Vandover, two men, saloonkeepers, awoke and lit their cigars and began a long discussion on the question of license. Two or three bunks
distant, a woman, a Salvation Army lassie, one of a
large party of Salvationists who were on board, began
to cough violently, choking for breath. Across the aisle
the little Jew of the plush skull-cap with ear-laps snored
monotonously in alternate keys, one a guttural bass, the
other a rasping treble. The *Mazatlan* was rolling worse
than ever, now up and down, now from side to side, and
now with long forward lurches that combined the other
two motions. During one of these latter the little Jew
was half awakened. He stopped snoring, leaving an
abrupt silence in the air. Then Vandover could hear him

threshing about uneasily; still half asleep he began to mutter and swear: "Dat's it, r-roll; I woult if I were you; r-roll, dat's righd—dhere, soh—ah, geep it oop—r-roll, you damnt ole tub, yust *r-r-roll*."

The continued pitching, the foul air, and the bitter smoke from the saloonkeepers' cigars became more than Vandover could stand. His stomach turned, at every instant he gagged and choked. He suddenly made up his mind that he could stand it no longer, and determined to go on deck, preferring to walk the night out rather than spend it in the cabin. He drew on his shoes without lacing them, and dressed himself hurriedly, omitting his collar and scarf; he put his hat on his tumbled hair, swung into his overcoat, and, wrapping his travelling-rug around him, started up toward the deck. On the stairs he was seized with such a nausea that he could hardly keep from vomiting where he stood, but he rushed out upon the lower deck, gaining the rail with a swimming head.

He sank back upon an iron capstan with a groan, weak and trembling, his eyes full of tears, a bursting feeling in his head. He was utterly miserable.

It was about half-past two in the morning, and a cold raw wind was whistling through the cordage and flinging the steamer's smoke down upon the decks and upon the water like a great veil of crêpe. A sickly half-light was spread out between the sea and the heavens. By its means he could barely distinguish great, livid blotches of fog or cloud whirling across the black sky, and the unnumbered multitude of white-topped waves rushing past, plunging and rising like a vast herd of black horses galloping on with shaking white manes. Low in the northeast horizon lay a long pale blur of light against which the bow of the steamer, inky black, rose and fell and heaved and sank incessantly. To the landward side and very near at hand, so near that he could hear the surf at their feet, the long procession of hills continually defiled, vague and formless masses between the sea and sky. The wind, the noise of the waves rushing past, the roll of the breakers and the groaning of the cordage all blended together and filled the air with a prolonged minor note, lamentable beyond words. The atmosphere was cold and damp, the spray flying like icy bullets. The sombre light that hung over the sea reflected itself in long blurred streaks upon the wet decks and slippery iron rods. Here and there about the rigging a tremulous ball of orange haze showed where the ship's lanterns were swung. Directly under him in the stern the screw snarled incessantly in a vortex of boiling water that forever swirled away and was lost in the darkness. From time to time the indicator of the patent log, just beside him, rang its tiny bell.

Vandover drew his rug about him and went up to the main deck, dragging his shoelaces after him. The wind was stronger here, but he bent his head against it and went on toward the smoking room, for the idea had occurred to him that he could shut himself in there and pass the rest of the night upon the cushions; anything was better than returning to the cabin downstairs.

The deck was jerked away from beneath his feet, and he was hurled forward, many times his own length, against a companionway, breaking his thumb as. he fell. A second shock threw him down again as he rose; everything about him shook and danced like glassware upon a jarred table. Then the whole ship rose under his feet as no wave had ever lifted it, and fell again, not into yielding water, but upon something that drove through its sides as if they had been paper. A deafening, crashing noise split the mournful howl of the wind, and far underneath him Vandover heard a rapid series of blows, a dreadful rumbling and pounding that thrilled and quivered through all the vessel's framework up to her very mast-tips. On all fours upon the deck, holding to a cleat with one hand, he braced himself, watching and listening, his senses all alive, his muscles tense. In the direction of the engine-room he heard the furious ringing of a bell. The screw stopped. The *Mazatlan* wallowed helplessly in the trough of the sea.

Vandover's very first impulse was a wild desire of saving himself; he had not the least thought for anyone else. Every soul on board might drown, so only he should be saved. It was the primitive animal instinct, the blind adherence to the first great law, an impulse that in this first moment of excitement could not be resisted. He ran forward and snatched a life-preserver from the pile that was stored beneath the bridge.

As he was fastening it about him, the passengers began to pour out upon the deck, from their staterooms, from the companionways, and from the dining saloon. In an instant the deck was crowded. Men and women ran about in all directions, pushing and elbowing each other, calling shrilly over one another's heads. Near to Vandover a woman, clothed only in her night-dress, clung to the arm of a half-dressed man, crying again and again for a certain "August." She wrung her hands in her excitement; at times the man shouted "August!" in a quavering bass voice. "August, here we are over *here !*" "Oh, where *is* Gussie?" wailed the woman. "Here, here I am," another voice answered at length; "here I am, I'm all right." "Oh," exclaimed the woman with a sob of relief, "here's Gussie; now let's all keep together whatever happens."

All about the decks just such scenes were going on; most of the women wore only their nightgowns or dressing-gowns, their hair tumbling down and blowing about their cheeks, their bare feet slipping and sliding on the heaving wet decks. The men were in shirt and drawers, standing in the centre of their family groups,

silent, excited, very watchful; others of them ran about
searching for life-preservers, shouting hoarsely, talking
to themselves, speaking all their thoughts aloud.

But there was no panic; there was excitement, confusion, bewilderment, but no excess of fear, no unreasoning terror, deaf, blind, utterly reckless.

All at once a man parted the crowd with shoulders
and elbows, passing along the deck with great strides.
It was the captain. The next instant Vandover saw him
on the bridge, hatless, without his vest or his coat, just
as he had sprung from his berth. From time to time he
shouted his orders, leaning over the rail, gesturing with
his arm. The crew ran about, carrying out his directions,
jostling the men out of the way, knocking over women
and children, speaking to no one, intent only upon their
work.

In a few moments the deck steward and one of the
officers appeared amid the crowd of passengers. They
were very calm, and at every instant shouted, "There
is no danger; everyone go back to his berth; clear the
deck, please; no danger, gentlemen; everybody be quiet;
go back to your berths!" The steward even came up to
Vandover and pulled at the straps of his life-preserver,
exclaiming, "Take this off! there is no danger; you're
only exciting the other passengers. Come on, take it off
and go back to your berth."

Vandover obeyed him, slowly loosening the buckles,
looking around him, bewildered, but still holding the
preserver in his hands.

Best of all, however, was the example of a huge old
fellow wearing the cap and clothes of a boatswain's mate
of a United States battleship; he seemed to dominate the
excited throng in a moment, going about from group to
group, quieting them all, spreading a feeling of confidence and courage throughout the whole ship. He was an
inspiration to Vandover, who began to be ashamed of hav-

ing yielded to the first selfish instinct of preservation.

Just as the boatswain's mate was offering his flask to the woman whom Vandover had heard calling for "August," the *Mazatlan* lurched heavily once or twice, and then slowly listed to the port side, going over farther and farther every instant. Vandover heard a renewed rumbling and smashing noise far beneath him, and in some way knew that the cargo was shifting. Instead of righting herself, the ship began to heave over more and more. The whole sea on the port side seemed to rise up to meet the rail; under Vandover's feet the incline of the deck grew steeper and steeper. All at once his excitement came back upon him with the sharpness of a blow, and he caught at the brass grating of a skylight exclaiming: "By God! we're going *over*." The women screamed with terror; one heard the men shouting, "Look out—hold on! catch hold there!" An old man, wearing only a gray flannel shirt, lost his footing; he fell, and rolled over and over down the deck stupidly, inertly, without making the slightest effort to save himself, without uttering the least cry; he brought up suddenly against the rail, with a great jar, the shock of his soft, withered body against the hard wood sounding like the sodden impact of a bundle of damp clothes. There was a cry; they thought him killed—Vandover had seen his head gashed against a sharp angle of iron—but he jumped up with sudden agility, clambering up the slope of the deck with the strength and rapidity of an acrobat.

There had been a great rush to the other side of the ship, a wild scrambling up the steep deck, over skylights and between masts and ventilators. People clung to anything, to cleats, to steamer chairs, to the brass railings, to the person who stood next to them. They no longer listened to the protestations of the brave boatswain's mate; that last long roll had terrified them. The sense of a great catastrophe began to spread and widen all about

394

like the rising of some fearful invisible mist. *"What* had happened? What was to become of them?"

While Vandover clung to the starboard rail, rolling his eyes wildly, trying to control himself again, a young man, a waiter in the dining saloon, rushed up to him from out of the crowd, holding out his hand. "It's all up!" he shouted.

Vandover grasped his extended palm, shaking hands with him fervently, without knowing why. The two looked straight into each other's eyes, their hands gripped close; then the waiter turned away, and dropping on his knees began to pray silently to himself.

Vandover saw a great many others praying; there was even a large group gathered about the band of Salvationists trying to raise a hymn. Every now and then their voices could be heard, singing all out of tune, a medley of discords.

At one time Vandover caught sight of the little Jew of the plush cap with the ear-laps; he was grovelling upon the deck, huddling a small black satchel to his breast; without a moment's pause he screamed, "God 'a' mercy! God 'a' mercy!"

The sight revolted Vandover and in a great measure helped to calm him. In a few moments he had himself in hand again, cool and self-collected, resolved not to act like a fool before the others, but to help them if he could.

Near to him a Salvation Army lassie was down upon her knees trying to cord up a huge bundle wrapped in sailcloth. "Here," exclaimed Vandover, coming up to her, "let me help. I'll tie this for you—you put *this* on." He took the wet, stiff ropes from between her fingers and held the life-preserver toward her; but she refused it.

"No," she cried, enthusiastically, "I'm going to be saved anyhow; I ain't going to drown; Jesus is watching

395

over me. Oh!" she suddenly exclaimed with a burst of fervour, "Jesus is going to save me. I *know* I'm going to be saved. I feel it, I feel it *here*," and she struck her palm on the breast of the man's red jersey she was wearing.

"Well, I wish *I* could have such a confidence," answered Vandover, sincerely envying the plain little woman under the ugly blue bonnet.

She seemed as if inspired, her face glowing. "Only *believe;* that's all," she told him. "It isn't too late for you now. Ah," she went on, smiling, "ah, you don't know what it is in a time like this! What a comfort! What a support! Oh, *look, look!*" she cried, breaking off and starting to her feet. "That man is going to jump!"

It was the boatswain's mate, the hero who had filled all the passengers with his own coolness and courage, who had been Vandover's inspiration. Some strange reaction seemed to have seized upon him. Of a sudden he rushed to the rail, the starboard rail that was heaved so high out of the water, stood upon it for a moment, and then with a great shout jumped over the side. His folly was as infectious as his courage. Four more men followed him, three going over all at the same time, and a fourth a little later, hanging an instant upon the outside of the rail, then dropping down feet first, disappearing with a great splash that made itself heard in the great silence that had suddenly fallen upon the throng.

Everyone had seen what had happened; a thrill of fear and apprehension passed over them all like a cold breath. They were silent, struck dumb, feeling the presence of death close by.

Suddenly a long flash of yellow upon the bridge made a momentary streak on the darkness, and there was the report of a gun. A minute later it was fired again, and alternating with it the *Mazatlan's* whistle began to roar,

396

like a hoarse shout for help. Between these sounds could be heard the renewed clamour upon the decks, the shouting, the screaming, and the rush of many feet; the little children clung about the knees of their mothers, shrieking and wailing monotonously, "Oh, ma*ma*—oh, ma*ma!*" rolling their eyes fearfully behind them.

Meanwhile the *Mazatlan* was settling forward, and already the spray was beginning to fly over the decks. Little by little the terror increased; people threw themselves down upon the deck, rising up again, their arms raised to heaven, praying aloud, screaming the same things over and over again. The Salvationists tried to raise another hym.1, but the sound of their voices was drowned out by the tumult, the roaring of the whistle, the barking of the minute guns, the straining and snapping of the cordage, and the sound of waves drawing closer and closer. Prone upon the deck, his arms still clasped about his black satchel, the little Jew of the plush cap went into some kind of fit, his eyes rolled back, his teeth grinding upon each other. Vandover turned from him in disgust. Then he looked around and above him, drawing a long breath, saying aloud to himself:

"It looks as though it were the end—well!"

All at once Vandover knew that the water had reached the boilers; there came a noise of hissing: deafening, stunning; white billows of steam poured up over the deck.

It was no longer the *Mazatlan*, no longer a thing of wood and iron, but some strange huge living creature that was dying there under his feet, some enormous brute that was plunging and writhing in its last agony, its belly ripped open by a hidden enemy that struck from beneath, its entrails torn out, its life-breath going from it in great gasps of steam. Suddenly its bellow collapsed; the great bulk was sinking lower; the enemy was in its very vitals. The great hoarse roar dwindled to a long death rattle, then to a guttural rasp; all at once it ceased; the brute was dead—the *Mazatlan* was a wreck.

Almost at the moment, he heard an order shouted twice from the bridge, where he could see the shadowy figures of the captain and officers moving about through the clouds of steam and smoke and mist. Immediately there followed the shrill piping of the boatswain's whistle; one of the officers, the first engineer, and some half dozen of the crew came dashing through the crowd, and there was a great shout of "The boats! The boats!"

The crowd broke up, rushing here and there about the ship, reforming again in smaller bands by the boats and life-rafts. Vandover followed the first engineer, running forward toward one of the boats in the bow.

"Come on!" he shouted to the little Salvationist lassie, pausing a moment to help her with her heavy canvas-covered bundle. "Come on! they're going to lower the boats."

She started up to follow him and the boom of the foremast, which the accident had in some way loosened, swung across the deck at the same moment. Vandover was already out of its path but it struck the young woman squarely across the back. She dropped in a heap upon the deck, then her body slowly straightened out, stiff and rigid, her eyes rapidly opened and shut, and a great puff of white froth slowly started from her mouth. Vandover ran forward and lifted her up, but her back was broken; she was already dead. He rose to his feet exclaiming to himself, "But she was so sure— she *knew* she was going to be saved," then suddenly fell silent again, gazing wonderingly at the body, disturbed, very thoughtful.

When Vandover finally reached the lifeboat, he found a great crowd gathered there; three people were already in the boat itself. The first engineer, who commanded that boat, and three of the crew stood by the falls preparing to cast off. Just below on the deck of the *Mazatlan* stood two sailors keeping the crowd in order, continually shouting, "Women and children first!" As the women passed their children forward, the sailors lifted them into the boats, some shrieking, others silent and stupid as if stunned. Then the women were helped up; the men, Vandover among them, climbing in afterward. The davits were turned out and the boat was swung clear of the ship's side.

Vandover looked out and below him and then made an involuntary movement to regain the ship's deck. Far below him, or so at least it seemed, were mountains of tumbling green water, huge, relentless, irresistible, rushing on by thousands, to shatter themselves with dreadful force against the ship's side. It seemed simple madness to attempt to launch the boat; even the sinking wreck would be safer than this change. Vandover was terrified, again deserted by all his calmness and self-restraint.

The sailors standing in the bow and the stern let out the ropes little by little, the vast black hulk of the ship began to loom up above them all, higher and higher, and to their eyes the lifeboat began to grow smaller and smaller, more and more frail, more and more pitiful.

All at once it struck the water with a crash, in an instant it was tossed up again in the air, heaving on the crest of a wave, was carried in and dashed up against the ship, all the oars on that side snapping in an instant. It was a fearful moment; the little boat was unmanageable in an instant, leaping and plunging among the waves like a terrified horse, banged and battered between the heaving water and the hull of the steamer itself. Vandover believed that all was over; he partially rose from his seat preparing to jump before the boat should swamp.

There was an interval of shouting and confusion, the
first engineer and the crew leaning over the sides fending
off the boat with the stumps of the oars and with long
boathooks. Some oars were shipped to the other side to
take the place of the broken ones, and a score of hands
tugging at them, the boat was at length pulled away out
of danger.

The lifeboat had been built to hold thirty-five people;
more than forty had crowded into it, and it needed all
prudence and care to keep it afloat in the heavy seas
that were running. The sailors and two of the passengers
were at the oars, while the first engineer took command,
standing in the stern at the steering-oar. He was dressed
in a suit of oilskins, a life-preserver strapped under his
arms; he wore no hat, and at every gust his drenched
hair and beard whipped across his face.

Just as the boat was pulling away from the wreck,
Vandover and the others saw the little Jew of the plush
cap with the ear-laps standing upon the rail of the
steamer, holding to a stanchion. He believed that he had
been abandoned, and screamed after them, stretching
out his hands. The engineer turned and saw him, but
shook his head. "Give way there!" he commanded the
men; "there's no more room."

The Jew flung his satchel from him and jumped; for a
moment he disappeared, then suddenly came up on the
crest of a wave, quite close to them, gasping and beating
his hands, the water running out of his mouth, and his
plush cap, glossy with wet, all awry and twisted so that
one ear-lap hung over his eye like a shade. In another
moment he had grasped one of the oar-blades. Everyone was watching and there was a cry, "Draw him in!"
But the engineer refused.

"It's too late!" he shouted, partly to the Jew and
partly to the boat. "One more and we are swamped.
Let go there!"

"But you can't let him drown," cried Vandover and the others who sat near. "Oh, take him in anyhow; we must risk it."

"Risk hell!" thundered the engineer. "Look here, you!" he cried to Vandover and the rest. "I'm in command here and am responsible for the lives of all of you. It's a matter of his life or ours; one life or forty. One more and we are swamped. Let go there!"

"Yes, yes," cried some. "It's too late! there's no more room!"

But others still protested. "It's too horrible; don't let him drown; take him in." They threw him their life-preservers and the stumps of the broken oars. But the Jew saw nothing, heard nothing, clinging to the oar-blade, panting and stupid, his eyes wide and staring.

"Shake him off!" commanded the engineer. The sailor at the oar jerked and twisted it, but the Jew still held on, silent and breathing hard. Vandover glanced at the fearfully overloaded boat and saw the necessity of it and held his peace, watching the thing that was being done. The sailor still attempted to tear the oar from the Jew's grip, but the Jew held on, panting, almost exhausted; they could hear his breathing in the boat. "Oh, don't!" he grasped, rolling his eyes.

"Unship that oar and throw it overboard," shouted the engineer.

"Better not, sir," answered the sailor. "Extra oars all broken." The Jew was hindering the progress of the boat and at every moment it threatened to turn broad on to the seas.

"God damn you, let go there!" shouted the engineer, himself wrenching and twisting at the oar. "Let go or I'll shoot!"

But the Jew, deaf and stupid, drew himself along the oar, hand over hand, and in a moment had caught hold of the gunwale of the boat. It careened on the instant.

There was a great cry. "Push him off! We're swamping! Push him off!" And one of the women cried to the mate, "Don't let my little girls drown, sir! Push him away! Save my little girls! Let him drown!"

It was the animal in them all that had come to the surface in an instant, the primal instinct of the brute striving for its life and for the life of its young.

The engineer, exasperated, caught up the stump of one of the broken oars and beat on the Jew's hands where they were gripped whitely upon the boat's rim, shouting, "Let go! let go!" But as soon as the Jew relaxed one hand he caught again with the other. He uttered no cry, but his face as it came and went over the gunwale of the boat was white and writhing. When he was at length beaten from the boat he caught again at the oar; it was drawn in, and the engineer clubbed his head and arms and hands till the water near by grew red. The little Jew clung to the end of the oar like a cat, writhing and grunting, his mouth open, and his eyes fixed and staring. When his hands were gone, he tried to embrace the oar with his arms. He slid off in the hollow of a wave, his body turned over twice, and then he sank, his head thrown back, his eyes still open and staring, and a silver chain of bubbles escaping from his mouth.

"Give way, men!" said the engineer.

"Oh, God!" exclaimed Vandover, turning away and vomiting over the side.

A little while later someone on the bow of the boat called to the engineer asking why it was they were not heading for the shore. The engineer did not answer, but Vandover in some way understood that it was too dangerous to attempt to run the breakers in such heavy weather, and that they must keep in the open, holding the boat head on to the seas until either the wind fell or they were picked up by some other vessel.

It was still very dark, and seen under the night from the little boat, the ocean and the sky seemed immense and terrible; the great waves grew out of the obscurity ahead of them, rushing down upon the boat, big, swelling, silent, their crests occasionally hissing and breaking into irruptions of cold white froth. As one of them would draw near, the boat would rise upon it as though it would never stop, would hang a moment upon its summit and then topple into the black gulf that followed, sending the bitter icy spray high into the air. The wind blew steadily. Suddenly toward three o'clock it began to rain.

Vandover, the engineer, all the five sailors, and two of the passengers were clothed. The rest of the passengers were little better than naked. Here and there a man had snatched a blanket from his berth, and one or two of them were wearing their trousers, but the rest were clothed for the most part only with their shirts and drawers. There were eighteen women and five little girls in the boat. The little girls were well looked after. Two were wrapped in Vandover's travelling-rug and a couple of men had put their coats around the third. But there were not wraps enough to go around among the women, by far the larger part of them were covered only by their night-dresses or their bed-gowns.

It was abominably cold; the rain fell continually, and the wind blew in long gusts, piercing, cutting. Every plunge of the boat threw icy bullets of spray into the air, which the wind caught up and flung down broad upon the boat. Sometimes even a huge wave would break just upon their quarter, and then great torrents of bitter, freezing water would fall over them in a deluge, leaving a sediment of salt that cracked the skin. The women were huddled upon the bottom of the boat near the waist, where they had been placed for greater safety. They were fouled with the muddy water that gathered there, their long hair dishevelled, dripping with sleet, clinging to their wet cheeks and throats, their bodies showing pink with cold, through their thin, soaked coverings, their limbs racked with long incessant shudderings, a wretched group, miserable beyond words. One of them close by Vandover's feet, he noticed particularly, had but a single garment to cover her. She was drenched through and through, her bare feet were blue with the cold, her head was thrown back, her eyes closed. She was silent except when an unusual gust of wind whipped the rain and spray across her body like the long, fine lash of a whip. Then with every breath she moaned, drawing in her breath between her teeth with a little whistling gasp, too weak, too exhausted, too nearly unconscious to attempt to shield herself in any way.

Vandover could do nothing; he had almost stripped himself to help clothe the others. Nothing more could be done. The suffering had to go on, and he began to wonder how human beings could endure such stress and yet live.

But Vandover himself suffered too keenly to take much thought for the sufferings of the others, while besides that anguish which he shared with the whole boat, the pain in his broken thumb gnawed incessantly like a rat. From time to time he stared listlessly about him, looking at the dark sky, the tumbling ocean, and the crowded groups in the plunging, rolling lifeboat.

There was nothing picturesque about it all, nothing heroic. It was unlike any pictures he had seen of lifeboat rescues, unlike anything he had ever imagined. It was all sordid, miserable, and the sight of the half-clad women, dirty, sodden, unkempt, stirred him rather to disgust than to pity.

At last the dawn came and grew white over a world of tumbling green billows and scudding wrack. Some three

404

miles distant, seen only when the boat topped a higher wave, the same procession of bleached hills moved gradually to the south under the fog, their feet covered by the white line of the surf. Not far behind in the wake of the boat the stern of the *Mazatlan* rose out of a ring of white foam, the waves breaking over her as if she had been there for ages, the screw writhing its flanges into the air like some enormous starfish already fastened upon the hulk.

One of the other boats could be seen now and then between them and the shore, a momentary dot of black on the vast blur of green and grey.

There was no conversation; the men relieved each other at the oars or bailed out the water with their caps and hands, scarcely interchanging a word. The only utterance was an occasional moaning from among the women and children. There was nothing to eat; long since the two whisky flasks had been exhausted. The rain fell steadily into the sea with a prolonged rippling noise.

Vandover was leaning upon the gunwale of the boat, his head buried in his arms, when suddenly he raised himself and asked of the man who sat next to him:

"What was the matter last night? What caused the accident?"

The other shook his head, wearily, turning away again. However, the engineer answered:

"We couldn't carry coal enough to keep up the right pressure of steam and drifted in upon a reef. I said once before that it would happen some time."

About an hour later Vandover dropped off to sleep, in spite of the cold, the wet, and the torment in his thumb. He dozed and woke, and dozed again all through the morning. About noon he was awakened by a more violent rolling of the boat, the sound of voices, and a stir among the other passengers.

405

It was still raining; the boat was no longer cutting the waves with her nose, but was being rowed seaward flank on; a sailor stood in the bow holding a coil of rope. Close in and seen over the tops of the waves were the shaking and slatting sails of a pilot-boat, lying to. One of the sails bore an enormous number six.

Vandover slept all that day and the night following, rolled in hot blankets. The next morning he awoke with a strange sense of unreality and of having dropped a day somewhere. As he lay in his stuffy little bunk between decks, and felt the rolling of the pilot-boat under him, he still fancied himself upon the *Mazatlan;* he felt the pain in his bandaged thumb and wondered how it came there. Then his fall on the deck came back to him, the wreck of the steamer, the excitement on board, the reports of the rifle fired as a minute gun, the clouds of steam that smelt of a great laundry, and the drowning of the little Jew with the plush cap with the ear-laps. He shuddered and grew sick again for a minute, telling himself that he would never forget that scene.

Such of the passengers as could get about breakfasted as best they could in the cabin with the boatkeeper and four of the pilots. Here they were informed as to what was to be done with them. The schooner would not go in for two weeks, and it was out of the question to keep the castaways on board for that length of time. However, at that moment the pilots were cruising in the neighbourhood on the lookout for two Cape Horners that were expected to be up at any moment. It was decided that when the first of these should be met with the party should be transferred.

An hour after they had been picked up, the wind had begun to freshen. By noon of the second day it had come on to blow half a gale. One could hope only for the best as regarded the rest of the *Mazatlan's* boats and rafts. Not another sign of the wreck was seen by the schooner.

The castaways filled the little schooner to overflowing, hindering her management, and getting in the way at every step. The pilot crew hustled them about without ceremony, and after dinner one had to intervene to prevent a fight between one of them and a sailor from the *Mazatlan* over the question of a broken pipe. The women of the *Mazatlan* kept in their berths continually, rolled in hot blankets, dosed with steaming whisky punches. In the afternoon, however, Vandover saw two of them in the lee of the house attempting to dry their hair: one of them was the woman he had particularly noticed in the lifeboat clad in a night-dress, and he wondered vaguely where the dress had come from she was now wearing.

About three o'clock of the afternoon of the following day Vandover was sitting on the deck near the stern, fastening on his shoes with a length of tarred rope, the laces which he had left trailing having long before broken and pulled out. By that time the wind was blowing squally out of the northeast. The schooner was put under try sails, "a three-reefed mitten with the thumb brailed up," as he heard the boatkeeper call it. This latter was at the wheel for a moment, but in a little while he called up a young man dressed in a suit of oilskins and a pea jacket and gave him the charge. For a long time Vandover watched the boy turning the spokes back and forth, his eyes alternating between the binocle and the horizon.

In the evening about half-past ten, the lookout in the crow's nest sang out: "Smoke—ho!" sounding upon his fish horn. The boatkeeper ran aft and lit a huge calcium flare, holding it so as to illuminate the big number on the mainsail. Suddenly, about a quarter of a mile off their weather-bow, a couple of rockets left a long trail of yellow against the night. It was the *Cape Horner*, and presently Vandover made out her lights, two glowing spots moving upon the darkness, like the eyes of some nocturnal sea-monster. In a few minutes she showed a blue light on the bridge; she wanted a pilot.

The schooner approached and was laid to, and the towering mass of the great deep-sea tramp began to be dimly seen through the darkness. There was little confusion in making the transfer of the castaways. Most of them seemed still benumbed with their recent terrible exposure. They docilely allowed themselves to be pushed into the pilot tender and again endured the experience of being lowered to the shifting waves below. Silently, like frightened sheep, they stood up in turn in the rocking tender and allowed the life preserver to be fitted about their shoulders to protect them from the bite of the rope's noose beneath their arms. There followed a sickening upward whirl between sea and sky, and then the comforting grasp of many welcoming hands from the deck above. By three o'clock in the morning the transfer had been made.

Vandover boarded the *Cape Horner* in company with the pilot and the rest and reached San Francisco late on the next day, which happened to be a Sunday.

About ten o'clock Vandover went ashore in the ship's yawl and landed in the city on a literally perfect day in early November. It seemed many years since he had been there. The drizzly morning upon which the *Santa Rosa* had cast off was already too long ago to be remembered. The city itself as he walked up Market Street toward Kearney seemed to have taken on a strange appearance.

It was Sunday, the downtown streets were deserted except for the cable-cars and an occasional newsboy. The stores were closed and in their vestibules one saw the peddlers who were never there on week-days, venders of canes and peddlers of glue with heavy weights attached to mended china plates.

Vandover had had no breakfast and was conscious of feeling desperately hungry. He determined to breakfast downtown, as he would arrive home too late for one meal and too early for the other.

Almost all of his money had been lost with the *Mazatlan;* he found he had but a dollar left. He would have preferred breakfasting at the Grillroom, but concluded he was too shabby in appearance, and he knew he would get more for his money at the Imperial.

It was absolutely quiet in the Imperial at the hour when he arrived. The single bartender was reading a paper, and in the passage between the private rooms a Chinese with a clean napkin wound around his head was polishing the brass and woodwork. In the passage he met Toby, the red-eyed waiter, just going off night duty, without his usual apron or white coat, dressed very carefully, wearing a brown felt hat.

"Why, how do you do, Mr. Vandover?" exclaimed Toby. "Haven't seen you round here for some time." Vandover was about to answer when the other interrupted:

"Well, what's happened to *you?* Look as though you'd been drawn through hell backward and beaten with a cat!"

In fact, Vandover's appearance was extraordinary. His hat was torn and broken, and his clothes, stained with tar and dirt, shrunken and wrinkled by sea-water. His shoes were fastened with bits of tarred rope; he was wearing a red flannel shirt with bone buttons which the boat-keeper on the pilot-boat had given him, tied at the neck with a purple handkerchief of pongee silk; his hair was long, and a week's growth of beard was upon his lip and cheeks.

"That's a fact," he answered grimly. "I do look queer. I was in a wreck down the coast," he added hastily.

"The *Mazatlan!*" exclaimed Toby. "That's a fact; the papers have been full of it. That's so, you were one of the survivors."

"The survivors!" echoed Vandover with wondering curiosity. "Tell me—you know I haven't heard a word yet—were there many lives lost?" He marvelled at the strangeness of the situation, that this bar waiter should know more of the wreck than he himself who had been upon it.

"You bet there were!" answered Toby. "Twenty-three altogether; one boat capsized; Kelly, 'Bug' Kelly, son of that fellow that runs the Crystal Grotto, *he* was drowned, and one of Hocheimer's—Hocheimer, the jeweller, you know—one of his travelling salesmen was drowned: a little Jew named Brann, diamond expert; he jumped overboard and——"

"Don't!" said Vandover with a sharp gesture. "I saw him drown—it was sickening."

"Were *you* in that boat?" exclaimed Toby. "Well, wait till I tell you; the authorities here are right after that first engineer with a sharp stick, and some of the passengers, too, for not taking him in. A woman in one of the other boats saw it all and gave the whole thing away. A thing like that is regular murder, you know." Vandover shut his teeth against answering, and after a little Toby went on, willing to talk. "You know, we've got a new man for the day-work down here now— George isn't here any more. No, he's going to start a roadhouse out on the almshouse drive in a few months; swell place, you know. I'll have him send you cards for the opening."

Vandover ordered oysters, an omelette, and a pint of claret from the new waiter who did the day-work, and ate and drank the meal—the like of which he had not tasted since leaving Coronado—with delicious enjoyment.

He delayed over it long, taking a great pleasure in satisfying the demands of the animal in him. The wine made him heavy, warm, stupid; he felt calm, soothed, and perfectly contented, and had to struggle against a desire to go to sleep where he was. The atmosphere of the Imperial was warm and there was a tepid languor in the air as of the traces of many past debauches, a stale odour of sweetened whisky and of musk. After the roughness and hardships of the last week he felt a pleasant sense of quiet, of relaxation, of enervation. He even began to wish that Flossie would come in. This, however, made him rouse himself; he shook himself, and started home, paying his carfare with his last nickel.

He sat on the outside of the car, wondering if anyone he knew would see him, half hoping that such a thing might happen, realizing the dramatic interest that would centre about him now in his present condition as a survivor of a wreck. The idea soon attracted him immensely and he began to look out for any possible acquaintance as the car began to climb over Nob Hill.

At the crossing of Polk Street he saw Ida Wade's mother in deep mourning, standing near a grocery store holding a little pink parcel.

It was like a blow between the eyes. Vandover caught his breath and started violently, feeling again for an instant the cold grip of the hysterical terror that had so nearly overcome him on the morning after Ida's death. It slowly relaxed, however, and by the time he had reached the house on California Street he was almost himself again.

It was about church time when Vandover arrived at home once more. There was a Sunday quiet in the air. The bells were ringing, and here and there family groups on their way to church, the children walking in front, very sedate in their best clothes, carrying the prayer-books carefully, by special privilege.

The butler was working in the garden, as he sometimes did of a Sunday morning, pottering about a certain bed of sweet-peas, and it was the housekeeper who answered his ring. She recognized him with a prolonged exclamation, raising her hands to heaven.

"O-oh, and is it you, Mr. Vandover, sir? Ah, how we've been upset about you and all, and it's glad to see you back again your father will be! Oh, such times as we had when we heard about the wreck and knowing you were on it! Yes, sir, your father's *pretty* well, though he was main poorly yesterday morning. But he's better now. You'll find him in the smoking room now, sir."

Vandover pushed open the door of the smoking room quietly. His father was sitting unoccupied in the huge leather chair before the fireplace. He was dead, and must have died some considerable time before, as he was already cold. He could have suffered no pain, hardly a muscle had moved, and his attitude was quite natural, the legs crossed, the right hand holding the morning's paper. However, as soon as Vandover touched the body it collapsed and slid down into a heap in the depth of the chair, the jaw dropping open, the head rolling side-wise upon his shoulder.

Vandover ran out into the hall, waving his arms, shouting for the servants. "Oh, why didn't you tell me?" he cried to the housekeeper. "Why did you let me find him so? When did he die?" The housekeeper was distraught. She couldn't believe it. Only a little while ago he had called her to say there were no more matches in the little brass matchsafe. She began to utter long cries and lamentations like a hen in distress, raising her hands to heaven. All at once they heard some-one rushing up the stairs. It was the butler, in his shirt-sleeves and his enormous apron of ticking, still carrying his trowel in his hand. He was bewildered, his eyes pro-truding, while all about him he spread the smell of fresh earth. At every instant he exclaimed:

"What? What? What's the matter?"

"Oh, my dear old governor—and all alone!" cried Vandover through shut teeth.

"Oh, oh, the good God!" exclaimed the housekeeper, crossing herself and rolling her eyes. "And him asking for matches in the little brass box only a minute since. Oh, the good, kind master!"

Suddenly Vandover rushed down the stairs and through the front hall, snatching his hat from the hat-rack as he passed. He ran to call the family doctor who lived some two blocks below on the same street. He caught him just as he was getting into the carry-all with his family, bound for church.

Vandover and the physician rode back together in the carry-all, the two grey horses going up the steep hill at a trot. The doctor was dressed for church; he wore red gloves with thick white seams, a spray of lilies-of-the-valley in his lapel.

"I'm afraid we can do nothing," he said, warningly. "It's your father's old enemy, I suppose. This was— it was sure to happen sooner or later. Any sudden shock, you know."

Vandover scarcely listened, holding the door of the carry-all open with one hand, ready to jump out, beating the other hand upon his knee.

"Go back and take the rest of them to church now," said the doctor to his coachman when the carry-all stopped in front of Vandover's house.

The whole house was in the greatest agitation all the rest of the day. The curtains were drawn, the door-bell rang incessantly, strange faces passed the windows, and the noise of strange footsteps continually mounted and descended the staircase. The hours for meals were all deranged, the table stood ready all day long, and one ate when there was a chance. The telephone was in constant use, and at every moment messenger boys came and went, people spoke in low tones, walking on tiptoe; the florist's wagon drove to the door again and again, and the house began to smell of tuberoses. Reporters came, waiting patiently for interviews, sitting on the leather chairs in the dining room, or writing rapidly on a corner of the dining table, the cloth pushed back. The under-taker's assistants went about in their shirt-sleeves, working very hard, and toward the middle of the after-noon the undertaker himself tied the crêpe to the bell handle.

Little by little a subdued excitement spread through-out the vicinity. The neighbours appeared at their win-dows, looking down into the street, watching everything that went on. It was a veritable event, a matter of com-ment and interest for the whole block. Women found excuses to call on each other, talking over what had happened, as they sat near their parlour windows, shaking their heads at each other, peering out between the lace curtains. The people on the cable-cars and the pedestrians looked again and again at the crêpe on the bell handle, and the curtained windows, craning their necks backward when they had passed. The neighbours' children collected in little groups on the sidewalk near the house, looking and pointing, drawn close together, talking in low tones. At last even a policeman appeared, walking deliberately, casting the shadow of his huge stomach upon the fence that was about the vacant lot. He frowned upon the children, ordering them away. But suddenly he discovered an acquaintance, the driver of an express-wagon that had just driven up with an enormous anchor of violets. He paused, exclaiming:

"Why, hello, Connors!"

"Why, hello, Mister Brodhead!"

Then a long conversation was begun, the policeman standing on the curbstone, one foot resting upon the hub of a wheel, the expressman leaning forward, his elbows on his knees, twirling his whip between his hands. The expressman told some sort of story, pointing with his elbow toward the house, but the other was incredulous, gravely shaking his head, putting his chin in the air, and closing his eyes.

Inside the house itself there was a hushed and subdued bustling that centred about a particular room. The undertaker's assistant and the barber called in low voices through the halls for basins of water and towels. There was a search for the Old Gentleman's best clothes and his clean linen; bureau drawers were opened and shut, closet doors softly closed. Relatives and friends called and departed or stayed to help. A vague murmur arose, a mingled sound of whispers and light footsteps, the rustle of silks, and the noise of stifled weeping, and then at last silence, night, solitude, a single gas-jet burning, and Vandover was left alone.

The suddenness of the thing had stunned and dizzied him, and he had gone through with all the various affairs of the day wondering at his calmness and fortitude. Toward eleven o'clock, however, after the suppressed excitement of the last hours, as he was going to bed, the sense of his grief and loss came upon him all of a sudden, with their real force for the first time, and he threw himself upon the bed face downward, weeping and groaning. During the rest of the night pictures of his father returned to him as he had seen him upon different occasions, particularly three such pictures came and went through his mind.

In one the Old Gentleman stood in that very room, with the decanter in his hand, asking him kindly if he felt very bad; in another he was on the pier with his handkerchief tied to his cane, waving it after Vandover as though spelling out a signal to him across the water. But in a third, he was in the smoking room, fallen into the leather chair, his arm resting on the table and his head bowed upon it.

After the funeral, which took place from the house, Vandover drove back alone in the hired carriage to his home. He would have paid the driver, but the other told him that the undertaker looked out for that. Vandover watched him a moment as he started his horses downhill, the brake as it scraped against the tire making a noise like the yelping of a dog. Then he turned and faced the house. It was near four o'clock in the afternoon, and everything about the house was very quiet. All the curtains were down except in one of the rooms upstairs. The butler had already opened these windows and was airing the room. Vandover could hear him moving about, sweeping up, rearranging the furniture, making up the bed again. In front of him, between the horse-block and the front door, one or two smilax leaves were still fallen, and a tuberose, already yellow. Behind him in the street he had already noticed the marks of the wheels of the hearse where it had backed up to the curb.

The crêpe was still on the bell handle. Vandover did not know whether it had been forgotten, or whether it was proper to leave it there longer. At any rate, he took it off and carried it into the house with him.

His father's hat, a stiff brown derby hat, flat on the top, hung on the hatrack. This had always been a sign to Vandover that his father was at home. The sight was so familiar, so natural, that the same idea occurred to him now involuntarily, and for an instant it was as though he had dreamed of his father's death; he even wondered what was this terrible grief that had overwhelmed him, and thought that he must go and tell his father about it. He took the hat in his hands, turning it about tenderly, catching the faint odour of the Old Gentleman's hair oil that hung about it. It all brought back his father to him as no picture ever could; he could almost *see* the kind old face underneath the broad curl of the brim. His grief came over him again keener than ever and he put his arms clumsily about the old hat, weeping and whispering to himself:

"Oh, my poor, dear old dad—I'm never going to see you again, never, never! Oh, my dear, kind old governor!"

He took the hat up to his room with him, putting it carefully away. Then he sat down before the window that overlooked the little garden in the rear of the house, looking out with eyes that saw nothing.

THE following days as they began to pass were miserable. Vandover had never known until now how much he loved his father, how large a place he had filled in his life. He felt horribly alone now, and a veritable feminine weakness overcame him, a crying need to be loved as his father had loved him, and also to love someone as he himself had loved his father. Worst of all, however, was his loneliness. He could think of no one who cared in the least for him; the very thought of Turner Ravis or young Haight wrought in him an expression of scorn. He was sure that he was nothing to them, though they were the ones whom he considered his best friends.

Another cause of misery was the fact that his father's death in leaving him alone had also thrown him upon his own resources. Now he would have to shoulder responsibilities which hitherto his father had assumed, and decide questions which until now his father had answered.

However, he felt that his father's death had sobered him as nothing else, not even Ida's suicide, had done. The time was come at length for him to take life seriously. He would settle down now to work at his art. He would go to Paris as his father had wished, and devote himself earnestly to painting. Yes, the time was come for him to steady himself, and give over the vicious life into which he had been drifting.

But it was not long before Vandover had become accustomed to his father's death, and had again rearranged himself to suit the new environment which it had occasioned. He wondered at himself because of the quickness with which he had recovered from his grief, just as before he had marvelled at the ease with which he had forgotten Ida's death. Could it be true, then, that nothing affected him very deeply? Was his nature shallow?

However, he was wrong in this respect; his nature was not shallow. It had merely become deteriorated.

Two days after his father's death Vandover went into the Old Gentleman's room to get a certain high-backed chair which had been moved there from his own room during the confusion of the funeral, and which, pending the arrival of the trestles, had been used to support the coffin.

As he was carrying it back his eye fell upon a little heap of objects carefully set down upon the bureau. They were the contents of the Old Gentleman's pockets that the undertaker had removed when the body was dressed for burial.

Vandover turned them over, sadly interested in them. There was the watch, some old business letters and envelopes covered with memoranda, his fountain-pen, a couple of cigars, a bank-book, a small amount of change, his pen-knife, and one or two tablets of chewing-gum.

Vandover thrust the pen and the knife into his own pocket. The bank-book, letters, and change he laid away in his father's desk, but the cigars and the tablets of gum, together with the crumpled pocket-handkerchief that he found on another part of the dressing-case, he put into the Old Gentleman's hat, which he had hidden on the top shelf of his clothes closet. The watch he hung upon a little brass thermometer that always stood on his centre table. He even wound up the watch with the resolve never to let it run down so long as he should live.

The keys, however, disturbed him, and he kept changing them from one hand to the other, looking at them very thoughtfully. They suggested to him the inquiry as to whether or no his father had made a will, and how much money he, Vandover, could now command. One of the keys was a long brass key. Vandover knew that this unlocked a little iron box that from time out of mind had been screwed upon the lower shelf of the clothes closet in his father's room. It was in this box that the Old Gentleman kept his ready money and a few important papers.

For a long time Vandover stood undecided, changing the keys about from one hand to the other, hesitating before opening this iron box; he could not tell why. By and by, however, he went softly into his father's room, and into the clothes closet near the head of the bed. Holding the key toward the lock, he paused, listening; it was impossible to rid his mind of the idea that he was doing something criminal. He shook himself, smiling at the fancy, assuring himself of the honesty of the thing, yet opening the box stealthily, holding the key firmly in order that it might not spring back with a loud click, looking over his shoulder the while and breathing short through his nose.

The first thing that he saw inside was a loaded revolver, the sudden view of which sent a little qualm through the pit of his stomach. He took it out gingerly, holding it at arm's length, throwing open the cylinder and spilling out the cartridges on the bed, very careful to let none of them fall on the floor lest they should explode.

Next he drew out the familiar little canvas sack. In it were twenty-dollar gold-pieces, the coin that used to be "Good for the Masses." Behind that was about thirty dollars in two rolls, and last of all in an old, oblong tin cracker-box a great bundle of papers. A list of these papers was pasted on one end of the box. They comprised deeds, titles, insurance policies, tax receipts, mortgages, and all the papers relating to the property. Besides these there was the will.

He took out this box, laying it on the shelf beside him.

He was closing the small iron safe again very quietly when all at once, before he could think of what he was doing, he ran his hand into the mouth of the canvas sack, furtively, sly, snatched one of the heavy round coins, and thrust it into his vest pocket, looking all about him, listening intently, saying to himself with a nervous laugh, "Well, isn't it mine anyway?"

In spite of himself he could not help feeling a joy in the possession of this money as if of some treasure-trove dug up on an abandoned shore. He even began to plan vaguely how he should spend it.

However, he could not bring himself to open any of the papers, but sent them instead to a lawyer, whom he knew his father had often consulted. A few days later he received a typewritten letter asking him to call at his earliest convenience.

It was at his residence and not at his office that Vandover saw the lawyer, as the latter was not well at the time and kept to his bed. However, he was not so sick but that his doctor allowed him to transact at least some of his business. Vandover found him in his room, a huge apartment, one side entirely taken up by book-shelves filled with works of fiction. The walls were covered with rough stone-blue paper, forming an admirable background to small plaster casts of Assyrian *bas-reliefs* and large photogravures of Renaissance portraits. Underneath an enormous baize-covered table in the centre of the room were green cloth bags filled apparently with books, padlocked tin chests, and green pasteboard deed-boxes. The lawyer was sitting up in bed, wearing his dressing-gown and occasionally drinking hot water from a glass. He was a thin, small man, middle-aged, with a very round head and a small pointed beard.

"How do you do, Mr. Vandover?" he said, very pleasantly as Vandover passed by the servant holding open the door and came in.

"How do you do, Mr. Field?" answered Vandover, shaking his hand. "Well, I'm sorry to see you like this."

"Yes," answered the lawyer, "I'm—I have trouble with my digestion sometimes, more annoying than dangerous, I suppose. Take a chair, won't you? You can find a place for your hat and coat right on the table there. Well," he added, settling back on the pillows and looking at Vandover pleasantly, "I think you've grown thinner since the last time I saw you, haven't you?"

"Yes," answered Vandover, grimly, "I guess I have."

"Yes, yes, I suppose so, of course," responded the lawyer with a vague air of apology and sympathy. "You have had a trying time of it lately, taking it by and large. I was *very* painfully shocked to hear of your father's death. I had met him at lunch hardly a week before; he was a far heartier man than I was. Eat? You should have seen—splendid appetite. He spoke at length of you, I re-remember; told me you expected to go abroad soon to study painting; in fact, I believe he was to go to Paris with you. It was very sad and very sudden. But you know we've all been expecting—been fearing—that for some time."

They both were silent for a moment, the lawyer looking absently at the foot-board of the bed, nodding his head slowly from time to time, repeating, "Yes, sir—yes, sir." Suddenly he exclaimed, "Well—now, let's see." He cleared his throat, coming back to himself again, and continued in a very businesslike and systematic tone:

"I have looked over your father's papers, Mr. Vandover, as you requested me to, and I have taken the liberty of sending for you to let you know exactly how you stand."

"That's the idea, sir," said Vandover, very attentive, drawing up his chair.

Mr. Field took a great package of oblong papers from the small table that stood at the head of his bed, and looked them over, adjusting his eyeglasses. "Well, now, suppose we take up the real property first," he continued, drawing out three or four of these papers and unfolding them. "All of your father's money was invested in what we call 'improved realty.'"

He talked for something over an hour, occasionally stopping to answer a question of Vandover's, or interrupting himself to ask him if he understood. At the end it amounted to this:

The bulk of the estate was residence property in distant quarters of the city. Some twenty-six houses, very cheaply built, each, on an average, renting for twenty-eight dollars. When all of these were rented, the gross monthly income was seven hundred and twenty-eight dollars. At this time, however, six were vacant, bringing down the gross receipts per month to five hundred and sixty dollars. The expenses, which included water, commissions for collecting, repairs, taxes, interest on insurance, etc., when expressed in the terms of a monthly average, amounted to one hundred and eight-six dollars.

"Well, now, let's see," said Vandover, figuring on his cuff, "one hundred and eighty-six from five hundred and sixty leaves me a net monthly income of three hundred and eighty-four—no, seventy-four. Three hundred and seventy-four dollars."

The lawyer shook his head while he drank another glass of hot water:

"You see," he said, wiping his moustache in the hollow of his palm, "you see, we haven't figured on the mortgages yet."

"Mortgages?" echoed Vandover.

"Yes," answered Mr. Field, "when I spoke of expenses I was basing them upon the monthly statements of Adams & Brunt, your father's agents. But they never looked after the mortgages. Your father acted directly with the banks in that matter. I find that there are mortgages that cover the entire property, even the homestead. They are for 6½ and 7 per cent. In some cases there are two mortgages on the same piece of property."

"Well," said Vandover.

"Well," answered the lawyer, "the interest on these foots up to about two hundred and ninety dollars a month."

Vandover made another hasty calculation on his cuff, and leaned back in his chair staring at the lawyer, saying:

"Why, that leaves eighty-four dollars a month, net."

"Yes," assented Field. "I made it that, too."

"Why, the governor used to allow *me* fifty a month," returned Vandover, "just for pocket money."

"I'm afraid you mustn't expect anything like that now, Mr. Vandover," replied Field, smiling. "You see, when your father was alive and pursuing his profession, he made a comfortable income besides that which he derived from his realty. His law business I consider to have been excellent when you take everything into consideration. He often made five hundred dollars a month at it. Such are the figures his papers show. He could make you a handsome allowance while he was alive, but all that is stopped now!"

"Well, but didn't he—didn't he leave any money, any—any—any lump sum?" inquired Vandover, incredulously.

"There was his bank account," answered the other. "You see, he invested most of his savings in this same realty, and since he stopped building he seems to have lived right up to his income."

"But eighty-four dollars!" repeated Vandover; "why, look at the house on California Street where we live. It costs that much to run it, the servants and all."

"Here's your father's domestic-account book," answered Field, taking it up and turning the leaves. "One hundred and seventy-five dollars a month were the average running expenses."

"*One hundred and seventy-five!*" shouted Vandover, feeling suddenly as if the ground were opening under him. "Why, great heavens, Mr. Field! where am I going to get—what am I going to *do?*"

Mr. Field smiled a little. "Well," he said, "you must make up your mind to live more modestly."

"Modestly?" exclaimed Vandover, scornfully.

"You'll have to rent the house and take rooms."

Vandover gave a gasp of relief.

"I hadn't thought of that," he answered, subsiding at once. "How much would it bring—the house?"

The lawyer hesitated as to this. "That I could hardly tell you definitely," he answered, shaking his head. "Adams & Brunt could give you more exact figures. In fact, I would suggest that you put it into their hands. California near Franklin, isn't it? Yes; the neighbourhood isn't what it used to be, you know. Everyone wants to live out on Pacific Heights now. Double house? Yes, well—with the furniture, I suppose—oh, I don't know—say, a hundred and fifty. But, you know, my estimate is only guesswork. Brunt is the man you want to see."

"Well," answered Vandover, solaced, "that makes— two thirty-four; that's more like it. But," he added, hastily, "you say the homestead is mortgaged as well; how about the interest on that?"

"You needn't be bothered about that," answered Mr. Field. "The interest on *that* mortgage is included in the two hundred and ninety that I spoke of, and the insurance interest on the homestead is included in Adams & Brunt's statement. That was on the whole estate *with* the homestead, you understand? But there is another thing you must look out for. Most of the mortgages are for one year, and every time they are renewed there is an expense of between forty and fifty dollars."

"Yes, I see," assented Vandover.

"Now," resumed the lawyer, "here is your father's bank account. He had in the First National to his credit between nine and ten thousand dollars; nine thousand seven hundred and ninety, to be exact. His professional account book shows that there is now due him in bills and notes eight hundred and thirty dollars; on the debit side he owes in all nine hundred; the difference, you see, is seventy. Nine thousand seven hundred and ninety less seventy leaves a balance of nine thousand six hundred and twenty. All clear?" he asked, interrupting himself. Vandover nodded and the other continued:

"Now, your father left a will; here it is. I drew it for him a year ago last September. He has given fifteen hundred dollars to some cousin in the southern part of the state, and six hundred to a few charities here in the city. The remainder, seven thousand five hundred and twenty, and all the rest of the estate is left to you with the wish that you pursue your art studies abroad. Brunt, of Adams & Brunt, and myself are appointed executors. So now, that is just how you stand as far as I can see; seventy-five hundred dollars in ready money and, if we suppose you rent the California Street house, income property that nets you two hundred and thirty-four a month. The will will have to be probated some time next month and you will have to appear; however, I shall let you know about that in time."

During the next two weeks Vandover was plunged into the affairs of business for the first time in his life. It interested and amused him, and he felt a certain self-importance in handling large sums of money, and in figuring interest, rents, and percentages. Three days after his interview with Mr. Field the sale of his father's office effects took place, and the consequent five hundred dollars Vandover turned over into the hands of the lawyer, who was already looking for an investment for the eighty-nine hundred. This matter had given Vandover considerable anxiety.

"I don't want anything fancy," he said to Field. "No big per cents. and bigger risks. If I've got to live economically I want something that's secure. A good solid investment, don't you know, with a fair interest; that's what I'm looking for."

"Yes," answered the lawyer, grimly; "I've been looking for that myself ever since I was your age."

They both laughed, and the lawyer added: "Has Brunt found a tenant for the California Street house yet? No? Well, perhaps you had better keep that five hundred for your running expenses until he does. It will probably take some time."

"All right," answered Vandover. "There were a couple of women up to look at the place yesterday, but they want to use it for a boarding house. I won't hear to that. Brunt says they would ruin it, dead sure."

"I suppose you are looking around, yourself, for rooms?" inquired Mr. Field. "Have you found anything to suit you?"

"No," answered Vandover, "I have not. I don't like the idea of living in one of the downtown hotels, and as far as I have looked, the uptown flats are rather steep. However, I haven't gone around very much as yet. I've been so busy. Oh, how about the paving of the street in front of those Bush Street houses of mine? Brunt says that the supervisors have passed a resolution of intention to that effect. Now shall I let the city contractor have the job or give it to Brunt's man?"

"Better let the city people do it," advised Field. "They may charge more, but you needn't pay *them* for a long time."

By the end of three weeks Vandover had sickened of

the whole thing. The novelty was gone, and business affairs no longer amused him. Besides this, he was anxious to settle down in some comfortable rooms. It was now the middle of winter and he had determined that it was not the season for a European trip. He would wait until the summer before going to Paris.

Little by little Vandover turned over the supervision and management of his affairs and his property to Adams & Brunt, declaring that he could not afford to be bothered with them any longer. This course was much more expensive and by no means so satisfactory from a business point of view, but Vandover felt as though the loss in money was more than offset by his freedom from annoyance and responsibility.

He was eager to get settled. The idea of taking rooms that should be all his own and that he could fit up to suit his taste attracted him immensely. Already he saw himself installed in charming bachelor's apartments, the walls covered with rough stone-blue paper forming an admirable background for small plaster casts of Assyrian *bas-reliefs* and photogravures of Velasquez portraits. There would be a pipe-rack over the mantelpiece, and a window-seat with a corduroy cushion such as he had had in his room in Matthew's.

Very slowly his father's affairs were settled, and by degrees the estate began to adjust itself to the new grooves in which it was to run. By the middle of December everything was beginning to go smoothly, and the day before Christmas Mr. Field announced to Vandover that he had invested his eighty-nine hundred in registered U. S. 4 per cents. They had had several long talks concerning this sum of money, and in the end had concluded that it would be better to invest it in some such fashion rather than to take up any of the mortgages that were on the houses.

During the first weeks of the new year the house on

California Street was rented for one hundred and twenty-
five dollars to an English gentleman, the president of a
fruit syndicate in the southern part of the state. There
were but three in the family, and though the rent was
below that which Vandover had desired, Brunt advised
him to close the transaction at once, as they were desirable tenants and would probably stay in the house a long
time.

On the last evening which he was to spend in his home,
Vandover cast up his accounts and made out a schedule
as to his monthly income.

Rent from realty, net average	$ 84.00
Rent from homestead property on California Street . .	125.00
Interest on U. S. bonds, 4 per cent.	23.00
Total	$232.00
In small iron safe	$170.00
Received from sale of office effects	500.00
	$670.00
Expenses, outstanding bills, lawyer's fees, undertaker's bill, expenses for collecting, etc.	587.00
Balance, January 16th	$83.00

Then with a shrug of the shoulders he dismissed the
whole burdensome business from his mind. Brunt would
manage his property, sending him regularly the monthly
statement in order to keep him informed. The English
gentleman of the fruit syndicate would add his hundred
and twenty-five, and the 4 per cents., faithfully brooding
over his eighty-nine hundred in the dark of the safety
deposit drawer, would bring forth their little quota of
twenty-three with absolute certainty. Two thirty-two
a month. Yes, he was comfortably fixed and was free
now to do exactly as he pleased.

His first object now was to settle down for the winter

in some pleasant rooms. He had decided that he would look for a suite of three—a bedroom, studio, and sitting room. The bedroom he was not particular about, the studio he hoped would have plenty of light from the north, but the sitting room *must* be sunny and overlook the street, else what would be the use of a window-seat? As to the neighbourhood, he thought he would prefer Sutter Street anywhere between Leavenworth and Powell.

In the downtown part this street was entirely given over to business houses; in the far, uptown quarter it was lined with residences; but between these two undesirable extremes was an intermediate district where the residences had given place to flats, and the business blocks to occasional stores. It was a neighbourhood affected by doctors, dentists, and reputable music-teachers; drug stores occupied many of the corners; here and there a fine residence still withstood the advance of business; there were a number of great apartment houses, and even one or two club buildings.

It was a gay locality, not too noisy, not too quiet. The street was one of the great arteries of travel between the business and the residence portions of the city, and its cable-cars were frequented by ladies going to their shopping or downtown marketing or to and from the matinées. Acquaintances of Vandover were almost sure to pass at every hour.

He took rooms temporarily at the Palace and at once set about locating on Sutter Street. He had recourse again to Brunt, who furnished him with a long list of vacancies in that neighbourhood. Apartment-hunting was an agreeable pastime to Vandover, though in the end it began to bore him. Altogether, he visited some fifteen or twenty suites, in each case trying to fit himself into the rooms, imagining how the window-seat would look in such a window, how the pipe-rack would show over such a mantel, just where on such walls the Assyrian *bas-reliefs* could be placed to the best advantage, and if his easel could receive enough steady light from such windows. Then he considered the conveniences, the baths, the electric light, and the heat.

After a two weeks' search, he had decided upon one of two suites; both of these were in the desired neighbourhood but differed widely in other respects.

The first was reasonable enough in the matter of rent, and had even been occupied by an artist for some three or four years previous. However, the room that Vandover proposed to use as a sitting room was small and had no double windows, thus making the window-seat an impossibility. There did not seem to be any suitable place for the Assyrian *bas-reliefs*, and the mantelpiece was of old-fashioned white marble like the mantelpiece in Mrs. Wade's front parlour, a veritable horror. It revolted Vandover even to think of putting a pipe-rack over it. These defects were offset by the studio, a large and splendid room with hardwood floors and an enormous north light, the legendary studio, the dream of an artist, precisely such a studio as Vandover had hoped he would occupy in the Quarter.

The other suite was in a great apartment house, a hotel in fact, but very expensive, with electric bulbs and bells, and with a tiled bathroom connecting with the bedroom. The room which he would be obliged to use as his studio was small, dark, the light coming from the west. But the sitting room was perfect. It had the sun all day long through a huge bay window that seemed to have been made for a window-seat; there were admirable, well-lighted spaces on the walls for casts and pictures, and the mantelpiece was charming, extremely high, and made of oak; in a word, the exact sitting room that Vandover had in mind. Already he saw himself settled there as comfortably and snugly as a kernel in a nutshell. It was true that upon investigation he found that the grate had been plastered up and the flue arranged for a stove. But for that matter there were open-grate stoves to be had that would permit the fire to be seen and that would look just as cheerful as a grate. He had even seen such a stove in the window of a hardware store downtown, a tiled stove with a brass fender and with curious flamboyant ornaments of cast-iron—a jewel of a stove.

For two days Vandover hesitated between these two suites, undecided whether he should sacrifice his studio for his sitting room, or his sitting room for his studio. At length he came to the conclusion that as he was now to be an artist a good studio ought to be the first consideration, and that since he was to settle down to hard, serious work at last, he owed it to himself to have a fitting place in which to paint; yes, decidedly he would take the suite with the studio. He went to the agent, told him of his decision, and put up a deposit to secure the rooms.

The same day upon which he took this decided step he had occasion to pass by both places in question. As he approached the apartment house in which the rejected suite was situated it occurred to him to tell the clerk in the office that he had decided against the rooms; he could take a last look at them at the same time.

He was shown up to the rooms again, and walked about in the sitting room, asking the same questions about the heat, the plumbing, and the baths. He even went to the window and looked out into the street. It *was* a first-rate berth just the same, and how jolly it would be to lounge in the window-seat of a morning, with a paper, a cigarette, and a cup of coffee, watching the people on their way downtown; the women going to their shopping and morning's marketing. Then all at once he remembered that at most he would only have these rooms for five months, and reflected that if his whole life was to be devoted to painting he might easily put up with an inconvenient studio for a few months. Once at Paris all would be different.

At that the rooms took on a more charming aspect than ever; never had they appeared cheerier, sunnier, more comfortable; never had the oak mantel and the tiled stove with the flamboyant ornaments been more desirable; never had a window-seat seemed more luxurious, never a pipe-rack more delectable, while at the same time, the other rooms, the rooms of the big studio, presented themselves to his imagination more sombre, uncomfortable, and forbidding than ever. It was out of the question to think of living there; he was angry with himself for having hesitated so long. But suddenly he remembered the deposit he had already made; it was ten dollars; for a moment he paused, then dismissed the matter with an impatient shrug of the shoulders. "So much the worse," he said. "What's ten dollars?" He made up his mind then and there and went downstairs, walking on his heels, to tell the clerk that after all he would engage the rooms from that date.

CHAPTER XII

Vandover took formal possession of his rooms on Sutter Street during the first few days of February. For a week previous they had been in the greatest confusion: the studio filled with a great number of trunks, crates, packing cases, and furniture still in its sacking. In the bedroom was stored the furniture that had been moved out of the sitting room, while the sitting room itself was given over to the paperhangers and carpenters. Vandover himself appeared from time to time, inquiring anxiously as to the arrival of his "stuff," or sitting on a packing-case, his hands in his pockets, his hat pushed back, and a cigarette between his lips.

He had passed a delightful week selecting the wall paper and the pattern for the frieze, buying rugs, screens, Assyrian *bas-reliefs*, photogravures of Renaissance portraits, and the famous tiled stove with its flamboyant ornaments. Just after renting his home he had had a talk with the English gentleman of the fruit syndicate and had spoken about certain ornaments and bits of furniture, valuable chiefly to himself, which he wished to keep. The president of the fruit syndicate had been very gracious in the matter, and as soon as Vandover had taken his rooms he had removed two great cases of such articles from the California Street house and had stored them in the studio.

After the workmen were gone away Vandover began the labour of arrangement, aided by one of the paperhangers he had retained for that purpose. It was a work of three days, but at last everything was in its place, and

434

one evening toward the middle of the month Vandover
stood in the middle of the sitting room in his shirt-
sleeves, holding the tweezers and a length of picture-
wire in his hand, and looked around him in his new
home.

The walls were hung with dull blue paper of a very
rough texture set off by a narrow picture moulding of
ivory white. A dark red carpet covered with rugs and
skins lay on the floor. Upon the left-hand wall, reaching
to the floor, hung a huge rug of sombre colours against
which were fixed a fencing trophy, a pair of antlers, a
little water-colour sketch of a Norwegian fjord, and
Vandover's banjo; underneath it was a low but very
broad divan covered with corduroy. To the right and
left of this divan stood breast-high bookcases with olive
green curtains, their tops serving as shelves for a multitude of small ornaments, casts of animals by Fremilt
and Barye, Donatello's lovely *femme inconnue*, beer
steins, a little bronze clock, a calendar, and a yellow
satin slipper of Flossie's in which Vandover kept Turkish
cigarettes. The writing-desk with the huge blue blotter
in a silver frame, the paper-cutter, and the enormous
brass inkstand filled the corner to the right of the divan,
while drawn up to it was the huge leather chair, the
chair in which the Old Gentleman had died. In the
drawer of the desk Vandover kept his father's revolver;
he never thought of loading it; of late he had only used
it to drive tacks with, when he could not find the hammer. Opposite the divan, on the other side of the room,
was the famous tiled stove with the flamboyant ornaments; back of this the mantel, and over the mantel a
row of twelve grotesque heads in plaster, with a space
between each for a pipe. To the left in the angle of the
room stood the Japanese screen in black and gold,
and close to this a tea-table of bamboo and a piano-lamp
with a great shade of crinkly red paper that Turner

Ravis had given to Vandover one Christmas. The bay window was filled by the window-seat, covered with corduroy like the divan and heaped with cushions, one of them of flaming yellow, the one spot of vivid colour amidst the dull browns and sombre blues of the room. A great sideboard with decanters and glasses and chafing-dishes faced the window from the end wall. The entrance to the studio opened to the left of it, which entrance Vandover had hung with curtains of dust-brown plush.

The casts of the Assyrian *bas-reliefs* were against the wall upon either side of the window. There were three of them, two representing scenes from the life of the king, the third the wounded lioness which Vandover never wearied of admiring.

Upon the wall over the mantel hung two very large photogravures, one of Rembrandt's Night Watch, the other a portrait of Velasquez representing a young man with a hunting spear. Above one of the bookcases was an admirable reproduction of the Mona Lisa; above the other, a carbon print of a Vandyke, a Dutch lady in a silk gown and very high ruff.

By the side of the Mona Lisa, however, was a cheap brass rack stuffed with photographs: actresses in tights, French quadrille dancers, high kickers, and chorus girls.

In the studio, Vandover had tacked great squares and stripes of turkey-red cloth against the walls to serve as a background for his sketches. Some dozen or more portfolios and stretchers were leaned against the baseboard, and a few ornaments and pieces of furniture, such things as Vandover set but little store by, were carelessly arranged about the room. The throne and huge easel were disposed so as to receive as much light as was possible.

Beyond the studio was the bedroom, but here there was only the regulation furniture. Some scores of photographs of Vandover's friends were tacked upon the walls, or thrust between the wood and glass of the mirror.

A new life now began for Vandover, a life of luxury and aimlessness which he found charming. He had no duties, no cares, no responsibilities. But there could be no doubt that he was in a manner changed; the old life of dissipation seemed to have lost its charm. For nearly twenty-six years nothing extraordinary had happened to break in upon the uneventful and ordinary course of his existence, and then, suddenly, three great catastrophes had befallen, like the springing of three successive mines beneath his feet: Ida's suicide, the wreck, and his father's death, all within a month. The whole fabric of his character had been shaken, jostled out of its old shape. His desire of vice was numbed, his evil habits all deranged; here, if ever, was the chance to begin anew, to commence all over again. It seemed an easy matter: he would merely have to remain inactive, impassive, and his character would of itself re-form upon the new conditions.

But Vandover made another fatal mistake: the brute in him had only been stunned; the snake was only soothed. His better self was as sluggish as the brute, and his desire of art as numb as his desire of vice. It was not a continued state of inaction and idleness that could help him, but rather an active and energetic arousing and spurring up of those better qualities in him still dormant and inert. The fabric of his nature was shaken and broken up, it was true, but if he left it to itself there was danger that it would re-form upon the old lines.

And this was precisely what Vandover did. As rapidly as ever his pliable character adapted itself to the new environment; he had nothing to do; there was lacking both the desire and necessity to keep him at his easel; he neglected his painting utterly. He never thought of attending the life-class at the art school; long since he had given up his downtown studio. He was content to be idle, listless, apathetic, letting the days bring whatever they chose, making no effort toward any fixed routine, allowing his habits to be formed by the exigencies of the hour.

He rose late and took his breakfast in his room; after breakfast he sat in his window-seat, reading his paper, smoking his pipe, drinking his coffee, and watching the women on their way downtown to their morning's shopping or marketing. Then, as the fancy moved him, he read a novel, wrote a few letters, or passed an hour in the studio dabbling with some sketches for the Last Enemy. Very often he put in the whole morning doing pen and inks of pretty, smartly dressed girls, after Gibson's manner, which he gave away afterward to his friends. In the afternoon he read or picked the banjo or, sitting down to the little piano he had rented, played over his three pieces, the two polkas and the air of the topical song. At three o'clock, especially of Wednesday and Saturday afternoons, he bestirred himself, dressed very carefully, and went downtown to promenade Kearney and Market streets, stopping occasionally at the Imperial, where he sometimes found Ellis and Geary and where he took cocktails in their company.

He rarely went out in the evenings; his father's death had changed all that, at least for a while. He had not seen Turner Ravis nor Henrietta Vance for nearly two months.

Vandover took his greatest pleasure while in his new quarters, delighted to be pottering about his sitting room by the hour, setting it to rights, rearranging the small ornaments, adjusting the calendar, winding the clock and, above all, tending the famous tiled stove.

In his idleness he grew to have small and petty ways. The entire day went in doing little things. He passed one whole afternoon delightfully, whittling out a new banjo bridge from the cover of a cigar-box, scraping it smooth afterward with a bit of glass. The winding of his clock was quite an occurrence in the course of the day, something to be looked forward to. The mixing of his tobacco was a positive event and undertaken with all gravity, while the task of keeping it moist and ripe in the blue china jar, with the sponge attachment, that always stood on the bamboo tea-table by the Japanese screen, was a wearing anxiety that was yet a pleasure.

It became a fad with him to do without matches, using as a substitute "lights," tapers of twisted paper to be ignited at the famous stove. He found amusement for two days in twisting and rolling these "lights," cutting frills in the larger ends with a pair of scissors, and stacking them afterward in a Chinese flower jar he had bought for the purpose and stood on top of the bookcases. The lights were admirably made and looked very pretty. When he had done he counted them. He had made two hundred exactly. What a coincidence!

But the stove, the famous tiled stove with flamboyant ornaments, was the chiefest joy of Vandover's new life. He was delighted with it; it was so artistic, so curious, it kept the fire so well, it looked so cheerful and inviting; a stove that was the life and soul of the whole room, a stove to draw up to and talk to; no, never was there such a stove! There was hardly a minute of the day he was not fussing with it, raking it down, turning the damper off and on, opening and shutting the door, filling it with coal, putting the blower on and then taking it off again, sweeping away the ashes with a little brass-handled broom, or studying the pictures upon the tiles: the Punishment of Caliban and His Associates, Romeo and Juliet, the Fall of Phaeton. He even pretended to the chambermaid that he alone understood how to manage the stove, forbidding her to touch it, assuring her that it had to be coaxed and humoured. Often late in the evening as he was going to bed he would find the fire in it drowsing; then he would hustle it sharply to arouse it, punching it with the poker, talking to it, saying: "Wake up there, you!" And then when the fire was snapping he would sit before it in his bathrobe, absorbing its heat luxuriously and scratching himself, as was his custom, for over an hour.

But very often in the evening he would have the boys, Ellis, Geary, and young Haight, up to a little improvised supper. They would bring home *tamales* with them, and Vandover would try to make Welsh rabbits, which did not always come out well and which they oftentimes drank instead of ate. Ellis, always very silent, would mix and drink cocktails continually. Vandover would pick his banjo, and together with young Haight would listen to Geary.

"Ah, you bet," this one would say, "I'm going to make my pile in this town. I can do it. Beale sent me to court the other morning to get the judge's signature. He had a grouch on, and wanted to put me off. You ought to have heard me jolly him. I talked right up to him! Yes, sir; you bet! Didn't I have the gall? That's the way you want to do to get along—get right in and not be afraid. I got his signature, you bet. Ah, I'm right in it with Beale; he thinks I'm hot stuff."

Now that there was nothing to worry him, and little to occupy his mind, Vandover gave himself over considerably to those animal pleasures which he enjoyed so much. He lay abed late in the morning, dozing between the warm sheets; he overfed himself at table, and drank too much wine; he ate between meals, having filled his sideboard with canned patés, potted birds, and devilled meats; while upon the bamboo table stood a tin box of chocolates out of which he ate whole handfuls at a time. He would take this box into the bathroom with him and eat while he lay in the hot water until he was overcome by the enervating warmth and by the steam and would then drop off to sleep.

It was during these days that Vandover took up his banjo-playing seriously, if it could be said that he did anything seriously at this time. He took occasional lessons of a Mexican in a room above a wigmaker's store on Market Street, and learned to play by note. For a little time he really applied himself; after he had mastered the customary style of play he began to affect the more brilliant and fancy performances, playing two banjos at once, or putting nickels under the bridge and picking the strings with a calling-card to imitate a mandolin. He even made up some comical pieces that had a great success among the boys. One of these he called the "Pleasing Pan-Hellenic Production"; another was the imitation of the "Midway Plaisance Music," and a third had for title "A Sailor Robbing a Ship," in which he managed to imitate the sounds of the lapping of the water, the creaking of the oarlocks, the tramp of the sailor's feet upon the deck, the pistol shot that destroyed him, and—by running up the frets on the bass-string— his dying groans, a finale that never failed to produce a tremendous effect.

CHAPTER XIII

JUST before Lent, and about three months after the death of Vandover's father, Henrietta Vance gave a reception and dance at her house. The affair was one of a series that the girls of the Cotillion had been giving to the men of the same club. Vandover had gone to all but the last, which had occurred while he was at Coronado. He was sure of meeting Geary, young Haight, Turner Ravis, and all the people of his set at these functions, and had always managed to have a very jolly time. He had been very quiet since his father's death and had hardly gone out at all; in fact, since Ida Wade's death and his trip down the coast he had seen none of his acquaintances except the boys. But he determined now that he would go to this dance and in so doing return once more to the world that he knew. By this time he had become pretty well accustomed to his father's death and saw no reason why he should not have a good time.

At first he thought he would ask Turner to go with him, but in the end made up his mind to go alone, instead; one always had a better time when one went alone. Young Haight would have liked to have asked Turner, but did not because he supposed, of course, that Vandover would take her. In the end Turner had Delphine act as her escort.

Vandover arrived at Henrietta Vance's house at about half-past eight. A couple of workmen were stretching the last guy ropes of the awning that reached over the sidewalk; every window of the house was lighted. The front door was opened for the guest before he could ring, and he passed up the stairs, catching a glimpse of the parlours through the portières of the doors. As yet they

442

were empty of guests, the floors were covered with canvas, and the walls decorated with fern leaves. In a window recess one of the caterer's men was setting out two punch bowls and a multitude of glass cups; three or four musicians were gathered about the piano, tuning up, and one heard the subdued note of a cornet; the air was heavy with the smell of pinks and of La France roses.

At the turn of the stairs the Vances' second girl in a white lawn cap directed him to the gentlemen's dressing room, which was the room of Henrietta Vance's older brother. About a dozen men were here before him, some rolling up their overcoats into balls and stowing them with their canes in the corners of the room; others laughing and smoking together, and still others who were either brushing their hair before the mirrors or sitting on the bed in their stocking feet, breathing upon their patent leathers, warming them before putting them on. There were one or two who knew no one and who stood about unhappily, twisting the tissue paper from the buttons of their new gloves, and looking stupidly at the pictures on the walls of the room. Occasionally one of the gentlemen would step to the door and look out into the hall to see if the ladies whom they were escorting were yet come out of their dressing room, ready to go down.

On the centre table stood three boxes of cigars and a great many packages of cigarettes, while extra hairbrushes, whiskbrooms, and papers of pins had been placed about the bureau.

As Vandover came in, he nodded pleasantly to such of the men as he knew, and, after hiding his hat and coat under the bed, shook himself into his clothes again and rearranged his dress tie.

The house was filling up rapidly; one heard the deadened roll of wheels in the street outside, the banging of carriage doors, and an incessant rustle of stiff skirts ascending the stairs. From the ladies' dressing room came an increasing soprano chatter, while downstairs the orchestra around the piano in the back parlour began to snarl and whine louder and louder. About the halls and stairs one caught brief glimpses of white and blue opera cloaks edged with swan's-down alternating with the gleam of a starched shirt bosom and the glint of a highly polished silk hat. Odours of sachet and violets came and went elusively or mingled with those of the roses and pinks. An air of gayety and excitement began to spread throughout the house.

"Hello, old man!" "Hello, Van!" Charlie Geary, young Haight, and Ellis came in together. "Hello, boys!" answered Vandover, hairbrush in hand, turning about from the mirror, where he had been trying to make his hair lie very flat and smooth.

"Look here," said Geary, showing him a dance-card already full, "I've got every dance promised. I looked out for that at the last one of these affairs; made all my arrangements and engagements then. Ah, you bet, I don't get left on any dance. That's the way you want to rustle. Ah," he went on, "had a bully sleep last night. I knew I was going to be out late to-night, so I went to bed at nine; didn't wake up till seven. Had a fine cutlet for breakfast."

It was precisely at this moment that Geary got his first advancement in life. Mr. Beale, Jr., head clerk in the great firm of Beale & Story, came up to him as he was drawing off his overcoat:

"How is Fischer?" asked Geary.

Beale, Jr., pulled him over into a corner, talking in a low voice. "He's even worse than yesterday," he answered. "I think we shall have to give him a vacation, and that's what I want to speak to you about. If you can, Geary, I should like to have you take his place for a

444

while, at least until we get through with this contract case. I don't know about Fischer. He's sick so often, I'm afraid we may have to let him go altogether."

Suddenly the orchestra downstairs broke out into a clash of harmony and then swung off with the beat and cadence of a waltz. The dance was beginning; a great bustle and hurrying commenced about the dressing rooms and at the head of the stairs; everybody went down. In the front parlour by the mantel Henrietta Vance and Turner stood on either side of Mrs. Vance, receiving, shaking hands, and laughing and talking with the different guests who came up singly, in couples, or in noisy groups.

No one was dancing yet. The orchestra stopped with a flourish of the cornet, and at once a great crowding and pushing began amidst a vast hum of talk. The cards were being filled up, a swarm of men gathered about each of the more popular girls, passing her card from hand to hand while she smiled upon them all helplessly and good-naturedly. The dance-cards had run short and some of the men were obliged to use their visiting cards; with these in one hand and the stump of a pencil in the other, they ran about from group to group, pushing, elbowing, and calling over one another's heads like brokers in a stock exchange.

Geary, however, walked about calmly, smiling contentedly, very good-humoured. From time to time he stopped such a one of the hurrying, excited men as he knew and showed him his card made out weeks before, saying, "Ah, how's that? *I* am all fixed; made all my engagements at the last one of these affairs, even up to six extras. That's the way you want to rustle."

Young Haight was very popular; everywhere the girls nodded and smiled at him, many even saving a place on their cards for him before he had asked.

Ellis took advantage of the confusion to disappear.

He went up into the deserted dressing room, chose a cigar, unbuttoned his vest and sat down in one chair, putting his feet upon another. The hum of the dance came to him in a prolonged and soothing murmur and he enjoyed it in some strange way of his own, listening and smoking, stretched out at ease in the deserted dressing room.

Vandover went up to Turner Ravis, smiling and holding out his hand. She seemed to be curiously embarrassed when she saw him, and did not smile back at him. He asked to see her card, but she drew her hand quickly from his, telling him that she was going home early and was not dancing at all, that in fact she had to "receive" instead of dance. It was evident to Vandover that he had done something to displease her, and he quickly concluded that it was because he had not asked her to go with him that evening.

He turned from her to Henrietta Vance as though nothing unusual had happened, resolving to see her later in the evening and in the meanwhile invent some suitable excuse. Henrietta Vance did not even see his hand; she was a very jolly girl, ordinarily, and laughed all the time. Now she looked him squarely in the face without so much as a smile, at once angry and surprised; never had anything seemed so hateful and disagreeable. Vandover put his hand back into his pocket, trying to carry it all off with a laugh, saying in order to make her laugh with him as he used to do, "Hello! how do you do this evening? It's a pleasant morning this afternoon." "How do you do?" she answered nervously, refusing to laugh. Then she turned from him abruptly to talk to young Haight's little cousin Hetty.

Mrs. Vance was neither embarrassed nor nervous as the girls had been. She stared calmly at Vandover and said with a peculiar smile, "I am surprised to see you here, Mr. Vandover."

446

An hour later the dance was in full swing. Almost every number was a waltz or a two-step, the music being the topical songs and popular airs of the day set to dance music.

About half-past ten o'clock, between two dances, the cornet sounded a trumpet call; the conversation ceased in a moment, and Henrietta Vance's brother, standing by the piano, called out, "The next dance will be the *first extra*," adding immediately, "a *waltz*." The dance recommenced; in the pauses of the music one heard the rhythmic movement of the feet shuffling regularly in one-two-three time.

Some of the couples waltzed fast, whirling about the rooms, bearing around corners with a swirl and swing of silk skirts, the girls' faces flushed and perspiring, their eyes half-closed, their bare, white throats warm, moist, and alternately swelling and contracting with their quick breathing. On certain of these girls the dancing produced a peculiar effect. The continued motion, the whirl of the lights, the heat of the room, the heavy perfume of the flowers, the cadence of the music, even the physical fatigue, reacted in some strange way upon their oversensitive feminine nerves, the monotony of repeated sensation producing some sort of mildly hypnotic effect, a morbid hysterical pleasure the more exquisite because mixed with pain. These were the girls whom one heard declaring that they could dance all night, the girls who could dance until they dropped.

Other of the couples danced with the greatest languor and gravity, their arms held out rigid and at right angles with their bodies.

About the doors and hallways stood the unhappy gentlemen who knew no one, watching the others dance, feigning to be amused. Some of them, however, had ascended to the dressing room and began to strike up an acquaintance with each other and with Ellis, smoking incessantly, discussing business, politics, and even religion.

In the ladies' dressing room two of the maids were holding a long conversation in low tones, their heads together; evidently it was concerning something dreadful. They continually exclaimed "Oh!" and "Ah!" suddenly sitting back from each other, shaking their heads, and biting their nether lips. On the top floor in the hall the servants in their best clothes leaned over the balustrade, nudging each other, talking in hoarse whispers or pointing with thick fingers swollen with dish-water. All up and down the stairs were the couples who were sitting out the dance, some of them even upon the circular sofa in the hall over the first landing.

The music stopped, leaving a babel of talk in the air, the couples fell apart for an instant, but a great clapping of hands broke out and the tired musicians heroically recommenced.

As soon as the short *encore* was done there was a rush for the lemonade and punch bowls. The guests thronged around them joking each other. "Hello! are you here *again?*" "Oh, this is dreadful!" "This makes *six* times I've seen you here."

A smell of coffee rose into the air from the basement. It was about half-past eleven; the next dance was the supper dance and the gentlemen hurried about anxiously searching the stairs, the parlours, and the conservatory for the girls who had promised them this dance weeks before. The musicians were playing a march, and the couples crowded down the narrow stairs in single file, the ladies drawing off their gloves. The tired musicians stretched themselves, rubbed their eyes, and began to talk aloud in the deserted parlours.

Supper was served in the huge billiard room in the basement and was eaten in a storm of gayety. The same parties and "sets" tried to get together at the same table; Henrietta Vance's party was particularly noisy: at her table there was an incessant clamour of screams and shouts of laughter. One ate oysters *à la poulette*, terrapin-salads, and croquettes; the wines were Sauternes and champagnes. With the nuts and dessert the caps came on, and in a few minutes were cracking and snapping all over the room.

Six of the unfortunates who knew no one, but who had managed through a common affliction to become acquainted with each other, gathered at a separate table. Ellis was one of their number; he levied a twenty-five-cent assessment, and tipped the waiter a dollar and a half. This one accordingly brought them extra bottles of champagne in which they found consolation for all the *ennui* of the evening.

After supper the dancing began again. The little stiffness and constraint of the earlier part of the evening was gone; by this time nearly everybody, except the unfortunates, knew everybody else. The good dinner and the champagne had put them all into an excellent humour, and they all commenced to be very jolly. They began a Virginia Reel still wearing the magician's caps and Phrygian bonnets of tissue paper.

Young Haight was with Turner Ravis as much as possible during the evening, very happy and excited. Something had happened; it was impossible for him to say precisely what, for on the face of things Turner was the same as ever. Nothing in her speech or actions was different, but there was in her manner, in the very air that surrounded her, something elusive and subtle that set him all in a tremor. There was a change in his favour; he felt that she liked to have him with her and that she was trying to have him feel as much in some mysterious way of her own. He could see, however, that she was hardly conscious of doing this and that the change was more apparent to his eyes than it was to hers.

"Must you really go home now?" he said, as Turner began to talk of leaving, soon after supper. They had been sitting out the dance under a palm at the angle of the stairs.

"Yes," answered Turner; "Howard has the measles and I promised to be home early. Delphine was to come for me and she ought to be here now."

"Delphine?" exclaimed young Haight. "Didn't you come with Van?"

"No," answered Turner quietly. Only by her manner, and by something in the way she said the word, Haight knew at once that she had broken definitely with Vandover. The talk he had had with her at her house came back to him on the instant. He hesitated a moment and then asked:

"There is something wrong? Has Van done anything —never mind, I don't mean that; it's no business of mine, I suppose. But I know you care for him. I'm sorry if——"

But he was not sorry. Try as he would, his heart was leaping in him for joy. With Vandover out of the way, he knew that all would be different; Turner herself had said so.

"Oh, everything is wrong," said Turner, with tears in her eyes. "I have been so disappointed in Van; oh, terribly disappointed."

"I know; yes, I think I know what you mean," answered young Haight in a low voice.

"Oh, please don't let's talk about it at all," cried Turner. But young Haight could not stop now.

"Is Van really out of the question, then?" he asked.

"Oh, yes," she exclaimed, not seeing what he was coming to. "Oh, yes; how could I—how *could* I care for him after—after what has happened?"

Very much embarrassed, young Haight went on: "I know it's unfair to take advantage of you now, but do

450

you remember what you said once? That if Vandover were out of the question, that '*perhaps*' you might—that it would be—that there might be a chance for me?"

Turner was silent for a long time, and then she said: "Yes, I remember."

"Well, how about that *now?*" asked young Haight with a nervous laugh.

"Ah," answered Turner, "how do I know—so soon!"

"But what do you *think*, Turner?" he persisted.

"But I haven't thought at all," she returned.

"Well, think now!" he went on. "Tell me—how about that?"

"About *what?*"

"Ah, you know what I mean," young Haight replied, feeling like a little boy, "about what you said at your house that Sunday night. Please tell me; you don't know how much it means to me."

"Oh, there's Delphine at the door!" suddenly exclaimed Turner. "Now, really, I *must* go down. She doesn't know where to go; she's so stupid!"

"No," he answered, "not until you tell me!" He caught her hand, refusing to let it go.

"Ah, how mean you are to corner me so!" she cried, laughing and embarrassed. "Must I—well—I know I shouldn't. *O-oh*, I just *detest* you!" Young Haight turned her hand palm upward and kissed the little circle of crumpled flesh that showed where her glove buttoned. Then she tore her hand away and ran downstairs, while he followed more slowly.

On her way back to the dressing room she met him again, crossing the hall.

"Don't you want to see me home?" she said.

"Do I *want* to?" shouted young Haight.

"Oh, but I forgot," she cried. "You can't. I won't let you. You have your other dances engaged!"

451

"Oh, damn the other dances!" he exclaimed, but instead of being offended, Turner only smiled.

Toward one o'clock there was a general movement to go. Henrietta Vance and Mrs. Vance were inquired for, and the blue and white opera cloaks reappeared, descending the stairs, disturbing the couples who were seated there. The banging of carriage doors and the rumble of wheels recommenced in the street. The musicians played a little longer. As the party thinned out, there was greater dance room and a consequent greater pleasure in dancing. These last dances at the end of the evening were enjoyed more than all the others. But the party was breaking up fast: Turner had already gone home; Mrs. Vance and Henrietta were back at their places in front of the mantel, surrounded by a group of gentlemen in cape-coats and ladies in opera wraps. Everyone was crying "Good-bye" or "Good-night!" and assuring Mrs. Vance and Henrietta of the enjoyableness of the occasion. Suddenly the musicians played "Home Sweet Home." Those still dancing uttered an exclamation of regret, but continued waltzing to this air the same as ever. Some began to dance again in their overcoats and opera wraps. Then at last the tired musicians stopped and reached for the cases of their instruments, and the remaining guests, seized with a sudden panic lest they should be the last to leave, fled to the dressing rooms. These were in the greatest confusion, everyone was in a hurry; in the gentlemen's dressing room there was a great putting on of coats and mufflers and a searching for misplaced gloves, hats, and canes. A base hum of talk rose in the air, bits and ends of conversation being tossed back and forth across the room. "*You* haven't seen my hat, have you, Jimmy?" "Did you meet that girl I was telling you about?" "Hello, old man! have a good time to-night?" "Lost your hat? No, I haven't seen it." "Yes, about half-past ten!" "Well, I

told him that myself!" "Ah, you bet it's the man that
rustles that gets there." "Come round about four,
then." "What's the matter with coming home in *our*
carriage?"

At the doors of the dressing rooms the ladies joined
their escorts, and a great crowd formed in the halls,
worming down the stairs and out upon the front steps.
As the first groups reached the open air there was a great
cry: "Why, it's pouring rain!" This was taken up and
repeated and carried all the way back into the house.
There were exclamations of dismay and annoyance:
"Why, it's raining right *down !*" "What *shall* we do!"
Tempers were lost, brothers and sisters quarrelling with
each other over the question of umbrellas. "Ah," said
Geary, delighted, peeling the cover from his umbrella in
the vestibule, "I *thought* it was going to rain before I
left and brought mine along with me. Ah, you bet I
always look out for rain!" On the horse-block stood the
caller, chanting up the carriages at the top of his voice.
The street was full of coupés, carriages, and hacks, the
raindrops showing in a golden blur as they fell across the
streaming light of their lamps. The horses were smoking
and restless, and the drivers in oilskins and rubber
blankets were wrangling and shouting. At every instant
there was a long roll of wheels interrupted by the banging of the doors. Near the caller stood a useless policeman, his shield pinned on the outside of his wet rubber
coat, on which the carriage lamps were momentarily reflected in long vertical streaks.

In a short time all the guests were gone except the
one young lady whose maid and carriage had somehow
not been sent. Henrietta Vance's brother took this one
home in a hired hack. Mrs. Vance and Henrietta sat
down to rest for a moment in the empty parlours. The
canvas-covered floors were littered with leaves of smilax
and La France roses, with bits of ribbon, ends of lace,

and discarded Phrygian bonnets of tissue paper. The butler and the second girl were already turning down the gas in the other rooms.

Long before the party broke up Vandover had gone home, stunned and dazed, as yet hardly able to realize the meaning of what had happened. Some strange and dreadful change had taken place; things were different, people were different to him; not everyone had been so outspoken as Turner, Henrietta Vance, and her mother, but even amongst others who had talked to him politely and courteously enough, the change was no less apparent. It was in the air, a certain vague shrinking and turning of the shoulder, a general atmosphere of aversion and repulsion, an unseen frown, an unexpressed rebuff, intangible, illusive, but as unmistakable as his own existence. The world he had known knew him now no longer. It was ostracism at last.

But why? Why? Sitting over his tiled flamboyant stove, brooding into the winking coals, Vandover asked himself the question in vain. He knew what latitude young men were allowed by society; he was sure nothing short of discovered crime could affect them. True enough he had at one time allowed himself to drift into considerable dissipation, but he was done with that now, he had reformed, he had turned over a new leaf. Even at his worst he had only lived the life of the other young men around him, the other young men who were received as much as ever, even though people, the girls themselves, practically knew of what they did, knew that they were often drunk, and that they frequented the society of abandoned women. What had he done to merit this casting off? What *could* he have done? He even went so far as to wonder if there was anything wrong about his father or his sudden death.

A little after one o'clock he heard Geary's whistle in

the street outside. "Hello, old man!" he cried as Vandover opened the window. "I was just on my way home from the hoe-down; saw a light in your window and thought I'd call you up. Say, have you got anything wet up there? I'm extra dry."

"Yes," said Vandover, "come on up!"

"Did you hear what Beale said to me this evening?" said Geary, as he mixed himself a cocktail at the sideboard. "Oh, I tell you, I'm getting right in, down at that office. Beale wants me to take the place of one of the assistants in the firm, a fellow who's got the consumption, coughing up his lungs all the time. It's an important place, hundred a month; that's right. Yes, sir; you bet, I'm going to get in and rustle now and make myself so indispensable in that fellow's place that they can't get along without me. I'll crowd him right out; I know it may be selfish, but, damn it! that's what you have to do to get along. It's human nature. I'll tell you right here to-night," he exclaimed with sudden energy, clenching his fist and slowly rapping the knuckles on the table to emphasize each word, "that I'll be the head of that firm some day, or I'll know the reason why."

When Geary finally became silent, the two looked into the fire for some time without speaking. At last Geary said:

"You came home early to-night, didn't you?"

"Yes," answered Vandover, stirring uneasily. "Yes, I did."

There was another silence. Then Geary said abruptly: "It's too bad. They are kind of stinky-pinky to you."

"Yes," said Vandover with a grin. "*I* don't know what's the matter. Everybody seems nasty!"

"It's that business with Ida Wade, you know," replied Geary. "It got around somehow that she killed herself on your account. Everybody seems to be on to it. I heard it—oh, nearly a month ago."

"Oh," said Vandover with a short laugh, "that's it, is it? I was wondering."

"Yes, that's it," answered Geary. "You see they don't know for sure; no one *knows,* but all at once every- one seemed to be talking about it, and they suspect an awful lot. I guess they are pretty near right, aren't they?" He did not wait for an answer, but laughed clumsily and went on: "You see, you always have to be awfully careful in those things, or you'll get into a box. Ah, you bet I don't let any girl *I* go with know *my* last name or *my* address if I can help it. I'm clever enough for that; you have to manage very carefully; ah, you bet! You ought to have looked out for that, old man!" He paused a moment and then went on: "Oh, I guess it will be all right, all right, in a little while. They will forget about it, you know. I wouldn't worry. I guess it will be all right."

"Yes," answered Vandover absently, "I guess so— perhaps."

A few days later Vandover was in the reading room of the Mechanics' Library, listlessly turning over the pages of a volume of *l'Art*. It was Saturday morning and the place was full of ladies who were downtown for their shopping and marketing, and who had come in either to change their books or to keep appointments with each other. On a sudden Vandover saw Turner just passing into the Biography alcove. He got up and followed her. She was standing at the end of the dim book-lined tunnel searching the upper shelves, her head and throat bent back, and her gloved finger on her lip. The faint odour of the perfume she always affected came to him mingled with the fragrance of the jonquils at her belt and the smell of leather and of books that exhaled from the shelves on either side. He did not offer to take her hand but came up slowly, speaking in a low voice.

It was the last time that Vandover ever met Turner

Ravis. They talked for upward of an hour, leaning against the opposite book-shelves, Vandover with his fists in his pockets, his head bent down, and the point of his shoe tracing the pattern in the linoleum carpet; Turner, her hands clasped in front of her, looking him squarely in the face, speaking calmly and frankly.

"Now, I hope you see just how it is, Van," she said at length. "What has happened hasn't made me cease to care for you, because if I had really cared for you the way I thought I did, the way a girl ought to care for the man she wants to marry, I would have stood by you through everything, no matter what you did. I don't do so now, because I find I don't care for you as much as I thought I did. What has happened has only shown me that. I'm sorry, oh, so sorry to be disappointed in you, but it's because I only think of you as being once a very good friend of mine, not because I love you as you think I did. Once—a long time ago—when we first knew each other, then, perhaps—things were different then. But somehow we seem to have grown away from that. Since then we have both been mistaken; you thought I cared for you in that way, and I thought so, too, and I thought you cared for me; but it was only that we were keeping up appearances, pretending to ourselves just for the sake of old times. We don't love each other now; you know it. But I have never intentionally deceived you or tried to lead you on; when I told you I cared for you I really thought I did. I meant to be sincere; I always thought so until this happened, and then when I saw how easily I could let you go, it only proved to me that I did not care for you as I thought I did. It was wrong of me, I know, and I should have known my own mind before, but I didn't, I didn't. You talk about Dolly Haight; but it is not Dolly Haight at all who has changed my affection for you. I will be just as frank as I can with you, Van. I may learn really to love Dolly Haight; I don't know, I

457

think perhaps I will, but it isn't that I care for him *just* because I don't care for you. Can't you see, it's just as if I had never met you. You know it's very hard for me to say this to you, Van, and I suppose it's all mixed up, but I can't help it. You don't know how sorry I am, because we have been such old friends—because I really did care for you as a friend; it's a proof of it, that there is no other man in the world I could talk to like this. I think, too, Van, that was the only way you cared for me, just as a good friend—except perhaps at first, when we first knew each other. You know yourself that is so. We really haven't loved each other at all for a long time, and now we have found it out before it was too late. And even if everything were different, Van, don't you know how it is with girls? They really love the man who loves them the most. Half the time they're just in love with being loved. That's the way most girls love nowadays, and you know yourself, Van, that Dolly Haight really loves me more than you do." She gathered up her books and went on after a pause, straightening up, ready to go: "If I should let myself think of what you have done, I feel—as if—why, dreadful—I—that I should hate you, loathe you; but I try not to do that. I have been thinking it all over since the other night. I shall always try to think of you at your best; I have tried to forget everything else, and in forgetting it I forgive you. I can honestly say that," she said, holding out her hand, "I forgive you, and you must forgive me because once, by deceiving myself, I deceived you, and made you think that I cared for you in that way when I didn't." As their hands fell apart Turner faced him and added with tears in her eyes: "You know this must be good-bye for good. You don't know how it hurts me to tell you. I know it looks as if I were deserting you when you were alone in the world and had most need of someone to influence you for the good. But, Van,

won't you be better now? Won't you break from it all
and be your own self again? I have faith in you. I
believe it's in you to become a great man and a good
man. It isn't too late to begin all over again. Just be
your better self; live up to the best that's in you; if not
for your own sake, then for the sake of that other girl
that's coming into your life some time; that other girl
who is good and sweet and pure, whom you will really,
really love and who will really, really love you."

All the rest of that month Vandover was wretched.
So great was his shame and humiliation over this fresh
disaster that he hardly dared to show himself out of
doors. His grief was genuine and it was profound. Yet he
took his punishment in the right spirit. He did not blame
anyone but himself; it was only a just retribution for the
thing he had done. Only what made it hard to bear was
the fact that the chastisement had fallen upon him long
after he had repented of the crime, long after he had
resolved to lead a new and upright life; but with shut
teeth he determined still to carry out that resolve; he
would devote all his future life to living down the past.
It might be hard; it might be one long struggle through
many, many years, but he would do it. Ah, yes, he would
show them; they had cast him off, but he would go away
to Paris now as he had always intended. As invariably
happened when he was deeply moved, he turned to his
art, blindly and instinctively. He would go to Paris now
and study his paintings, five, ten years, and come back
at last a great artist, when these same people who had
cast him off would be proud to receive him. Turner was
right in saying that he had in him the making of a great
man. He *knew* that she was right; knew that if he only
gave the better part of him, the other Vandover, the
chance, that he would become a great artist. Well, he
would do so, and then when he came back again, when

all the world was at his feet, and there were long articles in the paper announcing his arrival, these people would throng around him; he would show them what a great and noble nature he really had; he would forgive them; he would ignore what they had done. He even dramatized a little scene between himself and Turner, then Mrs. Haight. They would both be pretty old then and he would take her children on his lap and look at her over their heads—he could almost see those heads, white, silky, and very soft—and he would nod at her thoughtfully, and say, "Well, I have taken your advice, do you remember?" and she was to answer, "Yes, I remember." There were actually tears in his eyes as he saw the scene.

At the very first he thought that he could not live without Turner; that he loved her too much to be able to give her up. But in a little while he saw that this was not so. She was right, too, in saying that he had long since outlived his first sincere affection for her. He had felt for a long time that he did not love her well enough to marry her; that he did not love her as young Haight did, and he acknowledged to himself that this affair at least had ended rightly. The two loved each other, he could see that; at last he even told himself that he would be glad to see Turner married to Dolly Haight, who was his best friend. But for all that, it came very hard at first to give up Turner altogether; never to see her or speak to her again.

As the first impressions of the whole affair grew dull and blunt by the lapse of time, this humble penitential mood of Vandover's passed away and was succeeded by a feeling of gloomy revolt, a sullen rage at the world that had cast him off *only* because he had been found out. He thought it a matter of self-respect to resent the insult they had put upon him. But little by little he ceased to regret his exile; the new life was not so bad as he had at first anticipated, and his relations with the men whom he

knew best, Ellis, Geary, and young Haight, were in no-
wise changed. He was no longer invited anywhere, and
the girls he had known never saw him when he passed
them on the street. It was humiliating enough at first,
but he got used to it after a while, and by dint of thrusting the disagreeable subject from his thoughts, by refusing to let the disgrace sink deep in his mind, by
forgetting the whole business as much as he could, he
arrived after a time to be passably contented. His pliable
character had again rearranged itself to suit the new
environment.

Along with this, however, came a sense of freedom.
Now he no longer had anything to fear from society; it
had shot its bolt, it had done its worst, there was no
longer anything to restrain him, now he could do anything.

He was in precisely this state of mind when he received the cards for the opening of the roadhouse, the
"resort" out on the almshouse drive about which Toby,
the waiter at the Imperial, had spoken to him.

Vandover attended it. It was a debauch of forty-eight
hours, the longest and the worst he had ever indulged in.
For a long time the brute had been numb and dormant;
now at last when he woke he was raging, more insatiable,
more irresistible than ever.

The affair at the roadhouse was but the beginning.
All at once Vandover rushed into a career of dissipation,
consumed with the desire of vice, the perverse, blind,
and reckless desire of the male. Drunkenness, sensuality,
gambling, debauchery, he knew them all, He rubbed
elbows with street walkers, with bookmakers, with
saloonkeepers, with the exploiters of lost women. The
bartenders of the city called him by his first name, the
policemen, the night detail, were familiar with his face,
the drivers of the nighthawks recognized his figure by
the street lamps, paling in the light of many an early

461

dawn. At one time and another he was associated with all the different types of people in the low "sporting set," acquaintances of an evening, whose names grew faint to his recollection amidst the jingle of glasses and the popping of corks, whose faces faded from his memory in the haze of tobacco smoke and the fumes of whisky; young men of the city, rich without apparent means of livelihood, women and girls "recently from the East" with rooms over the fast restaurants; owners of trotting horses, actresses without engagements, billiard-markers, pool-sellers, and the sons of the proprietors of halfway houses and "resorts." With all these Vandover kept the pace at the Imperial, at the race-track, at the gambling tables in the saloons and bars along Kearney and Market streets, and in the disreputable houses amid the strong odours of musk and the rustle of heavy silk dresses. It lasted for a year; by the end of that time he had about forgotten his determination to go to Paris and had grown out of touch with his three old friends, Ellis, Geary, and Haight. He seldom saw them now; occasionally he met them in one of the little rooms of the Imperial over their beer and Welsh rabbits, but now he always went on to the larger rooms where one had champagne and terrapin. He felt that he no longer was one of them.

That year the opera came to San Francisco, and Vandover hired a messenger boy to stand in line all night at the door of the music store where the tickets were to be sold. Vandover could still love music. In the wreckage of all that was good that had been going on in him his love for all art was yet intact. It was the strongest side of his nature and it would be the last to go.

CHAPTER XIV

THE house was crowded to the doors; there was no longer any standing room and many were even sitting on the steps of the aisles. In the boxes the gentlemen were standing up behind the chairs of large plain ladies in showy toilets and diamonds. The atmosphere was heavy with the smell of gas, of plush upholstery, of wilting bouquets and of sachet. A fine vapour as of the visible exhalation of many breaths pervaded the house, blurring the lowered lights and dimming the splendour of the great glass chandelier.

It was warm to suffocation, a dry, irritating warmth that perspiration did not relieve, while the air itself was stale and close as though fouled by being breathed over and over again. In the topmost galleries, banked with tiers of watching faces, the heat must have been unbearable.

The only movement perceptible throughout the audience was the little swaying of gay-coloured fans like the balancing of butterflies about to light. Occasionally there would be a vast rustling like the sound of wind in a forest, as the holders of librettos turned the leaves simultaneously.

The orchestra thundered; the French horns snarling, the first violins wailing in unison, while all the bows went up and down together like parts of a well-regulated machine; the kettle-drums rolled sonorously at exact intervals, and now and then one heard the tinkling of the harp like the pattering of raindrops between peals of thunder. The leader swayed from side to side in his place, beating time with his baton, his hand, and his head.

On the stage itself the act was drawing to a close.

463

There had just been a duel. The baritone lay stretched upon the floor at left centre, his sword fallen at some paces from him. On the left of the scene, front, stood the tenor who had killed him, singing in his highest register, very red in the face, continually striking his hand upon his breast and pointing with his sword toward his fallen enemy. Next him on the extreme left was his friend the basso, in high leather boots, growling from time to time during a sustained chord,"*Mon honneur et ma foi.*" In the centre of the stage, the soprano, the star, the prima donna chanted a fervid but ineffectual appeal to the tenor who cried, "*Jamais, jamais!*" striking his breast and pointing with his sword. The prima donna cried, "*Ah, mon Dieu, ayez pitié de moi.*" Her confidante, the mezzo-soprano, came to her support, repeating her words with an impersonal meaning, "*Ayez pitié d'elle.*" "*Mon honneur et ma foi,*" growled the basso. The contralto, dressed as a man, turned toward the audience on the extreme right, bringing out her notes with a wrench and a twist of her body and neck, and intoning, "*Ah, malheureuse ! Mon Dieu, ayez pitié d'elle.*"

The leader of the chorus, costumed as the captain of the watch, leaned over the dead baritone and sang, "*Il est mort, il est mort. Mon Dieu, ayez pitié de lui.*" The soldiers of the watch were huddled together immediately back of him. They wore tin helmets, much too large, and green peplums, and repeated his words continually.

The chorus itself was made up of citizens of the town; it was in a semicircle at the back of the stage—the men on one side, the women on the other. They made all their gestures together and chanted without ceasing: "*O horreur, O mystére ! Il est mort. Mon Dieu, ayez-pitié de nous !*"

"*De Grace !*" cried the prima donna.

"*Jamais, jamais !*" echoed the tenor, striking his breast and pointing with his sword.

"*O mystére!*" chanted the chorus, while the basso struck his hand upon his sword hilt, growling "*Mon honneur et ma foi.*"

The orchestra redoubled. The finale began; all the pieces of the orchestra, all the voices on the stage, commenced over again very loud. They all took a step forward, and the rhythm became more rapid, till it reached a climax where the prima donna's voice jumped to a C in alt, holding it long enough for the basso to thunder, "*Mon honneur et ma foi*" twice. Then they all struck the attitudes for the closing tableau and in one last burst of music sang all together, "*Mon Dieu, ayez pitié de moi*" and "*de lui*" and "*d'elle*" and "*de nous.*" Then the orchestra closed with a long roll of the kettledrums, and the prima donna fainted into the arms of her confidante. The curtain fell.

There was a roar of applause. The gallery whistled and stamped. Everyone relaxed his or her position, drawing a long breath, looking about. There was a general stir; the lights in the great glass chandelier clicked and blazed up, and a murmur of conversation arose. The footlights were lowered and the orchestra left their places and disappeared underneath the stage, leaving the audience with the conviction that they had gone out after beer. All over the house one heard the shrill voices of boys crying out: "Op'ra books—books for the op'ra—words and music for the op'ra."

Throughout the boxes a great coming and going took place and an interchange of visits. The gentlemen out in the foyer stood about conversing in groups or walked up and down smoking cigarettes, often pausing in front of the big floral piece that was to be given to the prima donna at the end of the great scene in the fourth act.

There was a little titter of an electric bell. The curtain was about to go up, and a great rush for seats began. The orchestra were coming back and tuning up. They sent up a prolonged medley of sounds, little minor chirps and cries from the violins, liquid runs and mellow gurgles from the oboes, flutes, and wood-wind instruments, and an occasional deep-toned purring from the bass viòls. A bell rang faintly from behind the wings, the house lights sank, and the footlights blazed up. The leader tapped with his baton; a great silence fell upon the house, while here and there one heard an energetic "Ssh! ssh!" The fourth act was about to begin.

When the curtain rose on the fourth act one saw the prima donna standing in a very dejected pose in the midst of a vast apartment that might have been a bed-chamber, a council hall, or a hall of audience. She was alone. She wore a loose cream-coloured gown knotted about the waist; her arms were bare, and her hair un-bound and flowing loose over her shoulders to her girdle. She was to die in this act; it promised to be harrowing; and the first few notes she uttered recurred again later on as the motif for the famous quartet in the "great scene."

But for all this, the music had little by little taken possession of Vandover, and little by little he had for-gotten his surroundings, the stifling air of the house, the blinding glitter of the stage, and the discomfort of his limbs cramped into the narrow orchestra chair. All music was music to him; he loved it with an unreasoned, un-critical love, enjoying even the barrel organs and hand pianos of the streets. For the present the slow beat and cadence of the melodies of the opera had cradled all his senses, carrying him away into a kind of exalted dream. The quartet began; for him it was wonderfully sweet, the long-sustained chords breathing over the subdued orchestral accompaniment, like some sweet south wind passing in long sighs over the pulse of a great ocean. It seemed to him infinitely beautiful, infinitely sad, sub-dued minor plaints recurring persistently again and again like sighs of parting, but could not be restrained, like voices of regret for the things that were never to be again. Or it was a pathos, a joy in all things good, a vast tenderness, so sweet, so divinely pure that it could not be framed in words, so great and so deep that it found its only expression in tears. There came over him a vague sense of those things which are too beautiful to be comprehended, of a nobility, a self-oblivion, an immortal eternal love and kindness, all goodness, all benignity, all pity for sin, all sorrow for grief, all joy for the true, the right, and the pure.

To be better, to be true and right and pure, these were the only things that were worth while, these were the things that he seemed to feel in the music. It was as if for the moment he had become a little child again, not ashamed to be innocent, ignorant of vice, still believing in all his illusions, still near to the great white gates of life.

The appeal had been made directly to what was best and strongest in Vandover, and the answer was quick and overpowering. All the good that still survived in him leaped to life again in an instant, clamouring for recognition, pleading for existence. The other Vandover, the better Vandover, wrestled with the brute in him once more, never before so strong, never so persistent. He had not yet destroyed all that was good in him; now it had turned in one more revolt, crying out against him, protesting for the last time against its own perversion and destruction. Vandover felt that he was at the great crisis of his life.

After all was over he walked home through the silent streets, proceeding slowly, his hands in his pockets, his head bent down, his mind very busy. Once in his rooms he threw off his things and, having stirred up the drowsing fire in the tiled stove, sat down before it in his shirtsleeves, the bosom of his full dress shirt bulging from his

vest and faintly creaking as from time to time he drew a
long breath. He had been lured into a mood where he
was himself at his very best, where the other Vandover,
the better Vandover, drew apart with eyes turned
askance, looking inward and downward into the depths of
his own character, shuddering, terrified. Far down there
in the darkest, lowest places he had seen the brute, squat,
deformed, hideous; he had seen it crawling to and fro
dimly, through a dark shadow he had heard it growling,
chafing at the least restraint, restless to be free. For now
at last it was huge, strong, insatiable, swollen and distorted out of all size, grown to be a monster, glutted yet
still ravenous, some fearful bestial satyr, grovelling, perverse, horrible beyond words.

And with the eyes of this better self he saw again, little
by little, the course of his whole life, and witnessed again
the eternal struggle between good and evil that had been
going on within him since his very earliest years. He was
sure that at the first the good had been the stronger.
Little by little the brute had grown, and he, pleasure-
loving, adapting himself to every change of environment, luxurious, self-indulgent, shrinking with the
shrinking of a sensuous artist-nature from all that was
irksome and disagreeable, had shut his ears to the voices
that shouted warnings of the danger, and had allowed
the brute to thrive and to grow, its abominable famine
gorged from the store of that in him which he felt to be
the purest, the cleanest, and the best, its bulk fattened
upon the rot and the decay of all that was good, growing larger day by day, noisome, swollen, poddy, a filthy
inordinate ghoul, gorged and bloated by feeding on the
good things that were dead.

Besides this he saw how one by one he had wrenched
himself free from all those influences that had tended to
foster and to cultivate all the better part of him.

First of all, long ago it seemed now, he had allowed to

be destroyed that first instinctive purity, that fragile, delicate innocence which dies young in almost every human being, and that one sees evaporating under the earliest taint of vice with a smile partly of contempt, partly of pity, partly of genuine regret.

Next it had been his father. The Old Gentleman had exerted a great influence over Vandover; he had never forgotten that scene the morning after he had told him of his measure of responsibility in Ida Wade's suicide, the recovery from the first shock of dazed bewilderment and then the forgiveness, the solicitude, and the encouragement to begin over again, to live it down and to do that which was right and good and true. Not only had he stopped his ears to this voice, but also, something told him, he had done much to silence it forever. Despite the Old Gentleman's apparent fortitude the blow must have carried home. What must he not have suffered during those long weeks while Vandover was away, what lonely broodings in the empty house; and then the news of the wreck, the days of suspense!

It all must have told; the Old Gentleman was not strong; Vandover could not but feel that he had hastened his death, and that in so doing he had destroyed another influence which would have cultivated and fostered his better self, would have made it strong against the attacks of the brute.

The other person who had helped to bring out all that was best in Vandover had been Turner Ravis. There was no denying that when he had first known her he had loved her sincerely. Things were vastly different with him when Turner had been his companion; things that were unworthy, that were low, that were impure and vicious, did not seem worth while then; not only did they have no attraction for him, but he even shunned and avoided them. He knew he was a better man for loving her; invariably she made him wish to be better.

But little by little as he frequented the society of such girls as Ida Wade, Grace Irving, and Flossie, his affection for Turner faded. As the habits of passionate and unhealthy excitement grew upon him he lost first the taste and then the very capacity for a calm, pure feeling. His affection for her he frittered away with fast girls and abandoned women, strangled it in the foul, musk-laden air of disreputable houses, dragged and defiled it in the wine-lees of the Imperial. In the end he had quite destroyed it, wilfully, wantonly killed it. As Turner herself had said, she could only be in love with being loved; her affection for him had dwindled as well; at last they had come to be indifferent to each other, she no longer inspired him to be better, and thus he had shaken off his good influence as well.

Public opinion had been a great check upon him, the fear of scandal, the desire to stand well with the world he knew. Trivial though he felt it to be, the dread of what people would say had to a great extent held Vandover back. He had a position to maintain, a reputation to keep up in the parlours and at the dinner tables where he was received. It could not be denied that society had influenced Vandover for good. But this, too, like all the others, he had cast from him. Now he was ostracized, society cared no longer what he did, his position was gone, his reputation was destroyed. There was no one now to stand in his way.

Vandover could not fall back on any religious influence. Religion had never affected him very deeply. It was true that he had been baptized, confirmed, and had gone to church with considerable regularity. If he had been asked if he was a Christian and believed in God he would have answered "Certainly, certainly." Until the time of his father's death he had even said his prayers every night, the last thing before turning out the gas, sitting upon the edge of his bed in his nightgown, his

head in both his hands. He added to the Lord's Prayer
certain other petitions as to those who were in trouble,
sorrow, poverty, or any other privations; he asked for
blessings upon his father and upon himself, praying for
the former's health and prosperity, and for himself, that
he might become a great artist, that the Last Enemy
might be admitted to the Salon when he had painted it,
and that it might make him famous. But, as a rule, Vandover thought very little about religious matters and
when he did, told himself that he was too intelligent to
believe in a literal heaven, a literal hell, and a personal
God personally interfering in human affairs like any
Jove or Odin. But the moment he rejected a concrete
religion Vandover was almost helpless. He was not
mystic enough to find any meaning in signs or symbols,
nor philosophic enough to grasp vague and immense abstractions. Infinities, Presences, Forces, could not help
him withstand temptation, could not strengthen him
against the brute. He felt that somewhere, some time,
there was punishment for evildoing, but, as happened
in the case of Ida Wade's death, to dwell on such
thoughts disturbed and terrified him. He did not dare
to look long in that direction. Conscience, remorse,
repentance, all these had been keen enough at first,
but he had so persistently kicked against the pricks
that little by little he had ceased to feel them at all.

Then an immense and overwhelming terror seized
upon him. Was there nothing, then—nothing left which
he could lay hold of to save him? He knew that he could
not deliver himself by his own exertions. Religion could
not help him, he had killed his father, estranged the girl
he might have loved, outraged the world, and at a single
breath blighted the fine innate purity of his early years.
It was as if he had entered into his life in the world as into some vast labyrinth, wandering on aimlessly, flinging
from him one by one the threads, the clues, that might

have led him again to a safe exit, going down deeper and deeper until, when near the centre, he had suddenly felt the presence of the brute, had heard its loathsome muttering growl, had at last seen it far down at the end of a passage, dimly and in a dark shadow; terrified, he had started back, looking wildly about for any avenue of escape, searching with frantic haste and eagerness for any one of those clues he had so carelessly cast from him, realizing that without such guidance he would inevitably tend down again to that fatal central place where the brute had its lair.

There was nothing, nothing. He clearly saw the fate toward which he was hurrying; it was not too late to save himself if he only could find help, but he could find *no* help. His terror increased almost to hysteria. It was one of those dreadful moments that men sometimes undergo that must be met alone, and that when past, remain in the memory for all time; a glimpse far down into the springs and wheels of life; a glimpse that does not come often lest the reason brought to the edge of the fearful gulf should grow dizzy at the sight, and reeling, topple headlong.

But suddenly Vandover rose to his feet, the tears came to his eyes, and with a long breath he exclaimed: "Thank God for it!" He grew calmer in a moment, the crisis had passed, he had found a clue beneath his groping fingers.

He had remembered his art, turning to it instinctively as he always did when greatly moved. This was the one good thing that yet survived. It was the strongest side of him; it would be the last to go; he felt it there yet. It was the one thing that could save him.

The thought had come to him so suddenly and with such marvellous clearness that in his present exalted state of mind it filled him with a vague sense of awe, it seemed like a manifestation, a writing on the wall.

Might it not be some sort of miracle? He had heard of men reforming their lives, transformed almost in an instant, and had scoffed at the idea. But might it not be true, after all? What was this wonderful thing that had happened to him? Was this less strange than a miracle? Less divine?

The following day Vandover rented a studio. It was the lofty room with hardwood floors and the immense north light in that suite which he had rejected when looking for rooms on the former occasion. He gave notice to the clerk in the apartment house where his quarters were situated that he intended to vacate after the first of the month. Charming as he had found these rooms, he gave up, with scarcely a regret, the idea of living in them any longer. In a month it would be summer and he would be on his way to Paris.

But so great was his desire for work now, so eager was he to start the Last Enemy, so strong was the new energy that shook him, that Vandover could not wait until summer to begin work again. He grudged everything now that kept him away from his easel.

He disappeared from the sight of his ordinary companions; he did not even seek the society of Geary or of young Haight. All the sketches he had made for the Last Enemy, together with his easel and his disused palette, his colour-box, tubes, brushes, and all the other materials and tools for his work, he caused to be transferred to the new studio. Besides this he had the stretcher made, best twill canvas on a frame four feet long, two and a half feet high. This was for the large sketch of the picture. But the finished work he calculated would demand an eight by five stretcher.

He did not think of decorating the room, of putting any ornaments about the wall. He was too serious, too much in earnest now to think of that. The studio was not to be his lounging place, but his workshop. His art was work

473

with him now, hard, serious work. It was above all *work*
that he needed to set him right again, regular work,
steady, earnest work, not the dilettante fancy of an
amateur content with making pretty things.

Never in his life had Vandover been so happy. He
came and went continually between his rooms, his studio,
and his art dealers, tramping grandly about the city,
whistling to himself, strong, elated, filled with energy,
vigour, ambition. At times his mind was full of thank-
fulness at this deliverance at the eleventh hour; at times
it was busy with the details of the picture, its composition, its colour scheme. The main effects he wanted to
produce were isolation and intense heat, the shadows on
the sand would be blue, the horizon line high on the canvas, the sky would be light in tone, almost white near
the earth.

The morning when he first began to work was charming. His new studio was in the top floor of a five-story
building, and on arriving there, breathless from his long
climb up the stairs, Vandover threw open the window
and gazed out and down upon the city spread out below
him, enjoying the view a moment before settling to his
work.

A little later the trades would be blowing strong and
brisk from the ocean, driving steadily through the
Golden Gate, filling the city with a taint of salt; but at
present the air was calm, touched with a certain nim-
bleness, a sparkling effervescence, invigorating, ex-
hilarating.

It was early in the forenoon, not yet past nine o'clock,
and the mist that gathers over the city just before dawn
was steaming off under the sun, very thin and delicate,
turning all distant objects a flat tone of pale blue. Over
the roofs of the houses he could catch a glimpse of the
distant mountains, faint purple masses against the pale
edge of the sky, rimming the horizon round with a fillet

of delicate colour. But any larger view was barred by a huge frame house with a slated mansard roof, directly opposite him across the street, a residence house, one of the few in the neighbourhood. It had been newly painted white and showed brave and gay against the dark blue of the sky and the ruddy greens of the great garden in which it stood. Vandover from his window could from time to time catch the smell of eucalyptus trees coming to him in long aromatic breaths mingled with the odour of wet grass and fresh paint. Somewhere he heard a humming-bird singing, a tiny tweedling thread of song, while farther off two roosters were crowing back and forth at each other with strained and raucous trumpet calls.

Vandover turned back to his work. Under the huge north light was the easel, and clamped upon it the stretcher, blank, and untouched. The very sight of the heavy cream-white twill was an inspiration. Already Vandover saw a great picture upon it; a great wave of emotion suddenly welled up within him and he cried with enthusiasm:

"By God! it is in moods like this that *chef d'œuvres* are made."

Around the baseboard of the room were a row of *esquisses* for the picture, on small landscape-stretchers, mere blotches of colour laid on with the palette knife and large brushes, almost unintelligible to anyone but Vandover. He selected two or three of these and fastened them to the easel above the big stretcher where he could have them continually in his eye. He lit his pipe, rolled up his shirt-sleeves, and standing before the easel, began to sharpen a stick of charcoal with an old razor, drawing the blade toward him so as to keep the point of the stick from breaking. Then at last with a deep breath of satisfaction he began blocking in the first large construction lines of his picture.

It was one o'clock before he knew it. He went downtown and had a hasty lunch, jealous of every moment that was not spent on his picture. The sight of it as he reëntered the room sent a thrill all over him; he was succeeding better than he could have expected, doing better than he thought he would. He felt sure that now he should do good work; every stage ot the picture's progress was an inspiration for the next one. At this time the figures had only been "placed," broadly sketched in large lines, "blocked in" as he called it. The next step was the second drawing, much more finished.

He rapped the stretcher sharply with his knuckles; it responded sonorously like a drumhead, the vibration shaking the charcoal from the tracings, filling the air with a fine dust. The outlines grew faint, just perceptible enough to guide him in the second more detailed drawing.

He brought his stick of charcoal to a very fine edge and set to work carefully. In a moment he stopped and, with his chamois cloth, dusted out what he had drawn. He had made a false start, he began but could not recall how the lines should run, his fingers were willing enough; in his imagination he saw just how the outlines should be, but somehow he could not make his hand interpret what was in his head. Some third medium through which the one used to act upon the other was sluggish, dull; worse than that, it seemed to be absent. "*Well*," he muttered, "can't I make this come out right?" Then he tried more carefully. His imagination saw the picture clearer, his hand moved with more assurance, but the two seemed to act independently of each other. The forms he made on the canvas were no adequate reflection of those in his brain; some third delicate and subtle faculty that coördinated the other two and that called forth a sure and instant response to the dictates of his mind was lacking. The lines on his canvas were

476

those of a child just learning to draw; one saw for what they were intended, but they were crude, they had no life, no meaning. The very thing that would have made them intelligible, interpretive, that would have made them art, was absent. A third, a fourth, and a fifth time Vandover made the attempt. It was useless. He knew that it was not because his hand lacked cunning on account of long disuse; such a thing, in spite of popular belief, never happened to artists—a good artist might abandon his work for five years, ten years—and take it up again precisely where he had laid it down with no loss of technical skill. No, this thing seemed more subtle, so subtle that at first he could hardly grasp it. But suddenly a great fear came upon him, a momentary return of that wild hysterical terror from which he believed he had forever escaped.

"Is it gone?" he cried out. "Is it gone from me? My art? Steady," he went on, passing his hand over his face with a reassuring smile; "steady, old man, this won't do, again—and so soon! It won't do for you to get scared twice like that. This is just nervousness, you are overexcited. Pshaw! What's the matter with me? Let's get to work."

Still another time he dusted out what he had done and recommenced, concentrating all his attention with a tremendous effort of the will. Grotesque and meaningless shapes, the mocking caricatures of those he saw in his fancy, grew under his charcoal, while slowly, slowly, a queer, numb feeling came in his head, like a rising fog, and the touch of that unreasoning terror returned, this time stronger, more persistent, more tenacious than before.

Vandover nerved himself against it, not daring to give in, fearing to allow himself to see what this really meant. He passed one hand over his cheek and along the side of his head, the fingers dancing. "Hum!" he muttered,

477

looking vaguely about him, "this is bad. I mustn't let this get the better of me now. I'll knock off for to-day, take a little rest, begin again to-morrow."

In ten minutes he was back at his easel again. His charcoal wandered, tracing empty lines on his canvas, the strange numbness grew again in his head. All the objects in the range of his eyes seemed to move back and stand on the same plane. He became a little dizzy.

"It's the *tobacco*," he exclaimed. "That pipe always was too strong." He turned away to the open window, feeling an irresistible need of distraction, of amusement, and he remained there resting on his elbows, listening and looking, trying to be interested.

It was toward the middle of the afternoon. The morning mist was long since evaporated and the first faint puffs of the inevitable trade wind were just stirring the leaves of the eucalyptus across the street. In the music room of the white house the young lady of the family had opened the piano and was practising finger-exercises. The scales and arpeggios following one another without interruption, came to his ears in a pleasant monotone. A Chinese "boy," in a stiff blouse of white linen, made a great splashing as he washed down the front steps with a bucket of water and the garden hose. Grocery and delivery wagons came and went, rattling over the cobbles and car-tracks, while occasionally a whistle blew very far off. At the corner of the street by a livery-stable a little boy in a flat-topped leather cap was calling incessantly for some unseen dog, whistling and slapping his knees. An express-wagon stopped a few doors below the white house and the driver pulled down the back-board with a strident rattle of chains; the cable in its slot kept up an unceasing burr and clack while the cars themselves trundled up and down the street, starting and stopping with a jangling of bells, the jostled glass windows whir-

478

ring in a prolonged vibrant note. All these sounds played lightly over the steady muffled roar that seemed to come from all quarters at once; it was that deep murmur, that great minor diapason that always disengages itself from vast bodies, from mountains, from oceans, from forests, from sleeping armies.

The desire for movement, for diversion, for anything that would keep him from thinking was not to be resisted. Vandover caught up his hat and fled from the room, not daring to look again at the easel. Once outside, he began to walk, anywhere, straight before him, going on with great strides, his head in the air.

He found Charlie Geary and took him to supper. Vandover talked continually on all sorts of subjects, speaking very rapidly. In the evening he insisted on Geary going to the theatre with him. He paid the closest attention to the play, letting it occupy his mind entirely. When the play was over and the two were about to say good-night, Vandover began to urge Geary to sleep up at his rooms that night. He overrode his objections, interrupting him, taking hold of his arm, and starting off. But Geary, a little surprised at his manner, refused. There were certain law papers he had taken home with him from the office that afternoon and that it was necessary he should return in the morning. Ah, you bet, he would get it right in the neck if old Beale didn't have those depositions the first thing when the office was open. Ah, he was getting to be indispensable down there. He had had Fischer's place now for a year. Fischer had never come back, and he had the promise of being taken on as head clerk as soon as Beale Jr., went into the partnership with old Beale. "I'll make my way in this town yet," he declared. "I'll be in that partnership myself some day. You see; yes, sir; ah, you bet!"

The idea of passing the night alone terrified Vandover. He started toward home, walking up Sutter

Street, proceeding slowly, his hands in his pockets. All at once he stopped, without knowing why; he roused himself and looked about him. There was a smell of eucalyptus in the air. Across the street was the huge white house, and he found that he had stopped just before the door of the building on the top floor of which his studio was situated. All day Vandover's mind had been in the greatest agitation, his ideas leaping and darting hither and thither like terrified birds in a cage. Just now he underwent a sudden reaction. It had all been a matter of fancy, nothing but nervousness; he had not drawn for some time, his hand lacked cunning from long disuse. The desire for work came upon him again overpoweringly. He wanted to see again if he could not draw just as truly and freely as in the old days. No, he could not wait till morning; he must put himself to the test again at once, at the very instant. It was a sudden feminine caprice, induced, no doubt, by the exalted, strained, and unnatural condition of his nerves, a caprice that could not be reasoned with, that could not be withstood. He had his keys with him, he opened the outside door and groped his way up the four long flights of stairs to his studio.

The studio was full of a sombre half-light, like a fog, spreading downward from the great north light in the sloping roof. The window was still wide open, the stretcher showed a pale grey blur. Vandover was about to light the gas when he checked himself, his arm still raised above his head. Ah, no; he did not dare to look at the result of his day's work. It would be better to start in afresh from the beginning. He found the chamois skin on the tray of the easel and rubbed out all the drawing on the canvas. Then he lit the gas.

As he turned to his work once more a little thrill of joy and of relief passed over him. This time his hand was sure, steady, his head was clear. It had been nervousness, after all. As he picked up his charcoal he even exclaimed to himself, "Just the same, that *was* a curious experience this afternoon."

But the curious experience repeated itself again that night as soon as he tried to work. Once more certain shapes and figures were born upon his canvas, but they were no longer the true children of his imagination, they were no longer his own; they were changelings, grotesque abortions. It was as if the brute in him, like some malicious witch, had stolen away the true offspring of his mind, putting in their places these deformed dwarfs, its own hideous spawn.

Through the numbness and giddiness that gradually came into his head like a poisonous murk he saw one thing clearly: It was gone—his art was gone, the one thing that could save him. That, too, like all the other good things of his life, he had destroyed. At some time during those years of debauchery it had died, that subtle, elusive something, delicate as a flower; he had ruined it. Little by little it had exhaled away, wilting in the air of unrestrained debauches, perishing in the warm musk-laden atmosphere of disreputable houses, defiled by the breath of abandoned women, trampled into the spilt wine-lees of the Imperial, dragged all fouled and polluted through the lowest mire of the great city's vice.

For a moment Vandover felt as though he was losing his hold upon his reason; the return of the hysteria shook him like a dry, light leaf. He suddenly had a sensation that the room was too small to hold him; he ran, almost reeled, to the open window, drawing his breath deep and fast, inhaling the cool night air, rolling his eyes wildly.

It was night. He looked out into a vast blue-grey space sown with points of light, winking lamps, and steady, slow-burning stars. Below him was the sleeping city. All the lesser staccato noises of the day had long since died to silence; there only remained that prolonged and sullen diapason, coming from all quarters at once. It was like the breathing of some infinitely great monster, alive and palpitating, the sistole and diastole of some gigantic heart. The whole existence of the great slumbering city passed upward there before him through the still night air in one long wave of sound.

It was Life, the murmur of the great, mysterious force that spun the wheels of Nature and that sent it onward like some enormous engine, resistless, relentless; an engine that sped straight forward, driving before it the infinite herd of humanity, driving it on at breathless speed through all eternity, driving it no one knew whither, crushing out inexorably all those who lagged behind the herd and who fell from exhaustion, grinding them to dust beneath its myriad iron wheels, riding over them, still driving on the herd that yet remained, driving it recklessly, blindly on and on toward some far-distant goal, some vague unknown end, some mysterious, fearful bourne forever hidden in thick darkness.

CHAPTER XV

ABOUT a week later Hiram Wade, Ida's father, brought suit against Vandover to recover twenty-five thousand dollars, claiming that his daughter had killed herself because she had been ruined by him and that he alone was responsible for her suicide.

Vandover had passed this week in an agony of grief over the loss of his art, a grief that seemed even sharper than that which he had felt over the death of his father. For this last calamity was like the death of a child of his, some dear, sweet child, that might have been his companion throughout all his life. At times it seemed to him impossible that his art should fail him in this manner, and again and again he would put himself at his easel, only to experience afresh the return of the numbness in his brain, the impotency of his fingers.

He had begun little by little to pick up the course of his life once more, and on a certain Wednesday morning was looking listlessly through the morning paper as he sat in his window-seat. The room was delightful, flooded with the morning sun, the Assyrian *bas-reliefs* just touched with a ruddy light, the Renaissance portraits looking down at him through a fine golden haze; a little fire, just enough to blunt the keenness of the early morning air, snapping in the famous tiled and flamboyant stove. All about the room was a pleasant fragrance of coffee and good tobacco.

Vandover caught sight of the announcement of the suit with a sudden sharp intake of breath that was half gasp, half cry, starting up from the window-seat, reading it over again and again with staring eyes.

483

It was a very short paragraph, not more than a dozen lines, lost at the bottom of a column, among the cheap advertisements. It made no allusion to any former stage of the affair; from its tone Ida might have killed herself only the day before. It seemed hardly more than a notice that some enterprising reporter, burrowing in the records at the City Hall, had unearthed and brought to light with the idea that it might be of possible interest to a few readers of the paper. But there was his name staring back at him from out the grey blur of the type, like some reflection of himself seen in a mirror. Insignificant as the paragraph was, it seemed to Vandover as though it was the only item in the whole paper. One might as well have trumpeted his crime through the streets.

"But twenty-five thousand dollars!" exclaimed Vandover, terrified. "Where will *I* find twenty-five thousand dollars?" And at once he fell to wondering as to whether or no in default of payment he could be sent to the penitentiary. The idea of winning the suit did not enter his mind an instant; he did not even dream of fighting it.

For the moment it was like fire driving out fire. He forgot the loss of his art, his mind filled only with the sense of the last disaster. What could he do? Twenty-five thousand dollars! It would ruin him. A cry of exasperation, of rage at his own folly, escaped him. "Ah, what a fool I've been!"

For an hour he raged to and fro in the delightful sunlit room, pacing back and forth in its longest dimension between the bamboo tea-table and the low bookcase, a thousand different plans and projects coming and going in his head. As his wits steadied themselves he began to see that he must consult at once with some lawyer—Field, of course—perhaps something could be done; a clever lawyer might make out a case for him, after all.

But all at once he became convinced that Field would not undertake his defence; he knew he had no case; so what could Field do for him? He would have to tell him the truth, and he saw with absolute clearness that the lawyer would refuse to try to defend him. The thing could not honourably be done. But, then, what *should* he do? He must have legal advice from some quarter.

He was still in this state of perplexity when Charlie Geary arrived, pounding on the door and opening it immediately afterward as was his custom.

"Hello!" said Vandover, surprised. "Hello, Charlie! is that you?"

"Say," exclaimed Geary without returning his greeting, holding up his hand as if to interrupt him; "say, have you seen your lawyer yet—seen *any* lawyer?"

"No," answered Vandover, shaking his head gravely; "no, I've only this minute read about it in the paper." He was glad that Geary had come; at once he felt a desire to throw this burden upon his chum's shoulders, to let him assume the management of the affair, just as in the old college days he had willingly, weakly, submitted to the dictatorship of the shrewder, stronger man who smoothed out his difficulties for him, and extricated him from all his scrapes. He knew Geary to be full of energy and resource, and he had confidence in his ability as a lawyer, even though he was so young in years and experience. Besides this, he was his friend, his college chum; for all Geary's disagreeable qualities he knew he would do the right thing by him now.

"You're the one man of all others I wanted to see," he exclaimed as he gripped his hand. "By George! I'm glad you have come. Here, sit down and let's talk this over." Geary took the big leather chair behind the desk, and Vandover flung himself again upon the window-seat. It was as if the two were back in the room in Matthews; hundreds of times in those days they had occupied precisely these positions, Geary bending over at the study table, intent, nervous, very keen, Vandover lounging idly upon the window-seat, resting easily on his elbow listening to the other man's advice.

"Now, what must I do, Charlie?" Vandover began. "See my lawyer, I suppose? But do you think a lawyer like Field would take my case? You know I haven't a leg to stand on."

"But you haven't seen him?" inquired Geary, sharply. "Haven't seen anybody about it?" Vandover shook his head. "Sure?" insisted Geary anxiously.

"Why, I have only just heard about it twenty minutes ago," protested Vandover. "Why are you so particular about that?" he added. Then Geary exploded his mine.

"Because," he said, with a smile of triumph that he could not restrain, "because we are the counsel for the other side. I am on the case."

Vandover bounded from the window-seat speechless with astonishment, bitterly disappointed. "*You?*" he shouted. Geary slowly nodded his head, enjoying Vandover's bewilderment. Vandover dropped back upon the cushions again, staring at him wildly with growing suspicion and anger. He would not have thought it possible that Geary could so sacrifice their old friendship to his own personal interest. The two continued staring at each other across the table for a moment. In the silence they heard the long rumble of a cable-car passing the house, and the persistent jangling of its bell as it approached the street crossing. A grocery wagon went up the side street, the horses' hoofs making a cadenced clapping sound upon the asphalt.

"Well," exclaimed Vandover, scornfully, "I suppose that's business, but *I* would call it damned unkind!"

"Now, look here, old man," returned Geary, consolingly. "Don't you take the monkey-wrench off the safety valve like that. What am I here for if it isn't to help you? Maybe you don't know that this is a mighty unprofessional thing to do. Ah, you bet, if old Beale knew this I would get it right in the neck. Don't you suppose I can help you more as Wade's lawyer than I could as yours? And now that's the very first thing I've got to tell you—to keep this dark, that I have seen you. I can't do anything for you if you don't promise that."

"Oh, that's all right," returned Vandover, reassured. "That's all right, you can——"

"It's not considered the right thing to do," Geary continued, not heeding Vandover's answer, "but I just do it because"—he began to make awkward gestures with both his hands—"because we're old friends, like that. That was the very first thing I thought of when Beale, Jr., told me that we two had the case—that I could get you out of this hole better as Wade's lawyer than as your own. Ah, you bet, I was clever enough to see that the first thing."

"I'm sure it was awfully good of you, old man," said Vandover sincerely. "I'm in a lot of trouble nowadays!"

"Well, now, don't you bother, Van," answered Geary, consolingly. "I guess we can pull you out of this all right." He drew up to the table, looking about from side to side." "Got any writing paper concealed about the premises?" he asked. Vandover pushed him over his writing pad, and Geary, taking the cap from his fountain pen, began asking a series of questions, taking down his answers in shorthand. After he had asked him as to his age, length of residence in the city, his property, and some few other technical matters, he leaned back in his chair and said:

"Now, let's hear your side of the story, Van. I don't suppose you like to go over the thing again, but you see

I ought to know." Vandover told of the affair, Geary making notes as he went along. It was nearly noon before their interview was at an end. Then Geary gathered up the papers and reached for his hat and stick, saying:

"Well, now, that's all we can do to-day. I think I'll be up to see you again day after to-morrow, in the afternoon. Beale, Jr., and I have a date with Mr. Wade again to-morrow, I think, and I can talk to you more definitely after that. You know this is the devil of a thing to do," he suddenly exclaimed apprehensively, "this playing back and forth between the two parties like this; regularly dishonourable, don't you know?"

"If you think it's dishonourable," said Vandover as he accompanied Geary to the door, "if you think it's dishonourable, Charlie, why, don't do it! I don't want to ask you to do anything dishonourable for me."

"Oh, that's all right," replied Geary, uneasily; "I had just as soon do it for you, only listen to this: don't you say a word about the case to anybody, not to your lawyer, nor to anybody. If Field should write to you, you tell him you have counsel already. And, look here! you may have the reporters up here pretty soon, and don't you open your face to them; you mind that; don't you let them get a thing out of you. And there's another thing you must understand: I'm not your lawyer, of course; you see that. I could be disbarred if I was lawyer for both sides. It's like this, you see: I'm Wade's lawyer—at least the firm I am with are his lawyers—and of course I'm acting in Wade's interest. But you're an old chum of mine, and if I can I'm going to try and make it easier for you. You understand, don't you?"

"Yes, I understand, Charlie," answered Vandover, "and you are just a brick."

Vandover passed the rest of the day in his sitting room, the suspense of the situation slowly screwing his nerves tenser and tenser. He walked for hours back and forth, his hands clasped behind his back, his head bent down, his forehead drawn into a frown of anxiety and exasperation, or he stood for a long time at the window looking out into the street with eyes that saw nothing. At supper that night he found that his appetite had left him; the very thought of food revolted him. He returned to his room between seven and eight o'clock, his body and mind completely fagged, feeling a crying need of some diversion, some escape from the thoughts that had been hounding him all day.

He made up his mind to read a little before going to bed, and all at once remembered a book that he had once begun a long time ago but had never finished: the story of two men who had bought a wrecked opium ship for fifty thousand dollars and had afterward discovered that she contained only a few tins of the drug. He had never read on to find how that story turned out. Suddenly he found himself repeating, "Twenty-five thousand dollars, twenty-five thousand dollars—where will *I* find twenty-five thousand dollars?" He wondered if he would go to jail if he failed to pay. His interest in the book was gone in a moment, and he took up another of his favourite novels, the story of a boy at the time of Christ, a Jewish boy unjustly condemned to the galleys, liberated afterward, and devoting his life to the overthrow of his enemy, whom at last he overcame and humbled, fouling him in a chariot race, all but killing him.

He sat down in the huge leather chair, and, drawing it up to the piano lamp and cocking his feet upon the table, began to read. In a few moments the same numbness stole into his head like a rising fog, a queer, tense feeling, growing at the back of his forehead and at the base of his skull, a dulness, a strange stupefying sensation as of some torpid, murky atmosphere. He looked about him quickly; all the objects in the range of his vision—the corner of the desk, the corduroy couch, the low bookcase with Flossie's yellow slipper and Barye's lioness upon it—seemed to move back and stand upon the same plane; the objects themselves appeared immovable enough, but the sensation of them in his brain somewhere behind his eyes began to move about in a slow, dizzy whirl. The old touch of unreasoning terror came back, together with a sudden terror of the spirit, a sickening sinking of the heart, a loathing of life, terrible beyond words.

Vandover started up, striving to keep himself in hand, fighting against a wild desire to rush about from wall to wall, shrieking and waving his arms. Over and over again he exclaimed, "Oh, *what* is the matter with me?" The strangeness of the thing was what unsettled and unnerved him. He had all the sensations of terror, but without any assignable reason, and this groundless fear became in the end the cause of a new fear: he was afraid of this fear that was afraid of nothing.

Very gradually, however, the crisis passed away. He became a little calmer, and as he was mixing himself a glass of whisky and water at the sideboard he decided that he would go to bed. He was sure that he would be better for a good night's rest; evidently his nerves were out of order; it would not do for him to read late at night. He realized all at once that his mind and body alike were exhausted.

He passed a miserable night, dozing and waking at alternate hours until three o'clock, when he found it impossible to get to sleep; hour after hour he lay flat on his back staring open-eyed into the darkness, listening to the ticking of the clock, the mysterious footsteps that creaked the floors overhead, and the persistent drip of a water faucet. Outside in the street he heard at long intervals the rattling of wheels as the early milk wagons came and went; a dog began to bark, three gruff

490

notes repeated monotonously at exact intervals; all at
once there was a long muffled roll and an abrupt clack-
ing noise; it ceased, then broke out again sharply,
paused once more, then recommenced, settling to a prolonged minor hum; the cable was starting up; it was
almost morning, the window of his room began to show
a brighter blur in the darkness, while very far off he
could hear the steady puffing of a locomotive. As the
first cable-car trundled by the house he dropped off to
sleep for the last time, being waked again toward
nine o'clock by the sound of someone shovelling coal
outside under his window, the shovel clinking and
rasping upon the stone sidewalk.

He felt a little refreshed, but as he entered the dining
room for his late breakfast the smell of food repulsed
him; his appetite was gone; it was impossible for him to
eat. Toward eleven o'clock that same morning he was
pottering idly about his sitting room, winding his
clock and shaking down the ashes in the tiled flamboyant stove; his mind was still busy going over for the
hundredth time all the possibilities of Hiram Wade's
suit, and he was just wondering whether something in
the way of a compromise might not be arranged, when
with the suddenness of a blow between the eyes the
numbness in his head returned, together with the
same unreasoning fear, the same depression of spirits,
the same fearful sinking of the heart. What! it was
coming back again, this strange attack, coming back
even when his attention was not concentrated, even
when there was no unusual exertion of his brain!

Then the torment began. This time the crisis did not
pass off; from now on it persisted continually. Vandover began to feel strange. At first the room looked
unfamiliar to him, then his own daily life no longer
seemed recognizable, and, finally, all of a sudden, it
was the whole world, all the existing order of things, that

appeared to draw off like a refluent tide, leaving him alone, abandoned, cast upon some fearful, mysterious shore.

Nothing seemed worth while; all the thousand little trivial things that made up the course of his life and in which he found diversion and amusement palled upon him. A fearful melancholia settled over him, a despair, an abhorrence of living that could not be uttered. This only was during the day. It was that night that Vandover went down into the pit.

He went to bed early, his brain in a whirl, his frame worn out as if from long physical exertion. He was just dropping into a grateful sleep when his whole body twitched suddenly with a shock and a recoil of all his nerves; in an instant he was broad awake, panting and exhausted as if from a long run. Once more he settled himself upon the pillow, and once more the same leap, the same sharp spasm of his nerves caught him back to consciousness with the suddenness of a relaxed spring. At last sleep was out of the question; his drowsiness of the early part of the evening passed away, and he lay back, his hands clasped behind his head, staring up into the darkness, his thoughts galloping incessantly through his brain, suffering without pain as he had never imagined a human being could suffer though racked with torture from head to heel.

From time to time a slow torsion and crisping of all his nerves, beginning at his ankles, spread to every corner of his body till he had to shut his fists and teeth against the blind impulse to leap from his bed screaming. His hands felt light and, as he told himself, "jumpy." All at once he felt a peculiar sensation in them: they seemed to swell, the fingers puffing to an enormous size, the palms bulging, the whole member from the wrist to the nails distended like a glove when one has blown into it to straighten it out. Then he had a feeling that his head was swelling in the same way. He had to rub his hands together, to pass them again and again over his face to rid himself of the fancy.

But the strange numb feeling at the base of the skull did not keep him from thinking—he would have been glad if it had—and now at last when the terror overcame him it was no longer causeless; he knew now what he feared—he feared that he was going mad.

It was the punishment that he had brought upon himself, some fearful nervous disease, the result of his long indulgence of vice, his vile submission to the brute that was to destroy his reason; some collapse of all his faculties, beginning first with that which was highest, most sensitive—his art—spreading onward and downward till he should have reached the last stages of idiocy. It was Nature inexorably exacting. It was the vast fearful engine riding him down beneath its myriad spinning wheels, remorselessly, irresistibly.

The dreadful calamities that he had brought upon himself recoiled upon his head, crushing him to the dust with their weight of anguish and remorse: Ida Wade's suicide, his father's death, his social banishment, the loss of his art, Hiram Wade's lawsuit menacing him with beggary, and now this last, this approaching insanity. It was no longer fire driving out fire; the sense of all these disasters seemed to come back upon him at once, as keen, as bitter as when they had first befallen. He had told himself that he did not believe in a hell. Could there be a worse hell than this?

But all at once, without knowing why, moved by an impulse, a blind, resistless instinct, Vandover started up in bed, raising his clasped hands above him, crying out, "Oh, help me! Why don't you *help* me? You can if you only will!" Who was it to whom he had cried with such unerring intuition? He gave no name to this mysterious "You," this strange supernatural being,

493

this mighty superhuman power. It was the c y of a soul in torment that does not stop to reason, the wild last hope that feels its own helplessness, that responds to an intuition of a force outside of itself—the force that can save it in its time of peril.

Trembling, his hands still clasped above him, Vandover waited for an answer, waited for the miracle. In the tortured exalted state of his nerves he seemed suddenly possessed of a sixth sense; he fancied that he would know, there in that room, in a few seconds, while yet his hands remained clasped above his head. It was his last hope: if this failed him there was nothing left. Still he waited; he felt that he should know when the miracle came, that he would suddenly be filled with a sense of peace, of quiet joy. Still he waited—there was nothing, nothing but the vast silence, the unbroken blackness of the night, a night that was to last forever. There was no answer, nothing but the deaf silence, the blind darkness. But in a moment he felt that the very silence, the very lack of answer, was answer in itself; there was nothing for him. Even that vast mysterious power to which he had cried could not help him now, *could* not help him, could not stay the inexorable law of nature, could not reverse that vast terrible engine with its myriad spinning wheels that was riding him down relentlessly, grinding him into the dust. And afterward? After the engine had done its work, when that strange other time should come, that other life, what then? No, not even then, nothing but outer darkness then and the gnashing of teeth, nothing but the deaf silence, nothing but the blind darkness, nothing but the unbroken blackness of an eternal night.

It was the end of everything! With a muffled cry, "Oh, I can't stand this!" Vandover threw himself from his bed, groping his way out into the sitting room. By this time he was only conscious of a suffering too great to be borne, everything else was blurred as in a thick mist. For nearly an hour he stumbled about in the darkened room, bruising himself against the furniture, dazed, numb, trying in vain to find the drawer of the desk where he kept his father's revolver. At last his hand closed upon it, gripping it so tightly that the hundreds of little nicks and scratches made by the contact of the tacks and nails which he had hammered with it nipped and bit into his palm like the teeth of tiny mice. A vague feeling of shame overcame him at the last moment: he had no wish to be found sprawling upon the floor, dressed only in his nightgown. He lit the gas and put on his bathrobe, drawing the cords securely about his waist and neck.

When he turned about to pick up the revolver again he found that his determination had weakened considerably, and he was obliged to reflect again upon the wreck of his life and soul before he was back once more to the proper pitch of resolution. It was five minutes to two, and he made up his mind to kill himself when the clock struck the hour. He spent the intervening moments in arranging the details of the matter. At first he thought he would do it standing, but he abandoned that idea, fearing to strike his head against the furniture as he fell. He was about to decide upon the huge leather chair, when the remembrance of his father's death made that impossible. He finally concluded to sit upon the edge of his bed, leaning a little backward so as not to fall upon the floor, and he dragged the bed out into the sitting room, preferring somehow to die there. For a moment the idea of lying at length upon the bed occurred to him, but in an instant he recoiled from it, horrified at the thought of the death that struck from above; no, it would be best to sit upon the edge of the bed, falling backward with the shot. Then he wondered as to which it should be, his heart or his head; evidently the head

495

was the better; there upon the right side in the little hollow of the temple, and the next moment he found himself curiously touching and pressing the spot with his fingers. All at once he heard the little clicking noise that the clock makes a minute or so before the hour. It was almost two; he sat down upon the edge of the bed, cocking the revolver, waiting for the clock to strike. An idea came to him, and he looked at the calendar that stood at the right of the clock upon the top of the low bookcase. It was the twelfth of April, Thursday; that, then, was to be the date of his death—Thursday, April twelfth, at two in the morning, so it would read upon his gravestone. For an instant the awfulness of the thing he was to do came upon him, and the next instant he found himself wondering if they still coursed jackrabbits with greyhounds down at Coronado the way they used to do when he was there. All at once the clock struck two, and at the very last instant a strange impulse to seat himself before the mirror came upon him. He drew up a chair before it, watching his reflection intently, but even as he raised the revolver he suddenly changed his purpose without knowing why, and all at once crammed the muzzle into his mouth. He drew the trigger.

He heard no sound of a report; he felt no shock, but a great feebleness ran throughout his limbs, a relaxing and weakening of all his muscles; his eyes were open and he saw everything small and seemingly very far off as through the reversed end of an opera-glass. Suddenly he fainted.

When Vandover came to himself again it was early morning. The room was full of daylight, but the gas was still burning. Little by little the fearful things of the night came back to him; he realized that he had shot himself, and he waited for the end, not daring to move, his eyes closed, his hand still gripping the scratched butt of the revolver in his lap. For a long time he lay back in the chair, motionless, his consciousness slowly returning with an expression of scorn and incredulity; he was as sound as ever, there was neither scratch nor scar upon him; he had not shot himself after all.

Curiously, he looked at the revolver, throwing open the breech—the cylinder was empty; he had forgotten to load it. "What a fool!" he exclaimed, laughing scornfully, and still laughing he walked to the centre of the room under the chandelier and turned out the gas.

But when he turned about, facing the day once more, facing that day and the next and the next throughout all the course of his life, the sense of his misery returned upon him in its full strength and he raised his clenched fist to his eyes, shutting out the light. Ah, no, he could not endure it—the horror of life overpassed the horror of death; he could not go on living. A new thought had come to him. Wretched as he was, he saw that in time his anguish of conscience, even his dread of losing his reason, would pass from him; he would become used to them; yes, even become used to the dread of insanity, and then he would return once more to vice, return once more into the power of the brute, the perverse and evil monster that was knitted to him now irrevocably, part for part, fibre for fibre. He saw clearly that nothing could save him, he had had his answer that night, there was to be no miracle. Was it not right, then, that he should destroy himself? Was it not even his duty? The better part of him seemed to demand the act; should he not comply while there yet was any better part left? In a little while the brute was to take all.

On the shelves above his washstand Vandover found the cartridges in a green pasteboard box, and loaded all the chambers of the revolver, carefully. He closed the breech; but as he was about to draw back the hammer all his courage, all his resolution, crumbled in an instant like a tower of sand. He did not dare to shoot himself—he was afraid. The night before he had been brave enough; how was it now that he could not call up the same courage, the same determination? When he thought over the wreck, the wretched failure of his life, the dreadful prospect of the future years, his anguish and his terror were as keen as ever. But now there was a shrinking of his every nerve from the thought of suicide, the instinctive animal fear of death, stronger than himself. His suffering had to go on, had to run its course, even death would not help him. Let it go on, it was only the better part of him that was suffering; in a little while this better part would be dead, leaving only the brute. It would die a natural death without any intervention from him. Was there any need of suicide? Suicide! Great God! his whole life had been one long suicide.

That same morning Charlie Geary had eaten a very thick underdone steak for breakfast after enjoying a fine long sleep of eight hours. Toward eight o'clock he went downtown. He did not take a car; he preferred to walk; it helped his digestion and it gave him exercise. At night he walked home as well; that gave him an appetite; besides, with the ten cents that he saved in this way, he bought himself a nice cigar that he smoked in the evening to help digest his supper. He was very careful of his health. Ah, you bet, one had to look out for one's health.

At the office that morning he had had a long talk with Beale, Jr., as to Hiram Wade's suit. The great firm of Beale & Story, into whose office Geary had been received, made a specialty of damage suits, and especially those suits that were brought against a certain great monopoly which it was claimed was ruining the city and the state; such a case involving nearly a quarter of a million of dollars was now occupying the attention of the heads of the firm and, indeed, of the whole office. Hiram Wade's suit was assigned to the assistants. Beale, Jr., was one of these, and Charlie Geary had managed to push himself into the position of his confidential clerk. But Beale, Jr., himself took little interest in the Wade suit; the suit against the great monopoly was coming to a head; it was a battle of giants; the whole office found itself embroiled, and little by little Beale, Jr., allowed himself to be drawn into the struggle. The management of the Wade case was given over to Geary's hands.

When he had first heard of his assignment to the case Geary had been unwilling to act against his old chum, but it was the first legal affair of any great importance with which he had been connected, and he was soon devoured with an inordinate ambition to distinguish himself in the eyes of the firm to get a "lift," to take a long step forward toward the end of his desires, which was to become one of the firm itself. He knew he could make a brilliant success of the case. Geary was at this time nearly twenty-eight, keen, energetic, immensely clever, and the case against Vandover was strong. No one knew better than he himself how intimate Vandover had been with Ida Wade; Vandover had told him much of the details of their acquaintance. Besides this, a letter which Ida had written to Vandover the day before her suicide had been found, torn in three pieces, thrust between the leaves of one of the books that she used to study at the normal school. It directly implicated Vandover—it was evidence that could not be gainsaid. Geary had resolved to push the case against his old chum. Vandover ought to see that with Geary it was a matter of business; he, Geary, was only an instrument of the law; if Geary did not take the case some other lawyer would. At any rate, whether Van would see it

VANDOVER AND THE BRUTE

in this light or not, Geary was determined to take the
case; it was too good an opportunity to let slip; he was
going to make his way in the law or he would know the
reason why. Every man for himself, that was what he
said. It might be damned selfish, but it was human
nature; if he had to sacrifice Van, so much the worse.
It was evident that his old college chum was going to
the dogs anyway, but come whatever would, *he*,
Geary, was going to be a *success*. Ah, you bet, he would
make his way and he would make his money.

Ever since he had come into his little patrimony
Geary had been making offers to Vandover for his
block in the Mission. Geary would offer only eight
thousand dollars, but Brunt steadily advised Vandover
against listening to such a figure, assuring him that the
property was valued at twelve thousand six hundred.
Vandover had often wondered at Geary's persistence
in the matter, and had often asked him what he could
possibly want of the block. But Geary was very vague
in his replies, generally telling Vandover that there was
money in the investment if one could and would give
the proper attention to pushing it. He told Vandover
that he—Vandover—was no business man, which
was the lamentable truth, and would much prefer to
live upon the interest of his bonds rather than to be
continually annoyed by defective plumbing, complaints,
and repairs. The truth of the matter was that Geary
knew that a certain immense boot and shoe concern
was after the same piece of property. The houses themselves were nothing to the boot and shoe people; they
wanted the land in order to build their manufactory
upon it. A siding of the railroad ran down the alley
just back of the property, a fact that hurt the lot for
residence purposes, but that was indispensable for the
boot and shoe people. Geary knew that the heads of
the manufactory were determined to buy the lot, and

he was sure that if properly handled by clever brokers they could be induced to offer at least one third more than its appraised valuation. It was a chance for a fine speculation, and it was torture to Geary to think that Vandover, or in fact anyone besides himself, was going to profit by it.

The afternoon of the day upon which Hiram Wade had brought suit for twenty-five thousand dollars, while Geary was pottering about his swivel office chair with an oil can trying to find out where it creaked, a brilliant idea had suddenly occurred to him, a stroke of genius, a veritable inspiration. Why could he not make the Wade suit a machine with which to force Vandover into the sale of the property?

His first idea had been to push the case so vigorously that Vandover would surely lose it. But on second thought this course did not seem to promise any satisfactory results. Geary knew very well that though Hiram Wade had sued for twenty-five thousand dollars he could not recover more than five thousand, if as much as that. Geary did not know the exact state of Vandover's affairs, but he did not think that his chum would sell any property in order to make the payment of damages. It was much more likely that he would raise the five thousand, or whatever it might be, by placing a second mortgage on some of his property. This, however, was presuming that Wade would get judgment for about five thousand dollars. But suppose that Vandover thought that Wade could actually recover twenty-five thousand! Suppose that Geary himself should see Vandover and induce him to believe such a story, and to settle the affair out of court! Vandover was as ignorant of law as he was of business. Geary might frighten him into a sale. Yet this plan seemed very impracticable. In the first place, it would be unprofessional for Geary to have an interview with

Vandover under such circumstances, the story was almost too monstrous even for Vandover's credibility, and besides, Geary would not pay, could not pay twenty-five thousand for the property. This last was a serious tangle. In order to get Vandover to sell, Geary would have to represent the damage suit as involving a larger sum of money than Geary was willing to give for the block, even a far larger sum than that which the boot and shoe manufacturers could be induced to pay for it. It seemed to be a deadlock. Geary began to see that the whole idea was out of the question. Yet the desire of it came back upon him again and again. He dwelt upon it constantly, smelling out the chance for a "deal" somewhere in the tangle with the instinct of the keen man of business. At last he seemed to have straightened it out. The idea of a compromise came into his mind. What if Vandover and Hiram Wade could be made to compromise upon eight thousand dollars! Geary would be willing to pay Vandover eight thousand for the block. That was his original offer. Wade, though he had sued for twenty-five thousand, could easily be made to see that eight thousand was as much as he could reasonably expect, and Geary knew the boot and shoe manufacturers would pay fifteen thousand for the lot, perhaps more.

But in order to carry out the delicate and complicated affair it was absolutely necessary to keep Vandover from seeing a lawyer. Geary knew that any lawyer would fight the proposition of a compromise at eight thousand dollars; five thousand was as much as Wade could possibly get in court, and if judgment for such amount were rendered, Vandover's counsel would advise him to raise the sum by mortgaging some property instead of selling the block.

Yet as soon as Geary arrived at a solution of the problem, as soon as the "deal" began to seem feasible, he

commenced to hesitate. It was not so much that the
affair was crooked, that his rôle in it was, to say the
least, unprofessional, as it was the fact that Vandover
was his old college chum and that, to put the matter
into plain words, Geary was swindling his best friend
out of a piece of property valued at twelve thousand
six hundred dollars, and preventing him from reselling
the same piece at a very advanced figure. Again and
again he wished that it was some other than Vandover;
he told himself that in such case he would put the
screw on without the least compunction. All through
one night Geary was on the rack torn between his
friendship for his chum and his devouring, inordinate
ambition to make his way and to make his pile. In the
end Vandover was sacrificed—the opportunity was too
good—Geary could not resist the chance for a "deal."
Ah, you bet, just think of it, after all, not only would
Vandover believe that Geary was doing him a great
service, but the office would be delighted with him
for winning his first case, they would get a heavy fee
from Wade, and he would nearly double his money invested in the block in the Mission. As soon as he had
made up his mind to put the "deal" through, he had
seen Vandover at his rooms early in the morning and
had induced him to promise not to engage any other
counsel and in general keep very quiet about the whole
business.

The day after, he and Beale, Jr., had an appointment
with Hiram Wade, but toward noon Beale, Jr., disappeared, leaving word for Geary that he had gone to
court with his father to hear the closing arguments in
the great suit against the monopoly, the last struggle
in the tremendous legal battle that had embroiled the
whole office; Geary was to use his own judgment in the
Wade case. Geary laboured with Hiram Wade all that
afternoon. The old fellow mistrusted him on account of

his youth and his inexperience, was unwilling to arrive
at any definite conclusion without the sanction of
Geary's older associate, and for a long time would listen
to nothing less than ten thousand dollars, crying out
that his grey hairs had been dishonoured, and striking
his palm upon his forehead. Nothing could move him.
He, also, had his ambitions; it was his dream to own
the carpet-cleaning establishment in which he now had
but a three-fourths interest. Summer was coming, the
time of year when people were going into the country,
leaving their carpets to be cleaned in their absence.
If he could obtain complete ownership of his business
within the month he fancied that he saw an opportunity
to make more money than he had done before at any
previous season.

"Why, I tell you, Mister Geary," he exclaimed, indig-
nantly, wagging his head, "it would seem like selling
my daughter's honour if we should compromise at any
less figure. I am a father. I—I have my feelings, haven't
I?"

"Well, now, it isn't like that at all, Mr. Wade,"
answered Geary, making awkward gestures with both
his hands. "It isn't what we *ought* to get out of him.
Could any sum of money, could millions compensate you
for Miss Ida's death? I guess not. It's what we *can* get.
If this thing comes into court we won't get but five
thousand out of him; I'll tell you that right now. He
could raise that by a mortgage, easy; but if we compromise we can squeeze him for eight thousand. You
see the fact that we can act directly with him instead
of through counsel makes it easier for us. Of course, as
I tell you, it isn't just the legal thing to do, but I'm willing to do it for you because I think you've been wronged
and outraged."

Wade struck his hand to his head. "I tell you, he's
brought dishonour upon my grey hairs," he exclaimed.

"Exactly, of course, I understand how you feel," replied Geary, "but now about this eight thousand? I tell you what I'll do." He had resolved to stake everything upon one last hazard. "See here, Mr. Wade, there's a difference, of course, between eight thousand dollars and ten thousand, but the use of money is worth something, isn't it? And money down, cold hard cash, is worth something, isn't it? Well, now, suppose you got that eight thousand dollars money down within three days?"

Hiram Wade still demurred a little longer for the sake of his own self-respect and his dishonoured hairs, but in the end it was agreed that if the money were paid over to him in full before the end of the following week he would be content and would agree to the compromise. Eight thousand dollars would still be enough to buy out his partner's interest, and even then he would have a little left over with which to improve a certain steaming apparatus. If the amount was paid in full within a week he could get control of the cleaning-works in time to catch all of the summer trade.

Geary had calculated that this last argument would have its weight; the great difficulty now was to get Vandover to sell at such a low figure and upon such short notice. He almost despaired of his success in this quarter; however, it all depended upon Vandover now.

Early in the forenoon of the next day Geary pounded on the door of Vandover's sitting room, pushing it open without waiting for an answer. Vandover was lying in his shirt-sleeves on the corduroy divan under the huge rug of sombre colours that hung against the wall, and he did not get up as Geary came in; in fact, he hardly stirred.

"Hello!" cried Geary, closing the door with his heel. "Didn't expect to find *you* up so early. *I*'ve been up since half-past six; had breakfast at seven, fine cutlet, and then got down to the office at twenty minutes of eight. How's that for rustling, hey?"

"Yes?" said Vandover, dully.

"But, say," exclaimed Geary, "what's all the matter with *you?* You look all frazzled out, all pale around the wattles. Ah, you've been hitting up a pace again. You're a bird, Van, there's no use talking! All-night racket this trip?"

"I suppose so," answered Vandover, never moving.

"But you *do* look gone-in this morning, sure," continued Geary, seating himself on the edge of the table and pushing back his hat. "Never saw you looking so bad; you ought to be more careful, Van; there'll be a smash some time. Ah, you bet a man ought to look out for his health. I walk downtown every morning, and three times a week I take a cold shower as soon as I get up. Ah, I tell you, that braces a fellow up; you ought to try it; it's better than a dozen cocktails. You keep on getting thin like you have for the past few days and I'll have to be calling you Skinny Seldom-fed again, like we used to. Now, tell the truth, what time did you get to bed last night? Did you go to bed at all?"

"No," replied Vandover with a long breath, looking vaguely at the pipe-rack on the opposite wall.

"I thought as much," answered Geary. "Well, that's like you." He paused a moment, and then went on, nervously gesturing with both his hands simultaneously. "Well, I've had a long talk with Wade. I tell you, Van, that old boy is as stubborn as a mule. You see, he knows he's got a case. I couldn't talk him out of that. I'll tell you how it is," continued Geary, preparing to spring another mine; "he's found a letter Ida wrote you the day before she killed herself." He paused to watch the effect upon Vandover. Vandover waited for him to go on, but seeing that he did not and that he expected him to say something, nodded his head once and answered:

"I see."

"Don't you know, that letter that she wrote to you telling you how it was, how she was fixed?" repeated Geary, puzzled and irritated at Vandover's indifference.

"I know."

"Well, he's got it, anyhow," pursued Geary, "and of course that tells against you. Well, I had a long talk with him yesterday afternoon and I got him to compromise. Of course, you know in suits like this one a party sues for a great deal more than he expects to get. At first you know he said twenty-five thousand; that figure was decided upon at the first interview he had with us. Of course, he could never get judgment for that much. But he hung out at ten thousand; said it would be selling his daughter if he took any less. Now I knew you couldn't raise that much on any property you have, especially in these hard times——" Geary paused for the fraction of an instant; he had thrown out the last remark as a feeler, to see what Vandover would say; but his chum said nothing, staring vaguely at the opposite wall, merely making a faint sign to show that he understood, closing his eyes and bending his head. "And so," continued the other, "I jewed him down, and what do you suppose? Well, sir, from twenty-five thousand I brought him right down to, say, eight thousand. I could see that he had some scheme that he wants to go into right away, and that he wants ready money, right on the nail, you know, to carry it through. Ah, you bet, I was clever enough to see that. I waltzed him right over when I began to speak of ready money, cash down. As soon as he'd squeal I'd spring cold cash on him, money down, and he's hit gravel like an ostrich. Well," he went on deliberately after a pause, getting up from the table and standing before Vandover, his hands in his pockets, "well, I think that's the best I can do for you, Van. It's a good deal better than I expected, but I've done the best I could for you, and I would advise you to see him on the proposition."

"All right," said Vandover. "Go ahead."

Geary was perplexed. "Well, you think that's a good thing, don't you? You think I've done my best for you? You see it as I do, don't you?"

Vandover withdrew his eyes from the other wall, glancing under heavy eyelids at Geary, and with a slight movement of his head and shoulders replied: "Of course."

"Have you got the money?" asked Geary, eagerly; then, irritated at his indiscretion, hastened to interrupt himself. "You see, he hasn't put his proposition into writing yet, but it's like this: if you can pay him eight thousand dollars in cash before the end of next week he'll sign a document to the effect that he is satisfied."

"I've got no money," said Vandover, quietly.

"I was afraid you wouldn't have," said Geary, "but you can raise it somewhere. You had better close with the old man as soon as you can, Van, while he's in the mood for it; you'll make a clear two thousand by it. You can see that as well as I can. Now, where can you—how is your property fixed? Let's see! Here's the statement you made to me the other day," continued Geary, drawing his shorthand notes from his portfolio. "How about this piece on California Street, the one that you have rented, the homestead, you know?"

"Yes, there's that," answered Vandover, changing the position of his head upon his clasped hands.

"But that's pretty well papered up already," returned Geary, consulting his notes. "You couldn't very well raise another mortgage on *that*."

"I'd forgotten," answered Vandover. "There's the block in the Mission. He can have that."

Geary began to tremble with excitement. It looked as

though he might be able to make the deal, after all. But the next instant he grew suspicious. Vandover's indifference puzzled him. Might he not have some game of his own? The idea of playing off his cleverness against that of an opponent strung his nerves in an instant; the notion of an impending struggle was almost an inspiration, and his innate desire of getting the better of a competitor, even though it was his closest friend, aroused his wits and sharpened his faculties like a stimulant. He had no hesitancy in sacrificing his chum. It was business now; friendship ceased to be a factor in the affair. Ah, Van was going to be foxy; he'd show him that *he* could be foxy, too.

"He can have it?" echoed Geary. "You don't mean to sign it over to him bodily?"

"Oh, I suppose it could be mortgaged," answered Vandover.

"Yes, that's the idea," returned Geary. "You want me to figure that out for you? I can just as well as not. Well, now, let's see," he went on, settling himself at the desk, and figuring upon a sheet of Vandover's stamped letter-paper. "The banks will never give you more than two thirds of the appraised value; that's as much as we can expect; that would come to—well, let's see—that would come to six thousand on that piece; then you could mortgage something else to make up the difference."

"Wouldn't it be more than six thousand?" asked Vandover with a little show of interest. "I think that block has been appraised at something over twelve thousand."

"Ah, yes," returned Geary, putting his chin in the air, "that was your agent's valuation five years ago; but you know property out there, in fact, property all over the city, what they call inside property, has been going right down for the last ten years. That's what

I've always been telling you. You couldn't possibly get more than nine thousand for that block to-day. You see the railroad there hurts it."

"I suppose so," replied Vandover. "I've heard the governor say as much in his time."

"Of course," exclaimed Geary, delighted at this unexpected turn.

"Well, then, he can have my bonds," said Vandover. "I've got eighty-nine hundred in bonds; he can have those. Let him have anything he wants."

"Oh, don't touch your bonds," answered Geary. "Hang on to those. Bonds are always good—U. S. bonds. You don't want to sell those, Van. You see, the homestead is already mortgaged. And, besides, you know, too, that the banks are asking an awful big per cent. for mortgages on real estate; it's seven and a half nowadays. Don't sell your bonds. I'll tell you why: U. S. bonds are already good; they never depreciate, but it's different with realty, especially in this city just now. It's been depreciating ever since your father's time, and it's going to go right on depreciating. If you want to sell anything, sell your realty before it gets any lower. Now you don't want to sell your home, do you? You don't like that idea. You've lived there so long, and then what would you do with the furniture; besides, the rent of that," he glanced again at his notes, "is bringing you in a good hundred and twenty-five a month. If you've got to sell at all, why not sell your Mission block?"

"All right," said Vandover, as if wearied by Geary's clamour, "I'll sign it over to him."

"No, that's not the idea at all," Geary insisted. "He wants the ready money; he don't want depreciated real estate. You'll have to find a purchaser in the next week if you possibly can in such a short time, and make over the money to Wade. But if you can't sell in that time you will have to dig up ten thousand instead of eight. It's a hard position for you, Van; it's just a chance, you know, but I thought I would give you the benefit of that chance. If you want to give me a power of attorney I'll try and sell it for you."

"I guess Brunt would do that," replied Vandover.

"Yes," retorted Geary, watchful as a lynx, "but they would charge you a big commission. Of course *I* wouldn't think of asking you anything more than the actual costs. I am afraid that they would try to sell it at auction, too, if they knew you had to realize on it in so short a time, and it would go for a mere song then; you know how it is."

"I thought," inquired Vandover, "that you wanted that property."

"Yes," replied Geary, hesitating, "I—I did want to buy it of you once; well, for that matter I do now. But you know how it is with me."

"I might as well sell it to you as to anyone else," returned Vandover.

"Well, now, it's like this, Van," said Geary. "I know that block is worth nine thousand dollars; I won't deceive you. But I can only give you eight thousand for it. That's all the money I've got. But I'm not going to take advantage of your position to jew you down. I want the block, I'll admit that, but I'm not going to have you sacrifice it for me, or for anyone else. I think you can get nine thousand for it. I know you could if we had a little more time, and I'm not sure but what I could find a purchaser for you within the next week that would give you nine thousand."

"Oh, I don't care, Charlie; I'm sick of everything; eight thousand, nine thousand, anything you like; take it at your own figure."

Geary began to tremble once more, and this time his excitement was so great that he hardly dared to trust himself to speak; his breath grew short, his hands in his pockets twitched nervously, and curled themselves into fists, his heart seemed to him to beat high in his throat; he hesitated long, pretending to deliberate as he steadied himself.

Vandover remained silent, his hands still clasped back of his head, staring at the opposite wall with eyes that saw nothing. The little clock began to strike ten.

"I don't know, Van," said Geary; "I don't like to do this, and yet I would like to help you out of this muss. You see, if I should ever benefit by the property you would feel as though I had taken advantage of you at this time and worked a flim-flam on you!"

"Oh, I'll look out for that," returned Vandover.

"No, no, I don't feel quite right about it," answered Geary, wagging his head and shutting his eyes. "Better see what we can do at a forced sale."

"Why, don't you see you would be doing me a favour?" said Vandover, wearily. "I *ask* you to buy the block. I don't care what your figure is!"

Once more Geary hesitated, for the last time going over the whole deal in his mind from beginning to end, testing it, looking for weak points. It was almost perfect. Suppose the boot and shoe people did not buy the lot? He could resell it elsewhere, even below its appraised value, and yet make money by the transaction; the lot was cheap at ten thousand; it might bring twelve; even as an ordinary, legitimate speculation it was to be desired at such a figure. Suppose the boot and shoe people backed out entirely, suppose even he could not find another purchaser for the property, why, then he could hold on to it; the income from the rents was fully 10 per cent. of the price he would have paid for it.

"Well, Van," he said at last, making a slow, awkward

gesture with his left hand, all the fingers extended, "well, I'll take you up—but I don't feel as though I should——" He suddenly interrupted himself with a burst of sincerity, exclaiming: "Sure, old man, if I had nine thousand I'd give it to you for the block, that's straight goods." He felt that he was conscientious in saying this. It was true he would have given nine thousand if he had had it. For that matter, he might have given ten or twelve.

"Can't we settle the whole matter to-day?" said Vandover. "Right here—now. I'm sick of it, sick of everything. Let's get it done with."

Geary nearly bounded from his seat. He had been wondering how he might accomplish this very thing. "All right," he said, briskly, "no reason in waiting." He had seen to it that he should be prepared to close the sale the moment that Vandover was willing. Long ago, when he had first had the idea of buying the block, he had spent a day in the offices of the county recorder, the tax collector, and the assessor, assuring himself of the validity of the title, and only two days ago he had gone over the matter again in order to be sure that no encumbrances had been added to the block in the meanwhile. He found nothing; the title was clear.

"Isn't this rather rushing the thing through?" he asked. "Maybe you might regret it afterward. Don't you want to take two or three days to think it over?"

"No."

"Sure now?" persisted Geary.

"But I've *got* to sell before three days," answered Vandover. "Otherwise he'll want ten thousand."

"That's a fact," admitted the other. "Well," he went on, "if your mind's made up, why—we can go right ahead. As I say, there's no reason for waiting; better take up Wade while he's in the mood for it. You see, he hasn't signed any proposition as yet, and he might go back on us." Vandover drew a long breath and got up slowly, heavily, from the couch, saying:

"What's the odds to me what I sell for? *I* don't get the money."

"Well, what do you say if we go right down to a notary's office and put this thing right through," Geary suggested.

"Come on, then."

"Have you got your abstract here, the abstract of the block?" Vandover nodded. "Better bring it along, then," said Geary.

The office of the notary adjoined those of the firm of Beale & Story; in fact, he was in a sense an attaché of the great firm and transacted a great deal of legal business for them. Vandover and Geary fell upon him in an idle moment. A man had come to regulate the water filter, which took the place of an ice cooler in a corner of one of the anterooms, and while he was engaged at his work the notary stood at his back, abusing him and exclaiming at the ineffectiveness of the contrivance. The notary was a middle-aged man with a swollen, purple face; he had a toothpick behind each ear and wore an office coat of grey linen, ripped at the shoulders.

Then the transfer was made. It was all settled in less than half an hour, unceremoniously, almost hastily. For the sake of form Geary signed a check for eight thousand dollars which Vandover in his turn made over to Hiram Wade. The notary filled out a deed of grant, bargain, and sale, pasting on his certificate of acknowledgment as soon as Vandover and Geary had signed. Geary took the abstract, thrusting it into his breast-pocket. As far as Vandover was concerned, the sale was complete, but he had neither his property nor its equivalent in money.

"Well," declared Geary at length, "I guess that's all there is to be done. I'll get a release from old man Wade

514

and send it to you to-morrow or next day. Now, let's go down to the Imperial and have a drink on it." They went out, but the notary returned to the anteroom, turning the spigot of the filter to right and left, frowning at it suspiciously, refusing to be satisfied.

CHAPTER XVI

THAT particular room in the Lick House [8] was well
toward the rear of the building, on one of the upper
floors, and from its window, one looked out upon a vast
reach of roofs that rose little by little to meet the abrupt
rise of Telegraph Hill. It was a sordid and grimy wilderness, topped with a grey maze of wires and pierced with
thousands of chimney stacks. Many of the roofs were
covered with tin long since blackened by rust and soot.
Here and there could be seen clothes hung out to dry.
Occasionally upon the flanking walls of some of the
larger buildings was displayed an enormous painted
sign, a violent contrast of intense black and staring
white amidst the sooty brown and grey, advertising
some tobacco, some newspaper, or some department
store. Not far in the distance two tall smokestacks of
blackened tin rose high in the air, above the roof of a
steam laundry, one very large like the stack of a
Cunarder, the other slender, graceful, with a funnel-
shaped top. All day and all night these stacks were
smoking; from the first, the larger one, rolled a heavy
black smoke, very gloomy, waving with a slow and continued movement like the plume of some sullen warrior.
But the other one, the tall and slender pipe, threw off
a series of little white puffs, three at a time, that rose
buoyant and joyous into the air like so many white
doves, vanishing at last, melting away in the higher sun-
shine, only to be followed by another flight. They came
three at a time, the pipe tossing them out with a sharp
gay sound like a note of laughter interrupted by a
cough.

But the interior of the room presented the usual dreary aspect of the hotel bedroom—cheerless, lamentable.

The walls were whitewashed and bare of pictures or ornaments, and the floor was covered with a dull red carpet. The furniture was a "set," all the pieces having a family resemblance. On entering, one saw the bed standing against the right-hand wall, a huge double bed with the name of the hotel on the corners of its spread and pillow-cases. In the exact middle of the room underneath the gas fixture was the centre table, and upon it a pitcher of ice-water. The blank, white monotony of one side of the room was jarred upon by the grate and mantelpiece, iron, painted black, while on the mantelpiece itself stood a little porcelain matchsafe with ribbed sides in the form of a truncated cone. Precisely opposite the chimney was the bureau, flanked on one side by the door of the closet, and on the other in the corner of the room by the stationary washstand with its new cake of soap and its three clean, glossy towels. On the wall to the left of the door was the electric bell and the directions for using it, and tacked upon the door itself a card as to the hours for meals, the rules of the hotel, and the extract of the code defining the liabilities of innkeepers, all printed in bright red. Everything was clean, defiantly, aggressively clean, and there was a clean smell of new soap in the air.

But the room was bare of any personality. Of the hundreds who had lived there, perhaps suffered and died there, not a trace, not a suggestion remained; their different characters had not left the least impress upon its air or appearance. Only a few hairpins were scattered on the bottom of one of the bureau drawers, and two forgotten medicine bottles still remained upon the top shelf of the closet.

This had been the appearance of Vandover's new

517

home when he had first come to it, after leaving his
suite of rooms in the huge apartment house on Sutter
Street. He had lived here now for something over a
year.

It had all commenced with the seizure of his furniture
by the proprietors of the apartment house. Almost before he knew it he owed for six months' room and board;
when the extras were added to this bill it swelled to
nearly a thousand dollars. At first he would not believe
it; it was not possible that so large a bill could ac-
cumulate without his knowledge. He declared there was
a mistake, tossing back the bill to the clerk who had
presented it, and shaking his head incredulously. This
other became angry, offered to show the books of the
house. The manager was called in and attempted to
prove the clerk's statement by figures, dates, and extracts from the entries. Vandover was confused by their
noise, and grew angry, in his turn; vociferating that he
did not propose to be cheated, the others retorted in a
rage, the interview ended in a scene.

But in the end they gained their point; they were
right, and at length Vandover was brought around to see
that he was in the wrong, but he had no ready money,
and while he hesitated, unwilling to part with any of his
bonds or to put an additional mortgage upon the homestead, the hotel, after two warnings, suddenly seized
upon his furniture. What a misery!

In a moment of time it was all taken from him, all
the lovely bric-à-brac, all the heavy pieces, all the little
aritcles of *vertu* which he had bought with such intense
delight and amongst which he had lived with such happiness, such contentment, such never-failing pleasure.
Everything went—the Renaissance portraits, the pipe-
rack, the chair in which the Old Gentleman had died,
the Assyrian *bas-reliefs*, and, worst of all, the stove, the
famous tiled stove, the delightful cheery iron stove with

the beautiful flamboyant ornaments. For the first few months after the seizure Vandover was furious with rage and disappointment, persuaded that he could never live anywhere but in just such a room; it was as if he had been uprooted and cast away upon some barren, uncongenial soil. His new room in the hotel filled him with horror, and for a long time he used it only as a place where he could sleep and wash. For a long time even his pliable character refused to fit itself to such surroundings, refused to be content between four enormous white walls, a stuccoed ceiling, and a dark red carpet. He passed most of his time elsewhere, reading the papers at the Mechanics' Library in the morning, and in the afternoon sitting about the hotel office and parlours until it was time to take his usual little four o'clock stroll on Kearney and Market streets. He had long since become a familiar figure on this promenade. Even the women and girls of Flossie's type had ceased to be intersted in this tall, thin young man with the tired, heavy eyes and blue-white face. One day, however, a curious incident did for a moment invest Vandover with a sudden dramatic interest. It was just after he had moved down to the Lick House, about a month after he had sold the block in the Mission. Vandover was standing at Lotta's fountain[9] at the corner of Kearney and Market streets, interested in watching a policeman and two boys reharnessing a horse after its tumble. All at once he fell over flat into the street, jostling one of the flower venders and nearly upsetting him. He struck the ground with a sodden shock, his arms doubled under him, his hat rolling away into the mud. Bewildered, he picked himself up; very few had seen him fall, but a little crowd gathered for all that. One asked if the man was drunk, and Vandover, terrified lest the policeman should call the patrol wagon, hurried off to a basement barber shop near by, where he brushed his clothes, still bewildered, confused, wondering how it had happened.

The fearful nervous crisis which Vandover had undergone had passed off slowly. Little by little, bit by bit, he had got himself in hand again. However, the queer numbness in his head remained, and as soon as he concentrated his attention on any certain line of thought, as soon as he had read for any length of time, especially if late at night, the numbness increased. Somewhere back of his eyes a strange blurring mist would seem to rise; he would find it impossible to keep his mind fixed upon any subject; the words of a printed page would little by little lose their meaning. At first this had been a source of infinite terror to him. He fancied it to be the symptoms of some approaching mental collapse, but, as the weeks went by and nothing unusual occurred, he became used to it, and refused to let it worry him. If it made his head feel queer to read, the remedy was easy enough—he simply would not read; and though he had been a great reader, and at one time had been used to spend many delightful afternoons lost in the pages of a novel, he now gave it all up with an easy indifference.

But, besides all this, the attack had left him with nerves all unstrung; even his little afternoon walk on Kearney and Market streets exhausted him; any trifling and sudden noise, the closing of a door, the striking of a clock, would cause him to start from his place with a gasp and a quick catch at the heart. Toward evening this little spasm of nerves would sometimes come upon him even when there was nothing to cause it, and now he could no longer drop off to sleep without first undergoing a whole series of these recoils and starts, that would sometimes bring him violently up to a sitting posture, his breath coming short and quick, his heart galloping, startled at he knew not what.

At first he had intended to see a doctor, but he had put off carrying his intention into effect until he had grown accustomed to the whole matter; otherwise, he was well enough, his appetite was good, and when he finally did get to sleep he would not wake up for a good eight hours.

One evening, however, about three months after the first crisis and just as Vandover was becoming well accustomed to the condition of body and mind in which it had left him, the second attack came on. It was fearful, much worse than on the first occasion, and this time there was no room for doubt. Vandover knew that for the moment he was actually insane.

Ellis had been with Vandover most of that afternoon, the two had been playing cards in Vandover's room until nearly six o'clock. All the afternoon they had been drinking whisky while they played, and by supper-time neither of them had any appetite. Ellis refused to go down, declaring that if he should eat now it would make him sick. Vandover went down alone, but once in the dining room he found that *he* could not eat either. However, he knew that it was not the whisky. For two days his appetite had been failing him. The smell of food revolted him, and he left the supper-table, going up to his bare and lamentable room with the feeling that he was about to undergo a long spell of sickness. In the deserted hall, between the elevator and the door of his room, the second crisis came upon him all at once. It was so sudden that it was as if some enemy had leaped upon his back, springing out of the shadow, gripping from behind, holding him close. Once more the hysteria shook him like a dry leaf. The little nervous starts came so fast that they ran together, mingling to form one long thrill of terror, the blind, unreasoning terror of something unknown; the numbness weighted down upon his brain until consciousness dwindled to a mere point and mercifully dulled the torture of his crisping nerves. It seemed to him that his hands and head were rapidly swelling to enormous size.

All this he had felt before; it was his old enemy, but now with this second attack began a new and even stranger sensation. In his distorted wits he fancied that he was in some manner changing, that he was becoming another man; worse than that, it seemed to him that he was no longer human, that he was sinking, all in a moment, to the level of some dreadful beast.

Later on in that same evening Ellis met young Haight coming out of one of the theatres, and told him a story that Haight did not believe. Ellis was very pale, and he seemed to young Haight to be trying to keep down some tremendous excitement.

"If he was drunk," said Ellis, "it was the strangest drunk I ever saw. He came back into the room on all fours—not on his hands and knees, you understand, but running along the floor upon the palms of his hands and his toes—and he pushed the door of the room open with his head, nuzzling at the crack like any dog. Oh, it was horrible. *I* don't know what's the matter with Van. You should have seen him; his head was hanging way down, and swinging from side to side as he came along; it shook all his hair over his eyes. He kept rattling his teeth together, and every now and then he would say, way down in his throat so it sounded like growls, 'Wolf—wolf—wolf.' I got hold of him and pulled him up to his feet. It was just as though he was asleep, and when I shook him he came to all at once and began to laugh. 'What's the matter, Van?' says I. 'What are you crawling on the floor that way for?' 'I'm damned if I know,' says he, rubbing his eyes. 'I guess I must have been out of my head. Too much whisky!' Then he says: 'Put me to bed, will you, Bandy? I feel all gone in.' Well, I put him to bed and went out

to get some bromide of potassium; he said that made
him sleep and kept his nerves steady. Coming back, I
met a bell-boy just outside of Van's door, and told
him to ask the hotel doctor to come up. You see, I had
not opened the door of the room yet, and while I was
talking to the bell-boy I could hear the sound of something four-footed going back and forth inside the room.
When I got inside there was Van, perfectly naked, going
back and forth along the wall, swinging his head very
low, grumbling to himself. But he came to again as
soon as I shook him, and seemed dreadfully ashamed,
and went to bed all right. He got to sleep finally, and I
left the doctor with him, to come out and get something
for my own nerves."

"What did the doctor say was the matter?" asked
young Haight, in horror.

"*Lycanthropy-Mathesis.* I never heard the name
before—some kind of nervous disease. I guess Van had
been hitting up a pretty rapid gait, and then I suppose
he's had a good deal to worry him, too."

Once more the attack passed off, leaving Vandover
exhausted, his nerves all jangling, his health impaired.
Every day he seemed to grow thinner, great brown
hollows grew under his eyes, and the skin of his forehead
looked blue and tightly drawn. By degrees a deep gloom
overcame him permanently, nothing could interest him,
nothing seemed worth while. Not only were his nerves
out of tune, but they were jaded, deadened, slack; they
were like harpstrings that had been played upon so long
and so violently that now they could no longer vibrate
unless swept with a very whirlwind.

As he had foreseen, Vandover had returned again to
vice, to the vice that was knitted into him now, fibre for
fibre, to the ways of the brute that by degrees was taking
entire possession of him. But he no longer found pleasure

even in vice; once it had been his amusement, now it was his occupation. It was the only thing that seemed to ease the horrible nervousness that of late had begun to prey upon him constantly.

But though nothing could amuse him, on the other hand nothing could worry him; in the end the very riot of his nerves ceased even to annoy him. He had arrived at a state of absolute indifference. He had so often rearranged his pliable nature to suit his changing environment that at last he found that he could be content in almost any circumstances. He had no pleasures, no cares, no ambitions, no regrets, no hopes. It was mere passive existence, an inert, plantlike vegetation, the moment's pause before the final decay, the last inevitable rot.

One day after he had been living nearly a year at the Lick House, Adams & Brunt, the real estate agents, sent him word that they had an offer for his property on California Street. It was the homestead. The English gentleman, the president of the fruit syndicate who had rented the house of Vandover, was now willing to buy it. His business was by this time on a firm and paying basis and he had decided to make his home in San Francisco. He offered twenty-five thousand dollars for the house, including the furniture.

Brunt had several talks with Vandover and easily induced him to sell. "You can figure it out for yourself, Mr. Vandover," he said, as he pointed out his own calculations to him; "property has been going down in the city for the last ten years, and it will continue to do so until we can get a competing railroad through. Better sell when you can, and twenty-five thousand is a fair price. Of course, you will have to pay off the mortgage; you won't get but about fifteen thousand out of it, but at the same time you won't have to pay interest on that mortgage to the banks; that will be so much saved a month; add that to what you could get for your fifteen thousand at, say, 6 per cent., and you would have a monthly income nearly equal to the present rent of the house, and much more certain, too. Suppose your tenant should go out, then where would you be?"

"All right, all right," answered Vandover, nodding his head vaguely. "Go ahead, *I* don't care." He parted from his old home with as much indifference as he had parted from his block in the Mission.

Vandover signed the deed that made him homeless and at about the same time the first payment was made. Ten thousand dollars was deposited in one of the banks to his credit, and a check sent to him for the amount. The very next day Vandover drew against it for five hundred dollars.

At one time he had had an ambition to buy back his furniture from the huge apartment house in which he had formerly lived, and with it to make his cheerless bedroom in the Lick House seem more like a home. He felt it almost as a dishonour to have strangers using this furniture, sitting in the great leather chair in which the Old Gentleman had died, staring stupidly at his Renaissance portraits and copies of Assyrian *bas-reliefs*. Above all, it was torture to think that other hands than his own would tend the famous tiled and flamboyant stove, a stove that had its moods, its caprices, like any living person, a stove that had to be coaxed and humoured, a stove that he alone could understand. He had told himself that if ever again he should have money enough he would bring back this furniture to him. At first its absence had been a matter for the keenest regret and grief. He had been so used to pleasant surroundings that he languished in his new quarters as in a prison. His indulgent, luxurious character continually hungered after subdued, harmonious colours, pictures, ornaments, and soft rugs. His imagination was forever covering the white walls with rough stone-blue paper, and placing screens, divans, and window-seats in different parts of the cold bare room. One morning he had even gone so far as to pin about the walls little placards which he had painted with a twisted roll of the hotel letter-paper dipped into the ink-stand. "Pipe-rack Here." "Mona Lisa Here." "Stove Here." "Window-seat Here." He had left them up there ever since, in spite of the chambermaid's protests and Ellis' clumsy satire.

Now, however, he had plenty of money. He would have his furniture back within the week. He came back from the bank, the money in his pocket, and went up to the room directly, with some vague intention of writing to the proprietors of the apartment house at once. But as he shut the door behind him, leaning his back against it and looking about, he suddenly realized that his old-time desire was past; he had become so used to these surroundings that it now no longer made any difference to him whether or not they were cheerless, lamentable, barren. It was like all his other little ambitions—he had lost the taste for them, nothing made much difference, after all. His money had come too late.

Why should he spend his five hundred dollars on something that could no longer amuse him? It would be much wiser to spend it all in having a good time some-where—champagne dinners with Flossie, or betting on the races—he did not know exactly what. It was true that even these alternatives would not amuse him very much—he would fall back upon them as things of habit. For that matter everything was an *ennui*, and Vandover began to long for some new pleasure, some violent, untried excitement.

Since the sale of the block in the Mission he had seen but little of Geary; young Haight had not been his companion since the time when Turner Ravis had broken with him, but little by little he had begun to associate with Ellis and his friend the Dummy. Almost every evening the three were together, sometimes at the theatre, sometimes in the back rooms of the Imperial, sometimes even in the parlours of certain houses, amid the murmur of heavy silks and the rustle of stiffly starched skirts. At times they would be drunk four nights of the week, and on these occasions it was tacitly understood between Ellis and Vandover that they should try to get the Dummy so full that he could talk.

However, Ellis' vice was gambling; he and the Dummy often passed the whole night over their cards, and as Vandover came more and more under Ellis' influence—succumbing to it as weakly as he had succumbed to the influence of Charlie Geary—he began to join these parties. They played Van John at five dollars a corner. Vandover won as often as he lost, but the habit of cards grew upon him steadily.

Toward eleven o'clock the evening of the day upon which he had drawn his five hundred, Vandover went around to the Imperial looking for his two friends. He found Ellis drinking whisky all alone in one of the little rooms, as was his custom; fifteen minutes later the Dummy and Flossie joined them. Flossie had grown stouter since Vandover had first known her, nearly ten years ago. She had a double chin, and puffy, discoloured pockets had come under her eyes. Now her hair was dyed, her cheeks and lips rouged, and her former air of health and good spirits gone. She never laughed. She had smoked so many cigarettes that now her voice hardly rose above a whisper. At one time she had been accustomed to boast that she never drank, and it had been one of her peculiarities for which she was well known. But on this occasion she joined Ellis in his whisky. She had long since departed from her old-time rule of temperance, and nowadays drank nothing else but whisky. She had even become well known for the quantity of whisky she could drink.

For half an hour the four sat around the little table, talking about the new, enormous Sutro Baths that were building at that time.[10] After a while Flossie left them, and the Dummy began to imitate the notions of someone dealing cards, looking at the same time inquiringly into their faces.

"How about that, Bandy?" asked Vandover. "Shall we have a game to-night?"

The man of few words merely nodded his head and drank off the rest of his whisky at a swallow. They all went up to Vandover's room. Vandover got out the cards, the celluloid chips, and a fresh box of cigars. The Dummy held up two fingers of his left hand, shutting them together afterward with his right and making a hissing noise between his teeth. He raised his eyebrows at Vandover. Vandover understood, and, ringing for a bell-boy, ordered up three bottles of soda in siphon bottles.

The game was *vingt et un*, or, as they called it, Van John. They cut for banker. Ellis turned the first ace, and Vandover bought the bank from him. For the first hour they were very jolly, laughing and talking back and forth at each other; the Dummy especially communicative, continually scribbling upon his writing-pad, holding it toward the others. But it was not necessary for them to put their replies in writing—he understood from watching the movement of their lips. The luck had not declared itself as yet; none of them had lost or won very much. The bell-boy brought up the siphons. The Dummy took off his coat, and the other two followed his example. They were all smoking, and an acrid blue haze filled the room, making a golden blur about each gas globe.

But little by little the passion of the gambling seized

upon them. The luck had begun to declare itself, alternating between Ellis and the Dummy. Vandover lost steadily; twice already his bank had been broken, and he had been forced to buy in. The play resolved itself into two parts, Vandover struggling to keep up with the game on one side, and on the other a great battle going on between Ellis and the Dummy. Long since they had ceased to laugh, and not a word was spoken; each one was absorbed in the game, intently watching the cards as they were turned. The four gas-jets of the chandelier flared steadily, filling the room with a crude raw light that was reflected with a blinding glare from the four staring white walls, the room grew hot, the layer of foul warm air just beneath the ceiling, slowly descending. The acrid tobacco smoke no longer rose, but hung in long, slow-waving threads just above their heads. They played on steadily; a great stillness grew in the room, a stillness broken only by the little rattle of chips and subdued rustle of the shuffled cards. Once Vandover stopped, just time enough to throw off his vest, his collar, and his scarf. For a moment the luck seemed about to settle on him. He was still banking, and twice in succession he threw Van John, both times winning heavily from the Dummy, and a little later tied Ellis at twenty when the latter had staked on nearly a third of his chips. But in the next half-dozen hands Ellis got back the lead again, winning from both the others. From this time on it was settled. The luck suddenly declared openly for Ellis, the Dummy and Vandover merely fighting for second place. Ellis held his lead; at one o'clock he was nearly fifty dollars ahead of the game. The profound silence of the room seemed to widen about them. After midnight the noises in the hotel, the ringing of distant call bells, the rattle of dishes from the kitchens, the clash of closing elevator doors, gradually ceased; only at long intervals one heard the hurried step

of a bell-boy in the hall outside and the clink of the ice
in the water pitcher that he was carrying. Outside a
great quiet seemed in a sense to rise from the sleeping
city, the noises in the streets died away. The last electric
car went down Kearney Street, getting under way with
a long minor wail. Occasionally a belated coupé, a
nighthawk, rattled over the cobbles, while close by,
from over the roofs, the tall slender stack upon the
steam laundry puffed incessantly, three puffs at a time,
like some kind of halting clock. The room became more
and more close, none of them would take the time to
open the window, from ceiling to floor the air was
fouled by their breathing, by the tobacco smoke and by
the four flaring gas-jets. By this time a sombre excitement burnt in their eyes and quivered in their fingers.
Never for an instant did their glances leave the cards.
Ellis was drinking whisky again, mixed with soda, his
hand continually groping for the glass with a mechanical
gesture; the Dummy was so excited he could not keep
his cigar alight, and contented himself with chewing
the end with an hysterical motion of his jaws. The
perspiration stood in beads on the back of Vandover's
hands, running down in tiny rivulets between his fingers,
his teeth were shut close together and he was breathing
short through his nose, a fine trembling had seized upon
his hands so that the chips in his palm rattled like casta-
nets. In the stale and murky atmosphere of the overheated room in the midst of the vast silence of the sleeping city they played on steadily.

Then they began to "plunge," agreeing to play a no-
limit game and raising the value of a red chip to ten
dollars; at times they even played with the coins themselves when their chips were exhausted. Vandover had
lost all his ready money, and now for a long time had
been gambling with the five hundred dollars he had that
day drawn from the bank. Ellis had practically put the

Dummy out of the play, and now the game was between him and Vandover. Ellis was banking, and at length offered to sell the bank to either one of them. For the first time since the real gambling began they commenced to talk a little, but in short, brief sentences, answering by monosyllables and by signs.

"How much for the bank?" inquired Ellis, holding up the deck and looking from one to the other. Instantly the Dummy wrote ten dollars, in figures, on his pad, and showed it to him. Vandover looked at what the Dummy had written, and said:

"Fifteen."

"Twenty," scribbled the Dummy, as he watched Vandover's lips form the word.

"Twenty-five," returned Vandover. The Dummy hesitated a moment and then wrote "thirty." Ellis shook his head, saying, "I'll keep the bank myself at that."

"Forty dollars!" cried Vandover. The Dummy shook his head, leaning back in his chair. Ellis shoved the pack across the table to Vandover, and Vandover gave him a twenty-dollar bill and two red chips.

On Vandover's very first deal around, the Dummy "stood" on the second card, for twelve chips; Ellis bet twenty-five on his first card, and, as he got the second, turned both of them face up. He had two jacks. "Twenty-five on each of these," he said. "I'll draw to each one." Vandover looked at his own card; it was a ten-spot. All at once he grew reckless, and seized with a sudden folly, resolved to attempt a great *coup*. "Double up!" he ordered. The Dummy set out twelve more chips, and Ellis another fifty, making his bet an even hundred. Vandover began to deal to Ellis. On the first jack Ellis drew eighteen and stood at that; the first card that fell to the second jack was an ace. "Van John," he remarked quietly. The Dummy drew three cards and stood on nineteen. Vandover turned up his own card and began to deal for himself. He already had a ten; now he drew a seven-spot and king in succession.

"The bank pays," he exclaimed. He paid the Dummy twenty-four chips. He gave Ellis fifty for the eighteen he had drawn on his first jack, and one hundred for the Van John upon the second, since the latter combination called for double the amount wagered; besides this, the bank was lost to him. Including the forty that he had paid for the bank, he had lost in all two hundred and fourteen dollars.

Never in his life had Vandover played so high a game, never before had he won or lost more than fifty dollars at a sitting. But he was content to have it thus. Here at last was the new pleasure for which he had longed, the fresh violent excitement that alone could rouse his jaded nerves, the one thing that could amuse him. However, the failure of his *coup* had left him without chips; he was out of the game. He decided that he would stop; more than half of his five hundred dollars was gone already. He drank off a glass of soda, the dregs of one of the siphon bottles, and got up yawning, shivering a little and stretching his arms high above. The other two played on steadily. The Dummy began to gain slowly upon Ellis, playing very cautiously, betting only upon face cards, aces, and ten-spots. Twice Ellis offered to sell him the bank, but he refused, fearful lest it should change his luck.

Vandover sat behind the Dummy's chair, watching his game, but at length, worn out, he began to drop off to sleep, waking every now and then with a sudden leap and recoil of all his nerves. An hour later the persistent scratching of a match awoke him. Ellis and the Dummy were still playing, and the Dummy was once more re-lighting the stump of his cigar. Ellis continued to deal, winning at almost every play; a great pile of chips and money lay at his elbow. For a few minutes Vandover watched the Dummy's game, leaning forward in his chair, his elbows on his knees. But it was evident that the Dummy had lost his nerve. Ellis' continued winnings had at length demoralized him. At one time he would bet heavily on worthless cards, and at another would throw back nines and tens for no apparent reason. Finally Ellis dealt him a queen, which he kept, betting ten chips. His next card was a seven-spot. He signed to Ellis that he would stand. Ellis drew twenty in three cards. Vandover could not restrain an exclamation of impatience at the Dummy's stupidity. What a fool a man must be to stand on seventeen with only two in the game. All at once he tossed twenty dollars across the table to Ellis, saying, "Give me that in chips. I'm coming in again." Once more he resumed his seat at the table, and Ellis dealt him a hand.

But Vandover's interruption had for an instant taken Ellis' mind from the game. He stirred in his chair and looked about the room, puffing out his cheeks and blowing between his lips

"Say, this room is close enough to strangle you. Open the window behind you, Van, you're nearest to it." As Vandover raised the curtain he uttered a cry: "Look here! will you?"

It was morning; the city was flooded by the light of the sun already an hour high. The sky was without a cloud. Over the roofs and amongst the grey maze of telegraph wires swarms of sparrows were chittering hoarsely, and as Vandover raised the window he could hear the newsboys far below in the streets chanting the morning's papers.

"Come on, Van!" exclaimed Ellis, impatiently; "we're waiting for you."

That night decided it. From that time on, Vandover's only pleasure was gambling. Night and day he sat over

the cards, the passion growing upon him as he continued
to lose, for his ill luck was extraordinary. It was a veritable mania, a wild blind frenzy that knew no limit. At
first he had contented himself with a game in which
twenty or thirty dollars was as much as he could win or
lose at a sitting, but soon this palled upon him; he was
obliged to raise the stakes continually in order to arouse
in him the interest, the keen tense excitement, that his
jaded nerves craved.

The five hundred dollars that he had drawn from the
ten thousand, the first payment on his old home, melted
away within a week. Only a few years ago Vandover
would have stopped to reflect upon the meaning of this,
would have resisted the temptation that drew him constantly to the gambling-table, but the idea of resistance
never so much as occurred to him. He did not invest his
fifteen thousand, but drew upon it continually to satisfy
his last new craze. It was not with any hope of winning
that he gambled—the desire of money was never strong
in him—it was only the love of the excitement of the
moment.

Little by little the fifteen thousand in the bank dwindled. It did not all go in cards. Certain habits of extravagance grew upon Vandover, the natural outcome of
his persistent gambling, the desire of winning easily
being balanced by the impulses to spend quickly. He
took a certain hysterical delight in flinging away money
with both hands. Now it was the chartering of a yacht
for a ten-days' cruise about the bay, or it was a bicycle
bought one week and thrown away the next, a fresh suit
of clothes each month, gloves worn but once, gold-pieces
thrust into Flossie's pockets, suppers given to bouffe
actresses—twenty-four-hour acquaintances—a race-
horse bought for eight hundred dollars, resold for two
hundred and fifty—rings and scarf-pins given away to
the women and girls of the Imperial, and a whole world

of follies that his poor distorted wits conceived from hour to hour. His judgment was gone, his mind unbalanced. All his life Vandover had been sinking slowly lower and lower; this, however, was the beginning of the last plunge. The process of degeneration, though inevitable, had been gradual as long as he indulged generally in all forms of evil; it was only now when a passion for one particular vice absorbed him that he commenced to rush headlong to his ruin.

The fifteen thousand dollars—the price of his old home—he gambled or flung away in a little less than a year. He never invested it, but ate into it day after day, sometimes to pay his gambling debts, sometimes to indulge an absurd and extravagant whim, sometimes to pay his bill at the Lick House, and sometimes for no reason at all, moved simply by a reckless desire for spending.

On the evening of a certain Thanksgiving day, nine months after he had sold the house, Vandover came in through the ladies' entrance of the Imperial, going slowly down the passageway, looking into the little rooms on his right for Ellis or the Dummy. There had been a great intercollegiate football game that day, and Vandover, remembering that he had once found an interest in such things, had at first determined to see it. But toward eleven o'clock in the morning the rain had begun to fall, and Ellis, who was to have gone with him, declared that he did not care enough about the game to go out to it in the rain. Vandover was disappointed: he fancied that he could have enjoyed the game—as much as he could enjoy anything of late—but he hated to go to places alone. In the end, however, he resolved to go whether Ellis went or not. It was a holiday. Vandover had Ellis and the Dummy to lunch with him at the hotel, where they arranged the menu of a famous Thanksgiving dinner for that evening: they would meet in one of the little rooms of the Imperial and go from there to the restaurant. As they were finishing their lunch Vandover said:

"I got a new kind of liqueur yesterday—has a colour like violets and smells like cologne. You fellows better come up to my room and try it. I've got to go up and change anyway, if I go out to that game." They all went up to Vandover's cheerless room, and Ellis began to argue with Vandover against the folly of going anywhere in the rain.

"*You* don't want to go to that game, Van. Just look how it's raining. I'll bet there won't be a thousand people there. They'll probably postpone the game anyway. Say, this *is* queer-looking stuff. What do you call it?"

"*Crème violette.*"

The Dummy set down his emptied liqueur glass on the mantelshelf, and nodded approvingly at Vandover; then he scribbled, "Out of sight," on his tablet.

"Tastes like cough syrup and alcohol," growled Ellis, scowling and sipping. "I think a pint of this would make the Dummy talk Dutch. Keep it up, Dummy," he continued, articulating distinctly so that the other could catch the movement of his lips. "Drink some more—make you talk." Vandover was cutting the string around a pasteboard box that had just come from his tailor's; it was a new suit of clothes, rough cheviot, brown with small checks. He dressed slowly and tipped forward the swinging mirror of the bureau to see how the trousers set. Meanwhile Ellis and the Dummy had got out the cards and chips from the drawer of the centre table and had begun a game.

"Better change your mind, Van," said Ellis without raising his eyes from the cards.

"No, sir," answered Van. "You don't know how it is —you never were a college man. Why, I wouldn't miss a football game for anything. Talk about your horse-racing, talk about your baseball—I tell you there's nothing in the world so exciting as a hot football game." He swung into his long high-coloured waterproof and stood behind Ellis, watching his game for a moment while he tied a couple of long silk streamers to his umbrella handle.

"It's one of the college colours," he explained. "Seems like old times back at Harvard." Ellis snorted with contempt.

"Such kids!" he growled.

"I saw one of the coaches go down the street a little while ago," continued Vandover, still watching Ellis shuffle and deal. "There were about twenty college men on top, and they had a big bulldog all harnessed out in their colours, and they were blowing fish-horns, and I tell you it made me wish I was one of them again." Ellis did not answer; it was probable he did not hear. Both he and the Dummy were settling down for a game that no doubt would last all the afternoon. Vandover made them free of his room, and they often gambled there when he was away. But it invariably made Ellis nervous to have anyone stand behind his chair while he was playing; he began to move about uneasily. By and by he looked at his watch. "Better get a move on," he said, "you'll be late."

"Just a minute," answered Vandover, more and more interested in the game. "Go on playing; don't bother about me. Oh, I saw Charlie Geary, too," he continued, "on another coach; there was a party of them. Charlie was with Turner Ravis on the box seat. You remember Turner Ravis, don't you, Bandy? The girl I used to go with."

"There's a girl I never liked," observed Ellis. "She always struck me as being one of these regular snobs."

"Ah, snob is no name for it," assented Vandover.

"She thought she was too damned high-toned for me. As soon as I got into that mess about Ida Wade, she threw me over. No, she didn't want to be associated with me any longer. Well, she can go to the devil. Geary's welcome to her."

"I thought Dolly Haight was going to marry her," said Ellis. "What was the matter *there?*"

"*I* don't know," returned Vandover; "probably Dolly Haight didn't have enough money to suit her. Guess she wants a man that will make his pile in this town and make his way, too. Ah, you bet!"

Half an hour later he was still behind Ellis' chair. Ellis had become so fidgety that he was losing steadily. Once more he turned to Vandover, speaking over his shoulder, "Come on, come on, Van, go along to your football; you make me nervous standing there." Vandover pushed a ten-dollar gold-piece across the table to the Dummy, who was banking, and said:

"Give me that in chips. I'm coming in."

"I thought you were going to the game?" inquired Ellis.

"Ah, the devil!" answered Vandover. "Too much rain."

They had played without interruption all that afternoon, and for once Vandover had all the luck. When they broke up about five o'clock with the understanding to meet again in the Imperial at seven, he had won nearly a hundred dollars.

When Vandover went out to keep this appointment he found the streets—especially Kearney and Market streets—crowded. It was about half-past six. The football game was over and the college men had returned. They were everywhere, marching about in long files, chain-gang fashion, each file headed by a man beating upon a gong, or parading the sidewalks ten abreast, singing college songs or shouting their slogan. At every

moment one heard the college yells answering each
other from street corner to street corner, "Rah, rah,
rah—Rah, rah, rah!" Vandover found the Imperial
crowded with students. The barroom was packed to the
doors, every one of the little rooms in the front hall was
full, while Flossie and Nannie had a great party of the
young fellows in one of the larger rooms in the rear.
Among the crowd in the barroom, three members of the
winning team—heroes, with bandages about their heads
—were breaking training, smoking and drinking for the
first time in many long weeks.

Vandover found Ellis and the Dummy leaning against
the wall in the crowded front passage. They were both
in bad humour, the Dummy sulking because Flossie had
left him for one of the football men, the full-back, a
young blond giant with two dislocated fingers; Ellis in a
rage because he could get no cocktails at the bar, only
straight drinks that night—too much of a crowd. These
damn college sports thought they owned the town. "Ah,
let's get out of here, Van!" he called over the heads of
the throng as soon as Vandover came in sight.

They went out into the street and started in the direction of the restaurant where they had decided to eat
their Thanksgiving dinner. After leaving Vandover that
afternoon Ellis had seen the head waiter of this restaurant and had explained to him the bill of fare that Vandover, the Dummy, and himself had arranged during
their lunch at the Lick House. The streets had relapsed
into a momentary quiet—it was between half-past six
and seven—and most of the college men were gathered
into the hotels and cafés eating dinner. About an hour
later they would reappear again for a moment on their
way to the theatre, which they were to attend in a
body.

But Vandover suddenly discovered that he could not
eat a mouthful, the smell of food revolted him, and little

by little an irregular twitching had overcome his hands and forearms.

He had received a great shock. That same evening, as he was leaving the hotel, the clerk at the office had handed him some letters that had accumulated in his box. Vandover could never think to ask for his mail in the morning as he went in to breakfast. Something was surely wrong with his head of late. Every day he found it harder and harder to remember things. There were three letters altogether: one was the tailor's bill mailed the same day that his last suit had been finished; a second was an advertisement announcing the near opening of the Sutro Baths that were building at that time; and the third a notice from the bank calling his attention to the fact that his account was overdrawn by some sixty dollars.

At first Vandover did not see the meaning of this notice, and thrust it back in his pocket together with the tailor's bill; then slowly an idea struggled into his mind. Was it possible that he no longer had any money at the bank? Was his fifteen thousand gone? From time to time his bank-book had been balanced, and invariably during the first days of each month his checks had come back to him, used and crumpled, covered with strange signatures and stamped in blue ink; but after the first few months he had never paid the least attention to these; he never kept accounts, having a veritable feminine horror of figures. But it was absurd to think that his money was gone. Pshaw! one could not spend fifteen thousand in nine months! It was preposterous! This notice was some technicality that he could not understand. He would look into it the next day. And so he dismissed the wearisome matter from his mind with a shrug of his shoulders as though ridding himself of some troublesome burden. However, the idea persisted. Somehow, between the lines of the printed form he smelt out a fresh disaster. He read it over again and again. All at once as he stood in the doorway of the hotel, turning up the collar of his waterproof and watching the little pools in the hollows of the asphalt pavement to see if it were still raining, the conviction came upon him. In a second he knew that he was ruined. The true meaning of the notice became apparent with the swiftness of a great flash of light. He had spent his fifteen thousand dollars!

The blow was strong enough, sudden enough to penetrate even Vandover's clouded and distorted wits. His nerves were gone in a minute, a sudden stupefying numbness fell upon his brain, and the fear of something unknown, the immense unreasoning terror that had gripped him for the first time the morning after Ida Wade's suicide came back upon him, horrible, crushing, so that he had to shut his teeth against a wild hysterical desire to rush through the streets screaming and waving his arms.

By the time the three friends had reached the restaurant where they were to eat their Thanksgiving dinner, Vandover's appetite had given place to a loathing of the very smell of food, his nervousness was fast approaching hysteria, the little nerve clusters all over his body seemed to be crisping and writhing like balls of tiny serpents, at intervals he would twitch sharply as though startled at some sudden noise, his breath coming short, his heart beating quick.

They had their dinner in one of the private rooms of the restaurant on the second floor. All through the meal Vandover struggled to keep himself in hand, fighting with all his strength against this reappearance of his old enemy, this sudden return of the dreadful crisis, determined not to make an exhibition of himself before the others. He pretended to eat, and forced himself to talk, joining in with Ellis, who was badgering the Dummy about Flossie. The proper thing to do was to fill the Dummy's glass while his attention was otherwise absorbed, and in the end to get him so drunk that he could talk. Toward the end of the dinner Ellis was successful. All at once the Dummy got upon his feet, his eyes were glazed with drunkenness, he swayed about in an irregular circle, holding up, now by the table, now by the chair-back, and now by the wall behind him. He was very angry, exasperated beyond control by Ellis' raillery and abuse. He forgot himself and uttered a series of peculiar cries very faint and shrill, like the sounds of a voice heard through a telephone when some imperfection of transmission prevents one from distinguishing the words. His mouth was wide open and his tongue rolled about in an absurd way between his teeth. Now and then one could catch a word or two. Ellis went into spasms of laughter, holding his sides, gasping for breath. Vandover could not help being amused, and the two laughed at the Dummy's stammering rage until their breath was spent. Throughout the rest of the evening the Dummy recommenced from time to time, rising unsteadily to his feet, shaking his fists, pouring out a stream of little ineffectual birdlike twitterings, trying to give Ellis abuse for abuse, trying to talk long after it had ceased to amuse the other two. Ellis had been drinking for nearly six hours, without the liquor producing the slightest effect upon him; long since, the Dummy was hopelessly drunk; and now Vandover, who had been drinking upon an empty stomach, began to grow very noisy and boisterous. Little by little Ellis himself commenced to lose his self-control. By and by he and Vandover began to sing, each independent of the other, very hoarse and loud. The Dummy joined them, making a hideous and lamentable noise which so affected Ellis that he pretended to howl at it like a little dog overcome by mournful music. But suddenly Ellis had an idea, crying out thickly, between two hiccoughs:

"Hey, there, Van, do your dog-act for us! Go on! Bark for us!"

By this time Vandover was very nearly out of his head, his drunkenness finishing what his nervousness had begun. The attack was fast approaching culmination; strange and unnatural fancies began to come and go in his brain.

"Go on, Van!" urged Ellis, his eyes heavy with alcohol. "Go on, do your dog-act!"

All at once it was as though an angry dog were snarling and barking over a bone there under the table about their feet. Ellis roared with laughter, but suddenly he himself was drunk. All the afternoon he had kept himself in hand; now his intoxication came upon him in a moment. The skin around his eyes was purple and swollen, the pupils themselves were contracted; they grew darker, taking on the colour of bitumen. Suddenly he swept glasses, plates, castor, knives, forks, and all from off the table with a single movement of his arm. Then the alcohol overcame him all in an instant like a poisonous gas. He swayed forward in his chair and fell across the stripped table, his head rolling inertly between his outstretched arms. He did not move again.

In a neighbouring room young Haight had been dining with some college fellows, fraternity men, all friends of his, upon whose coach he had ridden to and from the game. He had heard Vandover and Ellis in the room across the hall and had recognized their voices. Haight had never been a friend of Ellis, but no one, not even Turner, had grieved more over Vandover's ruin than had his old-time college chum.

Young Haight heard the noise of the falling crockery as Ellis swept the table clear, and turned his head sharply, listening. There was a moment's silence after this, and Haight, fearing some accident had happened, stepped out into the hall and stood there a moment listening again, his head inclined toward the closed door. He heard no groaning, no exclamations of pain, not even any noise of conversation; only through the closed door came a steady sound of barking.

Puzzled, he tried the door and, finding it locked, as he had expected, put one foot upon the knob, and catching hold of the top jamb, raised himself up and looked down through the open space that answered for a transom.

The room was very warm, the air thick with the smell of cooked food, the fumes of whisky, and the acrid odour of cigar smoke. Ellis had rolled from his chair and lay upon the floor sprawling on his face in the wreck of the table. Near to him, likewise upon the floor, but sitting up, his back against the wall, was the Dummy. He was muttering incessantly to himself, as if delighted at having found his tongue, his head swaying on his shoulders, and a strange murmur, soft, birdlike, meaningless, like sounds heard from a vast distance, coming from his wide-open mouth.

Vandover was sitting bolt upright in his chair, his hands gripping the table, his eyes staring straight before him. He was barking incessantly. It was evident that now he could not stop himself; it was like hysterical laughter, a thing beyond his control. Twice young Haight called him by name, kicking the door as his leg hung against it. At last Vandover heard him. Then as he caught sight of his face over the door he raised his upper lip above his teeth and snarled at him, long and viciously.

As Haight dropped down into the hall a waiter came running up; he, too, had heard the noise of the breaking dishes. As he thrust his key into the lock he paused a moment, listening and looking in a puzzled way at young Haight. "They have a dog in here, then? They had no dog when they came. That's funny!"

"Open the door," said young Haight, quietly. Once inside Haight went directly to Vandover, crying out: "Come! come on, Van! come home with me." Vandover started suddenly, looking about him bewildered, drawing his hand across his face.

"Home," he repeated, vaguely; "yes, that's the idea. Let's go home. I want to go to bed. Hello, Dolly! where did *you* come from? Say, Dolly, let me tell you—listen here—come down here close; you mustn't mind me; you know I'm a wolf mostly!"

They went down toward the Lick House. Vandover grew steadier after a few minutes in the open air. Young Haight locked arms with him; they went on together in silence. By this time the streets were crowded again, the theatres were over, and the college men were once more at large. Now they were all gathered together into one immense procession, headed by a brass band in a brewer's wagon, and they tramped aimlessly to and fro about Kearney and Market streets, making a hideous noise. At the head the band was playing a popular quick-step with a great banging of a bass drum. The college men in the front ranks were singing one song, those in the rear another, while the middle of the column was given over to an abominable medley of fish-horns, policemen's rattles, and great Chinese gongs. At stated intervals the throng would halt and give the college yell.

"Dolly, you and I used to do that," said Vandover, looking after the procession. He had himself well in hand by this time. "What was the matter with me back there at the restaurant, Dolly?" he asked after a while.

"Oh, you'd been drinking a good deal, I guess," answered young Haight. "You—you had some queer idea about yourself!"

"Yes, I know," answered Vandover, quickly. "Fancied I was some kind of a beast, didn't I—some kind of wolf? I have that notion sometimes and I can't get it out of my head. It's curious just the same."

They went up to Vandover's room. Vandover lit the gas, but he could hardly keep back an exclamation as the glare suddenly struck young Haight's face. What in heaven's name was the matter with his old-time chum? He seemed to be blighted, shattered, struck down by some terrible, overwhelming calamity. A dreadful anguish looked through his eyes. The sense of a hopeless misery had drawn and twisted his face. There could be no doubt that something had made shipwreck of his life. Vandover was looking at a ruined man.

"My God, Dolly!" exclaimed Vandover, "what's happened to you? You look like a death's-head, man! What's gone wrong? Aren't you well?"

Haight caught his friend's searching gaze, and for a moment they looked at each other without speaking. There was no mistaking the fearful grief that smouldered behind Haight's dull, listless eyes. For a moment Vandover thought of Turner Ravis. But even if she had turned him off, that alone would not account for his friend's fearful condition of mind and body.

"What is it, Dolly?" persisted Vandover. "We used to be pretty good chums, not so long ago."

They sat down on the edge of the bed, and for a moment their positions seemed reversed: Haight the one to be protected and consoled, Vandover the shielding and self-reliant one.

Young Haight passed his hand over his face before he answered, and Vandover noticed that his fingers trembled like an old man's.

"Do you remember that night, Van, when you and Charlie and I all went out to Turner's house, and we had *tamales* and beer, and a glass broke in that peculiar way, and I cut my lip?"

Vandover nodded, forcing his attention against the alcoholic fumes, to follow his friend's words.

"We went down to the Imperial afterward," Haight continued, "and ran into Ellis, and we had something, more to eat. Do you remember that as we sat there, Toby, the waiter, brought Flossie in, and she sat there with us a while?"

He paused, choosing his words. Vandover listened closely, trying to recall the incident.

"She kissed me," said young Haight slowly, "and the court-plaster came off. You know I never had anything to do with women, Van. I always tried to keep away from them. But that's where my life practically came to an end."

"You mean——" began Vandover. "You mean— that you—that Flossie——?"

Haight nodded.

"Good God! I can't believe it. It's not possible! I *know* Flossie!"

Haight shook his head, smiling grimly.

"I can't help that, Van," said he. "There's no denying facts, there's no other possible explanation! As soon as I knew, I went to the doctors here, and then I went to New York for treatment, but there's no hope. I didn't know, you see. I didn't believe it possible. Turner Ravis and I were engaged. I waited too long! There's only one escape for me now." His voice dropped, he stared for a moment at the floor. Then he straightened up, and said in a different tone, "But, damn it, Van, let's not talk about it! I'm haunted with the thing day and night. I want to talk to you! I want to talk to you seriously. You know you are ruining yourself, old man!"

But Vandover interrupted him with a gesture, saying, "Don't go on, Dolly; it isn't the least use. There *was* a time for that, but that was long ago. I used to care, I used to be sorry and all that, but I'm not now. Ruining myself? Why, I *have* ruined myself long ago. We're both ruined—only in your case it wasn't your fault. It's too late for me now, and I'm even not sorry that it *is* too late. Dolly, I don't *want* to pull up. You can't imagine a man fallen as low as that, can you? I couldn't imagine it myself a few years ago. I'm going right straight to the devil now, and you might as well stand aside and give me a free course, for I'm bound to get there sooner or later. I suppose you would think that a man who could see this as plainly as I do would be afraid, would have remorse and all that sort of thing. Well, I did at first. I'll never forget the night when I first saw it; came near shooting myself, but I got over it, and now I'm used to the idea. Dolly, *I can get used to almost anything.* Nothing makes much difference to me nowadays—only I like to play cards. Look here!" he went on, laying out the notice from the bank upon the table, "this came to-day. You see what it is! I sold the old house on California Street. Well, I've gambled away that money in less than a year. It seems that I'm a financial ruin now, but"—and he began to laugh—"I live through it some-how. The news didn't prevent me from getting drunk to-night."

After young Haight was gone, Vandover went to bed, turning out the gas and drawing down the window half-way from the top. The wine had made him sleepy; he was dropping away into a very grateful doze when a sudden shock, a violent leap of every nerve in his body, brought him up to a sitting posture, gasping for breath, his heart fluttering, his hands beating at the empty air. He settled down again, turning upon his pillow, closing his eyes, very weary, longing for a good night's sleep. Dolly Haight's terrible story, his unjustified fate, and the hopeless tragedy of it, came back to him. Vandover would gladly have changed places with him. Young Haight had the affection and respect of even those that

knew. He, Vandover, had thrown away his friends' love
and their esteem with the rest of the things he had once
valued. His thoughts, released from all control of his
will, began to come and go through his head with incredible rapidity, confused ideas, half-remembered
scenes, incidents of the past few days, bits and ends of
conversation recalled for no especial reason, all galloping
across his brain like a long herd of terrified horses; an
excitement grew upon him, a strange thrill of exhilaration. He was broad awake now, but suddenly his left
leg, his left arm and wrist, all his left side jerked with
the suddenness of a sprung trap; so violent was the
shock that the entire bed shook and creaked with it.
Then the inevitable reaction followed, the slow crisping
and torsion of his nerves, twisting upon each other like
a vast swarm of tiny serpents; it seemed to begin with
his ankles, spreading slowly to every part of his body;
it was a veritable torture, so poignant that Vandover
groaned under it, shutting his eyes. He could not keep
quiet a second—to lie in bed was an impossibility; he
threw the bedclothes from him and sprang up. He did
not light the gas, but threw on his bathrobe and began
to walk the floor. Even as he walked, his eyelids drooped
lower and lower. The need of sleep overcame him like a
narcotic, but as soon as he was about to lose himself he
would be suddenly and violently awakened by the same
shock, the same jangling recoil of his nerves. Then his
hands and head seemed to swell; next, it was as though
the whole room was too small for him. He threw open
the window and, leaning upon his elbows, looked out.

The clouds had begun to break, the rain was gradually
ceasing, leaving in the air a damp, fresh smell, the smell
of wet asphalt and the odour of dripping woodwork.
It was warm; the atmosphere was dank, heavy, tepid.
One or two stars were out, and a faint grey light showed
him the vast reach of roofs below stretching away to

meet the abrupt rise of Telegraph Hill. Not far off the slender, graceful smokestack puffed steadily, throwing off continually the little flock of white jets that rose into the air very brave and gay, but in the end dwindled irresolutely, discouraged, disheartened, fading sadly away, vanishing under the night, like illusions disappearing at the first touch of the outside world. As Vandover leaned from his window, looking out into the night with eyes that saw nothing, the college slogan rose again from the great crowd of students who still continued to hold the streets.

"Rah, rah, rah! Rah, rah, rah!"

He turned back into the room, groping among the bottles on his washstand for his bromide of potassium. As he poured out the required dose into the teaspoon his hand twitched again sharply, flirting the medicine over his bared neck and chest, exposed by the bathrobe which he had left open at the throat. It was cold, and he shivered a bit as he wiped it dry with the back of his hand.

He knew very well that his nervous attack was coming on again. As he set down the bottle upon the washstand he muttered to himself, "Now I'm going to have a night of it." He began to walk the floor again with great strides, fighting with all his pitiful, shattered mind against the increasing hysteria, trying to keep out of his brain the strange hallucination that assailed it from time to time, the hallucination of a thing four-footed, a thing that sulked and snarled. The hotel grew quiet; a watchman went down the hall turning out each alternate gas-jet. Just outside of the door was a burner in a red globe, fixed at a stair landing to show the exit in case of fire. This burned all night and it streamed through the transom of Vandover's room, splotching the ceiling with a great square of red light. Vandover was in torment, overcome now by that same fear with

which he had at last become so familiar, the unreasoning
terror of something unknown. He uttered an exclamation, a suppressed cry of despair, of misery, and then
suddenly checked himself, astonished, seized with the
fancy that his cry was not human, was not of himself,
but of something four-footed, the snarl of some exasperated brute. He paused abruptly in his walk, listening, for what he did not know. The silence of the great
city spread itself around him, like the still waters of
some vast lagoon. Through the silence he heard the
noise of the throng of college youths. They were returning, doubling upon their line of march. A long puff of
tepid air breathing through the open window brought
to his ears the distant joyous sound of their slogan:
  "Rah, rah, rah! Rah, rah, rah!"
  They passed by along the adjacent street, their sounds
growing faint. Vandover took up his restless pacing
again. Little by little the hallucination gained upon
him; little by little his mind slipped from his grasp. The
wolf—the beast—whatever the creature was, seemed
in his diseased fancy to grow stronger in him from moment to moment. But with all his strength he fought
against it, fought against this strange mania, that overcame him at these periodical intervals—fought with his
hands so tightly clenched that the knuckles grew white,
and the nails bit into the palm. It seemed to him that
in some way his personality divided itself into three.
There was himself, the real Vandover of every day, the
same familiar Vandover that looked back at him from
his mirror; then there was the wolf, the beast, whatever
the creature was that lived in his flesh, and that struggled with him now, striving to gain the ascendency, to
absorb the real Vandover into its own hideous identity;
and last of all, there was a third self, formless, very
vague, elusive, that stood aside and watched the strife
of the other two. But as he fought against his madness,

concentrating all his attention with a tremendous effort of the will, the queer numbness that came upon his mind whenever he exerted it enwrapped his brain like a fog and this third self grew vaguer than ever, dwindled and disappeared. Somehow it seemed to be associated with consciousness, for after this the sense of the reality of things grew dim and blurred to him. He ceased to know exactly what he was doing. His intellectual parts dropped away one by one, leaving only the instincts, the blind, unreasoning impulses of the animal.

Still he continued his restless, lurching walk back and forth in his room, his head hanging low and swinging from side to side with the movement of his gait. He had become so nervous that the restraint imposed upon his freedom of movement by his bathrobe and his loose night-clothes chafed and irritated him. At length he had stripped off everything.

Suddenly and without the slightest warning Vandover's hands came slowly above his head and he dropped forward, landing upon his palms. All in an instant he had given way, yielding in a second to the strange hallucination of that four-footed thing that sulked and snarled. Now without a moment's stop he ran back and forth along the wall of the room, upon the palms of his hands and his toes, a ludicrous figure, like that of certain clowns one sees at the circus, contortionists walking about the sawdust, imitating some kind of enormous dog. Still he swung his head from side to side with the motion of his shuffling gait, his eyes dull and fixed. At long intervals he uttered a sound, half word, half cry, "Wolf—wolf!" but it was muffled, indistinct, raucous, coming more from his throat than from his lips. It might easily have been the growl of an animal. A long time passed. Naked, four-footed, Vandover ran back and forth the length of the room.

By an hour after midnight the sky was clear, all the

stars were out, the moon a thin, low-swinging scimitar, set behind the black mass of the roofs of the city, leaving a pale bluish light that seemed to come from all quarters of the horizon. As the great stillness grew more and more complete, the persistent puffing of the slender tin stack, the three gay and joyous little noises, each sounding like a note of discreet laughter interrupted by a cough, became clear and distinct. Inside the room there was no sound except the persistent patter of something four-footed going up and down. At length even this sound ceased abruptly. Worn out, Vandover had just fallen, dropping forward upon his face with a long breath. He lay still, sleeping at last. The remnant of the great band of college men went down an adjacent street, raising their cadenced slogan for the last time. It came through the open window, softened as it were by the warm air, thick with damp, through which it travelled:

"Rah, rah, rah! Rah, rah, rah!"

Naked, exhausted, Vandover slept profoundly, stretched at full length at the foot of the bare, white wall of the room beneath two of the little placards, scrawled with ink, that read, "Stove here"; "Mona Lisa here."

O N A certain Saturday morning two years later Vandover awoke in his room at the Reno House, the room he had now occupied for fifteen months. [11]

One might almost say that he had been expelled from the Lick House. For a time he had tried to retain his room there with the idea of paying his bills by the money he should win at gambling. But his bad luck was now become a settled thing—almost invariably he lost. At last Ellis and the Dummy had refused to play with him, since he was never able to pay them when they won. They had had a great quarrel. Ellis broke with him sullenly, growling wrathfully under his heavy moustache, and the Dummy had written upon his pad— so hastily and angrily that the words could hardly be read—that he would not play with professional gamblers, men who supported themselves by their winnings. Damn it! one had to be a gentleman.

Next, Vandover had tried to borrow some money of Charlie Geary. Geary had told him that he could not afford as much as Vandover needed. Then Vandover became enraged. He had long since seen that Geary had practically swindled him out of his block in the Mission, and at that very moment the huge boot and shoe "concern" was completing the factory built upon the ground that Vandover had once owned. Geary had cleared seven thousand dollars on his "deal." His refusal to loan his old-time friend fifty dollars upon this occasion had exasperated Vandover out of all bounds. There was a scene. Vandover told Geary what he thought of his "deal" in very plain words. They shouted "swindler" and "gambler" into each other's faces; the whole office was aroused; Vandover was ejected by force. On a stair landing halfway to the street he sat down and cried into his arms folded upon his knees. When he returned to his room he had a sudden return of his dreadful nervous malady and barked and whined under the bed.

Then Vandover wrote a fifty-dollar check on the bank—the same bank that had just notified him that he was overdrawn—and passed it upon young Haight. How he came to do the thing he could not tell; it might have been the influence of Geary's successful robbery, or it might have been that he had at last lost all principle, all sense of honour and integrity. At any rate, he could not bring himself to feel very sorry. He knew that young Haight would not prosecute him for the dishonesty; he traded upon Haight's magnanimity; he only felt glad that he had the fifty dollars. But by this time Vandover did not even wonder at his own baseness and degradation. A few years ago this would have been the case; now his character was so changed that the theft seemed somehow consistent. He had destroyed young Haight's friendship for him. He had cast from him his college chum, his best friend, but neither did this affect him. Nothing made much difference to him now.

Nevertheless, Vandover was evicted from the Lick House three days after he had stolen young Haight's money. Instead of paying his bills with the amount, he gambled it away in a back room of a new café on Market Street with Toby, the red-eyed waiter from the Imperial and a certain German "professor," a billiard marker, who wore a waistcoat figured with little designs of the Eiffel Tower, and who was a third owner in a trotting mare named Tomato Ketchup.

Vandover was now left with only his bonds, his U. S. 4 per cents. These brought him but sixty-nine dollars a quarter, or as he had had it arranged, twenty-three dollars a month. Just at this time, as if by a miracle, a veritable God from the Machine, Vandover's lawyer, Mr. Field, found him an opportunity to earn some money. For the first and only time in his life Vandover knew what it was to work for a living. The work that Field secured for him was the work of painting those little pictures on the lacquered surface of iron safes, those little oval landscapes between the lines of red and gold lettering—landscapes, rugged gorges, ocean steamships under all sail, mountain lakes with sailboats careening upon their surfaces, the boat indicated by two little triangular dabs of Chinese white, one for the sail itself and the other for its reflection in the water. Sometimes even he was called upon to paint other little pictures upon the sides of big express wagons—two horses, one white and the other bay, galloping very free in an open field, their manes and tails flying, or a bulldog, very savage, sitting upon a green and black safe, or the head of a mastiff with a spiked collar about his neck.

What with the pay for this sort of work and the interest of his bonds, Vandover managed to lead a haphazard sort of life, living about in cheap lodging-houses and cheap restaurants. But he was never more than a second-class workman, and he was so irregular that he could never be depended upon.

The moment he began to paint again—even to paint such pitiful little pictures as these—the same familiar experience repeated itself, the unwillingness of his fingers, their failure to rightly interpret his ideas, the resulting crudity of his work, the sudden numbness in his brain, the queer, tense sensation behind his eyes. But Vandover had long since become accustomed to these symptoms and would not have minded them at this time had it not been that they were occasionally followed by a nervous twitching and jerking of his whole arm, so that sometimes he could not hold the brush steady a minute at a time.

For two years he had drifted about the city, living now here and now there, a real hand-to-mouth existence, sinking a little lower each day. Now, no one knew him. He had completely passed out of the lives of Haight, Geary, and Ellis, just as before he had passed out of the life of Turner Ravis. At the end of the first year they had ceased even to think about him. For a long time they thought that he was dead, until one day Ellis declared that he had seen him far down on Kearney Street, near the Barbary Coast, looking at the pictures in the illustrated weeklies that were tacked upon the showboard on the sidewalk in front of a stationer's. Ellis had told the others that on this occasion Vandover seemed to be more sickly than ever; he described his appearance in detail, wagging his head at his own story, pursing his lips, putting his chin in the air. Vandover had worn an old paint-stained pair of blue trousers, fastened with a strap, so that his shirt showed below his vest; he had no collar, and he had allowed his beard to grow, a straggling thin beard, through which one could see the buttons of his shirt, a dirty beard full of the cracker crumbs from the free lunch-counters of cheap saloons; he had on a hat which he had worn when they had known him; but one should see that hat now!

It was all true: little by little Vandover had abandoned all interest in his personal appearance. Of course it was impossible for him to dress well at this time, but he had even lost regard for decency and cleanliness. He washed himself but rarely. He had even acquired the habit of sleeping with all his clothes on during the colder nights of the year.

Nothing made any difference. Gradually his mind grew more and more clouded; he became stupid, sluggish.

He went about the city from dawn to dark, his feet dragging, his head hanging low and swinging from side to side with the motion of his gait. He rarely spoke; his eyes took on a dull, glazed appearance, filmy, like the eyes of a dead fish. At certain intervals his mania came upon him, the strange hallucination of something four-footed, the persistent fancy that the brute in him had now grown so large, so insatiable, that it had taken everything, even to his very self, his own identity—that he had literally *become the brute*. The attack passed off and left him wondering, perplexed.

The Reno House, where Vandover had lived for some fifteen months, was a sort of hotel on Sacramento Street below Kearney. The neighbourhood was low—just on the edge of the Barbary Coast, abounding in stores for second-hand clothing, saloons, pawnshops, gun-stores, bird-stores, and the shops of Chinese cobblers. Around the corner on Kearney Street was a concert hall, a dive, to which the admission was free. Near by was the old Plaza.

Underneath the hotel on the ground floor were two saloons, a barber shop, and a broom manufactory. The lodgers themselves were for the most part "transients," sailors lounging about shore between two voyages, Swedes and Danes, farmhands, grape-pickers, and cow-punchers from distant parts of the state, a few lost women, and Japanese cooks and second-boys remaining there while they advertised for positions.

Vandover sank to the grade of these people at once with that fatal adaptability to environment which he had permitted himself to foster throughout his entire life, and which had led him to be contented in almost any circumstances. It was as if the brute in him were forever seeking a lower level, wallowing itself lower and lower into the filth and into the mire, content to be foul, content to be prone, to be inert and supine.

It was Saturday morning about a quarter of nine. The wet season had begun early that year. Though this was but the middle of September, the rain had fallen steadily since the previous Wednesday. Its steady murmur, prolonged and soothing like the purring of a great cat, filled Vandover's room with a pleasant sound. The air of the room was thick and foul, heavy with the odour of cooking, onions, and stale bedding. It was very warm; there was no ventilation. Vandover lay upon the bed half awake, dozing under the thick coarse blankets and soiled counterpane. With the exception of his shoes and coat he wore all his clothes. He was glad to be warm, to be stupefied by the heat of the bedding and the bad air of the room.

In the next room a Portuguese fruit vender, very drunk, was fighting with the tin pitcher and pasteboard bowl on his wash-stand, trying to wet his head, swearing and making a hideous clatter. At length he tipped them over upon the floor and gave the pitcher a great kick. The noise roused Vandover; he sat up in bed, stretching, rubbing his hands over his face. About the same moment the clock in the office downstairs struck nine. Vandover let his feet drop to the floor and sat on the edge of the bed, looking vaguely about him. His face, ordinarily very pale, was oily from sleep and red upon one side from long contact with the pillow, the marks of the creases still showing upon his cheek. His long straight hair fell about his eyes and ears like a tangled mane. A thin straggling beard and moustache, of a brown much lighter than his hair, covered the lower part of his face. His nose was long and pinched, while brown and puffed pockets hung beneath his eyes.

He wore a white shirt very crumpled and dirty, a low standing collar, and a black four-in-hand necktie, very greasy. His trousers were striped and of a slate-blue colour—the "blue pants" of the ready-made clothing stores. Still sitting on the bed, Vandover continued his stupid gaze about the room.

The room was small, and at some long-forgotten, almost prehistoric period had been covered with a yellowish paper, stamped with a huge pattern of flowers that looked like the flora of a carboniferous strata, a pattern repeated to infinity wherever the eye turned. Newspapers were pasted upon the ceiling and a great square of very dirty matting covered the floor. There were a few pieces of furniture, very old-fashioned, made of pine, with a black walnut veneer, two chairs, a washstand, and the bed. A great pile of old newspapers tied up with bale rope was kicked into one corner. Two gas brackets without globes stretched forth their long arms over the empty space where the bureau should have been. Under the single window was Vandover's trunk, and upon it his colour box and pots of paint. His hat hung upon a hook screwed to the door. The hat had once been black, but it had long since turned to a greenish hue, and sweat stains were showing about the band.

Vandover dressed slowly. He straightened his hair a bit before the cheap mirror that hung over the washstand, putting on his hat immediately after to keep it in place. He washed his hands in the dirty water that had stood in his pasteboard bowl since the previous afternoon, but left his face as it was. He put on his coat, an old cutaway which had been his best years ago, but which was now absurdly small for him, the breast all spotted and streaked with old stains of soup and gravy. Last of all he drew on his shoes. They were new. Vandover had bought them two days before for a dollar and ninety cents. They were lined so as to make socks superfluous.

It had been a bad week with Vandover. The paint-shop had given him no work to do for ten days, and he had been forced to get along in some way upon the interest of his bonds—that is to say, upon five dollars and seventy-five cents a week. Two dollars and seventy-five cents of this went for his room rent, one dollar and ninety for his shoes, and Tuesday afternoon he had bought a package of cigarettes for ten cents. By Saturday morning he had spent seventy-five cents for food.

When the paint-shop gave him enough work it was Vandover's custom to buy a week's commutation ticket at a certain restaurant. He never ate at the hotel; it was too expensive. By the commutation system he could buy two dollars and twenty-five cents' worth of meals for two dollars, paying in tickets at each meal.

But such a thing had been impossible this week. He had been forced to fall back upon the free-lunch system. In two years Vandover had learned a great deal; even his dulled wits had been sharpened when it had come to a question of food. The brute in him might destroy all his finer qualities, but even the brute had to feed. When work failed him at the beginning of the week Vandover was not unprepared for the contingency; the thing had happened before and he knew how to meet it.

On Monday he beat up and down the Barbary Coast, picking out fifteen or twenty saloons which supported a free-lunch counter in connection with the bar. He took his breakfast Monday morning at the first of these. He paid five cents for a glass of beer and ate his morning's meal at the lunch counter: stew, bread, and cheese. At noon he made his dinner at the second saloon on his route. Here he had another glass of beer, a great plate of soup, potato salad, and pretzels. Thus he managed to feed himself throughout the week.

It was always his great desire to feed well at Sunday's dinner, to spend at least a quarter on that meal. It was something to be looked forward to throughout the entire week. But to get twenty-five cents ahead when he was out of work was bitter hard. That week he had started out with the determination to eat but two meals a day. He would thus save five cents daily and by Sunday morning would be thirty cents to the good. But each day his resolution broke down. At breakfast he would resolve to go without his lunch, at lunch he would make up his mind to go without supper, and at supper he would tell himself that now at least his determination was irrevocable—he would eat no breakfast the next morning. But on each and every occasion his hunger proved too strong, his feet carried him irresistibly to the saloon lunch counters, whether he would or no. At no time in his life had Vandover accustomed himself to self-denial; he could hardly begin now.

At length Saturday morning had come, and while he was dressing he realized that he could not look forward to any unusual dinner the next day at noon. The disappointment had all the force of an unexpected disaster and he began keenly to regret his weakness of the past week. Suddenly Vandover resolved that he would go without food all that day; it would be a saving of fifteen cents, which, added to the five cents that he would spend anyway for his dinner, would almost make a quarter. He knew where he could dine excellently well for twenty cents. However, he could not make up his mind to go without his Sunday morning's breakfast. That, he told himself, he must eat.

Once dressed, Vandover went out. Fortunately, the rain had stopped. He went on down through the reeking, steaming streets to one of the big fruit markets not far from the water front. The Portuguese fruit vender who roomed next to him at the Reno House was employed at a stall here. Vandover knew him a little, and it was not hard for him to get a thin slice of cocoanut out from the inside rind of one of those that were lying cracked open among his other wares.

All the morning Vandover chewed this slice of cocoa-

nut, at the same time drinking a great deal of water; for
hours he deadened the pang of hunger by this means.
He passed the time for the most part sitting on the
benches in the Plaza reading an old newspaper that he
had found under a seat. The sun came out a little; Vandover found the warmth very grateful. He told himself
that he could easily hold out until the next morning.

He had forgotten about the time and was surprised
when the whistles all over the town began to blow for
noon. In an instant Vandover was hungry again. It was
all one that he chewed the little pulp of cocoanut rind
more vigorously than ever, swallowed great draughts
of water of the public fountains; the little gnawing just
between his chest and his stomach began to persist. He
got up and began to walk. He left the Plaza behind him,
crossed Kearney Street and went on down Clay Street
till he reached the water front. For a time he found a
certain diversion among the shipping and especially in
watching a gang of caulkers knocking away at the seams
of an immense coal steamer. He sat upon a great iron
clamped pile, spitting into the yellow water below. The
air was full of the smell of bilge and oakum and fish; the
thousands of masts made a grey maze against the sky;
occasionally an empty truck trundled over the hollow
docks with a sound of distant cannon. A weakness, a
little trembling that seemed to come from the pit of his
stomach, began upon Vandover. He was very hungry.
Evidently the slice of cocoanut was no longer effective.
He swallowed it and lit a cigarette, one of the half-
dozen still left of the pack he had bought the Tuesday
before.

He smoked the cigarette slowly, inhaling as much of
the smoke as he could. This quieted him for an hour,
but he had the folly to smoke again at the end of that
time, and at once—as he might have known—was
hungry again. Until dark he struggled along, drinking

563

water continually, chewing chips of wood, toothpicks, bits of straw, anything so that the action of his jaws might cheat the demands of his stomach. Toward half-past seven in the evening he returned to his room in the Reno House. If he could get to sleep that would be best of all. On the stairs of the hotel, while going up to his room, the strong smell of cooking onions came suddenly to his nostrils. It was delicious. Vandover breathed in the warm savour with long sighs, closing his eyes; a great feebleness overcame him. He asked himself how he could get through the next twelve hours.

An hour later he went to bed, hiccoughing from the water he had been drinking all day. By this time he had torn the paper from one of his cigarettes and was chewing the tobacco. This was his last resort, an expedient which he fell back upon only in great extremity, as it invariably made him sick to his stomach. He slept a little, but in half an hour was broad awake again, gagging and retching dreadfully. There was nothing on his stomach to throw up, and now at length the hunger in him raged like a wolf. Vandover was in veritable torment.

He could not keep his thoughts away from the money in his pocket, a nickel and two dimes. He could eat if he wanted to, could satisfy this incessant craving. At every moment the temptation grew stronger. Why should he wait until morning? He had the money; it was only a matter of a few minutes' walk to the nearest saloon. But he set his face against this desire; he had held out so long that it would be a pity to give in now; he was not so very hungry, after all. No, no; he would not give in, he was strong enough; as long as he used his will he need not succumb. It was just a question of asserting his strength of mind, of calling up the better part of him. Even better than eating would be the satisfaction of knowing that he had shown himself stronger than his lower animal appetite. No; he would not give in.

Hardly a minute after he had arrived at this resolution Vandover found himself drawing on his coat and shoes making ready to go out—to go out and eat.

The gas in the room was lit, his money, the nickel and the two dimes, was shut in one of his fists. He was dressing himself with one hand, dressing with feverish, precipitate haste. What had happened? He marvelled at himself, but did not check his preparations an instant. He could not stop, whether he would or no; there was something in him stronger than himself, something that urged him on his feet, that drove him out into the street, something that clamoured for food and that would not be gainsaid. It was the animal in him, the brute, that would be fed, the evil, hideous brute grown now so strong that Vandover could not longer resist it—the brute that had long since destroyed all his finer qualities but that still demanded to be fed, still demanded to live. All the little money that Vandover had saved during the day he spent that night among the coffee houses, the restaurants, and the saloons of the Barbary Coast, continuing to eat even after his hunger was satisfied. Toward daylight he returned to his room, and all dressed as he was flung himself face downward among the coarse blankets and greasy counterpane. For nearly eight hours he slept profoundly, with long snores, prone, inert, crammed and gorged with food.

It was the middle of Sunday afternoon when he awoke. He roused himself and going over to the Plaza sat for a long while upon one of the benches. It was a very bright afternoon and Vandover sat motionless for a long time in the sun while his heavy meal digested, very happy, content merely to be warm, to be well fed, to be comfortable.

THAT winter passed, then the summer; September and October came and went, and by the middle of November the rains set in. One very wet afternoon toward the end of the month Charlie Geary sat at his desk in his own private office. He was unoccupied for the moment, leaning back in his swivel chair, his feet on the table, smoking a cigar. Geary had broken from hid old-time habit of smoking only so many cigars as he could pay for by saving carfare. He was doing so well now that he could afford to smoke whenever he he chose. He was still with the great firm of Beale & Story, and while not in the partnership as yet, had worked up to the position of an assistant. He had cases of his own now, a great many of them, for the most part damage suits against that certain enormous corporation whom it was said was ruining the city and entire state. Geary posed as one of its bitterest enemies, pushing each suit brought against it with a tireless energy, with a zeal that was almost vindictive. He began to fit into his own niche, in the eyes of the public, and just in proportion as the corporation was hated, Geary was admired. Money came to him very fast. He was hardly thirty at this time, but could already be called a rich man.

His "deal" with Vandover had given him a taste for real estate, and now and then, with the greatest caution, he made a few discreet investments. At present he had just completed a row of small cottages across the street from the boot and shoe factory. The cottages held two rooms and a large kitchen. Geary had calculated that the boot and shoe concern would employ nearly a thousand operatives, and he had built his row with the view of accommodating a few of them who had families and who desired to live near the factory. His agents were Adams & Brunt.

It was toward half-past five, there was nothing more that Geary could do that day, and for a moment he leaned back in his swivel chair, before going home, smiling a little, very well pleased with himself. He was still as clever and shrewd as ever, still devoured with an incarnate ambition, still delighted when he could get the better of anyone. He was yet a young man; with the start he had secured for himself, and with the exceptional faculties, the faculties of self-confidence and "push" that he knew himself to possess, there was no telling to what position he might attain. He knew that it was only a question of time—of a short time even —when he would be the practical head of the great firm. Everything he turned his hand to was a success. His row of houses in the Mission might be enlarged to a veritable settlement for every workman in the neighbourhood. His youth, his cleverness, and his ambition, supported by his money on the one hand, and on the other by the vast machinery of the great law firm, could raise him to a great place in the world of men. Gazing through the little blue haze of his cigar smoke, he began to have vague ideas, ideas of advancement, of political successes. Politics fascinated him—such a field of action seemed to be the domain for which he was precisely suited—not the politics of the city or of the state; not the nasty little squabbling of boodlers, lobbyists, and supervisors, but something large, something inspiring, something on a tremendous scale, something to which one could give up one's whole life and energy, something to which one could sacrifice everything—

friendships, fortunes, scruples, principles, life itself, no matter what, anything to be a "success," to "arrive," to "get there," to attain the desired object in spite of the whole world, to ride on at it, trampling down or smashing through everything that stood in the way, blind, deaf, fists and teeth shut tight. Not the little squabbling politics of the city or state, but national politics, the sway and government of a whole people, the House, the Senate, the Cabinet, and the next —why not?—the highest, the best of all, the Executive. Yes, Geary aspired even to the Presidency.

For a moment he allowed himself the indulgence of the delightful dream, then laughed a bit at his own absurdity. But even the entertainment of so vast an idea had made his mind, as it were, big; it was hard to come down to the level again. In spite of himself he went on reasoning in stupendous thoughts, in enormous ideas, figuring with immense abstractions. And then, after all, why not? Other men had striven and attained; other men were even now striving, other men would "arrive"; why should not he? As well he as another. Every man for himself—that was his maxim. It might be damned selfish, but it was human nature: the weakest to the wall, the strongest to the front. Why should not he be in the front? Why not in the very front rank? Why not be even before the front rank itself—the leader? Vast, vague ideas passed slowly across the vision of his mind, ideas that could hardly be formulated into thought ideas of the infinite herd of humanity, driven on as if by some enormous, relentless engine, driven on toward some fearful distant bourne, driven on recklessly at headlong speed. All life was but a struggle to keep from under those myriad spinning wheels that dashed so close behind. Those were happiest who were farthest to the front. To lag behind was peril; to fall was to perish, to be ridden down, to be beaten to the dust, to be inexorably crushed and blotted out beneath that myriad of spinning iron wheels. Geary looked up quickly and saw Vandover standing in the doorway.

For the moment Geary did not recognize the gaunt, shambling figure with the long hair and dirty beard, the greenish hat, and the streaked and spotted coat, but when he did it was with a feeling of anger and exasperation.

"Look here!" he cried, "don't you think you'd better knock before you come in?"

Vandover raised a hand slowly as if in deprecation, and answered slowly and with a feeble, tremulous voice, the voice of an old man: "I did knock, Mister Geary; I didn't mean no offence." He sat down on the edge of the nearest chair, looking vaguely and stupidly about on the floor, moving his head instead of his eyes, repeating under his breath from time to time, "No offence—no, sir—no offence!"

"Shut that door!" commanded Geary. Vandover obeyed. He wore no vest, and the old cutaway coat, fastened by the single remaining button, exposed his shirt to view, abominably filthy, bulging at the waist like a blouse. The "blue pants," held up by a strap, were all foul with mud and grease and paint, and there hung about him a certain odour, that peculiar smell of poverty and of degradation, the smell of stale clothes and of unwashed bodies.

"Well?" said Geary, abruptly.

Vandover put the tips of his fingers to his lips and rolled his eyes about the room, avoiding Geary's glance; then he dropped them to the floor again, looking at the pattern in the carpet.

"Well," repeated Geary, irritated, "you know I haven't got all the time in the world." All at once Vandover began to cry, very softly, snuffling with his nose, his chin twitching, the tears running through his thin, sparse beard.

"Ah, get on to yourself!" shouted Geary, now thoroughly disgusted. "Quit that! Be a man, will you? Stop that! do you hear?" Vandover obeyed, catching his breath and slowly wiping his eyes with the side of his hand.

"I'm no good!" he said at length, wagging his head and blinking through his tears. "I'm—I'm done for and I ain't got no money; yet, of course, you see I don't mean no offence. What I want, you see, is to be a man and not give in and not let the wolf get me, and then I'll go back to Paris. Everything goes round here, very slow, and seems far off; that's why I can't get along, and I'm that hungry that sometimes I twitch all over. I'm down. I ain't got another cent of money and I lost my job at the paint-shop. There's where I drew down twenty dollars a week painting landscapes on safes, you know, and then——"

Geary interrupted him, crying out, "You haven't a cent? Why, what have you done with your bonds?"

"Bonds?" repeated Vandover, dazed and bewildered. "I ain't never had any bonds. What bonds? Oh, yes," he exclaimed, suddenly remembering, "yes, I know, *my* bonds, of course; yes, yes—well, I—those—those, I had to sell those bonds—had some debts, you see, my board and my tailor's bill. They got out some sort of paper after me. Yes, I had forgotten about my bonds. I lost every damned one of them playing cards— gambled 'em all away. Ain't I no good? But I was winner once—just in two nights I won ten thousand dollars. Then I must have lost it again. You see, I get so hungry sometimes that I twitch all over—so, just like that. Lend me a dollar."

For a few moments Geary was silent, watching Vandover curiously, as he sat in a heap on the edge of the chair, fumbling his greenish hat, looking about the floor. Presently he asked:

"When did you lose your job at the paint-shop?"

"Day before yesterday."

"And you are out of work now?"

"Yes," answered Vandover. "I'm broke; I haven't a cent. I'm blest if *I* know how I'm to get along. Lately I've been working for a paint-shop, painting landscapes on safes. I drew down twenty dollars a week there, but I've lost my job."

"Good Lord, Van!" Geary suddenly exclaimed, nodding his head toward him reflectively, "I'm sorry for you!"

The other laughed. "Yes; I suppose I'm a pitiable looking object, but I'm used to it. I don't mind much now as long as I can have a place to sleep and enough to eat. If you can put me in the way of some work, Charlie, I'd be much obliged. You see, that's what I want—work. I don't want to run any bunco game. I'm an honest man—I'm too honest. I gave away all my money to help another poor duck; gave him thousands; he was good to me when I was on my uppers and I meant to repay him. I was grateful. I signed a paper that gave him everything I had. It was in Paris. There's where my bonds went to. He was a struggling artist."

"Look here!" said Geary, willing to be interested, "you might as well be truthful with me. You can't lie to me. Have you gambled away all those bonds, or have you been victimized, or have you still got them? Come, now, spit it out."

"Charlie, I haven't a cent!" answered Vandover, looking him squarely in the face. "Would I be around here and trying to get work from you if I had? No; I gambled it all away. You know I had eighty-nine hundred in U. S. 4 per cents. Well, first I began to pawn things when my money got short—the Old Gentleman's watch that I said I never would part with, then my clothes. I couldn't keep away from the cards. Of course, you can't understand that; gambling was the only thing that could amuse me. Then I began to mortgage my bonds, very little at first. Oh, I went slow! Then I got to selling them. Well, somehow, they all went. For a time I got along by the work at the paint-shop. But they have let me out now; said I was so irregular. I owe for nearly a month at my lodging-place." His eyes sought the floor again, rolling about stupidly. "Nearly a month, and that's what makes me jump and tremble so. You ought to see me sometimes—*b-r-r-r-h!*—and I get to barking! I'm a wolf mostly, you know, or some kind of an animal, some kind of a brute. But I'd be all right if everything didn't go round very slowly, and seem far off. But I'm a wolf. You look out for me; best take care I don't bite you! Wolf—wolf! Ah! It's up four flights at the end of the hall, very dark, eight thousand dollars in a green cloth sack, and lots of lights a-burning. See how long my finger nails are— regular claws; that's the wolf, the brute! Why can't I talk in my mouth instead of in my throat! That's the devil of it. When you paint on steel and iron your colours don't dry out true; all the yellows turn green. But it would 'a' been all straight if they hadn't fined me! I never talked to anybody—that was *my* business, wasn't it? And when all those eight thousand little lights begin to burn red, why, of course that makes you nervous! So I have to drink a great deal of water and chew butcher's paper. That fools him and he thinks he's eating. Just so as I can lay quiet in the Plaza when the sun is out. There's a hack-stand there, you know, and every time that horse tosses his head so's to get the oats in the bottom of the nose-bag he jingles the chains on the poles and, by God! that's funny; makes me laugh every time; sounds gay, and the chain sparkles mighty pretty! Oh, I don't complain. Give me a dollar and I'll bark for you!"

Geary leaned back in his chair listening to Vandover, struck with wonder, marvelling at that which his old chum had come to be. He was sorry for him, too, yet, nevertheless, he felt a certain indefinite satisfaction, a faint exultation over his misfortunes, glad that their positions were not reversed, pleased that he had been clever enough to keep free from those habits, those modes of life that ended in such fashion. He rapped sharply on the table. Vandover straightened up, raising his eyes.

"You want some work?" he demanded.

"Yes; that's what I'm after," answered Vandover, adding, "I must have it!"

"Well," said Geary, hesitatingly, "I can give you something to do, but it will be pretty dirty."

Vandover smiled a little, saying, "I guess you can't give me any work that would be too dirty for me!" With the words he suddenly began to cry again. "I want to be honest, Mister Geary," he exclaimed, drawing the backs of his fingers across his lips; "I want to be honest; I'm down and I don't mean no offence. Charlie, you and I were old chums once at Harvard. My God! to think I was a Harvard man once! Oh I'm a goner now and I ain't got a friend. When I was in the paint-shop they paid me well. I've been in a paint-shop lately painting the little pictures on the safes, little landscapes, you know, and lakes with mountains around them. I pulled down my twenty dollars and findings!"

"Oh, don't be a fool!" cried Geary, ashamed even to see such an exhibition. "If you can't be a man, you can get out. Now, see here, you came up here once and insulted me in my office, and called me a swindler. Ah, you bet you had the swelled head then and insulted me, attacked my honesty and charged me with shoving the queer. Now I never forget those things generally, but I am willing to let that pass this time. I could be nasty now and tell you to rustle for yourself. If you want half a dollar now to get something to eat, why, I'll give it to you. But I don't propose to support you. Ah, no; I guess not! If you want to work I'll give you a chance, but I shall expect you to do good work if I give you my good money for it. You may be drunk now or—*I* don't know what's the matter with you. But you come up here to-morrow at noon, and if you come up here sober or straight or"—Geary began to make awkward gestures in the air with both hands—"come up here to talk *business*, I may have something for you, but I can't stop any longer this evening."

Vandover got upon his feet slowly, turning his greenish hat about by the brim, nodding his head. "All right, all right," he answered. "Thank you very much, Mister Geary. It's very good of you, I'm sure. I'll be around at noon sure."

When Geary was left alone, he walked slowly to his window, and stood there a moment looking aimlessly down into the street, shaking his head repeatedly, astonished at the degradation of his old-time chum. While he stood there he saw Vandover come out upon the sidewalk from the door of the great office building. Geary watched him, very interested.

Vandover paused a moment upon the sidewalk, turning up the collar of his old cutaway coat against the cold trade wind that was tearing through the streets; he thrust both his hands deep into his trousers pockets, gripping his sides with his elbows and drawing his shoulders together, shrinking into a small compass in order to be warm. The wind blew the tails of his cutaway about him like flapping wings. He went up the street, walking fast, keeping to the outside of the sidewalk, his shoulders bent, his head inclined against the wind, his feet dragging after him as he walked. For a moment Geary lost sight of him amid a group of men who were hoisting a piano upon a dray. The street was rather crowded with office boys, clerks, and typewriters going home to supper, and Geary did not catch sight of him again immediately; then all at once he saw him hesitating on a corner of Kearney Street, waiting for an electric car to pass; he crossed the street, running, his hands still in his pockets, and went on hurriedly, dodging in and out of the throng, his high shoulders, long neck, and greenish hat coming into sight at intervals. For a moment he paused to glance into the show window of a tobacconist and pipe-seller's store. A Chinese woman passed him, pattering along lamely, her green jade ear-rings twinkling in the light of a street lamp, newly lighted. Vandover looked after her a moment, gazing stupidly, then suddenly took up his walk again, zigzagging amid the groups on the asphalt, striding along at a great pace, his head low and swinging from side to side as he walked. He was already far down the street; it was dusk; Geary could only catch glimpses of his head and shoulders at long intervals. He disappeared.

About ten minutes before one the next day as Geary came back from lunch he was surprised to see Vandover peeping through the half-open door of his office. He had not thought that Vandover would come back.

Of the many different stories that Vandover had told about the disappearance of his bonds, the one that was propably truest was the one that accounted for the thing by his passion for gambling. For a long time after his advent at the Reno House this passion had been dormant; he knew no one with whom he could play, and every cent of his income now went for food and lodging. But one day, about six months before his visit to Geary's office, Vandover saw that the proprietor of the Reno House had set up a great bagatelle board in a corner of the reading room. A group of men, sailors, ranchmen, and fruit venders were already playing. Vandover approached and watched the game, very interested in watching the uncertain course of the marble jog-jogging among the pins. The clear little note of the bell or the dry rattle as the marble settled quickly into one of the lucky pockets thrilled him from head to foot; his hands trembled, all at once his whole left side twitched sharply.

From that day the fate of the rest of Vandover's little money was decided. In two weeks he had lost twenty dollars at bagatelle, obtaining the money by selling a portion of his bonds at a certain broker's on Montgomery Street. As soon as he had begun to gamble again the old habits of extravagance had come back upon him. From the moment he knew that he could get all the money he wanted by the mere signing of a paper, he ceased to be economical, scorning the former niggardliness that had led him to starve on one day that he might feast the next; now, he feasted every day. He still kept his room at the Reno House, but instead of taking his meals by any ticket system, he began to affect the restaurants of the Spanish quarter, gorging himself with the hot spiced meals three and four times a day. He quickly abandoned the bagatelle board for the card-table, gambling furiously with two of the ranchmen. Almost invariably Vandover lost, and the more he lost the more eager and reckless he became.

In a little time he had sold every one of his bonds and had gambled away all but twenty dollars of the money received from the last one sold. This sum, this twenty dollars, Vandover decided to husband carefully. It was all that was left between him and starvation. He made up his mind that he must stop gambling and find something to do. He had long since abandoned his work at the paint-shop, but at this time he returned there and asked for his old occupation. They laughed in his face. Was that the way he thought they did business? Not much; another man had his job, a much better man and one who was regular, who could be depended on. That same evening Vandover broke his twenty dollars and became very drunk. A game of poker was started in a back room of one of the saloons on the Barbary Coast. One of the players was a rancher named Toedt, a fellow-boarder at the Reno House, but the two other players were strangers; and there in that narrow, dirty room, sawdust on the floor, festoons of fly-specked red and blue tissue paper adorning the single swinging lamp, figures cut from bill-posters of the Black Crook pasted on the walls, there in the still hours after midnight, long after the barroom outside had been closed for the night, the last penny of Vandover's estate was gambled away.

The game ended in a quarrel, Vandover, very drunk, and exasperated at his ill luck, accusing his friend Toedt, the rancher, of cheating. Toedt kicked him in the stomach and made him abominably sick. Then they went away and left Vandover alone in the little dirty room, racked with nausea, very drunk, fallen forward upon the table and crying into his folded arms. After a little he went to sleep, but the nausea continued, nevertheless, and in a few moments he gagged and vomited. He never moved. He was too drunk to wake. His hands and his coat-sleeves, the table all about him, were foul beyond words, but he slept on in the midst of it all, inert, stupefied, a great swarm of flies buzzing about his head and face. It was the day after this that he had come to see Geary.

"Ah," said Geary, as he came up, "it's you, is it?

Well, I didn't expect to see you again. Sit down outside there in the hall and wait a few minutes. I'm not
ready to go yet—or, wait; here, I tell you what to do."
Geary wrote off a list of articles on a slip of paper and
pushed it across the table toward Vandover, together
with a little money. "You get those at the nearest
grocery and by the time you are back I'll be ready to
go."

That day Geary took Vandover out to the Mission.
They went out in the cable-car, Geary sitting inside
reading the morning's paper, Vandover standing on the
front platform, carrying the things that Geary had
told him to buy: a bar of soap, a scrubbing brush,
some wiping cloths, a broom, and a pail.

Almost at the end of the car-line they got off and
crossed over to where Geary's property stood. Vandover
looked about him. The ground on which his own block
had once stood was now occupied by an immense red
brick building with white stone trimmings; in front
on either side of the main entrance were white stone
medallions upon which were chiselled the head of a
workman wearing the square paper cap that the workman never wears, and a bent-up forearm, the biceps
enormous, the fist gripping the short hammer that the
workman never uses. An enormous round chimney
sprouted from one corner; through the open windows
came the vast purring of machinery. It was a boot
and shoe factory, built by the great concern who
had bought the piece of property from Geary for fifteen thousand dollars, the same property Geary had
bought from Vandover for eight.

Across the street from the factory was a long row of
little cottages, very neat, each having a tiny garden
in front where nasturtiums grew. There were fifteen
of these cottages; three of them only were vacant.

"That was *my* idea," observed Geary, as they approached the row, willing to explain even though he thought Vandover would not comprehend, "and it pays like a nitrate bed. I was clever enough to see that cottages like these were just what's wanted by the workmen in the factory that have families. I made some money when I sold out my block to the boot and shoe people, and I invested it again in these cottages. They are cheap and serviceable and they meet the demand." Vandover nodded his head in assent, looking vaguely about him, now at the cottages, now at the great building across the street. Geary got the keys to one of the vacant cottages and the two went inside.

"Now here's what I want you to do," began Geary, pointing about with his stick. "You see, when some of these people go out they leave the rooms nasty, and that tells against the house when parties come to look at it. I want you to go all over it, top and bottom, end to end, and give it a good cleaning, sweep the floor, and wash the paint, you know. And now these windows, you see how dirty they are; wash those inside and out, but don't disturb the agents' signs; you understand?"

"Yes, I understand."

"Now come out here into the kitchen. Look at these laundry tubs and that sink. See all that grease! Clean that all out, and underneath the sink here. See that rubbish! Take that out, too. Now in here—look at that bathtub and toilet. You see how nasty they have left them. You want to make 'em look like new!"

"Yes."

"Now come downstairs. You see I give 'em a little floored basement, here; kind of a storeroom and coal-room. Here's where most of the dirt and rubbish is. Just look at it! See all that pile over there?"

"I see."

"Take it all out and pile it in the back yard. I'll have

an ash-man come and remove it. Whew! there is a dead hen under here; sling that out the first thing."

They went back through the house again, and Geary pointed out the tiny garden to Vandover. "Straighten that up a bit, pick up those old newspapers and the tin cans. Make it look neat. Now you understand just what I want? You make a good job of it, and when you are through with this house, you begin on the next vacant one farther down the row. You can get the keys at the same place. You get to work right away. I should think you ought to finish this house this afternoon."

"All right," answered Vandover.

"I'm going to look around a little. I'll drop in again in about an hour and see how you're getting on."

With that Geary went away. It was Saturday afternoon, and as the law office closed at noon that day, Geary very often spent the time until evening looking about his property. He left Vandover and went slowly down the street, noting each particular house with immense satisfaction, even entering some of them, talking with the womenfolk, all the men being at the factory.

Vandover took off his coat, his old and greasy cutaway, and began work. He drew a pail of water from the garden faucet in a neighbour's yard, and commenced washing the windows. First he washed the panes from the inside, very careful not to disturb Adams & Brunt's signs, and then cleaned the outside, sitting upon the window ledge, his body half in and half out of the house.

Geary enjoyed himself immensely. The news of the landlord's visit had spread from cottage to cottage, awakening a mild excitement throughout the length of the row. The women showed themselves on the steps or on the sidewalks, very slatternly, without corsets, their hair coming down, dressed in faded calico wrappers just as they had come from the laundry tubs or the cook-stove. They bethought them of their various grievances, a leak here, a broken door-bell there, a certain bad smell that was supposed to have some connection with a rash upon the children's faces. They waited for Geary's appearance by ones and twos, timid, very respectful, but querulous for all that, filling the air with their lamentations.

Vandover had finished with the windows. Now he was cleaning out the sink and the laundry tubs. They smelt very badly and were all foul with a greasy mixture of old lard, soap, soot, and dust; a little mould was even beginning to form about the faucets of the tubs. The escape pipe of the sink was clogged, and he had to run his finger into it again and again to get it free. The kitchen was very dirty; old bottles of sweet oil, mouldy vinegar, and flat beer cluttered the dusty shelves of the pantry.

Meanwhile Geary continued his rounds. He went about among the groups of his tenants, very pleased and contented, smiling affably upon them. He enlarged himself, giving himself the airs of an English lord in the midst of his tenantry, listening to their complaints with a good-humoured smile of toleration. A few men were about, some of whom were out of work for the moment; others who were sick. To these Geary was particularly condescending. He sat in their parlours, little, crowded rooms, smelling of stale upholstery and of the last meal, where knitted worsted tidies, very gaudy, covered the backs of the larger chairs and where one inevitably discovered the whatnot standing in one corner, its shelves filled with shell-boxes, broken thermometers, and little alabaster jars, shaped like funeral urns, where one kept the matches. The wife brought the children in, very dirty, looking solemnly at Geary, their eyes enlarged in the direct unwinking gaze of cows.

By this time Vandover had finished with the sinks and tubs and was down upon his hands and knees scrubbing the stains of grease upon the floor of the kitchen. It was very hard work, as his water was cold. He was still working about this spot when Geary returned. By this time Vandover was so tired that he trembled all over, his spine seemed to be breaking in two, and every now and then he paused and passed his hand over the small of his back, closing his eyes and drawing a long breath.

"Well, how are you getting on?" asked Geary, as he came into the kitchen, drawing on his gloves, about ready to go home.

"Oh, I'm getting along," replied Vandover, rising up to his knees.

"You want to hurry up," answered Geary. "You must be done with this house by this evening. You see, I want to advertise it in to-morrow's papers."

"All right; I'll have it done."

"Pretty dirty, wasn't it?"

"Yes, pretty dirty."

"You may have to work here a little later than usual this afternoon, but be sure you have everything cleaned up before you leave," Geary said.

"All right," answered Vandover, bending to his work again.

Just as Geary was leaving he had the admirable good fortune to meet on the steps of the cottage a little group who were house-hunting; two young women and a little boy. The mother of the little boy, so she explained to him, was married to one of the burnishers in the factory; the other woman was her sister.

Geary showed them about the little house, very eager to secure them as tenants then and there. He began to sing its praises, its nearness to the factory, its excellent plumbing, its bathroom and its one stationary washstand; its little garden and its location on the sunny side of the street. "I'm a good landlord," he said to them, as he ushered them into the kitchen. "Anyone in the row will tell you that. I make it a point to keep my houses in good repair and to keep them clean. You see, I have a man here now cleaning out." Vandover glanced up at the women an instant. The two of them and the little boy looked down at him on all fours upon the floor. Then he went on with his work.

"This is the kitchen, you see," pursued Geary. "Notice how large it is; you see, here are your laundry tubs, your iron sink, your boiler, everything you need. Of course, it's a little grimy now, but by the time the man gets through, it will be as clean as your face. Now come downstairs here and I'll show the basement."

In a moment their voices sounded through the floor of the kitchen, an indistinct, continuous murmur. Then the party returned and passed by Vandover again and stood for a long time in the front room haggling. The cottage rented for fifteen dollars. The young woman was willing to take it at that, but with the understanding that Geary should pay the water rent. Geary refused, unwilling even to listen to such a thing. Every other tenant in the row paid for his own water. The young women went away shaking their heads sadly. Geary let them get halfway down the front steps and then called them back. He offered a compromise, the young women should pay for the water, but half of their first month's rent should be remitted. The burnisher's wife still hesitated, saying, "You know yourself this house is awfully dirty."

"Well, you see I'm having it cleaned!"

"It'll have to be cleaned pretty thoroughly. I can't stand *dirt*."

"It *will* be cleaned thoroughly," persisted Geary. "The man will work at it until it is. You can keep an eye on him and see that the work is done to suit you."

"You see," objected the burnisher's wife, "I would want to move in right away. I don't want to wait all week for the man to get through."

"But he is going to be through with this house to-night," exclaimed Geary, delighted. "Come, now, I know you want this cottage and I would like to have such nice-looking people have it. I know you would make good tenants. I can find lots of other tenants for this house, only you know how it is, a nasty, slovenly woman about the house and a raft of dirty children. And you don't like dirt, I can see that. Better call it a bargain, and let it go at that."

In the end the burnisher's wife took the house. Geary even induced her to deposit five dollars with him in order to secure it.

Vandover was down in the basement filling a barrel with the odds and ends of rubbish left by the previous tenants; broken bottles, old corsets, bones, rusty bed-springs. The dead hen he had taken out first of all, carrying it by one leg. It was a gruesome horror, partly eaten by rats, swollen, abnormally heavy, one side flattened from lying so long upon the floor. He could hardly stand; each time he bent over it seemed as though his backbone was disjointing. After cleaning out the débris he began to sweep. The dust was fearful, choking, blinding, so thick that he could hardly see what he was about. By and by he dimly made out Geary's figure in the doorway.

"Those people have taken the house," he called out, "and I promised them you would be through with it by this evening. So you want to stay with it now till you're finished. I guess there's not much more to do. Don't forget the little garden in front."

"No; I won't forget!"

Geary went away, and for another hour Vandover

kept at his work, stolidly, his mind empty of all thought, knowing only that he was very tired, that his back pained him. He finished with the basement, but as he was pottering about the little garden, picking up the discoloured newspapers with which it was littered, the burnisher's wife returned, together with her sister and the little boy; the little boy eating a slice of bread and butter. They reëntered the house; Vandover heard their voices, now in one room, now in another. They were looking over their future home again; evidently they lived close by.

Suddenly the burnisher's wife came out upon the front steps, looking down into the little garden, calling for Vandover. She was not pretty; she had a nose like a man and her chin was broad.

"Say, there," she called to Vandover, "do you mean to say that you've finished inside here?"

"Yes," answered Vandover, straightening up, nodding his head. "Yes, I've finished."

"Well, just come in here and look at this."

Vandover followed her into the little parlour. Her sister was there, very fat, smelling somehow of tallow candles and cooked cabbage; near by stood the little boy still eating his bread and butter.

"Look at that baseboard," exclaimed the burnisher's wife. "You never touched that, I'll bet a hat." Vandover did not answer; he brought in the pail of water, and soaping his scrubbing brush, went down again on his hands and knees, washing the paint on the baseboard where the burnisher's wife indicated. The two women stood by, looking on and directing his movements. The little boy watched everything, never speaking a word, slowly eating his bread and butter. Streaks of butter and bread clung to his cheeks, stretching from the corners of his mouth to his ears.

"I don't see how you come to overlook that," said

the burnisher's wife to Vandover. "That's the dirtiest baseboard I ever saw. Oh, my! I just can't naturally stand *dirt!* There, you didn't get that stain off. That's tobacco juice, I guess. Go back and wash that over again." Vandover obeyed, holding the brush in one hand, crawling back along the floor upon one palm and his two knees, a pool of soapy, dirty water very cold gathered about him, soaking in through the old "blue pants" and wetting him to the skin, but he slovened through it indifferently. "Put a little more elbow grease to it," continued the ·burnisher's wife. "You have to rub them spots pretty hard to get 'em out. Now scrub all along here near the floor. You see that streak there— that's all gormed up with something or other. Bugs get in there mighty quick. There, that'll do, I guess. Now, is everything else all clean? Mister Geary said it was to be done to my satisfaction, and that you were to stay here until everything was all right."

All at once her voice was interrupted by the pro-longed roar of the factory's whistle, blowing as though it would never stop. It was half-past five. In an instant the faint purring of the machinery dwindled and ceased, leaving an abrupt silence in the air. A moment later the army of operatives began to pour out of the main entrance; men and girls and young boys, all in a great hurry, the men settling their coat collars as they ran down the steps. The usually quiet street was crowded in an instant.

The burnisher's wife stood on the steps of the vacant house with her sister, watching the throng debouch into the street. All at once the sister exclaimed, "There he is!" and the other began to call, "Oscar, Oscar!" waving her hand to one of the workmen on the other side of the street. It was her husband, the burnisher, and he came across the street, crowding his lunch basket into the pocket of his coat. He was a thin little

man with a timid air, his face white and fat and covered
with a sparse unshaven stubble of a pale straw colour.
An odour as of a harness shop hung about him. Vandover gathered up his broom and pail and soap preparing to go home.

"Well, Oscar, I've taken the house!" said his wife to
the burnisher as he came up the steps. "But I couldn't
get him to say that he'd let me have it for fifteen, water
included. The landlord himself, Mr. Geary, was here
to-day and I made the dicker with him. He's had a
man here all day cleaning up." She explained the bargain, the burnisher approving of everything, nodding
his head continually. His wife showed him about the
house, her sister and the little boy following in silence.
"He's a good landlord, I guess," continued the young
woman; "anybody in the row will tell you that, and he
means to keep his houses in good repair. Now you see,
here's the kitchen. You see how big it is. Here's our
laundry tubs, our iron sink, our boiler, and everything
we want. It's all as clean as a whistle; and get on to this
big cubby under the sink where I can stow away things."
She opened its door to show her husband, but all at
once straightened up, exclaiming, "Well, dear me *suz* [12]
—did you *ever* see anything like that?" The cubby
under the sink was abominably dirty. Vandover had
altogether forgotten it.

The little burnisher himself bent down and peered in.

"Oh, that'll never do!" he cried. "Has that man gone
home yet? He mustn't; he's got to clean this out first!"
He had a weak, faint voice, small and timid like his
figure. He hurried out to the front door and called
Vandover back just as he was going down the steps.
The two went back into the kitchen and stood in front
of the sink. "Look under there!" piped the burnisher.
"You can't leave that, that way."

"You know," protested his wife, "that this all was

to be done to our satisfaction. Mr. Geary said so. That's the only way I came to take the house."

"It's about six o'clock, though," observed her fat sister, who smelt of cooked cabbage. "Perhaps he'd want to go home to his dinner." But at this both the others cried out in one voice, the burnisher exclaiming: "I can't help *that*, this has got to be done first," while his wife protested that she couldn't naturally stand dirt, adding, "This all was to be done to our satisfaction, and we ain't satisfied yet by a long shot." Delighted at this excitement, the little boy forgot to eat into his bread and butter, rolling his eyes wildly from one to the other, still silent.

Meanwhile, without replying, Vandover had gone down upon the floor again, poking about amid the filth under the sink. The four others, the burnisher, his wife, his sister-in-law, and his little boy, stood about in a half-circle behind him, seeing to it that he did the work properly, giving orders as to how he should proceed.

"Now, be sure you get everything out that's under there," said the burnisher. "Ouf! how it smells! They made a regular dump heap of it."

"What's that over in the corner there?" cried the wife, bending down. "I can't see, it's so dark under there—something grey; can't you see, in under there? You'll have to crawl way in to get at it—go way in!" Vandover obeyed. The sink pipes were so close above him that he was obliged to crouch lower and lower; at length he lay flat upon his stomach. Prone in the filth under the sink, in the sour water, the grease, the refuse, he groped about with his hand searching for the something grey that the burnisher's wife had seen. He found it and drew it out. It was an old hambone covered with a greenish fuzz.

"Oh, did you *ever!*" cried the burnisher, holding up his hands. "Here, don't drop that on my clean floor;

put it in your pail. Now get out the rest of the dirt, and
hurry up, it's late." Vandover crawled back, half the
way under the sink again, this time bringing out a rusty
pan half full of some kind of congealed gravy that exhaled a choking, acrid odour; next it was an old stocking, and then an ink bottle, a broken rat-trap, a battered teapot lacking a nozzle, a piece of rubber hose,
an old comb choked with a great handful of hair, a torn
overshoe, newspapers, and a great quantity of other
débris that had accumulated there during the occu-
pancy of the previous tenant.

"Now go over the floor with a rag," ordered the little
burnisher, when the last of these articles had been
brought out. "Wipe up all that nasty muck! Look there
by your knee to your left! Scrub that big spot there with
your brush—looks like grease. That's the style—scrub
it hard!" His wife joined her directions to his. Then it
was over here, and over there, now in that corner, now
in this, and now with his brush and soap, and now with
his dry rag, and hurry up all the time because it was
growing late. But the little boy, carried away by the
interest of the occasion, suddenly broke silence for the
first time, crying out shrilly, his mouth full of bread
and butter, "Hey there! Get up, you old lazee-bones!"

The others shouted with laughter. *There* was a smart
little boy for you. Ah, he'd be a man before his mother.
It was wonderful how that boy saw everything that
went on. He took an *interest*, that was it. You ought to
see, he watched everything, and sometimes he'd plump
out with things that were astonishing for a boy of his
years. Only four and a half, too, and they reminded each
other of the first day he put on knickerbockers; stood
in front of the house on the sidewalk all day long with
his hands in his pockets. The interest was directed from
Vandover, they turned their backs, grouping themselves
about the little boy. The burnisher's sister-in-law felt

called upon to tell about her little girl, a matter of family pride. *She* was going on twelve, and would you suppose that little thing was in next to the last grade in the grammar school? Her teacher had said that she was a real wonder; never had had such a bright pupil. Ah, but one should see how she studied over her books all the time. Next year they were to try to get her into the high school. Of course she was not ready for the high school yet, and it was against the rule to let children in that way, she was too young, but they had a pull, you understand. Oh, yes, for sure they had a pull. *They'd* work her in all right. The burnisher's wife was not listening. She wanted to draw the interest back to her own little boy. She bent down and straightened out his little jacket, saying, "Does he like his bread 'n butter? Well, he could have all he wanted!" But the little boy paid no attention to her. He had made a *bon-mot*, ambition stirred in him, he had tasted the delights of an appreciative audience. Bread and butter had fallen in his esteem. He wished to repeat his former success, and cried out shriller than ever:

"Hey, there! Get up, you old lazee-bones!"

But his father corrected him—his mother ought not to encourage him to be rude. "That's not right, Oscar," he observed, shaking his head. "You must be kind to the poor man."

Vandover was sitting back on his heels to rest his back, waiting till the others should finish.

"Well, all through?" inquired the burnisher in his thin voice. Vandover nodded. But his wife was not satisfied until she had herself carefully peered into the cubby while her husband held a lighted match for her. "Ah, that's something like," she said finally.

It was nearly seven. Vandover prepared to go home a second time. The little boy stood in front of him, looking down at him as he made his brush and rags and broom into a bundle; the boy slowly eating his bread and butter the while. In one corner of the room an excited whispered conference was going on between the burnisher, his wife, and his fat sister-in-law. From time to time one heard such expressions as "Overtime, you know—not afraid of work—ah! think I'd better, looks as though he needed it." In a moment the two women went out, calling in vain for the little boy to follow, and the burnisher crossed the room toward Vandover. Vandover was on his knees tying up his bundle with a bit of bale rope.

"I'm sorry," began the burnisher, awkwardly. "We didn't mean to keep you from your supper—here," he went on, holding out a quarter to Vandover, "here, you take this, that's all right—you worked overtime for us, that's all right. Come along, Oscar; come along, m' son."

Vandover put the quarter in his vest pocket.

"Thank you, sir," he said.

The burnisher hurried away, calling back, "Come along, m' son; don't keep your mama waiting for supper." But the little boy remained very interested in watching Vandover, still on the floor, tying the last knots. As he finished, he glanced up. For an instant the two remained there motionless, looking into each other's eyes, Vandover on the floor, one hand twisted into the bale rope about his bundle, the little boy standing before him eating the last mouthful of his bread and butter.

NOTES

Blix

1. In the serialization of *Blix* that preceded book publication, Chapters I and II were combined. The opening scene was set at five o'clock tea, and other particulars differed. However, the gist was much the same, though there was more emphasis on Travis herself and less detail about her family.

2. This spelling of Saucelito, rather than the currently accepted Sausalito, was common until 1900.

3. Norris consistently misspells the street named for General Kearny as though it honored the San Francisco labor agitator, Denis Kearney.

4. Robert Louis Stevenson often visited Portsmouth Plaza in the winter of 1879, and the first monument ever erected to him was placed there: a little bronze sailing vessel atop a shaft designed by Norris' friend Bruce Porter.

The political enmity of U.S. Senator David C. Broderick and the state's chief justice, David S. Terry, arose from the senator's anti-slavery views and the judge's proslavery sentiment. They fought the state's last duel, southwest of San Francisco on September 13, 1859. Terry mortally wounded Broderick. Five days later Colonel Edward D. Baker (later senator) delivered the funeral oration before a crowd of people in the city's major square.

5. *Life's Handicap* is a volume of short stories by Kipling, published in 1891.

6. Marie Corelli and the Duchess were pen names of tremendously popular English novelists of cheap romances, like *The Sorrows of Satan* (1895) by the former and *Airy, Fairy Lilian* (1879) by the latter.

7. This doggerel about the ounce, a moderate-sized feline resembling a lynx, probably was written by Norris when he was a stu-

dent in LeConte's classes, which had once inspired him to write the limerick:

> "There once was an ichthyosaurus,
> Who lived when the world was all porous.
> When he first heard his name,
> He fainted from shame,
> And departed a long time before us."

8. *Plain Tales* and *Many Inventions* are additional collections of stories by Kipling, published respectively in 1888 and 1893.

9. E. L. Thayer's popular *Casey at the Bat*, from which Condy is quoting, was first published in the *San Francisco Examiner* in 1888.

10. Lake San Andreas is part of a fish and game refuge in a fenced watershed preserve south of San Francisco.

11. Luna's Restaurant, in the Mexican Quarter, was actually located at 1236 Dupont Street, the northern extension of Grant Avenue that then ended at Bush Street.

12. The U.S. Coast and Geodetic Survey marker, dated 1869–1880, sets forth the longitude and latitude of the site.

13. In this contemptuous allusion to Browning circles, Norris was probably twitting his mother, who was the perennial president of San Francisco's Browning Society.

14. A Krag-Jörgensen was a widely used rifle of Scandinavian design.

15. The Seri Indians are known as a hardy, warlike tribe, said to have practiced cannibalism on their enemies.

16. The Pacific Northwest, from Vancouver down to Seattle, was a place of settlement for many expatriated Britons, among them some remittance men. Determined not to be Americanized, a number of them might have established an organization like The Exiles, although local historians cannot identify a real prototype for it nor a model for Billy Isham.

17. Kipling's volume of poems *The Seven Seas* was published in 1896.

18. Redfern and Virot were famous dressmakers of the time.

19. Loudon Dodds is a character in *The Wrecker* (1892) by Robert Louis Stevenson and Lloyd Osbourne.

20. In associating "costume reading" with the prim K.D.B., Norris was not only drawing upon knowledge gained from his mother, who gave such readings for ladies' clubs, but was probably also twitting her again.

21. The time span of the novel—the period of the romance

—seems to be confused, since earlier in this chapter and again in the next one it is said to be three months, not two.

22. The Whitehall boat was a wherry, sometimes carrying a sail. First developed as a water taxi off the foot of Whitehall Street, New York City, it was also used in San Francisco Bay to carry men and goods to and from deep-water ships.

Vandover and the Brute

1. In *The Harvard Book* (1875) James Russell Lowell describes the "rush" in this way: "At five o'clock comes the dance round the Liberty Tree, but long before that every inch of vantage-ground whence even a glimpse at this frenzy of muscular sentiment may be hoped for has been taken up . . . First, the Seniors whirl hand in hand about the tree with the energy of excitement gathered through the day; class after class is taken in, till all the College is swaying in the unwieldy ring, which at last breaks to pieces of its own weight. Then come the frantic leaping and struggling for a bit of the wreath of flowers that circles the tree at a fairly difficult height."

2. Van John is a nickname for "vingt-et-un," the card game twenty-one.

3. San Francisco restaurants often served the small unpeeled bay shrimps gratis with an order of drinks.

4. More properly named Mechanics' Institute, this privately financed organization was established for workingmen but had long since been a society for cultivated readers.

5. Probably a reference to a brooch or pendant copied from a royal Russian decoration bearing a miniature of the glamorous young Czarina Alexandra suspended from a replica of the imperial crown, created as a souvenir to celebrate her marriage to Nicholas in November 1894. This was the date when Norris not only set but probably wrote this part of the novel, which just precedes the material in his November 19 Harvard Theme 8. Theme 6 presents evidence that Norris liked to make immediately topical references.

6. Well-known gay but respectable restaurants of the period.

7. A distinguished club for gentlemen, emphasizing the arts.

8. Located at Montgomery and Sutter Streets, the Lick House was a good hotel built by James Lick, a wealthy San Francisco real estate investor who for a long time lived in the hotel.

9. A cast iron column with drinking fountains surrounding it,

presented to the citizens of San Francisco in 1875 by Lotta Crabtree, a popular California actress.

10. An elaborate glass-roofed bathing pavilion with several salt water swimming pools constructed over a long period of time by Adolph Sutro, a San Francisco millionaire, but finally opened in March 1896.

11. The Reno House was a cheap lodging place located on Sacramento Street between Montgomery and Kearny Streets.

12. *Suz* was an interjection commonly used by women in the latter part of the nineteenth century, particularly in New England. It was employed again by Norris in *The Pit*.